Leonard Bernstein
and His
Young People's Concerts

Leonard Bernstein and His
Young People's Concerts

Alicia Kopfstein-Penk

ROWMAN & LITTLEFIELD
Lanham • Boulder • New York • London

Published by Rowman & Littlefield
A wholly owned subsidiary of The Rowman & Littlefield Publishing Group, Inc.
4501 Forbes Boulevard, Suite 200, Lanham, Maryland 20706
www.rowman.com

Unit A, Whitacre Mews, 26-34 Stannary Street, London SE11 4AB

British Library Cataloguing in Publication Information Available

Library of Congress Cataloging-in-Publication Data

Kopfstein-Penk, Alicia.
  Leonard Bernstein and his young people's concerts / Alicia Kopfstein-Penk.
     pages cm
  Includes bibliographical references and index.
  ISBN 978-0-8108-8849-4 (hardcover : alk. paper) — ISBN 978-0-8108-8850-0
(ebook)
  1. Bernstein, Leonard, 1918–1990. 2. Young people's concerts (Television program).
3. Music—Social aspects—United States—History—20th century. 4. Music—United
States—20th century—History and criticism. I. Title.
  ML410.B566K66 2015
  780.92—dc23   2014032082

Printed in the United States of America

To George Schuetze, who kindly and
patiently first set my feet on this path;
Mark Horowitz, who guided me to
this particular path; and Leonard Bernstein,
who makes every step a joy.

"What [President John Fitzgerald] Kennedy did for the affairs of the world, you do for the heart of the world. It seemed to me, tonight, that you two are not (were not) unalike—in courage, in conscience, in warmth and in purpose."

—Mary Rodgers Guettel to Leonard Bernstein,
24 November 1963

Contents

Illustrations

27   Bernstein and André Watts in rehearsal (1960s). Watts performed a total of twenty-three times with the Philharmonic. Photo by Eugene Cook. New York Philharmonic Digital Archives, used by permission.

28   The globe-trotting conductor brought his children, Jamie and Alexander, on the Philharmonic tour of Europe and Israel, here in New York preparing to leave for Brussels (22 August 1968). New York Philharmonic Digital Archives, used by permission.

29   Bernstein and Stravinsky while filming the CBS television program *The Creative Performer* (1960). Also appearing were Eileen Farrell, Glenn Gould, and the New York Philharmonic. Courtesy of the Library of Congress.

30   Bernstein with his good friend Aaron Copland during a rehearsal in Philharmonic Hall for the world premiere of Copland's *Connotations* on 22 September 1962. New York Philharmonic Digital Archives, used by permission.

31   Bernstein and his friend Lukas Foss, Carnegie Hall (October 1960). New York Philharmonic Digital Archives, used by permission.

32   A display ad for a televised *Young People's Concert* from the *Los Angeles Times*, designed to attract viewers who would avoid anything connected to modern music (27 December 1970).

33   A collage of *Young People's Concerts* fan mail addressed to Bernstein from young viewers. Courtesy of the Library of Congress and the Leonard Bernstein Office.

34   Bernstein's fame spread through the world via television and recordings as seen in this brief collage of international fan mail from adults to the maestro. Courtesy of the Library of Congress.

35   Charles Schulz's *Peanuts* strip for Sunday, 7 June 1959. Bernstein's *Young People's Concerts* were so popular a year and a half after their debut that Schulz devoted a full Sunday strip to Bernstein. Of course Schroeder is familiar with Bernstein, but even Lucy knows about the maestro! Peanuts © 1959 Peanuts Worldwide LLC, distributed by Universal Uclick, reprinted with permission, all rights reserved.

36   Charles Schulz's *Peanuts* strip from a weekday at the beginning of the tenth season of the *Young People's Concerts* (1 September 1966). Peanuts © 1966 Peanuts Worldwide LLC, distributed by Universal Uclick, reprinted with permission, all rights reserved.

37   Bernstein studying a score, cigarette in hand (1970s). Courtesy of the Library of Congress and the Leonard Bernstein Office.

TABLES

Foreword

Music can name the unnameable and communicate the unknowable.

—Leonard Bernstein

$\mathcal{B}$ernstein uniquely understood the transformative power of music: how it connected people on a fundamental level, transcended language and spoke across barriers, bridged differences and promoted tolerance, and, in the end, captured the best humanity had to offer. And he believed with all of his heart that every human being is born with a limitless capacity to understand, access, and experience that transformative power of music.

All anyone needed was access and a bit of guidance. He decided to use the brand-new medium of television as the vehicle to throw open the doors to the world of classical music and, in the process, became the ultimate musical guide and storyteller for generations of young people.

Alicia Kopfstein-Penk's *Leonard Bernstein and His* Young People's Concerts captures the magic and brilliance of those groundbreaking presentations but also offers insight into Bernstein's deeply felt political and social beliefs, manifest so adeptly in the concerts themselves.

Like so many, I, too, fell under Bernstein's spell. I was only nine years old the day my father took me to see him with the New York Philharmonic, but I instinctually knew that this man conducting the orchestra and enthusiastically explaining everything to the audience was much more than a conductor. He was a preacher and a storyteller, a man with an unabashed passion for music and sharing. He was fearless and incredibly cool and, from that day on, he was my hero.

I turned to my father and whispered: "That's what I'm going to do when I grow up; I want to be a conductor!"

With Bernstein as my inspiration, I pursued this dream.

And that dream came true when I became one of Bernstein's conducting students at Tanglewood in 1988. Only then did I begin to understand the depth of his humanity and experience his profound generosity of spirit.

As his student, I had the privilege to see firsthand how his genius lay not only in his brilliance as a composer and conductor, writer and communicator, thinker and teacher, but in his ability to bring all of these areas together in himself. Bernstein's ultimate genius was his ability to connect all of life's dots!

I remember a wonderful evening talking to him about Robert Schumann's Second Symphony. When I said something about a phrase reminding me of a Beatles song, he promptly sat down at the piano and played (and then sang) *all* of the Beatles' songs!

There was no differentiation for him between highbrow and lowbrow. As he said "there is only 'brow'"—because we all come from one human race.

Leonard Bernstein was more than my musical hero. He was my role model for how to be a citizen of the world. He was a man of profound principle who was willing to stand up, even alone, for what he believed. Whether one agreed with his politics or not, there was no denying his convictions. Having a hero is a rare gift, but having a hero who exceeds all expectations is a priceless one.

Alicia Kopfstein-Penk explores the complexities and many dimensions of Leonard Bernstein through the lens of his *Young People's Concerts.* Bernstein's seemingly simple objective of giving young people access to a great art form was, as Kopfstein-Penk underscores, a vehicle for dramatic social commentary and change.

Just like the man, there is nothing simple about any of it. But, at the same time, it is all so very simple!

> Sing God a simple song, lauda laude
> Make it up as you go along, lauda laude
> Sing like you like to sing, God loves all simple things.
> For God is the simplest of all, For God is the simplest of all.

—Text from *MASS: A Theatre Piece for Singers, Players, and Dancers,*
Leonard Bernstein

—Marin Alsop, music director,
Baltimore Symphony Orchestra,
São Paulo Symphony Orchestra, and
Cabrillo Festival of Contemporary Music

Preface

Surprisingly, few sources provide significant information about Leonard Bernstein and his *Young People's Concerts*. Many short articles published during the years the programs were broadcast offer negligible insights. The personal reminiscences by those close to the series published years later in *prelude, fugue & riffs* (the newsletter of the Leonard Bernstein Office) offer a wider, yet still superficial, view of the series.[1] Meryl Secrest's interview-focused biography (1994) and Peyser's slanted biography (1998) do include some useful tidbits about the series.[2] The most carefully researched, most reliable, and most detailed of the Bernstein biographies is by his friend and colleague Humphrey Burton (1994). Written shortly after Bernstein's death, this is the "official" biography endorsed by the family. Although this important book is invaluable in placing this youth education series into the context of Bernstein's life and times, its coverage is also sparse. The same is true for Jonathan Cott's recent *Dinner with Lenny*. Jack Gottlieb's *Working with Bernstein: A Memoir* (2010) is valuable for his essays on Bernstein's *Young People's Concerts* as well as placing them within the context of the maestro's life.[3]

Bernstein's *Young People's Concerts* are the subject of few substantial academic studies. Brian David Rozen's 1997 dissertation focuses entirely on Bernstein's pedagogical techniques, hoping to inspire music educators to emulate Bernstein's success, and James Lester Rees's 1966 thesis studies the rhetoric of Bernstein's writing and presentation in his *Young People's Concerts*. Rees interviewed members of the staff, production crew, and the maestro himself and attended conferences for the preparation of the script for "A Birthday Tribute to Shostakovich" (5 January 1966), all of which proved invaluable in establishing the creative process and verifying Bernstein's total control of the final product. Sharon Gelleny offers a brief overview of the series in her 1991 thesis, covering many of the same topics discussed here but without much depth, which sometimes led her to erroneous conclusions.[4] She does include a short survey of the critical reception of the series, which is not covered here (Gelleny 1991, 41–72). John Christian MacInnis also provides a sketch of the 1961–1962 season in his 2009 thesis, focusing on Roger Englander (producer/director of the series) and television production.

Some more general sources are quite informative. Brian G. Rose's two books (1986 and 1992) place Bernstein's *Young People's Concerts* in the context of early cultural/educational television programming and technology, as he traces cultural television in the United States (1950s–1980s) and interviews important producers such as Englander. Howard Shanet's 1975 history of the Philharmonic relates the series to a timeline of the orchestra and gives invaluable lists of concerts with repertory and soloists. James H. North's 2006 discography of the Philharmonic and Shanet's history makes it possible to compare the repertory of the educational television series with works performed or recorded by the Philharmonic.

Until recently, little had been done on the social, political, and cultural contexts of any aspect of Leonard Bernstein's work. *Mass*, as a reaction to the turbulent social and political changes of the 1960s, was the subject of dissertations by Don A. André (1979) and William A. Cottle (1978), and the influence of McCarthyism on *Candide* was investigated in articles by Elizabeth Bergman Crist (2006 and 2007). Drew Massey's article "Leonard Bernstein and the Harvard Student Union: In Search of Political Origins" (2009) gives some of the results from a team-research seminar presented at a symposium at Harvard University in 2006 titled "Leonard Bernstein: Boston to Broadway."[5] Barry Seldes examines the troubled partnership between American politics and high art as seen in Bernstein's career in his valuable but occasionally problematic study *Leonard Bernstein: The Political Life of an American Musician* (2009).

Other than Christopher Jarrett Page's thorough study of Bernstein's advocacy of Gustav Mahler, no significant research has been done on the maestro's thoughts regarding composers or trends (2000). Bernstein's energetic advocacy of American music and his mixed attitudes toward modernism have been largely overlooked.

Comprehensive collections of existing primary sources on his *Young People's Concerts* reside in the Leonard Bernstein Collection at the Library of Congress and the New York Philharmonic Archives at Lincoln Center; some items are also found at the Leonard Bernstein Office in New York City. The Library of Congress began receiving Bernstein documents in 1953, and donations continue today; Senior Music Specialist and curator Mark Eden Horowitz notes that the Leonard Bernstein Collection "offers a remarkably complete record of his life and is one of the Music Division's richest repositories in the variety and scope of its materials."[6]

The Leonard Bernstein Collection has a special section devoted to the documents of his *Young People's Concerts*. It includes scraps of paper on which Bernstein brainstormed ideas for specific programs, initial outlines for most programs, first and final drafts for every program with a varying number of intermediary drafts, an occasional synopsis, many cue and routine/rundown sheets, items that assisted Bernstein in creating the programs (such as newspaper articles, translations, a 45-rpm record, or the score of a popular song), as well as ancillary documents. The fan mail in the Leonard Bernstein Collection is possibly the most extensive collection of such letters in existence according to Horowitz.[7] Bernstein paid close attention to fan mail, as seen in *Dinner with Lenny* when he observed that he thinks he got more fan mail for his program on modes than for any other (Cott 2013, 71). Letters from viewers play a vital role in the reception and history of his *Young People's Concerts*.

Bernstein tended to notate the scripts in a rather consistent manner over the fourteen years. Pages of ideas are usually in pencil scribbled on anything from memo pads and hotel stationery to his favored lined, yellow legal pad sheets, the same yellow paper on which he wrote his outlines and scripts. Often the brainstorming sheets resemble the final outline so closely that it is difficult to tell the difference. Outlines are consistently written in pencil on yellow legal paper and tend to be somewhat more formal. For the earliest programs, second and subsequent drafts were typed on either carbon paper or mimeograph masters and then reproduced to facilitate distribution to the production crew; later in the series, such documents are typed then photocopied. Sometimes the paper for the drafts is colored, for instance, yellow, pink, or blue. Handwritten additions appear in blue, red, and black pencil.[8] In addition to the final drafts contributed to the collection by Bernstein's secretary (Helen Coates), personal working copies were contributed by members of the production crew, which explains differences between presumably "final" scripts seen at the Library of Congress and those at the Leonard Bernstein Office. The Library of Congress has scanned and made available online what was determined to be the first and last draft of all fifty-three programs, as well as a few related documents, such as outlines.

As of 2013 DVDs exist for all fifty-three programs. Bernstein's management company, Amberson Enterprises, energetically sought copies of all the films when the decision was made to make VHS tapes of selected programs from the series (documents in box 924 trace this process).[9] Many were preserved by McGraw-Hill, the company that distributed films of the programs for classroom use; some came from CBS, the network that broadcast the series and owned the copyright. Once copies of all the programs were found, a committee (including Bernstein) watched them and chose the twenty-five most appealing for volume 1, released in 1993. An effort was made to include representatives of the different technologies: the earliest concerts on kinescope, then those on two-inch quadruplex videotape (the early ones in black and white and the later ones in color). The remaining twenty-eight programs are now available in volume 2. All can also be seen at the Paley Center for Media in New York City.[10]

I must begin expressing my profound thanks to Mark Eden Horowitz, Senior Music Specialist at the Library of Congress and curator of the Leonard Bernstein Collection (as well as many other collections) at the Library of Congress. When I decided to investigate Bernstein, I asked Mark for guidance. After a few pointed questions, he immediately suggested Bernstein's *Young People's Concerts*—as they say, the rest is history. Anyone who has worked in the Library's musical theater or Bernstein archives knows of his readiness to help, his expertise, and warmth. My gratitude to Mark for his help and friendship is immense.

I am also grateful to Marie Carter (vice president of licensing and publishing for the Leonard Bernstein Music Publishing Company) for her support from the beginning of my project. She has readily shared her vast knowledge and sent me incredibly valuable copies of the scripts for all fifty-three *Young People's Concerts*, as well as those for his programs in Moscow, Berlin, and Tokyo. Occasionally she would be so thoughtful as to send something unasked that she felt would be helpful.

Bennett Graff, senior editor at Rowman and Littlefield, has been amazing. He quickly saw the value of my project and had faith in a new author. Bennett has always been there to quickly answer any question, deal with any problem that arose, and patiently guide a novice author through the mysteries of publishing. I cannot thank him enough for his faith in me as well as his most excellent support and advice.

A number of libraries and archives deserve my gratitude. When I originally did my research, only twenty-five of the programs were available on DVD. I saw the others at either the Paley Center for Media in New York or at the Library of Congress. I would like to thank the staff of the Paley Center for free unlimited access and their warm, efficient assistance. Of course, the Leonard Bernstein Collection at the Library of Congress has been a mainstay of my research. My thanks go to both the Library and the Bernstein family for making so much of the Leonard Bernstein Collection available online. The Library's staff has willingly dealt with any questions that arose, in particular Josie Walters-Johnston (Moving Image Reference Librarian) and Karen Moses (Senior Music Specialist). My week at the Archives of the New York Philharmonic in New York City was superb due to the friendly staff and the efficient assistance of Richard C. Wandel and later Gabe Smith (Associate Archivists of the New York Philharmonic). I would like to express my gratitude to the Philharmonic Archives for open access to the photocopier and the permission to quote documents. I also owe a debt to the librarians and faculty at American University, including: Nobue Matsuoka-Motley (Head Music/ Performing Arts Librarian); Jim Heintze (Head of the Music Library, emeritus, and Assistant University Librarian, emeritus); Christopher Lewis (Head Media Librarian); and Robert Griffith (Chair of the History Department). The American University library is known for its comprehensive music collection thanks to the efforts of these three librarians.

I have been extremely fortunate in receiving help from a number of individuals. Faculty members at other universities kindly answered questions and offered insights, specifically Elizabeth Bergman and Carol Oja. Humphrey Burton, who worked with Bernstein, consented to interviews and email communications, shared invaluable information, then kindly permitted me to quote him. Mary Rodgers Guettel permitted me to quote her letter to Bernstein. Jennifer Goldhammer, Stefanie Stahlnecker, David Ottinger, and my young students Emma Buzbee and Julia Smith were a pleasure to work with, as well as efficient, capable research assistants. George C. Schuetze first set me on the path of musicology as an undergraduate when he saw and nurtured my enthusiasm, taught me incredibly high standards, and guided me to opportunities. The world would be a better place if every young student could find such a marvelous mentor. My debt to him for opening this door is enormous.

Grants for research in musicology are as rare as hen's teeth, yet I was fortunate to receive partial funding for this project from two sources: the Cosmos Club Foundation in Washington, DC, and the Mu Phi Epsilon International Professional Music Fraternity.

I am grateful for the editing suggestions of Grayson Wagstaff, Andrew H. Weaver, Sarah Forman, and fellow Bernstein scholar Elizabeth Wells. Beth and I have thoroughly enjoyed sharing our love of Lenny, which has led to a lovely friendship.

I have been deeply touched by the interest and support my students and friends have shown for my work. David Benson took time to explain the mysteries of the Nielsen ratings to me. Many pointed out new sources, translated Russian, printed materials, brought me copies of articles, videos, broadcasts, books, and even concert tickets, frequently asked for updates on my work, and happily discussed my research; others kindly offered practical support in times of need. Particular thanks go to: Ralph Alterowitz, Fred Begun (Principal Timpanist, Emeritus, National Symphony Orchestra, deceased), Dr. Jane Bonin, Donna Cleverdon, Jennifer Damme, Martha Ellison (chair of Vocal Arts

DC), Dr. Barbara Farishian, Sarah Forman, David Geyer, Susan Goldsamt, Dr. Suzanne Hemberger, Patti Iglarsh, Ksenya Litvak, Marilyn Macy, Cantor Mikhail Manevich, Dr. Marianne Phelps, Dr. Robert Rifkin, Olaf Schoenrich, and Angela Wozencroft.

My husband, Charles Kopfstein-Penk (yes, the entire last name came from him), deserves an entire paragraph dedicated to him alone. He generously spent innumerable hours improving the quality of old photographs and grainy images, making collages, and creating possible book covers (I am happy to report that our design was selected, with some tweaks). He has acted as a research assistant, editor (sparking several energetic discussions), invaluable IT professional (keeping me calm while finding lost documents, learning new computer programs, and so forth), sounding board, listener, and adviser through every step of my life. Charles is the warmest, kindest, most generous, supportive, and helpful companion one could ever hope to have, and he makes me laugh! This book would not be what it is without him. And I would not be who I am or where I am without him. Each day I am amazed at how lucky I am to travel with this wonderful life partner.

A Note on Permissions

Leonard Bernstein's words, recordings, letters, lectures, scripts, drafts, outlines, and other writings of Leonard Bernstein are used by permission of the Leonard Bernstein Office, Marie Carter, vice president of licensing and publishing. Documents found in the archives of the New York Philharmonic are printed with their permission.

"Aquarius" (from *Hair*), lyrics by James Rado and Gerome Ragni, music by Galt MacDermot, © 1966, 1967, 1968, 1970 (copyrights renewed); James Rado, Gerome Ragni, Galt MacDermot, Nat Shapiro, and EMI U Catalog, Inc. All rights administered by EMI U Catalog, Inc. (publishing) and Alfred Music Publishing Co., Inc. (print). All rights reserved. Used by permission of Alfred Music Publishing Co., Inc.

The Unanswered Question: Six Talks at Harvard by Leonard Bernstein, pp. 55, 140, 153, 245, 269–270, copyright © 1976 by Leonard Bernstein, reprinted by permission of the publisher (Cambridge, Mass.: Harvard University Press).

Library Sigla and Other Information

The primary documents for my research came from three archives: the Library of Congress, the New York Philharmonic Archives, and the Leonard Bernstein Office. Most came from the Leonard Bernstein Collection at the

Library of Congress, hence these will be noted simply by "box/folder" or "scrapbook" without library siglum. Many items in this collection may be viewed online at http://memory.loc.gov/ammem/collections/bernstein/ (accessed 22 January 2014). Since there is no RISM siglum for the archives of the New York Philharmonic, I created one: NYpa. Bernstein's *Young People's Concerts* scripts are usually referenced by their title and date, followed by the page number where relevant, such as "What Is Orchestration" (8 March 1958, 4). In extensive lists, only the program number is given (see appendix A). Thanks to the generosity of Marie Carter, I was privileged to work from copies of the scripts housed in the Leonard Bernstein Office, which differ in small ways from those at the Library of Congress. Upon occasion, script pages have been revised, so the page number reads "2rev" or "2Rev" or "2revised." For the sake of clarity and consistency, these have been changed to all read "2 revised." Italics indicate that a program was televised and quotes that the program was live and never broadcast, for instance, *Young People's Concert* versus "Young People's Concert." All titles and composers are given as Bernstein did specifically in his *Young People's Concerts*, which means titles are usually in English.

When discussing art music (also called "classical" music) as compared to popular music, terminology becomes important. The word "classical" has many meanings: from Greek or Roman times; of acknowledged excellence; or respected for a long time. Musically, "classical" is also ambiguous and could indicate music composed circa 1750 to 1800; with clarity and balance that emphasizes formal beauty; that has a permanent rather than ephemeral quality; or classified as art music rather than as popular music. Bernstein himself understood this dilemma and attempted to define "classical" music in "What Is Classical Music?" (24 January 1959). Since Bernstein chose to call art music "classical," that term is used here.

Introduction

Some of the gifted among us are twice blessed: they yoke arresting talents to historic coincidences that enable them to make the most of their gifts. Leonard Bernstein is one of these: it was his—and our—good fortune that he and American television grew to maturity together.

—Robert S. Clark, "Congruent Odysseys: Bernstein and the Art of Television"

The long sixties were fraught with strife, stress, and change. The controversial Vietnam War raged with young men drafted amidst peace protests. Fear of nuclear annihilation permeated the world. The Red Scare persisted—those even suspected of Communist leanings were persecuted. Society itself underwent violent (sometimes bloody) upheavals as civil rights for African Americans, women, Latinos, and homosexuals moved to the fore. Divisions between social classes were breaking down. In difficult times like this, mankind turns to the arts for solace, but even classical music seemed to ignore the typical music-lover with dissonant, complex music many found repugnant.

Leonard Bernstein's *Young People's Concerts* offered a fascinating and pleasurable oasis of calm and beauty through all this. From the 1950s until his death in 1990, Leonard Bernstein was the face of classical music in America. The world knew him as a charismatic conductor and teacher, largely due to his many appearances on the new medium of television. His most significant, far-reaching, and longest-running television series was his *Young People's Concerts*. From 1958 through 1972, throughout the United States and in over forty countries throughout the world, these fifty-three programs were arguably the most influential phenomenon in music education in the second half of the twentieth century, helping to "convert an entire generation of casual

American [and international] music listeners into avid music lovers" (Gottlieb [1962] 2005, xi). Many professional musicians and music teachers whom I interviewed cited his *Young People's Concerts* as a moment of discovery that guided their steps toward a career in music. The Music Director of the Baltimore Symphony Orchestra Marin Alsop decided to become a conductor at the age of nine when she saw Bernstein conduct at a *Young People's Concert*.[1] Non-musicians tell me they are grateful that Bernstein gave them the gift of a lifelong love affair with classical music. People still watch selected episodes to learn about sonata form or modes, and the programs still appear on some cable stations. But were these programs untouched by their times?

Outside of superlative music education, what images did these programs create in the minds of the viewers—images of classical music, of modernist music, of American music, of society at large, or of Bernstein himself? Musicians are aware of how Bernstein changed the performing canon: how he brought Mahler back to the concert hall and how he supported American and selected modernist composers (albeit favoring those who embraced tonality). What role did his *Young People's Concerts* play in those changes? The programs spanned the Golden Age of Television through the turbulent long decade of the sixties. Are any of the political, social, or cultural clashes reflected in the programs? While there are no documents clearly stating that Bernstein decided to react to current events in this television series, he was a vocal, self-proclaimed liberal activist. It would be out of character for him to remain silent. Did Bernstein's own life shape some of his decisions for the series? His *West Side Story* certainly was in part an artistic reaction to events in the news (Wells 2011, 32). Can it be a coincidence that Bernstein discussed the beauty of Cuban music in the "Latin American Spirit" (8 March 1963) only months after the Cuban Missile Crisis? Or that he brought African American pianist André Watts back to this internationally viewed series, calling him a prince and treating him with tremendous respect several months after the 1966 race riots? *Leonard Bernstein and His* Young People's Concerts looks at how the cultural, political, social, and musical issues of his day influenced him and may have seeped into the scripts.

This book consists of eight chapters in four parts. The first part sets the stage through a detailed study of archival documents, as well as a comparison of the scripts with the television programs, histories of the Philharmonic, and its recordings. Chapter 1 describes the target audience, structure of the programs and series, broadcast information, and the production crew and its role in the creative process. Chapter 2 describes for the first time how Bernstein chose topics, orchestral works, and young performers. A comparison of the repertory performed on his *Young People's Concerts* with Howard Shanet's history of the orchestra and James North's discography confirms a sound economic basis for his repertory decisions.

The second part examines the cultural context through a study of archival documents, Nielsen ratings, secondary sources, and cultural references in the scripts. Russell Lynes's seminal 1949 article "Highbrow, Lowbrow, Middlebrow" in *Harper's* began the game of dividing everything in America, from furniture and clothing to art and libations, into social categories. Chapter 3 examines these concepts and places these pedagogical television shows within this cultural context. Bernstein easily wove in references from highbrow to lowbrow, from art and literature to comic strips and commercials, seemingly without class awareness, thereby touching all brow levels. His *Young People's Concerts* demonstrate not only his successful, eclectic, almost "postmodern" inclusiveness but also the most powerful cultural trends of the day. Chapter 4 focuses on television and the performing arts, revealing new information about the inception of the programs at the hands of Bernstein and William S. Paley of CBS, and how the American Bernstein, through the medium of television, replaced the Italian Toscanini as the "culture-god" for music in the second half of the twentieth century. The time slots of the broadcasts and the Nielsen ratings show how the number of viewers peaked, then fell off, reflecting the changing status of classical music. A study of sponsors with their target markets reveals that they aimed not for the highbrow, but for the middlebrow and family market.

The third part delves into how the political and social contexts of his time influenced Bernstein, how they may have been brought into the scripts, and how he upon occasion apparently sought to sway audiences. This is achieved through matching timelines (supported by accompanying secondary sources and newsreels) with a sensitive reading of the scripts, coupled with an understanding of Bernstein's life and known opinions. Chapter 5 focuses on the Cold War. One proposed program was far too incendiary for the political climate and never passed the outline stage. Overt political messages had no place in Bernstein's *Young People's Concerts*, yet the evidence is strong that he proselytized indirectly. This chapter offers a portrait of the veiled connection between these programs and world events, as seen, for example, in the show "The Latin American Spirit." The maestro had a lifelong affection for Latin America. Within weeks of the Cuban Missile Crisis, he dispelled the prevailing image people had formed of Latin America as being comprised only of bellicose, unruly "peasants" by dedicating an entire program to the educated, elegant, urban, and urbane aspects of Latin American countries. Bernstein proved himself a master of the subliminal message. Chapter 6 covers how social issues crept into the programs: civil rights, feminism, hippies, excessive illegal drug use, faith in astrology, international unity, and the responsibilities of citizens in a democracy. His comments became bolder after he announced his resignation from the Philharmonic, in part, perhaps, because the topics became less fraught with controversy.

The final part studies Bernstein's interaction with the canons of modernism and American music. Information taken from secondary sources, as well as the writings of Bernstein and his contemporaries, provides the background for a careful examination of the scripts and repertory. Chapter 7 examines Bernstein's predilection for "reactionary" (that is, tonal, melodic) music and his troubled relationship with the avant garde (both fellow composers and critics). After a brief survey of the different approaches to musical composition (with their concomitant political ramifications) in the twentieth century, the focus moves to Bernstein's troubles as a reactionary composer and his various pro-tonal writings. The chapter concludes with a study of Bernstein's programming and comments on the various types of modernism seen in his *Young People's Concerts*. Although he programmed atonal works, his tonal bias negatively colors his comments throughout. The final chapter focuses on American music, beginning with a brief survey of the role that the New York Philharmonic (from its inception) and later Bernstein (once he became Music Director) played as advocates for American music. The maestro's concept of American music reached its maturity while he was at Harvard (as seen in his Harvard thesis) and only expands without changing substance throughout his life. In Bernstein's opinion, music does not sound American unless it includes some element of jazz, so this chapter concludes with a study of American music and jazz in his *Young People's Concerts*. He was a creature of his time, and his *Young People's Concerts* were a mirror of their time.

The detailed appendices list chronological and alphabetical lists of the programs with possible motivations for topics, production information, the youngsters on the "Young Performers" programs (with age, country of origin, and repertory performed), Nielsen ratings, twentieth-century works separated into reactionary and avant garde, pieces by American composers, and a list of *Young People's Concerts* from 1958 to 1972 (both televised and not televised) under the hand of presenters other than Bernstein.

A BRIEF BIOGRAPHY OF LEONARD BERNSTEIN

Bernstein is the subject of many biographies, children's books, timelines, and photographic essays in many languages. Rather than reiterating information that is well known, this offers a short biography of Bernstein focusing primarily on those aspects of his life that influenced or contributed in some fashion to his *Young People's Concerts*: his family background, love of popular music, television work, political difficulties, and experiences as both student and teacher.

Bernstein was born on 25 August 1918 in Lawrence, Massachusetts, to immigrant Russian Jews, Jennie (née Charna Resnick, 1898–1992) and

Samuel Joseph (Schmuel Josef, 1892–1969) Bernstein. The immigrant Jewish community of Boston played a profound role in his life, from family and classmates to friends and synagogue.

Bernstein's father left his *shtetl* in the Ukraine in 1908, leaving behind its certain military conscription and anti-Semitic persecution.[2] Once arriving in the United States, he worked hard to succeed in his new country. His first job was cleaning fish at Boston's Fulton Fish Market. Sam eventually lived the American dream, becoming a prosperous middle-class businessman owning his own hair and beauty supply company. He hoped that his son would follow him into the business, but Leonard took his own path toward what his father assumed would be an unreliable and unrespectable career—music. Later, with pride in both his son and his adopted country, he described Leonard as "my gift to Uncle Sam" (H. Burton 1994, 122).

Although Leonard did not come from a musical family, he was drawn to music even as a toddler. Little Lenny would cry "moynik, moynik!"—music, music—until someone would put a recording on the Victrola. The family 78s included Galli-Curci, Jewish cantors, and pop songs like "Oh by Jingo," which the child adored (7). Radio opened new musical worlds, supplying innumerable popular songs and commercial jingles for him to absorb and "rattle off" (7–8). His great-uncle Harry Levy's expensive Victrola introduced the boy to a different collection of diverse music, from Rosa Ponselle singing "Suicidio" (from *La Gioconda*) to Billy Rose's comedy song "'Barney Google,' with the Goo, Goo, Googly Eyes," as Bernstein called it (12). Thus, his earliest musical experiences (like many Americans of his time) had no artificial barriers between highbrow and lowbrow, art music and popular music; it was all simply food for his young ears. After fights with his father over the cost of music lessons, Bernstein discovered he could earn money to pay for his own piano lessons by following his natural bent toward teaching. His first student was his childhood friend and later colleague, Sid Ramin. His sensitivity to the emotional content in music is seen in the terms for chords he designed and taught Ramin before he knew music theory—finishing chords, pre-finishing, governing chords, and so forth, probably referring to the tonic, subdominant chords, and dominant (Simeone 2013, 556). The young musician also raised money for lessons by playing in jazz bands at weddings, which he said "filled me with a new kind of knowledge of popular music and black music that was far beyond anything I knew from the radio . . . and it became part of my musical bloodstream" (H. Burton 1994, 17). Bernstein and Ramin also played piano four-hand duets of such works as George Gershwin's *Rhapsody in Blue*, the "St. Louis Blues," and various songs by Jerome Kern (18). By the age of twelve, Bernstein's life as a pedagogue had officially begun, and the great variety of musical styles later seen in his *Young People's Concerts*—jazz, blues, opera, Broadway, American music, and high art—were already in his musical bloodstream.

Ironically, Bernstein never attended children's symphony concerts as a child. In "Overtures and Preludes" (8 January 1961), he tells the audience, "I heard most of my music at an early age over the radio, because I wasn't lucky enough then to attend children's concerts" (4). Typical of people who grew up with little money, his father's idea of entertainment was to stay home listening to the radio; tickets to live concerts, theater performances, or even movies were very rare. Radio played an important role in the development of the maestro's musical tastes.

Bernstein's lifelong relationship with Helen Coates began in 1932 when she became his piano teacher (Secrest 1994, 22). Coates was the first to recognize his genius and became an integral part of Bernstein's life until she died in 1989 (about a year and a half before Bernstein), their relationship spanning nearly sixty years (H. Burton 1994, 25). "Miss Coates" evolved from teacher, to mentor, to friend, and eventually private secretary. Her foresight and organizational abilities have left an amazingly complete documentary portrait of Bernstein's life. She saved every scrap of paper imaginable (now the core of the Leonard Bernstein Collection at the Library of Congress)—an extremely valuable achievement.

Bernstein's tendency to near total control of a production, seen in his *Young People's Concerts*, appears early in his life. As a teenager he, his younger sister Shirley Anne, and his friends put on a parody of the opera *Carmen* at the family's summer home in Sharon, Massachusetts. He wrote the parody with a friend, recruited the performers, borrowed costumes (including wigs from his father's company), ran the rehearsals, choreographed the dances, performed the title role (!), and played piano, all at the young age of fifteen (22–23).

Immigrants often value education for its own sake but also as a path to success. Sam Bernstein gave his son the best possible: Boston Latin School and Harvard University. Leonard knew his father was a great Hebrew scholar who highly respected learning and considered himself a "chip off the old Tanach" (16). The young conductor spent summers at the musical mecca at Tanglewood in Massachusetts, studying under his future mentor, Serge Koussevitzky, and earned a diploma from the famed Curtis Institute (Secrest 1994, 60–72, 83–85).[3] Bernstein honored his teachers from these institutions (along with Coates and others) in his *Young People's Concert* "A Tribute to Teachers" (29 November 1963) (Bernstein 1982, 178–210). These teachers, along with his father, informed Bernstein's pedagogical style.

Teaching permeated Bernstein's life: from local children when he himself was a child; to students at Tanglewood, Berkshire, and Brandeis University; to professionals in the orchestras he conducted; as well as his audiences. His work at Tanglewood inspired him to establish conducting schools late in his life in Fontainbleau at the Schleswig-Holstein Music Festival in northern Germany (late 1980s), and the Pacific Music Festival in Sapporo, Japan (1990). His pedagogical bent is also apparent in his film and television work.[4] His first original television script (on Beethoven's sketches for the Fifth Symphony) was in 1954 for the weekly cultural series *Omnibus* on CBS. Bernstein's overtly pedagogical television programs include: *Omnibus* (ten programs, 1954–1961), *Lincoln Presents* (four programs, 1958–1959), *Ford Presents* (eleven programs, 1959–1962), *Young People's Concerts* (fifty-three programs, 1958–1972), as well as twenty other scripts. *The Unanswered Question* (six programs, 1976) are among the nearly 200 films he made for Unitel-Amberson Music Films from 1971 to 1991, many of which had pedagogical elements.

Jamie Bernstein, his eldest daughter, feels the Hebrew phrase "Torah Lishmah" (loosely translated as a raging thirst for knowledge) was at his core, "what he loved most was to communicate his excitement to others."[5] In fact, one of his earliest statements as the new Music Director of the Philharmonic was, "my job is an educational mission" (H. Burton 1994, 290). Toward the end of his life, he said that he was proudest of his own accomplishments as a teacher saying, "I don't feel vindicated as a composer, but I do as a teacher" (W. W. Burton 1995, xxxiii). Many who knew him agree.[6] Bernstein's podium often served as a lectern. Every rehearsal was a chance to teach the orchestra, and almost every concert was a chance to teach the audience, as evidenced by the Thursday Evening Preview series that he ran from 1958 through 1962; he would informally speak to the audience about the works on the program and would readily stop the orchestra to make a point (H. Burton 1994, 290–291).

Bernstein sprang into the conducting limelight with his dramatic debut directing the New York Philharmonic on radio for the ailing Bruno Walter on 14 November 1943. He eventually conducted around the world, breaking ground as the first American to conduct at La Scala and the first American-born and -trained music director of the New York Philharmonic (1958–1969). As a conductor, he actively programmed American music and twentieth-century music and was a tremendous advocate for Gustav Mahler and Aaron Copland. Bernstein was so revered by the Philharmonic that they named him Laureate Conductor on his departure. He later developed a close relationship with the Vienna Philharmonic.

Throughout his life, Bernstein often placed himself in the thick of political as well as social controversy. Specific instances are mentioned in later chapters. Recently, Seldes (2009) thoroughly studied the maestro's FBI files and then related them and politics in America to aspects of Bernstein's life and works. One incident in particular cast a shadow over Bernstein's early career, influencing the nature and extent of many of his later actions. Like many artists during the McCarthy era, the evidence is strong that the young maestro was blacklisted just as his professional life was taking off. His name appearing in *Red Channels* of 1950 had far-reaching and profound results: Bernstein's compositions (along with those by fellow "communists" such as Copland, Gershwin, Roger Sessions, Virgil Thomson, and Roy Harris) were removed from the International Information Administration libraries and Voice of America broadcasts (Seldes 2009, 66); Bernstein knew the blacklist extended to CBS radio and Hollywood (53); both Paley, chairman of the board of CBS who was "an aggressive blacklister," and conservative Arthur Judson were on the board of the Philharmonic, which, along with other factors, may have barred the young maestro from any appointments with the orchestra between 1951 and 1956 (55–56). Bernstein rehabilitated himself by signing a humiliating affidavit, which allowed Robert Saudek to hire him in 1954 for the television series *Omnibus* without complaint from CBS (67–72). Bernstein's nightmare was over but not forgotten; traces seep out at times in his *Young People's Concerts*.

Bernstein's love for and success with musicals, coupled with his enjoyment of popular styles such as boogie-woogie, negatively influenced his early conducting career. Secrest (1994, 144) asserts that the obvious pleasure he took in this type of music was partly responsible for his not being given the post of director of the Boston Symphony Orchestra. Bernstein received similar messages from his greatest mentor, Koussevitzky. At the Boston opening of Bernstein's 1944 musical *On the Town*, Koussevitzky gave Bernstein a furious, three-hour lecture about how a potentially great conductor must not "dissipate his talents" (H. Burton 1994, 136). From then on, Bernstein restricted his composing to holidays. Bernstein's "surrender to Koussevitzky was almost as unconditional as that of the Nazis to the Allied Forces in May 1945" (137). Nonetheless, the maestro went on to write several successful musicals, but only after Koussevitzky's death.

As a composer, Bernstein created works in a great variety of styles and genres.[7] For the concert hall, he wrote three symphonies (*Jeremiah*, 1943; *The Age of Anxiety*, 1949; and *Kaddish*, 1962–1963), song cycles (such as *I Hate Music*, 1943; *La bonne cuisine*, 1948), and solo piano pieces (many short works called "Anniversaries" written over many years for friends and family). For the stage, he wrote Broadway shows (*On the Town*, 1944; *Wonderful Town*, 1953; *West Side Story*, 1957), a chamber opera (*Trouble in Tahiti*, 1952), an operetta (*Candide*, 1955–1956), an opera (*A Quiet Place*, 1983), as well as ballets (*Fancy Free*, 1944; *Dybbuk*, 1974), and incidental music for plays (*Peter Pan*, 1950, play by J. M. Barrie; *The Lark*, 1955, play by Anouilh). He also ventured into other forms such as traditional choral works (*Chichester Psalms*, 1965) and film music (*On the Waterfront*, 1954). It could be said that his characteristic blending of high- and lowbrow music culminated in the 1971 work *Mass*, which includes choral anthems, electronic music, folksong, rock, jazz, marching band, and almost Mahlerian finales.

His three children by the Chilean actress Felicia Montealegre Cohn (whom he married in 1951) continue Bernstein's work: daughter Jamie (born 1952), son Alexander Serge (1955), and daughter Nina (1962).[8] The children founded JALNI Publications (Jamie, ALexander, NIna), a subsidiary of Bernstein's company Amberson Enterprises. Jamie is the public face of the Bernstein family, touring and giving talks and interviews. Nina remains behind the scenes dealing with the Bernstein legacy, such as the Leonard Bernstein Collection at the Library of Congress. Alexander founded and runs the Leonard Bernstein Center for Artful Learning. Following Bernstein's model of an integrated education, the Center shows primary- and secondary-school teachers how to teach all subjects by relating them to a practical understanding of music and the arts. The Center's success and influence continues to grow.[9]

Bernstein was showered with an almost overwhelming number of honors in his life. The Leonard Bernstein Office website offers, under "Research," a selected list: twenty-two honorary degrees (which he stopped accepting in the late 1980s) (Rozen 1998, 33); thirteen decorations from foreign governments; twenty Grammies; twenty platinum, gold, and international record awards; eleven Emmy Awards; fourteen other television awards; sixty arts awards; twenty-seven civic awards (keys to the city/state proclamations); fourteen honorary memberships in various societies; and five honorary offices. These 206 honors represent only a *selected* list. The encomiums on his death attest to his accomplishments and to the great affection a large portion of the artistic world had for him.

• 1 •

Background

Who, When, and How

> My dear young friends: I am happy and proud to welcome you
> to our tenth season of *Young People's Concerts*. Imagine, it's been
> a whole decade we've been playing and talking about music for
> you. And I don't know how much you've actually learned, but I
> like to think we must be doing something right, because—well,
> because it's our tenth season.
>
> —Leonard Bernstein, "What Is a Mode?" (23 November 1966)

$\mathscr{L}$eonard Bernstein must indeed have been doing something right with his
Young People's Concerts. To help orient the reader for later discussions, I will
begin with some basic background information on this unique international
television series: the general structure, broadcast times, technologies employed, people involved, and creative process.

GENERAL STRUCTURE OF
BERNSTEIN'S *YOUNG PEOPLE'S CONCERTS*

Bernstein controlled almost all aspects of these televised concerts. He decided on the topics, wrote the scripts, selected the compositions and guest
artists (assisted by the production crew), narrated the programs, conducted,
and performed. He collaborated on the production of the first shows with
producer Roger Englander and director Charles Dubin (who was blacklisted
and removed after three shows). Soon, Bernstein liked what Englander did
and left production entirely to him (Rose 1992, 132). A Young People's Concerts Committee, comprised of dedicated women (who met periodically at a
member's house), acted as liaison between the audiences and the orchestra's

1

management.[1] They coordinated school groups, surveyed teachers' attitudes toward content, summarized promotional efforts, and so forth.[2]

The fifty-three one-hour programs spanned fourteen years or fifteen seasons, from the first program (18 January 1958) during the 1957–1958 season through the final program (26 March 1972) during the 1971–1972 season. The experimental opening season had three televised *Young People's Concerts*, and seasons 2 through 12 (1958–1969) had four each. For the final three seasons (1969–1972, after he retired as music director of the Philharmonic), Bernstein televised only two of four, while various conductors, composers, performers, and actors (such as Peter Ustinov) covered the other two which were not broadcast.[3] Perhaps these were intended as auditions to see who would be his successor.[4]

The target age for the audience was vague at first. Before Bernstein assumed control of the *Young People's Concerts* in 1958, no particular standard was established—children of any age could attend. By 1959, however, children under six were deemed too disruptive and excluded.[5] In 1966, Carlos Moseley, the manager of the Philharmonic, reported that the target audience was children eight to thirteen, although those both younger and older did attend.[6] Bernstein himself said that he felt his audience was best represented by the "typical 13-year old" (the age of his eldest daughter, Jamie, at the time) and wrote for that age (Rees 1966, 28).[7] This seems an accurate description of the majority of those who attended the live performances in New York City.[8] However, apparently more adults watched the programs on television than children.[9] Englander affirmed that adults "wanted their kids to watch. Or just adults [would watch]. Our fan mail came more from adults than kids" (Rose 1992, 135). In fact, in 1964 CBS reported that 83 percent of the viewers were adults (37 percent men and 46 percent women) and 17 percent young people; of these only 6 percent were Bernstein's target audience of teenagers, while 11 percent were younger.[10]

The pedagogical design of the programs essentially remained the same: an opening question or statement that was then answered or discussed, followed by a performance (Rozen 1998, 146). Brian David Rozen classified the pedagogical organization of the programs and described variations to this basic plan.[11]

BROADCAST AND PRODUCTION

Bernstein's *Young People's Concerts* were performed in and televised from two prestigious halls: Carnegie Hall until April 1962, then the newly constructed Concert Hall at Lincoln Center. The performances were almost always on Saturday afternoons for the convenience of children and their parents.[12] The first seven seasons (1957–1964) were Saturdays at noon; beginning with the eighth season (1964–1965), the performances were changed to Saturdays, usually from 2:35 to 3:35 p.m.[13]

The broadcast time shifted throughout the days of the week. Slightly over half (at the beginning and end of the series) were shown on weekends, with the remainder during the "golden hours" of primetime on different weekdays. Early television technology required that programs 1 through 9 (6 March 1960) be broadcast live. Once the programs were recorded in advance, the broadcast time became flexible but remained on weekends (programs 10 through 15), aiming for the family audience in a less than desirable time slot (not primetime). In May 1961, FCC Chair Newton Minow gave his "Vast Wasteland" speech that chided broadcasters to choose diverse programming, including cultural fare, instead of only questing for the highest ratings with popular genres such as Westerns and sitcoms (Barnouw 1970, 196–201). After this famous address and beginning with the fifth season (1961–1962), Bernstein's *Young People's Concerts* were paraded during primetime, usually 7:30–8:30 p.m., on various weeknights as evidence of the artistic merit CBS provided. Also starting with the fifth season, the concerts were broadcast internationally beginning with Canada.[14] As the television market changed in the mid-1960s, the Nielsen ratings dropped, and the *Young People's Concerts* began having trouble. Documents reveal great struggles to find a sponsor for the eleventh season (1967–1968). For seasons eleven through fifteen (1967–1972), the series was moved back to Sunday afternoons at 4:30, in what noted journalist Edward R. Murrow called the "intellectual ghetto."[15]

Three different technologies preserve Bernstein's *Young People's Concerts*. Seasons 1 and 2 (1957–1959) were broadcast live in black and white and recorded on kinescope. Seasons 3 through 9 (1959–1966) were recorded in black and white on two-inch Quadruplex (Quad) video tape. Programs from 10 (27 March 1960) onward saw two technological advances—separate times for taping (allowing for later broadcast) and use of the teleprompter (allowing greater freedom of movement but requiring an extra rehearsal).[16] From the tenth season (1966–1967) to the end of the run in 1972, the performances were recorded in color on two-inch Quad tape.[17] Twenty-five of the programs representative of all three technologies became commercially available when they were selected for transfer to VHS tape in the 1980s and later to DVD.[18] The remainder of the series became available in 2013 when volume 2 was released on DVD.

THE CREATIVE PROCESS

Understanding the creative process is vital to realizing that most of each script sprang from Bernstein's mind and how little others influenced the final product. The maestro felt an exemplary teacher would, "Tell them what you're going to do. Then do it. Then tell them what you did" (Rose 1992, 131). This familiar adage by an unknown humble rural preacher has achieved fame in many speech textbooks and aptly describes the creation and execution of these programs (Rees 1966, 73). Fortunately, existing documents make it possible to trace their evolution from inception to execution. After Bernstein wrote the outline and script, the production crew met several times, generating multiple drafts until the final product was approved.[19] Once the ideal script was written, he made only minor changes during performance.

The notes, outline, and first draft of each script were solely the work of Bernstein. To shape the final draft the maestro met many times with a talented group of individuals who would energetically evaluate the proposed script, make certain it read well, offer suggestions on wording or structure, suggest possible cuts, and discuss which pieces would be performed. Changes continued through the dress rehearsal.

Producer/director Englander's contract stipulated that the completed script must be in his hands one month before the air date (Rose 1992, 133). Bernstein found this difficult since he tended to write the scripts at the last minute. This narrow, pre-set window between the script being finished and being broadcast coupled with the need for scheduling the topics before the beginning of each season becomes important when considering how the shows might have been influenced by current events.

Once he had a topic, Bernstein scribbled thoughts on any scrap of paper handy, but usually in pencil on his favored yellow-lined legal-sized paper. He then created a general outline that was quite close to the script's final form in organization if not in detail.[20] He preferred the quiet intimacy of handwriting to the clatter of a typewriter or the stress of dictating.[21] When comparing the final script with the outline, all the primary elements and many of the secondary elements are already there, occasionally reorganized. Sometimes he listed a plethora of options for pieces, with composers and/or titles written in, crossed out, and scribbled in margins. For instance, the first page of notes for "Folk Music in the Concert Hall" (9 April 1961) has general brainstorming; the second page gives all the general ideas and potential musical examples, with the first names of thirty-eight composers marching down the right margin. Most of the songs proposed for demonstrating the differences in style and language are nestled in the upper left margin. The bottom of the page is covered with the ubiquitous time estimates for talk and music. Sometimes, Bernstein simply left a blank line where a piece should be listed, and works were later chosen as the script evolved.[22] Clearly, the pedagogical concept was more important than the work in such cases.

Next Bernstein wrote the first draft, again using pencil and yellow-lined legal-sized paper.[23] He always wrote more than necessary allowing for later refinement. He was frequently commended for not "talking down" to his audience, always choosing words and syntax familiar to his young audience. The *Newark News* (New Jersey) reported that "a new way to teach music to the young has been found—treat them as adults."[24] The *Musical Leader* in Chicago specifically mentioned that Bernstein "did not talk down to his listeners, in fact the things he said to them could easily have held the attention of adults, and probably did in many homes."[25] Miss Bill wrote a letter in 1958 on behalf of many students and teachers saying, "we think your Youth Concerts on CBS are simply delightful! They are entertaining and instructional, and many adults have expressed their admiration of the way you talk to your audience—'down to earth' and in their language." The same year Donald N. Luckenbill (Chairman of the Music Department for the Oyster Bay New York Public Schools) agreed, adding how good it was to see an American conductor who speaks American English as well as the language of "teen-age America, and who is actively acquainted with American musicals and American jazz." Joseph Horowitz attributes Bernstein's ability to avoid being "patronizing or sanctimonious" to his passion and naïve enthusiasm as he discussed music (2007, 478). The *Times Dispatch* of Richmond, Virginia, reported that Bernstein "has the rare quality of making everything he does seem terribly important" and that he "laid down a contagious fire of enthusiasm for 'just music.'"[26] The maestro would speak the words aloud as he wrote since he was "attempting to hear it as the audience would."[27] He further mentioned that "I find myself mumbling when I write, because it is to be spoken, not read. Sometimes I realize that my voice has been going for an hour." He knew the concerts were witnessed by two audiences (television and live), but focused entirely on the audience in the concert hall while writing and presenting the script (Rees 1966, 27). Bernstein was aware that young people have a shorter attention span and tried to anticipate when the program might lose their attention, lest the dreaded paper airplanes made from programs begin soaring about the concert hall (Cott 2013, 68). After describing his first *Young People's Concert* to Jonathan Cott, he proudly announced that there were "no paper airplanes" (69).

Apparently, Bernstein censored himself before committing the scripts to paper (as did many at that time), yet controversial ideas do sometimes creep into the outlines, as in either "The Latin American Spirit" (8 March 1963) in which he seems to skirt the Cuban Missile Crisis or "The Genius of Paul Hindemith" (23 February 1964) in which he compared music critics to Nazis.[28] Such problematic prose may even have survived until a final draft to be deleted at the last minute, as in "A Birthday Tribute to Shostakovich" (5 January 1966).[29] Surprisingly and sadly, such windows into Bernstein's innermost thoughts are usually missing.

Meetings with the production crew began only after Bernstein completed the first draft.[30] Englander selected most of the staff for the first
season, specifically director Charles Dubin and Mary Rodgers as Englander's
assistant (Rose 1992, 131).[31] Elizabeth (Candy) Finkler was added somewhat
later by CBS. At first, the production crew ranged from three to five, then
grew to six after the 1964–1965 season, including Jack Gottlieb despite the
absence of his name on the scripts' title pages. Bernstein needed a very special group of people for this job. He had to be comfortable with them lest
his creative flow be inhibited. Each person contributed a different skill, was
congenial, and had similar goals for the programs. Several of these extraordinary individuals worked on his *Young People's Concerts* for nearly the entire
run, so the crew must have been well chosen. Since they played a significant
role in editing the scripts, we should start with brief biographies of the most
important figures and their roles in the concerts.

Englander became good friends with Bernstein when they were both
at Tanglewood, eleven years before Bernstein's *Young People's Concerts* (Englander 1985, 29–35).[32] Englander is a highly respected television pioneer
who produced all fifty-three programs and directed seasons 2 through 15
(1958–1972).[33] He reminisced, "because I had known Leonard Bernstein for
many years I sensed that our re-association would be a happy one" and that
the series proved to be "the most rewarding experience of my professional life"
(Englander 1985, 30).

No one but Bernstein and Englander worked on the entire series, but
several people assisted with multiple programs: Rodgers, Finkler, John Corigliano Jr., and Gottlieb. Rodgers is the daughter of Richard Rodgers, composer of such well-known shows as *The Sound of Music*.[34] With Bernstein's love
of musical theater, it is no surprise that she was his friend before his *Young
People's Concerts* began.[35] From the beginning, she served as an assistant to the
producer, working on a total of fifty of the fifty-three shows. As a successful
author of children's books, she clarified and simplified the text (Englander
1985, 32). Finkler was a non-musician assigned by CBS and was the only
member of the crew not known to Bernstein beforehand. She worked on the
first program as assistant producer and became associate producer in the tenth
season (1966–1967), working on thirty-nine programs. She recorded the word
changes and, in Englander's words, "insist[ed] that we maintain some level of
decorum" and bring the show out on time (ibid.). Bernstein knew Corigliano
through his father John Corigliano Sr. (concertmaster of the Philharmonic).
Before he became a renowned composer, Corigliano was Englander's assistant for twenty-five shows from the eighth season to the end of the series
(1964–1972).[36] He provided musicological expertise (ibid.). Gottlieb studied
under Bernstein at Brandeis University in the fall of 1954 and wrote his 1964

DMA dissertation on Bernstein's music.[37] In the summer of 1958, Bernstein hired Gottlieb as his regular musical assistant with a portion of Gottlieb's pay coming from the Philharmonic; he became Bernstein's "amanuensis and colleague and occasionally his musical spokesman, and remained so, with only one break, until Bernstein's death" (H. Burton 1994, 302).[38] It is likely that he worked on all the shows from mid-1958 until 1966. As a musician and a scholar, his duties included research, suggesting repertory to meet a specific need (Peyser 1998, 299–300), and creating detailed cue sheets for the orchestra to ensure a smooth performance (Englander 1985, 32).

Gottlieb reports that the "family-style script meetings" had a "lot of easygoing give-and-take with Bernstein welcoming the banter and commentary of his production team" (2010, 176–177). But the maestro maintained total creative control, writing or approving every word himself. He insisted that "since he was doing the speaking, he could not comfortably deliver someone else's words," and that he would also have trouble remembering words that he had not written (Englander 1985, 32). There were three to seven conferences, typically scheduled two weeks before the first rehearsal. A difficult subject, such as "What Is Sonata Form?" (6 November 1964), or a program with many musical examples, such as "What Is a Mode?," needed more conferences (and more drafts) than simple programs such as a Young Performers program. Finkler remembers that, "sometimes it would be a breeze, with everything falling into place; other times a real sweat" (Finkler 1993). Conferences would run from around noon until sometime after 2:00 p.m. (Rees 1966, 40).

Most confirm Gottlieb's fond memories of these gatherings. Englander says that the "script conferences were happily anticipated rituals held at Bernstein's apartment. Our staff was small, but boisterous and creative" (Englander 1985, 32). Rodgers (1993) recalls, "Oh God, we all had such a good time," and Finkler (1993) remembers "the giggles and groans, the inspirations and perspirations." The friendly atmosphere is seen in anonymous sketches of the staff on a script page (see figure 10 in the center).

Bernstein's love of words and games can be seen in one of the entertaining ways he had of soliciting ideas: a competition for the perfect word.[39] As the performance deadline drew closer, the conferences became more focused and thoughtful. Even though most of the rewriting had been done, cuts had been made, prose tightened, Englander expressed it best when he said, "the search for the exact word, the most illuminating phrase, continued right up until we went on the air" (Englander 1985, 32).

Before the first script conference, the first draft was typed (with wide margins for notes), copied, and distributed to the members of the production crew, allowing them to write in suggestions before the first gathering (Rees 1966, 41). The typical meeting would begin with Bernstein reading the script aloud, singing the chosen musical examples (44). As he read, the interruptions for discussion were so frequent that whoever was timing the script was constantly turning the stopwatch on and off. Suggestions were made and debated—subject to the maestro's final decision—and revisions entered into the script. He would then read the altered passage again, allowing the group to immediately make a decision about the changes. The draft was retyped, copied, and redistributed for continued debate at the next meeting. Although this was sometimes a long, agonizing process that ran to five or six drafts, it usually required only one or two (36). Notes made at the last conference were added by hand directly to the final draft (50).[40]

Like Gottlieb, James Lester Rees (1966) described the meetings of the production crew as having an "atmosphere of cooperative criticism" in which Bernstein "displayed little ego-defensiveness" (41). Corigliano had a somewhat different experience, as he explained to Meryl Secrest: "[Bernstein] did the entire script. You couldn't suggest anything to him. Not always better, but it was his. . . . And yet . . . he's brilliant. The man's a genius. We'd make suggestions in an incomplete way, so that he could add his own flourishes. I don't mean this as a criticism. The results were the best ever" (Secrest 1994, 245). Since Bernstein felt all the words needed to be his own, perhaps he rejected certain suggestions that either veered off the track he had in mind or could not be adapted to his speaking style. Perhaps specific suggestions stifled his creativity whereas general ideas would fuel his imagination leading to a more effective presentation.

Rees sat in on two production meetings for "A Birthday Tribute to Shostakovich" (Rees 1966, 41–55). A few of the script changes he mentions are below. The overriding reason for alterations was, "will the kids get it?" (39). Prose was reduced or simplified. For instance, the partial line "Yevtushenko's famous poem 'Babi Yar' (an outcry against anti-Semitism)" was simplified to read "Yevtushenko's famous poem against anti-Semitism" (42). The unfamiliar title was removed, and the strong emotional content of the original line was diminished. The latter change verifies that Bernstein pointedly avoided potential controversy in his *Young People's Concerts*.[41] Long lists were eliminated or reduced. In "A Birthday Tribute to Shostakovich," a collection of unfamiliar Russian names recounting Shostakovich's heritage was reduced to "after all, he is basically a traditional Russian composer—a true son of Tchaikovsky" (42). Irrelevancies were removed. For instance, when discussing why the unexpected is funny, Bernstein initially wrote, "scientists have tried to explain this for centuries, and they still don't know why surprises are funny" (44). The word *scientists* was deemed inaccurate and changed to *experts*; in the second meeting the entire sentence was deemed irrelevant and removed for the sake of time. The scripts were tightly constructed.

Bernstein gave careful thought to reaching his audience with the most appealing and effective words and analogies. Bernstein's brother, Burton Bernstein, wrote about the maestro's quest for just the right allusion with which to reach a German audience, a search that took a couple of days, research, and the advice of several people.[42] In the Shostakovich program, Bernstein rejected the sentence, "It's like sitting down to a big serious banquet, and finding that someone has pulled away your chair," saying that it is not really like that. After discussion, he rewrote the sentence to read "and being served hot dogs and potato chips." Everyone agreed this was "better for kids, and a better and more apropos analogy" (48).

Occasionally, the production crew would help censor the text prior to review by the network and sponsors. When Bernstein wrote, "thank God! He's made it at last," referring to a seemingly tardy trombone entrance at the end of the first movement of Symphony no. 9, Englander reminded him that the sponsor might not sanction that particular expression. Bernstein laughed. "Heavens be praised" was suggested and rejected because the maestro felt the phrase would not "come easily out of my mouth," so "thank Goodness" was finally chosen (ibid.). Bernstein's contract required him, among other things, to avoid controversial topics; when the first truly controversial issue arose during the third season (1959–1960), he censored himself in advance.[43] If he missed something that might prove objectionable, his stalwart production crew would catch the offending words before they made it to the screen.

Once the teleprompter was used (beginning with "Unusual Instruments of the Past, Present, and Future," 27 March 1960), there was a teleprompter rehearsal, after which the production crew would gather on stage for a brief evaluation of the script and its presentation. As Englander said, alterations continued even then. For instance, a bassoon solo near the end of the final movement of Shostakovich's Ninth Symphony had been described as "saucy," but Bernstein felt a better word could be found. After many different suggestions from everyone, Rodgers offered "kittenish," which the maestro happily accepted (58). After this, Englander and Bernstein would adjourn to the upstairs studio to "go over the script and paste and cut to make it come out to 52:40" (Rose 1992, 134).

This final point highlights a problem that pervaded every aspect of Bernstein's *Young People's Concerts*, and indeed everything on television from the very beginning: time. The exigencies of network television were so overwhelming that, when Rose interviewed him twenty years after the last program in the series, Englander still remembered how long the programs needed to be down to the second. Bernstein described staying within the time frame of a broadcast and including appropriate breaks as "an impossible business" but a "small sacrifice" compared to the opportunity (Simeone 2013, 380). For the first ten years of the show, there was a commercial only at the beginning and end; the program was seen without interruption.[44] By the end of the series, two commercial breaks had been added, dividing the show into thirds and causing pre-set interruptions. From that time forward, all the prose, the short demonstrations, and the longer pieces performed by Bernstein or the Philharmonic had to be wedged logically into these sections without destroying the flow of the overall concert.[45] Finkler, who was in charge of time issues for most of the series, said, "there was no editing and the network tended to be humorless about a show running three seconds late" (Finkler 1993).

The concern with time permeates the documents for Bernstein's *Young People's Concerts*. Timings were scribbled at the bottom of his initial notes, on outlines, and in the margins of scripts (see figure 12). To ascertain more exact timings, the production crew created charts (such as that provided in figure 11) that detailed estimated time, time at first rehearsal, and time at second rehearsal, cued by instrument.[46] The difficulties with time were exacerbated by the fact that there was never a complete dress rehearsal (Finkler 1993).[47] Another job of the production crew was to puzzle out possible cuts, labeled "Poss cuts" in the scripts; these often became reality if a program went over time (Rodgers 1993). Time constraints were beneficial in that redundancies were removed; wordiness replaced by conciseness. Time was a guiding force.

Some of the other problems the production crew encountered are seen in a rare critical evaluation that Bernstein typed at the end of a draft for "Musical Atoms: A Study of Intervals" (29 November 1965):

> PROBLEMS 1. Ork [orchestra]. Doesn't play a note for ages. 2. Is there a piece to end part I? (5') 3. Is there time for such a piece? (Wagner?) Seems to me it's the game or the piece. 4. Invent a game with viable rules, that will be fun, to make the audience participation more than just a quiz. Att: Mary Rodgers 5. Talka too much. How involve ork. nearer top of show? Apropos of 4. Can this game involve the orchestra? Can it be a contest: everyone given a card and pencil to write down intervals of famous tunes, and send them in to me or Bell Tel. and winners receive a—oh, balls.[48]

Four problems are apparent. What is the balance between talk and music? What piece will fit into the time available? How should the music and talk be distributed within the program? What kind of audience participation will be both challenging and fun? Bernstein and the production crew certainly faced a formidable task.

Once the final script was completed, Bernstein moved forward with enthusiasm. Corigliano said, "He'd look at the positive side. He wouldn't go on tearing it apart, as he had at the beginning. He suspended judgment. He wanted to be pleased with it" (Secrest 1994, 245). The fact that he accepted it with such relish no doubt facilitated his ability to memorize and effectively deliver the script.

From all reports, being on the production crew was a wonderful experience. Rodgers expresses it well: "We had great pride in what we were doing; and we had great affection and respect for each other. Most of all, we had love. For Lenny, and from Lenny, and, as I've already said, Oh God, we all had such a good time" (Rodgers 1993).

After such elaborate labors to create the seemingly perfect script, Bernstein nevertheless often departed from the carefully prepared words in live performance. These changes, however, were insubstantial since he wrote the scripts, made sure that he felt comfortable with the ideas and wording, and practiced them repeatedly. The maestro said, "I used to stay up nights, not just writing it but memorizing. I remember my wife Felicia hearing my lines and falling asleep, and then Adolph Green would come over and spell her—one would take a nap while the other one heard me. Those were tough days, and whatever went out on the air, that's what people heard and saw—and if there were mistakes, there were mistakes!" (Burton 1995, 38). Bernstein worked tremendously hard in both crafting natural-sounding scripts and practicing an unaffected delivery, so he must have been pleased to see from the fan mail that viewers noticed and approved. Ruth Burks, a writing teacher, said that she watched "throughout with intense interest—and I learned a great deal . . . not only in how you went about presenting your subject, but actually learning what you were trying to teach. It was exciting and moving, and I am still carrying the exhilaration. . . . You could not have *contrived* the manner, the informality of language, the friendly relationship, and had it strike the bell." Actress, director, and playwright Caleen Jennings attended the live performances and was quite surprised to discover that the scripts had been carefully crafted.[49]

Bernstein was so integral to the success of his televised *Young People's Concerts* that in the ninth season the Philharmonic sought contingency plans in case he was unable to perform. In a memo, William L. Weissel recommended to Moseley that two assistant conductors be present at all "YPC-TV" rehearsals ready to conduct.[50] The program would be changed: "Since Mr. Bernstein's talk fills about half the time of the program and nobody could learn Mr. Bernstein's script 'at a moment's notice', musical numbers (chosen by Bernstein in advance) have to be substituted for the narrative part of the program." The appropriate people would have to be notified. Without Bernstein, the live audience would see a concert conducted by an assistant without narration, and the televised concert would be cancelled. Fortunately, these contingency plans were never needed. Bernstein was simply irreplaceable.

For more than thirty years—from his early *Omnibus* shows in the mid-1950s to his 1973 Harvard lectures—Leonard Bernstein wove pedagogy and performance together for television audiences. Extending for fifteen seasons in the middle of his career, from 1958 to 1972, Bernstein's fifty-three hour-long *Young People's Concerts* are undoubtedly his most important and far-reaching contribution to music education on television. Every aspect of every program was either Bernstein's idea or approved by him, and he personally carefully considered every word. In *Newsweek*, he said that these children's shows "have a quality that I particularly love. When you know that you're reaching children without compromise or the assistance of acrobats, marching bands, slides, and movies, but that you are getting them with hard talk, a piano, and an orchestra . . . it gives you a gratification that is enormous."[51]

This book seeks to understand the influence of Bernstein's life and times on his *Young People's Concerts* and how they probably were a forum for his musical and non-musical ideas, subtly or obviously. Through it all, he had to maintain the goodwill of CBS, the sponsors, and the audience (both the live and television audiences), hold the audience's interest, and create a positive atmosphere for the children, while honoring the main goal of the series: to teach young people how to understand and enjoy music. Somehow, Bernstein managed simultaneously to juggle all these goals, react to current events, and slip in his own messages—both for a more inclusive musical world and for a better world in general.

• *2* •

Decisions

Topics, Pieces, and Performers

> It's wonderful to be back with you again, after what I hope was
> a nice restful summer vacation, and since you're all looking so
> bright and ready to work, I've picked a real hard subject for this
> opening program.
>
> —Leonard Bernstein, "What Is Sonata Form?"
> (6 November 1964)

$\mathscr{T}$he first season of Bernstein's *Young People's Concerts* was a grand experiment by CBS and the Philharmonic when television was young. The future would hold either success or failure, determined in part by the young maestro's choices. He had to ensure that the shows not only taught but drew in the television audience. Here we see how he achieved this so successfully over fourteen years by providing an overview of the previously undocumented processes for deciding on topics, repertory, and young soloists.

SELECTING TOPICS

The first task was choosing a topic. As a lover of language and an intelligent thinker, Bernstein understood the difficulties of trying to explain the inexplicable, that is, "the unique phenomenon of human reaction to organized sound" (Bernstein 1959, 11). He was aware of the pitfalls of what Virgil Thomson (1962, 111–120) referred to as the "appreciation-racket" that (according to Bernstein) frequently bored people and whose chief goal was the mass marketing of music (Bernstein 1959, 13). But the maestro also realized

13

that the public of his time was "an intelligent organism" longing for knowledge and insight, and that teachers must try to "shed some light on the mystery [of music]" (13). He details the two different approaches that the "racket" usually took in the introduction to his book *The Joy of Music*, suggesting that "one is duller than the other." Type A fills the audience with "homey tales" and "anecdotes" while telling them "nothing about music." Type B focuses on analysis—"a laudably serious endeavor," but the second is as dull as the first is coy (14). After denigrating the traditional music appreciation approach, he expounds on what he feels is the mystery of "meaning" in music. His description basically follows an outline he prepared for the first year of his *Young People's Concerts*, which pre-dates *The Joy of Music* by approximately a year.[1] Both suggest that music has four possible meanings: narrative-literary meanings (for example, Richard Strauss's *Till Eulenspiegel*); atmospheric-pictorial meanings (Claude Debussy's *La Mer*); affective-reactive meanings (triumph, melancholy, and the like); and purely musical meanings. While Bernstein asserted that only the last is "worthy of *musical* analysis," he did allow that "certain extra-musical ideas, like religion, or social factors, or historical forces" might influence music (16). He observed that finding a middle ground between "the music-appreciation racket and purely technical discussion" is difficult, but was confident that it could be found (ibid.). Bernstein felt whenever his talks about music succeeded (as in his *Young People's Concerts*), it was because he achieved this goal. While the scripts did fluctuate between music appreciation (such as "Fantastic Variations [*Don Quixote*]," 25 December 1968) and purely technical discussions (such as the award-winning "What Is Sonata Form?"), his choice of topics helped him maintain that happy medium.

Topics were inextricably linked to the repertory of the Philharmonic's current season.[2] They either were inspired by the season or suitable works would be chosen from the season to fit the demands of the script. Bernstein felt that no subject was too difficult for his young viewers, so he felt confident choosing ideas and music from the regular Philharmonic season for adults (Cott 2013, 68).

Topics were chosen during the spring or summer prior to each season, then submitted to CBS and the sponsor (Rees 1966, 36).[3] From the third season (1959–1960) through the twelfth season (1968–1969), topics were chosen from four general areas: technical investigations, composers, music appreciation, and young performers, usually one program per subject area. In the first two seasons (1957–1959), Bernstein only delved into music appreciation and technical investigations as he experimented with format. In the last three seasons, after he retired as music director of the Philharmonic (1969–1972), the focus shifted almost entirely to composers. As he gradually distanced himself from the Philharmonic, he abandoned technical investigations and young performers programs, then finally appreciation. For his last two seasons, the sole remaining topic was composer/works. The maestro had the flexibility to revise or substitute other topics as the broadcast date approached, which allowed current events to influence his choices.

Every decision about topics was controlled by one especially important factor: how to showcase the Philharmonic (Rees 1966, 36). The orchestra's management sponsored these programs to feature not only their famed Music Director but also the orchestra. Bernstein said that although he would have enjoyed doing a program on the music of India, he could not since the focus would be on instruments of India (sitars, tablas, and the like) rather than those of the Philharmonic (ibid.). Financial factors also had to be considered as these broadcasts not only provided extra income for the players, but doubled as rehearsals for many recording sessions, as discussed below.[4]

CLASSIFICATION AND DISTRIBUTION OF TOPICS

The programs of Bernstein's *Young People's Concerts* were officially classified by topic three times. Bernstein himself categorized them during the eighth season (1965–1966).[5] PBS did the same in 1975 when the network was considering rebroadcasting the entire series, and Unitel followed suit in 1989 (when they were organizing the transfer of twenty-five programs to VHS).[6] The maestro said that he usually emphasized four general areas each season: technical musical concepts; the symphony orchestra, or music in general; composers; and young performers (Rees 1966, 35). The subject categories created later by PBS and Unitel are essentially the same. The Young Performers programs are the least technical and showcase young talent without musical explanations.

While Bernstein's overview for the topics covered in a typical season is appropriate for the ninth season (1965–1966) when he was interviewed, it does not hold true for the entire series. That particular season either represents the maestro's model or may simply be a reflection of what was on his mind at the time he was interviewed.[7] Despite Bernstein's avowal, only one-third of the seasons follow his ideal scenario.

Table 2.1 offers an overview of the seasons according to the four subject categories suggested by Bernstein: technical investigations (that is, form, compositional techniques, and the like), appreciation, composers, and young performers. In cases where the program has elements of more than one category, the classification is determined by the primary characteristic. Bernstein took his pedagogical obligations very seriously: twenty of the fifty-three

Table 2.1.   Classification of Bernstein's *Young People's Concerts* by Season and Subject Area

Season	Technical Investigations	Composers	Appreciation	Young Performers
1		*1, 2, 3*		
2	*4, 7*		5, 6	
3		8, *11*	10	9
4	*15*	13	12	14*
5	17*	18	16	19
6	20, 21		23*	22*
7	27	26	24	25*
8	28	31	29	30
9	32	34*	33	35
10	36	38		37, 39*
11	43	41*	40	42
12	45	44, 46*, 47		
13		48*	49*	
14		50, 51		
15		52, 53*		

Only the program number is given. Programs connected somehow to their cultural, political, and/or social contexts (even only slightly) are indicated by an asterisk (*); for more, see chapters 5 and 6. Programs related to the canons of modernism and/or American music (even only slightly) are indicated in *italics*. For more, see chapters 7 and 8.

programs examined individual composers or works, twelve were technical investigations of musical concepts, eleven covered music appreciation, and ten showcased young performers. But more than music education resides in these shows. Twelve programs included his musings (brief or extended) on cultural, social, or political contexts; thirty-four programs related in some way to the canons of modernism and American music; seven programs addressed both contexts and canons. Bernstein held such strong personal opinions it is no surprise that they slipped into thirty-nine programs.

IDEAS FOR TOPICS THAT CAME
FROM OUTSIDE AND INSIDE THE PHILHARMONIC

Even before the first broadcast, suggestions for topics arrived from many sources. Throughout the run, unsolicited ideas came from outside the Philharmonic from publishers, personalities, sponsors, schools, fan letters, colleagues, and family members. Bernstein also took inspiration from the Philharmonic's earlier "Young People's Concerts," and the production crew always played an active role.

Ideas from Outside the Philharmonic That Were Rejected

Before the first program, publishers sent Bernstein letters and catalogues with repertory suggestions. An insurmountable problem with performing many of these works was financial; pieces not part of the regular Philharmonic season would require extra, prohibitively expensive rehearsal time. One letter (from Southern Publishing) proposed works that catered to the assumed tastes of children, such as *Gerald McBoing Boing*.[8] Because Bernstein never "talked down" to his young audiences, he presumably would have disdained such compositions. He did, however, include four quality works aimed at young people, pointedly scheduled during programs that featured young performers.[9]

Bernstein was contacted at least twice by people who worked with children or educators, and once by a comedian. After the first season Bob Kesshan (Captain Kangaroo of the eponymous, popular 1950s children's television show) offered his services.[10] His offer was not accepted, perhaps because the character of Captain Kangaroo appealed to a younger audience than the Philharmonic sought, or the appearance of a costumed character would diminish the dignified tenor of the program. In 1963, the Dalcroze School of New York suggested a program to commemorate the hundredth birth-anniversary of the famous eurhythmics teacher Emile Jaques-Dalcroze that would include works by some of his students, such as Arthur Honegger, Ernst Bloch, or Frank Martin.[11] The suggestion was rejected for unknown reasons. Harpo Marx of the famed Marx brothers even offered to conduct his version of Haydn's *Toy Symphony* (Simeone 2013, 459).

When AT&T joined Bell System Associated Companies to sponsor the 1966–1967 season, AT&T began investigating the market for the programs. In the first half of 1966, a lengthy questionnaire was sent out to teachers by the Public Relations Department of AT&T (regarding distribution of their 16-mm films of Bernstein's *Young People's Concerts*).[12] Most comments were very positive. The survey also requested ideas for future programs, but many had already been done (e.g., American music, jazz, concerto, and folk music). Bernstein did not incorporate any of the suggestions into the series. A member of the production crew reports that the sponsors had no influence on the choice of topics.[13]

In one instance, a desired and promising idea for a program was blocked by an outside source. Englander wrote and received many letters actively seeking the rights to produce an abridged version of Maurice Ravel's opera *L'enfant et les sortilèges*, on a libretto by the French author Sidonie Gabrielle Colette Gauthier-Villars, known simply as Colette.[14] Colette's daughter refused to allow the work to be simplified, abridged, or reduced in any way, but would have permitted a concert version, which unfortunately was too long for one program.

Ideas from Outside the Philharmonic That Were Accepted

The opening of "Humor in Music" (28 February 1959) offers evidence of the rare influence fan mail had on the subjects of programs. Bernstein says, "since ['What Is Classical Music?' (24 January 1959)], we've had so many letters and requests for more about the subject of humor in music that I've decided to spend a whole program on it" (1). No other evidence of such influence was found.

Stephen Sondheim, the lyricist for *West Side Story* who became Bernstein's good friend, suggested "Quiz-Concert: How Musical Are You?" (26 May 1968). Sondheim was working for quiz programs at the time and even wrote some of the questions for Bernstein's Quiz-Concert.[15]

Bernstein's family also offered suggestions. A two-page list of "Ideas from Shirley [Bernstein, his sister]" in pencil offered five possible topics: nationalism in music, music for the ballet, music to pray by, opera, and orchestration; each is fleshed out with a few sentences (box/folder 1024/8, "Ideas from Shirley," n.d.). The sentences make it clear that these were general ideas for any Bernstein television show with the Philharmonic. Several of Shirley's ideas saw fruition in this series: two shows on nationalism, "Folk Music in the Concert Hall" (9 April 1961) and "Farewell to Nationalism" (30 November 1964); two on orchestration, "The Sound of an Orchestra" (21 November 1962) and "The Anatomy of a Symphony Orchestra" (24 May 1970); one on ballet music, "Two Ballet Birds" (14 September 1969); two on opera, "*The Second Hurricane* by Copland" (24 April 1960) and "*Fidelio*: A Celebration of Life" (29 March 1970).[16] However it is not possible to know if any of these programs are the result of Shirley's suggestions, since her list is undated.

Bernstein readily accepted a suggestion from his daughter Jamie for "What Is a Mode?" (23 November 1966). Fourteen-year-old Jamie had been trying to harmonize a Beatles song on her guitar but was confused by the "funny harmony," so she turned to her father. He describes the scene in his opening remarks: "she got so excited she wanted to know more and more about it, until finally she said: 'Why not tell all this on a Young People's Program? Nobody ever heard of modes!' Well, I thought, Jamie is just a natural music-lover with the usual weekly piano lesson, and if she finds this material fascinating, why shouldn't you? So here goes, and you can blame it all on Jamie" (5). This program, like many, had multiple layers. It showed links between classical music and the popular music of the time, and it made the children of the great conductor into real human beings, while displaying him as a concerned and involved father.

Inside the Philharmonic: Ideas from the "Young People's Concerts"
before Bernstein

The New York Philharmonic had experimented with and developed effective approaches for "Young People's Concerts" during the first half of the twentieth century. A document from the beginning of the 1952–1953 season in the Philharmonic archives titled "A Resume [*sic*] of Children's Concert Activities" describes the nature of these programs in the early 1950s.[17] Programs within each year were unified by themes that included: history (for instance, early music, classical, romantic, contemporary), form (sonata form, melody, the symphony, opera, dance or folk music), and the orchestra (how the development of instruments related to the growth of the orchestra, special uses of individual instruments or sections) (ibid.). They noted how essential it is to hold the children's interest and suggested frequent audience participation (ibid.). Devices used were from the stage:

- Professional soloists, child soloists, school choruses
- Stories with music (such as *Tubby the Tuba*)
- Dancers interpreting the music
- Children's operas
- Slides during commentaries

And from the audience:

- Group singing at each concert
- Composition contests
- Notebook contests (children submit notebooks with answers to quizzes in programs, or arrange notebooks with pictures and essays)
- Art projects (graphic impressions of music heard; posters on specific musical themes; and the like)
- Program notes written by music pupils (ibid.)

The document also mentions competitions for the youngsters (1) and that "each season at least two to five outstanding, talented children are given an opportunity to perform as soloists with the orchestra, to the great delight of their contemporaries" (2).

As mentioned previously, Bernstein did not attend youth concerts as a child but presumably found out what his predecessors at the Philharmonic did (Cott 2013, 44). He eschewed many of these established approaches, such as composition or notebook contests, art projects, dancers, and program notes by music students, even the "lantern slides" that had been such a successful accompaniment to Ernest Schelling's precedent-setting youth concerts with the Philharmonic in the first quarter of the twentieth century.[18] He did, however, have the audience sing twice early in the series (imitating the sounds of instruments in "What Is Orchestration" [8 March 1958] and "Frère Jacques" in "What Makes Music Symphonic?" [13 December 1958]). One entire show rather late in the series was devoted to a contest ("Quiz-Concert: How Musical Are You?"). The only time he employed a student chorus was in "*The Second Hurricane* by Copland" in the third season; both the soloists and the chorus were from the High School of Music and Art of New York City. The nine concerts featuring young performers were distributed throughout the series.[19]

Inside the Philharmonic: Ideas and the Production Crew

The process of choosing a topic was not a solitary one for Bernstein, who was always stimulated by collaboration with others. The entire production crew would discuss various options, fire his imagination, and act as sounding boards, as confirmed by memos and letters that Englander sent Bernstein. For instance, a note from Englander to Bernstein dated 23 June 1967 suggests eight subjects, only two of which were subsequently scheduled (albeit in altered form) (box/folder 1024/7). Other memos from Englander to Bernstein in the same box begin with "This is a recap of specific subjects we have discussed" (29 October 1967) or "I've had a chance while in Iowa to look over a bag of notes from last year, and came across some subjects for YPC that you have been interested in" (1 July no year). The implication is that these memos referred to earlier meetings, and were a reminder that Bernstein should reach a timely decision on topics so publicity could be prepared.

A 5 January [1960] memo gives an interesting view of this process.[20] Englander wrote to Bernstein, "Thought you'd enjoy going over this on the plane rather than British crosswords." The six options (each fleshed out with a few sentences) for the 1959–1960 season were: "Odd Instruments (old and new instruments, special effects)," "The Strength of Music (*Peter and the Wolf* as a youth concert)," "Music as a Universal Language, Taste in Music (bad vs. good arrangements and performances)," "Religious Music," and "Styles in Music" (ibid.). The four subjects Bernstein chose (only two from this list) are nestled in the upper right margin in pencil: Strength, Youth (*Peter and the Wolf*), Odd Instruments, and Copland's opera *The Second Hurricane*. The four programs broadcast were: "Who Is Gustav Mahler?" (7 February 1960), the first young performers program (with *Peter and the Wolf*, 6 March 1960), "Unusual Instruments of the Past, Present, and Future" (27 March 1960), and "*The Second Hurricane* by Copland."[21]

BERNSTEIN'S OWN IDEAS FOR TOPICS

The earliest programs focused on music appreciation or technical investigations with a special Bernstein twist—rather than dry statements of the subjects, the titles are couched as questions. Conductor Michael Tilson Thomas, one of Bernstein's protégés and the person whom Bernstein personally selected as his successor for these televised youth concerts, states that from the moment he met Bernstein

> I understood that he was an asker of questions. "What is your favorite music?" "Why do you phrase it *that* way?" "How do you know that?" "Who's writing new good music and where can I hear it?" Questions were essential for him because questions led to answers, more knowledge, and, of course, to more questions . . . most of his thoughts on music could be condensed into three questions: What is happening? Why is it happening? What's the best way to communicate what's happening? (Thomas (1962) 2005, vii)

Twelve program titles are phrased as questions, immediately arousing the curiosity of potential viewers.

In some cases, various musical events inside or outside the Philharmonic may have led Bernstein toward a topic. A Philharmonic survey of the concerto led to "What Is a Concerto?" (28 March 1959), and festivals of Liszt and Mahler to "Liszt and the Devil" (13 February 1972), and "Who Is Gustav Mahler?"[22] The opening of Lincoln Center in September 1962 and the concert hall's problematic acoustics were explored in "The Sound of a Hall" (21 November 1962), and the 125th birthday of both the New York Philharmonic and the Vienna Philharmonic were celebrated on Christmas Day in "A Toast to Vienna in 3/4 Time" (25 December 1967). Many composers were honored with dedicated programs. With a public statement from President Lyndon Johnson, the United States officially recognized 1965 as Jean Sibelius year on the centennial of the Finnish composer's birth; "A Tribute to Sibelius" (19 February 1965) contributed to that celebration. Composers' birthdays were celebrated by five programs: "Aaron Copland Birthday Party" (12 February 1961), "Happy Birthday Igor Stravinsky" (26 March 1962), "A Birthday Tribute to Shostakovich" (5 January 1966), "Forever Beethoven!" (28 January 1968), and "A Copland Celebration" (27 December 1970). The first of these was a special birthday present to his friend Copland that "nobody else can do for your 60th" that Bernstein said "should be fun" (Simeone 2013, 429–430).

Bernstein wove popular culture into many programs, but sometimes this unlikely source probably provided the impetus for an entire program. The maestro referenced the popular 1968 film *2001: A Space Odyssey* by discussing Strauss's tone poem *Also Sprach Zarathustra* in "Thus Spake Richard Strauss"

(4 April 1971); an excerpt is prominently featured in the popular film. "Bach Transmogrified" (27 April 1969) was likely inspired by the popular LP by Walter (later Wendy) Carlos, *Switched-On Bach*.[23] In this first classical album certified platinum by the Recording Industry Association of America (RIAA), various pieces by Johann Sebastian Bach were performed on the Moog synthesizer.[24] Bernstein mentions the recording in the program and includes a Moog performance of a Bach work.

Bernstein's own musical interests led him to use concepts from his Harvard thesis in the programs "What Is American Music?" (1 February 1958) and "Jazz in the Concert Hall" (11 March 1964), and his love of folk music prompted "Folk Music in the Concert Hall" (9 April 1961). In a speech reproduced in *Findings*, he said, "apart from anything else, I long to sit again in a little room on the outskirts of Santiago and listen to the magical folk singing of Violeta Parra. I have always been a folk-music fan, ever since I can remember—any kind: Hindu, Swahili, hillbilly (Bernstein 1982, 221)." He also referred to folk music in a number of other programs.[25]

Bernstein's own memories suggested topics close to his heart. In "Overtures and Preludes" (8 January 1961), he explains, "why a program of just Overtures? Well, I'll tell you. When I was a boy and first discovering music, the biggest kicks I got always seemed to come from Overtures. . . . I used to wait breathlessly for each new program in hopes that an overture would be played. . . . So today I'm going to try and recapture some of that excitement for myself, and I hope for you too, by playing a whole program of nothing but overtures (3–4)." "A Tribute to Teachers" (29 November 1963) must have been especially moving for Bernstein. The relationship between Bernstein and Helen Coates in particular was a deep and longstanding one; both were in tears much of the time during the preparations for this program.[26] From the podium, he gratefully acknowledged fourteen teachers and mentors (many of whom were in the audience) for their "lasting influence" on him and spoke eloquently about how a "great teacher is one who can light a spark in you, the spark that sets you on fire with enthusiasm . . . for whatever you are studying" (13, 7). Nostalgia also inspired "Fantastic Variations (*Don Quixote*)." Bernstein opens the program saying,

> My dear young friends: This is going to be my last season as Music Director of the New York Philharmonic and naturally I'm already feeling a bit nostalgic. I can't help looking back to the beginning of my relationship with this great orchestra, twenty-five years ago (heavens), when I was its *assistant* conductor, and made my debut unexpectedly by replacing Bruno Walter who had caught the flu. On that program, the main event was the fabulous tone-poem *Don Quixote* by Richard Strauss, and I would like to indulge my nostalgic mood today by playing it again, and sharing it with you. (4 revised)

Bernstein was guided to topics by his own pedagogical approach, various musical events, popular culture, suggestions from a select few, and his own life. Contemporaneous political and social issues may have led him to consciously or subconsciously select certain topics (discussed in later chapters). His production crew would offer input, and the maestro would discuss his ideas with Englander to make certain the proposed show would look good on television. Nonetheless the final decision was always Bernstein's.

A VERY PERSONAL TOPIC: CRITICS

The drafts for "The Genius of Paul Hindemith" (23 February 1964)[27] are unique and very revealing—no other script offers such a window into Bernstein's heart. The maestro had learned by the third season (1959–1960) to censor his ideas before touching pencil to paper.[28] While a few controversial thoughts occasionally slipped into the drafts, they were always deleted by the broadcast. The drafts for this tribute to Hindemith show that initially there was much more to this particular program than the obvious encomium upon the death of a revered composer. Bernstein's feelings on many issues seeped onto these pages, including his anger at the way critics evaluated Hindemith, his own problems with music critics and his complex opinion of music criticism in general, his fondness for Hindemith and his works, his profound sorrow at Kennedy's assassination, as well as his fury at the Nazis.[29] Few of these comments survive in the final script. The evolution of this program is the most angst-ridden of all his *Young People's Concerts.*

Paul Hindemith died on 28 December 1963. On 30 December, the *New York Times* published music critic Harold Schonberg's "appreciation" for Hindemith titled "Musical Logician." Although Schonberg offered a few straightforward compliments, praising Hindemith's abilities as a violinist, violist, conductor, theorist, and author, the article is full of rather backhanded praise. To cite just two examples, Schonberg wrote, "he represents harmonic daring and acerbity rather than melodic genius," and "perhaps Hindemith is the kind of composer who will always make more of an impact among the professionals than the public." He observed that some of Hindemith's scores (which he said were "strong with vicious dissonances and wild rhythms") reflected the "bitterness" of the period between the World Wars in Germany, and that the composer was considered a revolutionary in his youth but at his death was considered an anachronistic academician by the new revolutionaries who espoused atonality. The article even recounts a story in which Richard Strauss told Hindemith, "Why do you write like this? You don't have to. You have talent."

Schonberg regularly wrote reviews of Bernstein that ranged from good to bad to horrendously insulting, so the critic's comments about Hindemith touched a raw nerve.[30] From the beginning of his conducting career, some critics objected to his flamboyant "antics on the podium" that included "fencing, hula-dancing, and calling upon the heavens to witness his agonies."[31] Schonberg was a constant thorn in Bernstein's side, rarely writing anything positive about the maestro's conducting. He even attacked Bernstein's programming and talks: "This is bad: bad psychology, bad music-making, bad show business, bad everything."[32] Bernstein's compositions also elicited mixed reviews; although some were well received, others were not. For instance, his First Symphony, *Jeremiah*, was described as a good first effort, but the Second Symphony, *The Age of Anxiety*, was considered by some to be a disappointment (W. W. Burton 1995, xxi). The *New York Times* critic Olin Downes declared that *The Age of Anxiety* was "wholly exterior in its style, ingeniously constructed, effectively orchestrated, and a triumph of superficiality" (24 February 1950). Bernstein suffered attacks for his adherence to tonality, with critics dismissing his compositions as "drab, tawdry and derivative—leaving the listener with the feeling of having spent the time nibbling on a dietetic cotton candy."[33] The eclecticism and tonality of the work many consider his best, *Mass*, engendered tremendous controversy. While critics like Paul Hume of the *Washington Post* (9 September 1971) called it "a rich amalgam of the theatrical arts" and a "brilliant array of musical forms and styles," the most influential review was by Schonberg (*New York Times*, 19 September 1971), who called it "a combination of superficiality and pretentiousness, and the greatest mélange of styles since the ladies' magazine recipe for fried steak in peanut butter and marshmallow sauce." Even his *Young People's Concerts* were not immune from scathing remarks. Amid comments that the first broadcast was "a razzle dazzle tour de force," "a fascinating mixture," and an "excellent program," Seymour Raven of the *Chicago Tribune* gave the first broadcast a poor review. Raven called it a "failure," saying that Bernstein's presentation "bogged down," "it didn't work," and spoke of the "bored" child on camera, and the *New York Herald Tribune* commented on Bernstein's "inexperience" that led him "to commit one blunder after another."[34] The reception history of Bernstein's life and works is replete with contradictory evaluations.

Evidently, Bernstein empathized with Hindemith, was quite distressed by Schonberg's "appreciation," and felt compelled to contradict the critic's comments with a *Young People's Concert* dedicated to "The Genius of Paul Hindemith."

Bernstein wrote the first pencil draft on 14 January 1964, seventeen days after Hindemith's death and fifteen days after Schonberg's backhanded appreciation; the program was taped on 25 January 1964, and broadcast on 23

February 1964. Bernstein did not have to discard a planned program to add this one since a memo from 7 October 1963 indicates that no topic had been finalized for the 25 January concert.[35]

Comments about critics pervade the drafts. In all the quotes below, the cross-outs were made by Bernstein, and the page number from the draft is given in parenthesis at the end of the quote. The first pencil draft began, "since we were last together—which was a very joyful occasion, with all those talented young performers—two things have happened which made me feel sad. First came the death of one of the greatest composers on earth, Paul Hindemith" (1). Bernstein praised Hindemith's various abilities in music, then wrote about Hindemith's troubles in Germany when the country was "being run by the Hitler mob" (1). As he wrote the first draft, he became so angry that he had trouble shaping sentences that would be appropriate for young audiences. His words almost sputter on the page as he added and revised, trying to rephrase his thoughts in a more positive way appropriate for his young viewers. The impetus was the obituary that described how Hindemith was "a master—a master of form, logic, counterpoint, systems," but omitted any hint that

> he had ever written one bar of *beautiful* music which is a terrible thing; because that's really what music is about after all—to be expressive of what's inside us; & when we feel that expression to be true, we call it beautiful. But music critics are a strange bunch of people, & they often forget this simple truth. In a way, I pity them—running from one concert to another, day after day, until their ears are clogged and having to write *something* in the few minutes before their paper goes to press—something readable & intelligent, they hope. It's a very hard job; I wouldn't be a music critic for anything. But as much as I pity them, I still find it hard to take when they get so wound up in their own important words & judgments that they forget what's *really* important in music—beauty. And when a composer as great as Hindemith dies, ~~it's not their business to~~. The least they can do is ~~have the grace to admit~~ to honor him for all the beauty that he has given to the world. But instead they analyze him, pick him apart, call him old-fashioned, (compared to the newer twelve-tone composers), make him out to be like an academic old schoolteacher, & say that he couldn't write a decent melody. (2)

Bernstein refutes the non-melodic accusation by playing Hindemith's *Concert Music for Strings & Brass*, saying "If this isn't a great melodic line, I'll eat it" (2–3). Here, Bernstein stated what he believed was most important in music—beauty—calling critics "a strange bunch of people" and heatedly adding a few deprecating comments (2).

In this first draft, Bernstein complains that critics (like inexperienced students) have to "pigeonhole" composers by putting "convenient labels" on everything "to keep it all straight," and that they classified Hindemith as "*unmelodic* or *atonal* or *academic*" (3). He continues with a story (which survived to the final script) about his discovery of Hindemith's piano music while he was at Harvard—how he thought Hindemith was "revolutionary," "a Bolshevik," defiant, shocking, an angry young man, observations that are similar to Schonberg's comments about "vicious dissonances" and bitterness. Bernstein then says that he grew out of these thoughts as he became a mature musician and wondered why Schonberg had not. He then performs the very work Schonberg had chosen to prove his point, the Third String Quartet, noting that it "couldn't be prettier" and that it's "kind of sad, that something as lovely as that music can be chosen precisely as an example of non-prettiness. But what can you do? The critics have to stick to their labels." Bernstein asserts that "this critic has Hindemith all wrong. He even spoke about the bitterness of Hindemith's music after the 1st World War—a bitterness that reflected the general disillusionment of those post-war years. And to prove *this* new silly point, he picked, again exactly wrongly, one of the most cheerful & heartwarming pieces Hindemith ever wrote: The Little Chamber Music for 5 wind instruments" (6–7). After Bernstein enumerated Hindemith's accomplishments in life, we find Bernstein's clearly stated opinion of music critics: "But [Hindemith] was never bitter, never ugly, never revolutionary. Only the Nazis said he was, & our dear music critics" (7). After Bernstein's death, Schonberg asserted that the writings of critics had no influence whatsoever on the maestro.[36] Yet this script proves otherwise. Bernstein—a Jew who lost some twenty-seven family members to the Holocaust—equated music critics with the Nazis (B. Bernstein (1982) 2000, 101).[37]

In his revisions, Bernstein continued attempting to craft a script that would be appropriate for his young audience but again failed, overcome by anger and sorrow. He tried opening the program with a greeting not specifically to "my dear young friends" (as he often did) but to a more general audience of "my dear friends," perhaps intentionally including adults as well. The sorrow over Hindemith evoked the sorrow he felt when President Kennedy was assassinated just a few months earlier (22 November 1963), that consolation in the "death of a great man" can be found in a full life well-lived, and that Kennedy died too soon: "youth cut down: it is like the death of Apollo" (1). The critics intrude again: "The other day, reading Hindemith's obituary in a leading NY newspaper, instead of finding consolation in a statement of the man's greatness, I found myself grieving doubly. For here was one of our master-minds of musical journalism pronouncing the final judgment" (ibid.). He writes of "glib music-journalism" and says "thank God we do not have to depend on the highhanded final judgments of critics; the music will always speak louder." Bernstein then scheduled the slow movement of Hindemith's "great symphony" *Mathis der Maler*, saying that it is "among the most beautiful pieces of music ever written." He dedicates the performance "not only in living memory of the composer, but also in sorrowful reply to those who gleefully deny beauty, & who delight in taking the joy out of music, & out of life" (2).

Two statements Bernstein made about critics in the drafts never made it to the screen: his equating music critics with the Nazis and his describing them as "those who gleefully deny beauty, & who delight in taking the joy out of music, & out of life." It seems clear that, as his friend and collague John Mauceri said, the maestro was deeply hurt by the critics and their comments.[38]

The last draft clarifies additional reasons for Bernstein's vehement reactions. He says that Hindemith's music was not bitter, but "gay, light, and full of fun," then adds

> That was one of Hindemith's main qualities—the joy he put into music. He was a fun-loving man, for whom music was everything in life. He was my idea of the *total* musician: he played music, wrote it, taught it, *breathed* it. He played jazz in cafes; he was a concertmaster of an orchestra; he played the viola in a string quartet; he wrote books about music—big, little, serious, light, noble and jazzy, hard and easy, music for professionals, for amateurs, and for children. (15)

Bernstein was also "a fun-loving man, for whom music was everything." Hindemith seemed to have done almost everything in music—a goal the maestro had set for himself. Bernstein said that he always wanted to do one of everything in music, and he succeeded handily (H. Burton 1994, 139). He is now acknowledged as one of the most versatile American musicians of the twentieth century. He certainly empathized with Hindemith's being misunderstood and belittled by critics and music intellectuals. Both composers were considered out-of-touch since they did not totally subscribe to the revered twelve-tone practices of the time. For Bernstein, Hindemith was a kindred spirit in many ways, and he defended him with an entire *Young People's Concert*.

SELECTING ORCHESTRAL REPERTORY

As we have seen, Bernstein did not patronize youngsters by providing traditional children's fare like *Tubby the Tuba*. Rather, he enjoyed challenging his young audiences with pieces selected directly from the Philharmonic's performing or recorded repertory. Of the four quality works that might appeal to

young people on the series, two were from the Philharmonic's recorded repertory: Prokofiev's *Peter and the Wolf* in "Young Performers No. 1" (6 March
1960) and Saint-Saëns's *Carnival of the Animals* in "Young Performers No. 3"
(13 April 1962).[39] Neither part of the performing nor of the recorded repertory, Mark Bucci's Concerto for a Singing Instrument (III: "Tug of War"),
originally scored for violin and strings, was performed as a kazoo concerto to
appeal to his young audience in "Unusual Instruments of the Past, Present,
and Future."

Whether the work or topic was selected first depended upon the nature of the program. For programs that focused on a work or composer, the
pieces were selected first, and for programs that were more pedagogical in
nature, the idea came first. The outlines range from listing a few pieces or a
few composers to as many as thirty-nine composers.[40] Sometimes Bernstein
would know the nature of the music he wanted and would leave a blank line
for Gottlieb to fill (Peyser 1998, 300).

For sound economic reasons, Bernstein intentionally chose works that
required little or no extra rehearsal time. One way he achieved this was by
selecting pieces that had been recently performed or were about to be performed on the subscription season. The outline for "What Is a Melody?" (21
December 1962) provides insight into this process. Several works came to
mind as Bernstein brainstormed for this program, most came from the subscription series (see table 2.2).[41] The Brahms (from the Philharmonic season)
was the featured work. The LP was recorded on 9 October 1962 and the
Young People's Concert on 3 November 1962.

Table 2.2.   Bernstein's Outline for "What Is a Melody?"

Prok[ofiev, Symphony] #5	[not on season]
[Tchaikovsky,] Francesca [da Rimini] (cl solo)	[not on season]
* Mozart [Symphony No. 40,] Gm (bit)	[16, 17, 18, 19 May 1963 (651)]
Mendelssohn Vln Conc (bit)	[15, 16, 17, 18 Nov 1962 (651)]
[Stravinsky] Sacre [du printemps] (motives)	[26 Sep 1962 (652)]
?? [Copland] Connotations	[23 Sep 1962; 31 Jan, 1, 2 Feb 1963 (651)]
[T]Chai[kovsky, Symphony no.] 4 (ob solo)	[8, 9, 10 Feb 1963 (652)]
?Schubert song (pno.)	[not on season]
* Tristan Prelude (complete?)	[not on season]
Mozart [Symphony no. 40 in] gm 1st mvt.	[16, 17, 18, 19 May 1963 (651)]
Hind[emith]y–[Kammermusick] Pt I	[not on season]
* Brahms [Symphony no.] 4	[4, 5, 6, 7 Oct 1962 (650)]
(? encore) Strauss waltz—Danube or Emperor	[not on season]

* Performed on the program. Note that the dates indicate when the works appeared on the subscription
series, and the numbers in parentheses refer to Shanet 1975.

Bernstein also intentionally selected works in conjunction with a recording session. This was both a good business practice and a good musical
decision for an orchestra that was liable to forget a work if the gap between
rehearsal and performance (or between performances) was too long. Bernstein wrote apologizing to William Schuman for deleting Schumann's Sixth
Symphony from the Latin American tour. He said it was necessary because
the orchestra was unable to retain the work when the time lapse between
appropriate venues was more than a week (Simeone 2013, 400).[42] Over half
of the broadcasts included works within two months of a recording session
(see table 2.3). Most were between season four (1960–1961) and season ten
(1966–1967) inclusively in the middle of Bernstein's tenure as music director, with a precipitous drop after Bernstein announced in October 1966 that
he would retire from that position in May 1969 (H. Burton 1994, 360). The
recordings for the tenth season programs were probably already scheduled by
the time of his announcement.[43] All in all, fewer recordings were made near
the beginning and end of the series.[44]

Only four *Young People's Concerts* featured music that was not part of
either the subscription or recording repertory—a clear demonstration of the
efficient use of time.[45] For three of these, the choice of works was most likely
restricted by the abilities of the young performers.

Table 2.3. Programs Associated with Recording Sessions
(Shortly before or after a *Young People's Concert*)

Program	Before	After	Program	Before	After
1	1	1	23	4	
5		1	24		2
6	1		25	1	
7	1		27	2	
8	1		29		4
9	1		30		1
11		1	31		1
12	2	1	32	1	
15	3	1	34	1	
16	1	2	38		3
17	1		40	1	
19		1	42	1	
20	1		44	1	
21	1		51	1	
22		1			

This chart catalogs recording sessions that were associated with a *Young People's Concerts*
program. They were recorded within two months either before or after the taping (not the
broadcast). These references come from North 2006.

The idea of synergy (programming works for the television program as an advertisement for selling LPs) apparently occurred to Bernstein, the Philharmonic, and/or Columbia Records (owned by CBS at the time).[46] Bernstein and William S. Paley, of CBS and Columbia Records, were smart businessmen who probably realized the value of using the television programs to remind enthusiastic viewers of Philharmonic recordings they could purchase on LP. Assuming that Bernstein read the fan letters or was told about their content, two fan letters in particular attested to a link between broadcasts and LP sales. A sixteen-year-old wrote: "I was so impressed with your show at Christmas, that I bought your album of Handel's 'Messiah.'" A parent wrote: "Being wise in the ways of sponsors, my 14-year-old son asked me what we had to buy to keep you on the air. Since we don't have to buy any Scrunchies, we are going into town to buy your record of Ravel 'La Valse.' I want to add that my 12-year-old daughter was equally fascinated and that *I* am simply overwhelmed—since they own every record Elvis Presley has made."[47] Twenty-eight works seen on Bernstein's *Young People's Concerts* were released on LP sometime during the year following the broadcast (see table 2.4). Usually only one was released, but multiple pieces were released after three programs: two after "What Is a Melody?," three after "Overtures and Preludes," and four after "The Latin American Spirit" (8 March 1963). Bernstein may have created the latter program to counter the negative emotions mistakenly aimed at his beloved Latin America after the Cuban Missile Crisis, so this show must have been of great significance to him.[48] Perhaps he made a point of ensuring those recordings of Latin American music were available as soon as possible; certainly more LPs were released after this program than any other. As with recording sessions, the release of LPs after a broadcast dropped in 1966 after Bernstein's retirement announcement.

Table 2.4. LPs Released within One Year of a *Young People's Concert* Broadcast

Program	LPs	Program	LPs	Program	LPs
1	1	11	1	31	1
2	1	12	3	38	1
3	1	15	1	46	1
4	1	20	1	47	1
5	1	21	2	49	1
6	1	22	1	51	1
8	1	23	4		
9	1	29	1		

These references come from North 2006; for more information, see appendix 6. North only gives the year the recording was released, not the month and year.

"Charles Ives: American Pioneer" (23 February 1967) in particular created synergy between topics, pieces, and recording sessions. At first glance, the topic of this program seems an oddity. Ives lived from 1874 to 1954, so 1967 was not a birth or death anniversary year, and none of the works on the program were performed either on the subscription series or on tour. However, Bernstein championed both Mahler and Ives in his role as conductor of the Philharmonic. He was the first to conduct Ives at the Philharmonic,[49] the first to record the same work (in 1961; North 2006, 349), and the first to parade Ives in Europe (Horowitz 2007, 479). Bernstein possibly offered this concert to bring Ives into the public eye, as an exploration of one facet of American music (a subject dear to Bernstein's heart), as a rehearsal for a recording session, and/or as an advertisement for LP sales. Performed on this program were: *The Gong on the Hook and Ladder, or the Fireman's Parade on Main Street*; "Washington's Birthday" from *Holiday Symphony*; *The Circus Band March*; and *The Unanswered Question*. The taping of the *Young People's Concert* on 21 January 1967 acted as a rehearsal for recording sessions on 31 January 1967 for all but the last of these (North 2006, 349). The LP of Ives's *Holiday Symphony* was released in 1967 (191);[50] Ives's *The Unanswered Question* had just been released in 1966 (167).[51] Two of the four Ives pieces on this program were thus available on LP shortly before or after the broadcast. Perhaps Bernstein felt that introducing the music on television (accompanied by explanations of the unusual sounds) might encourage the television audience to purchase his LPs of Ives's music.

Pieces tended to be either truncated to accommodate the demands of television and/or interrupted to accommodate Bernstein's narration. James H. North (2006, 423) points out that "the music played consists primarily of excerpts" and offers that while Ravel's *La Valse* (ends the first program) sounds complete, a quarter of it is missing. The maestro tells the story of the puppet between selected movements from *Petrushka* in "Happy Birthday, Igor Stravinsky," and in "The Anatomy of a Symphony Orchestra," he separates the movements of Respighi's *The Pines of Rome* with discussions of the music's structure and its descriptive program.

Very brief excerpts from entirely unrelated works (often just a few seconds) are consistently added to illustrate a point. For instance, in "What Is a Mode?" the musical excerpts of less than 30 seconds included: plainsong; the popular songs Tandyn Almer's "Along Comes Mary," Paul McCartney and John Lennon's "Norwegian Wood," and Jeff Barry and Ellie Greenwich's "Hanky Panky"; and such classical pieces as the second movement of Nikolai Rimsky-Korsakov's *Scheherazade*, the second movement of Johannes Brahms's Fourth Symphony, and Sergei Prokofiev's *Lieutenant Kije Suite*. By the last eight shows (six of which occurred after Bernstein had become Lau-reate Conductor), he had reduced the number of works to only one or two pieces per program with no brief musical examples.[52]

At first, production values did not factor into selecting repertory, and Bernstein left all production decisions up to Englander. Later when no other factors (such as pedagogical needs or repertory available) demanded specific music, Bernstein would turn to Englander with a few pieces, then they would discuss which work would be "more photogenic" (Rose 1992, 133). The two men would choose the piece that allowed Englander to design the most cre-ative, interesting, and eventually award-winning camera work.

SELECTING YOUNG PERFORMERS

The process of selecting young performers and works for their solo debuts in Bernstein's *Young People's Concerts* was somewhat complicated by the necessity of obtaining legal permission for minors to appear on television. The young musicians ranged in age from twelve to twenty-four, with many being in their mid-teens; the youngest performer was a nine-year-old nar-rator for *Peter and the Wolf* in "Young Performers No. 1." Apparently the Philharmonic did not advertise these auditions as no notices or ads survive. The application required information about training, recommendations, a list of repertory with orchestral accompaniment, photo, newspaper articles and/or reviews, and personal information (age, address, and the like).[53] Those selected were notified one month before the audition. Hopeful perform-ers came to and stayed in New York at their own expense and, if possible, brought their own accompanist. The preliminary audition was run by three assistant conductors and Englander; finalists played for Bernstein the next day. For the winners, the Philharmonic would fill out the "Application for Consent to Exhibit Child" form (listing all rehearsals and performances) to be signed by the parent or guardian, then sent to the Mayor of New York; the mayor's office would provide a permit.[54] The maestro did not limit young per-formers to those auditioning. When a clarinetist auditioned and brought his own accompanist (David Oei), the clarinetist was rejected, but Bernstein and the audition committee gave a contract to the accompanist since they were enchanted by [Oei's] "superb musicianship" and "charm" ("Young Performers No. 7," 22 February 1966, 20). The soloists were paid by the Philharmonic.[55]

Bernstein had the gift of finding talented young performers, as a glance at appendix D will show. The most stellar young soloist on the series was famed pianist André Watts. Bernstein's effusive enthusiasm while introducing Watts in his series debut at the age of sixteen in "Young Performers No. 4" (15 January 1963) and on Watts's return in "Alumni Reunion" (19 April 1967) affirms that Bernstein realized that he had found a rare treasure.[56] Many of the other young people who received the honor of being chosen by Bernstein for these programs became noted performers, among them, cellist Lynn Harrell (sixteen years old when he performed on the series), pianist Jung Ja Kim (sixteen yrs.), violinist Young Uck Kim (nineteen yrs.), composer Shulamit Ran (sixteen yrs.), flutist Paula Robison (twenty yrs.), and soprano Veronica Tyler (twenty-two yrs.). The young conductors were in their twenties and were already assistant conductors at the Philharmonic. Many became well known, such as Edo De Waart, Serge Fournier, Seiji Ozawa, Maurice Peress, and James DePreist. Adult fans wrote to say how much they enjoyed seeing the gifted young performers. Bob Pittsley wrote that the performance by "the [Young Uck] Kim boy . . . is one I shall never forget. Throughout his playing it was necessary to keep dabbing the eyes so that I could see the TV screen clearly" (1967). He also wrote "with deepest gratitude for the beauty you are constantly giving to America's youth." Harold S. Walker, a sergeant in the US Army stationed in Tacoma, Washington, also wrote about Kim's "outstanding performance" (1967).

The Young Performers programs were particularly popular with young musicians and their teachers. When the Bell System distributed films of the concerts to schools without charge, they chose only seven of the thirty-five that had been broadcast—two were Young Performers programs.[57] The AT&T survey sent to music teachers reported that their young pupils showed interest in the "performances by Young Artists" (box/folder 1027/7). Carol Turpen, concertmistress of the Albuquerque Youth Symphony Orchestra, wrote that her orchestra watched the telecast at their rehearsal and that "everyone thoroughly enjoyed the performance, at the same time sharing a unique musical experience." Several children described their music lessons in their fan letters, and some said that they practiced with more enthusiasm after seeing the programs. For instance, Geraldine Maddocks (thirteen years old) studied piano, and Ira Mellman (third grade) played flute in the Philadelphia Elementary School Orchestra. Norman Aaronson (eleven-and-a-half yrs.) announced, "I guess I am just any boy who plays an instrument that wants to get all the praise for doing it nicely without practicing. I do practice but I do it more willingly after I watch your program" (1958). Many requested a photograph of Bernstein to provide inspiration for practicing.[58]

Bernstein was extraordinarily successful in guiding audiences to understand music in an effective and interesting fashion while avoiding the ineffectual methods that reeked of what Thomson called the music "appreciation-racket." The guiding forces behind all his selections of topics and pieces were appealing pedagogy, sound economic decisions, and effective use of the Philharmonic, both musically and visually. While publicity from the Leonard Bernstein Office stated that "Bernstein usually planned the programs for the Young People's Concerts based on repertory from the New York Philharmonic's regular concert season," the recording repertory also played an important role.[59] The maestro instinctively understood what worked best and what he hoped to achieve, so he generally preferred to keep his own counsel, accepting suggestions only from people he knew well and who knew him well. This examination of the overt influences on Bernstein as he made his decisions clarifies the freedom he had in shaping the programs.

• 3 •

The Postmodernist

Highbrow, Lowbrow, and Middlebrow Joined

> Certain people were amazed when I told them I was going to
> play [*Das Lied von der Erde*] for you today. They said, "What?
> You're going to play that long, slow, highbrow music for young
> people? You're crazy—they'll get restless and noisy. They won't
> understand it. It's just too highbrow. And it doesn't even end
> with a bang-up finish. . . . Nobody will clap." Well, I know my
> young people, and I'm not afraid to play this music for you. I
> know you'll understand it, and even love it, because you already
> know more about Mahler than most people do.
>
> —Leonard Bernstein, "Who Is Gustav Mahler?"
> (7 February 1960)

*B*ernstein knew how to engage to his audiences. He also intimately understood from personal experience the class divisions in the United States.
In all of his televised or filmed presentations, he enthused, captivated, and
challenged viewers by setting the bar slightly beyond their comfort zone,
then thoughtfully walked them through new concepts without intimidating
or confusing them. After a summary of the tripartite taste divisions in the
mid-twentieth century—which is vital to understanding the cultural contexts
surrounding Bernstein—a look at his three filmed or televised pedagogical
series for different "brow" levels (emphasizing his *Young People's Concerts*)
will show us how he comfortably bridged class divisions while achieving this
seemingly impossible task.

BACKGROUND OF THE TRIPARTITE TASTE DIVISIONS

While the terms "highbrow," "lowbrow," and "middlebrow" date from the late-nineteenth and early-twentieth centuries, debates about the distinctions between high culture and popular culture occurred as far back as ancient Greece. One's choice of cultural products was inextricably linked with one's social class, even from the earliest writings on the subject. Heated exchanges about taste cultures appeared in books and articles, particularly after the mid-twentieth century in the United States, Britain, and France.[1] Recurring arguments (until recently) stated that highbrow art was superior and should be revered, while the acceptance of low, inferior art would inevitably lead to social chaos.

Linking the concept of "brow" to taste began with the mistaken idea that the physical shape of an individual's brow reflected his intellectual capacities and taste culture. The origins are found in the eighteenth-century pseudo-science of phrenology, but the terms "highbrow" and "lowbrow" did not take shape until the turn of the twentieth century. A "highbrow" is someone who has (or has pretentions of) superior intellect, learning, and interests—attributes (it was said) found among the wealthy and cultivated.[2] In the United States, highbrows were said to be from the Anglo-American elites (Travis 2002, 339). A "lowbrow" is someone who is not aesthetically refined, lacks intellectual curiosity, and reacts to things purely sensually and emotionally. Phrenologists and a large portion of society believed that lowbrows were found among immigrants, dark-skinned ethnic groups, and the poorly educated working class (ibid.)—the "folk." According to this definition, Bernstein's family origins were lowbrow in every way.[3] The definition of lowbrow culture changed in the twentieth century. At first, it was simply culture of the people, but as new technologies (such as records, radio, movies, easily available books, and later television) became part of daily life, the concept of mass culture evolved. An important shift was seen from "a culture *of* the people to a culture *for* the masses" (Garofalo 2002, 3). As late as the mid-1960s, Stuart Hall and Paddy Whannel asserted that "popular art seen in mass media at the time was not popular art, but a corruption of it" (Hall and Whannel 1965, 67–68).

Pundits separated lowbrow or folk culture from popular culture, but many simply referred to them both as lowbrow. Appearing in the 1920s (with no parallel in phrenology), "middlebrow" refers to one who is moderately intellectual with average or limited cultural interests. As an adjective, it can allude to "an artistic work, etc.: of limited intellectual or cultural value; demanding or involving only a moderate degree of intellectual application, *typically as a result of not deviating from convention*" (my italics; s.v. middlebrow, OED). All three terms can be used in a derogatory fashion. The words highbrow, middlebrow, and lowbrow will be used here since Bernstein himself employed them in his *Young People's Concerts*, and they still occasionally appear today. Although considerable market research existed concerning classes and the choices they made, there was little academic research until the 1970s, so much of the following information relating to this educational television series must come from articles written by magazine authors such as Russell Lynes and Dwight Macdonald, whose job it was to observe and comment on society.[4]

Early in the twentieth century, it was thought that economic level and/or breeding influenced a person's choice of taste culture, but "class, age, religion, ethnic and racial background, regional origin, and place of residence, as well as personality" factored in as well (Lynes 1949a, 19; Gans 1974, 70). By mid-century wealth and breeding were still important, but intellectual accomplishments gained dominance (Lynes 1949a, 19; Gans 1974, 70). Such societal changes are energized by youth, the target audience of Bernstein's *Young People's Concerts* (Gans 1974, 70).

By the time Bernstein's series began, highbrows were primarily the highly educated upper and upper-middle classes who had academic and professional occupations (76).[5] They valued nuance and subtlety, sought "careful communication of mood and feeling," preferred introspection over action, and were intrigued by how cultural products were constructed (form, method, content, and the like) (76). Highbrow culture was dominated by creators (and critics). Other highbrows (such as highly educated professionals and managers) bowed to the evaluations of these sages (75–76, 79). Highbrows typically found culture within daily activities (Lynes 1949a, 20). They ignored mass opinion and mass salesmanship, deeming broad commercial success a clear indicator of inferiority; Winthrop Sargeant (with tongue-in-cheek) suggested that highbrows devoted themselves to culture that was not successful commercially (Sargeant 1949).

Lowbrows in the 1960s were mainly skilled and semiskilled factory and service workers, and low-level white collar workers who often dropped out of high school after the tenth grade (Gans 1974, 89). Lowbrows typically rejected culture even with some hostility as "dull, effeminate, immoral, and sacrilegious." They felt eroticism should be censored but not violence and preferred action and melodrama (ibid.). Lowbrows like what they like and do not care about understanding history, process, or implications, which suggests that children are lowbrows (Lynes 1949a, 23). Lynes called lowbrows the *"hoi polloi"* who (he felt) were found at all economic levels of society but had a kind of integrity because they did not care about being fashionable (19–20, 23, 25). Art for art's sake is unimportant, and form should follow function

(23). Macdonald, however, disdainfully reported that lowbrows were the immigrants who were the "bottom-dogs of Europe," who took the "dirtiest jobs at the lowest pay," were the "ready-made consumers of *kitsch* who abandoned their native culture for mass-produced American culture" (Macdonald 1960b, 590). Low culture was dominant in America before the 1950s, but the lower-middle increased as working-class youths left their rural communities and urban ethnic ghettos, and by the 1950s, increased availability of education helped them move into the lower middle class, thereby shrinking the lower class (Gans 1974, 89).

Middlebrows were divided into upper-middle and lower-middle; Macdonald simply referred to both as Midcult. The upper-middle class was comprised of "professionals, executives, managers, and their wives who have attended the 'better' colleges and universities" who eschewed innovation and felt that high culture did not satisfy them (81). While seeking substantive culture, they were unconcerned with innovation or methodology (81–82). This was the fastest growing of all groups due to a "boom in college attendance" (84). The lower-middle class came from lower-status professionals such as accountants, public school teachers, as well as those in most white-collar jobs. The older members graduated from high school, while many of the younger members had college degrees from state universities or small colleges (84–85). In the past, this public rejected culture. Although they continued to reject high and much upper-middle culture, lower-middlebrows began to accept the idea of "culture" itself and began embracing some art forms. The lower-middle brow level was dominant in America during the long decade of the 1960s, and revered institutions such as the Metropolitan Museum of Art began courting them (85).

Attitudes toward different brow cultures changed in the mid-twentieth century—from the worshipful reverence accorded to all things highbrow and the dismissive disdain accorded to all things lowbrow, to the elevation of popular culture, and finally to "postmodernism" and the collapse of cultural barriers at the end of the century. In the 1940s, critics and philosophers stated unequivocally that highbrow culture was superior, "aesthetically rich," and "vital," whereas lowbrow culture (which then included both folk and popular culture) valued only immediate pleasure or usefulness (Lynes 1949a, 23).[6] Highbrow culture required a "skilled" creator and an "elite, cultured" audience, while lowbrow culture (the mass culture version) was the "standardized and homogenized" product of venal corporations who preyed on the "unsophisticated mass public." Hollywood films in the two decades after World War II were "denigrated" by critics (mostly from New York) as the "epitome of commercial, mass culture" (Halle 2007). Controversy over the subject swelled.

Lowbrow or popular culture was universally denigrated until the 1950s and early 1960s when scholars began challenging the assumption that popular/lowbrow culture lacked aesthetic value—while highbrow culture was still considered superior, lowbrow culture was not as bad as previously thought (Kammen 1999, 95–102). Others had the radical idea that popular/lowbrow culture was actually aesthetically superior to highbrow in some respects (Halle 2007). While some busily maintained an aesthetic hierarchy by separating and categorizing, others gradually made pleas for balance. The changing cultural world in which Bernstein dwelled powerfully influenced his decisions.

Two important aspects inform aesthetic choice: the "built-in educational requirement" of the product (for example, low for comics, high for T. S. Eliot's poetry), and the aesthetic standards the individual learned at home and school (Gans 1974, 70–71). An individual's education and type of school were probably the best predictors of his cultural level and choices (ibid.). Both were closely related to his socioeconomic level (and that of his parents), so there was a strong though not infallible correlation between taste cultures and classes in American society (71). Selected items and pastimes relevant to Bernstein's *Young People's Concerts* (with a few extras to establish context) have been gathered from the sources mentioned above and classified in table 3.1.

Factors important in assigning an item to a taste culture were its educational requirement, cost, and appeal. Anything that required higher education or a great expenditure of money was categorized as highbrow or upper middlebrow, as only people at this level have the education to appreciate the artifact and/or have the discretionary income. Anything that was designed to appeal to the greatest number of people was categorized as popular culture or lowbrow, such as most sports, amusement parks, and the majority of television programs. Macdonald points to Norman Rockwell, rock 'n' roll, Elvis Presley, and the offerings of various media (radio, television, movies) as examples of Masscult (1960a, 203–204, 232).[7] Both Lynes and Macdonald believed that middlebrow cultural products were parodies of high culture that had been altered, watered down, or otherwise debased to make them marketable to the masses. Gans made no such value judgments.

Macdonald named a few items he felt were clearly Midcult. For instance, the acclaimed cultural television series *Omnibus* (so important in Bernstein's life) met his two criteria for Midcult: the series was an effort by moneyed middlebrows to teach other curious middlebrows, and it "aimed straight at the average American audience, neither highbrow nor lowbrow, the audience that read *Readers Digest*, *Life*, *The Ladies Home Journal*, the audience which is the sole backbone of any business as it is of America itself" (1960b, 595). Macdonald asserted that Midcult endeavors were "a corruption of High Culture" (593). *Omnibus* was founded by a "great foundation to raise the level of

Table 3.1. Cultural Artifacts or Activities Classified by Taste Culture

Cultural Artifact	Highbrow	Upper Middlebrow	Lower Middlebrow/ Midcult (M)	Lowbrow/ Masscult (M)
Education	University	College	High school	Tenth grade
Profession	Academic or professional, atomic scientist, cultural historian, commentator	Professional, executive, manager	Accountant, public school teacher, most white collar workers	Skilled & semi-skilled factory worker or low level white collar worker
Art	Original oils, Picasso	Quality reproductions	Representational art, mass-produced originals & dept. store reproductions (e.g., Cezanne, Van Gogh, Degas, Buffet)	Very poor: calendars & magazine pictures; Norman Rockwell (M)
Drama (need for)	Legitimate theater	Movies & television	Movies & television	Football games, boxing, wrestling matches
Entertainment	Live	Live	Musicals on film	Western movies, amusement parks, most radio & mass media; bargain sales (M)

Film	Sophisticated films of Chaplin & D.W. Griffiths	Foreign films	Big Hollywood films of musicals (if they attend)	Action comedies; Cecil B. DeMille (M)
Food		*Gourmet*	Homestyle cooking	
Magazines	*Horizon Magazine:: A Review of Literature and Art*	*New Yorker, Harper's*	*Reader's Digest, Ladies Home Journal, Life,* (M)	*Argosy*
Music	Baroque and earlier, post-1900 (e.g., J.S. Bach, Ives, Bartók)	Symphonies, operas (e.g., Brahms)	Popular ballads, old Broadway musicals, Perry Como	Jukeboxes, jazz, folk; rock 'n' roll, Elvis Presley (M)
Reading	Avant garde literature	Solid non-fiction, better novels	Book club books; H. G. Wells (M)	Comic books, pulps, adventure stories (e.g., Edna Ferber, Fanny Hurst, James Michener, Leon Uris) (M)
Sports	[Golfing, sailing, skiing]	Tennis	Bowling	Most, horse races, boxing
Television		Public television	Family or action comedies, commercial TV; *Omnibus* (M)	Most TV, esp. westerns & sports

The information in this chart is compiled from Gans 1974, Lynes 1949a, Macdonald 1960a, and 1960b. Other enriching examples from Lynes 1949b (e.g., drinks, furniture, books, records, sculpture) are not listed here but can be seen at http://kieranhealy.org/files/misc/highbrow-lowbrow.png (accessed 14 November 2013). Macdonald's midcult refers to both upper and lower middlebrow column, so such entries have been arbitrarily placed in lower middlebrow column and notated with an (M). Macdonald's masscult or popular culture entries are placed in the lowbrow column and differentiated from purely lowbrow entries by an (M). I added the sports in brackets based on the expense involved.

television," but rather than elevating television fare, the series failed. "The level of television was not raised, for some reason" (595). Eventually, *Omnibus* earned over 65 awards including seven Emmys (*The Current*).

To prove his point, Macdonald described an issue of *Life* magazine that embraced all brows by juxtaposing a serious article on atomic energy, one on Rita Hayworth's love life, photos of starving children in Calcutta, nine color pages of Renoir paintings, and a picture of a roller-skating horse; he disdainfully declared that "these scramblings together seem to work all one way, degrading the serious rather than elevating the frivolous" and left the final impression "that both Renoir and the horse were talented" (Macdonald 1960a, 213).[8] As he spoke of the "tepid ooze of Midcult" that was spreading everywhere, he asserted that Midcult had "the essential qualities of Masscult—the formula, the built-in reaction, the lack of any standard except popularity—but it decently covers them with a cultural fig-leaf" (Macdonald, 592). Gans, with his egalitarian point of view, believed that members of any taste culture should enjoy whatever cultural items pleased them.

As the lines of demarcation between brows became more clearly drawn, conflicts were fueled that continued throughout the twentieth century.[9] Individuals and institutions began seeking ways to assist lowbrows in their bid to become more learned, which irritated some highbrows. Middlebrows were seen (depending on the point of view) as either altruists genuinely helping or greedy businessmen who degraded high art. The fires of debate were fanned in the early twentieth century by dramatic social and technological changes, including nearly universal public education, which resulted in the literacy of most Americans. Reading the "best books" was the best way of obtaining culture, and they were becoming increasingly cheap due to improvements in paper making, printing, and publishing (Rubin 1992, 1; Travis 2002, 339). People like Dr. Charles W. Eliot, president of Harvard University, assisted harried but curious middlebrows by selecting books for collections of great literature like Eliot's Five-Foot Shelf of Books; the Book-of-the-Month Club brought books to readers who lived too far from good bookstores (Travis 2002, 339). The lower middle class would be familiar with the work of high culture artists such as Cezanne, Van Gogh, Degas, and Buffet through reproductions (Gans 1974, 87–88). The New York Philharmonic joined in the efforts to bring culture to the people in the 1920s with low-priced summer concerts, radio broadcasts, and collections of phonograph recordings (Shanet 1975, 244). Here, middlebrows were seen as modern white-collar individuals doing their best to educate themselves and keep up with an ever-increasing overabundance of literature and art, while responsibly honoring their professional duties (Travis 2002, 361). This model reveals a sympathy and willingness to help middlebrows in their quest for knowledge, although some achieved this while making money.

All these changes, however, proved very disturbing to some highbrows, and the battles seemed continuous, from cultural critic and British poet Matthew Arnold in 1869 through Macdonald in 1960 and onward. For centuries, owning, displaying, reading, and understanding books had been the special province of the privileged classes (the "elites"), as was understanding and enjoying music of "high seriousness," as Arnold called it (Travis 2002, 339; Grant 1998, 196). Highbrow writers deemed these middlebrows a "bloodless and pernicious pest" and a "corrupting influence," blaming them for venally mass-marketing a "parody of high culture" ("non-art," even "anti-art") to middle- and lowbrows (Lynes 1949a, 25; Macdonald 1960a, 204). They opined that these bourgeoisie businessmen who mass-marketed culture were venal villains, despised as a "serious threat" to high culture either because they put money above aesthetics, or because they demeaned high culture by making it too available to the masses, who were constitutionally unable to appreciate high culture despite their best attempts (Lynes 1949a, 25). Authority figures in literature and the arts believed that items from high culture should have aesthetic value and work for progressive change in society. Yet they also felt that the mass-marketing of literature and "high" arts drained those cultural products of both their aesthetic as well as their progressive function, leaving the focus on only profits and manipulation for self-serving, hollow ends (Travis 2002, 358–360).

The attitude toward lowbrow culture depended upon whether it was mass marketed or not. By 1960, Macdonald made the most scathing comments among the primary sources considered here. He purposefully differentiated between "mass culture" and "popular culture," saying that "'popular' culture implies a spontaneity and an authenticity which is a quality of folk art but is not a quality of [Masscult] (1960a, 203)." Macdonald bitingly ridiculed mass culture with such comments as "never underestimate the ignorance and vulgarity of publishers, movie producers, network executives and other architects of Masscult" (211). He intentionally shocked with such statements as "Nazism and Soviet Communism, however, show us how far things can go in politics, as Masscult does in art" (ibid.). Only fifteen years after World War II, while the wounds were still raw for many people, he equated Masscult with Nazism. With his list of items created "for crowds," he even linked Masscult with murder: "a football game, a bargain sale, a lynching" (208). Those who sought to integrate Masscult with high art, like Leonard Bernstein, had to contend with these attitudes.

Other highbrows held a condescending attitude toward lowbrows and their art forms, as seen in the satirical article by the self-proclaimed highbrow Sargeant: "The oafish classes [lower middlebrow and lowbrow that made up 90 percent of the population, according to Sargeant], being overwhelmingly numerous, are the biggest consumers of everything from salad to music, and an investment in their tastes is correspondingly profitable. They therefore dominate taste in nearly all our big industries where taste is a factor." He felt "the most horrible examples" were radio and movies made in Hollywood (Sargeant 1949, 102). He voiced the thoughts of those who felt that anything popular with the "masses" was to be disparaged and dismissed. Highbrow culture was superior, "aesthetically rich," and "vital," requiring a "skilled" creator and an "elite, cultured" audience, whereas lowbrow culture (both folk and popular culture) was the "standardized and homogenized" product of venal corporations (run by middlebrows) who preyed on the "unsophisticated mass public" that valued only immediate pleasure or usefulness (Lynes 1949a, 21–23). On the other hand, Lynes believed that highbrows respect lowbrow culture when it is an honest statement of the people (such as form following function or folk culture), stating that "the highbrow enjoys and respects the lowbrow's art—jazz for instance" when it is "a spontaneous expression of folk culture" (ibid.).

Jazz began life as lowbrow music at the end of the nineteenth century, became a popular form during the 1920s through 1940s, then highbrow in the late twentieth century.[10] Classical composers like Copland and Milhaud had embraced aspects of this musical tradition during the jazz age of the 1920s, and the 1950s saw a "booming commercial market in recordings and live performances" (Lopes 2002, 1).[11] All this, however, was insufficient to overcome the tenacious associations of jazz with drugs and immorality held by society at large, and jazz continued to struggle to gain cultural legitimacy, as revealed by jazz great Dizzy Gillespie in 1957:

> [Jazz] has never really been accepted as an art form by the people of my own country. . . . I believe that the great mass of the American people still consider jazz as lowbrow music. . . . To them, jazz is music for kids and dope addicts. Music to get high to. Music to take a fling to. Music to rub bodies to. Not "serious" music. Not concert hall material. Not music to listen to. Not music to study. Not music to enjoy purely for its listening kicks.[12]

Social distinctions between race, class, and ethnicity were reflected in the arts favored by each group, and social, cultural, and institutional forces tacitly joined to uphold the barriers that separated both people and their arts (Lopes 2002, 6–7). The greatest challenge jazz had to conquer was the racial hierarchy dividing American culture (9). The jazz renaissance was the result of efforts by those who produced records and concerts, club owners, critics, publishers of magazines, and the diverse audiences who sought the music (2). Many people from varied backgrounds worked toward the same goal of making jazz into a respected art form—Bernstein among them.

Some highbrows reacted to art in a similar manner as lowbrows, that is, they chose culture "for the feelings and enjoyment it evoked" without worrying about how it was created (Gans 1974, 79). They did care, however, about the "insight and information they could obtain." Great art tends to be serious, so these highbrows did not hesitate to follow carefully selected entertainment from lower cultures, such as sports (specifically football and baseball, but not the very lowbrow sport of wrestling) or certain television programs (81). This resulted in a phenomenon called cultural straddling, in which any brow would occasionally partake of something from another taste culture. This could lead to a reassessment of an item or activity. When a lower culture would appropriate something from a higher culture, the higher culture would lose interest, dropping it from its "cultural repertoire," for example the films of Ingmar Bergman (80–81, 83, 115). Alternatively, some lowbrow products were considered part of folk culture, and as such were worthy of highbrow respect, such as jazz (Lynes 1949a, 23). Even the firebrand Macdonald concurred: "jazz is the only art form that appeals to both the intelligentsia and the common people" (1960a, 214n).

Cultural straddling or "crossing over" the artificial barrier between the worlds of classical and popular music became commonplace in 1940s and 1950s America. Instances include Leopold Stokowski's conducting for Walt Disney's 1940 movie *Fantasia*, Agnes De Mille's choreography for the American Ballet Theater and several musicals such as *Oklahoma* (1943), and the 1950 premiere of Gian Carlo Menotti's opera *The Consul* on Broadway (Bernstein and Haws 2009, 62, 66). Television programs such as the *The Voice of Firestone* and the recording of blues and Tin Pan Alley songs by opera singer Eileen Farrell can be added to this list. Bernstein migrated between the two taste cultures "in high style" (59). His greatest Broadway hit, *West Side Story*, opened in 1957, the same year he was appointed Music Director of the New York Philharmonic.

High culture was so widespread in the 1950s and early 1960s that it actually became popular culture in what was referred to at the time as a "cultural explosion" (Grad 2006, 3). Studies of American culture in the twentieth century tend to focus on only popular (such as rock) music or the more esoteric high art forms (such as avant garde), entirely omitting most high art (such as symphonies and operas formerly considered upper middlebrow). Yet surveys of various cultural groups in America reveal the pervasiveness of high culture in the 1950s and early 1960s: two hundred dance companies, seven hundred opera groups, twelve hundred symphony orchestras, five thousand theater groups, and twenty thousand dramatic workshops.[13] Opera singers appeared on *The Ed Sullivan Show*, and Sears sold great art as part of the Vincent Price Collection. Despite such occurrences as Elvis Presley appearing on *The Ed*

Sullivan Show in 1956, these acceptable crossovers, however, did not initially include rock 'n' roll.

The youth of America in the 1950s were entranced by "race records," that is, music recorded by African Americans for an African American audience. According to many adults, this music would lead to "miscegenation, sexuality, violence, juvenile delinquency, and general moral decline" (Garofalo 2002, 140). Sociologically, many feared that the tidy separation between races was breaking down, so many of the songs originally recorded by African Americans were sanitized, "covered" by white artists, then called "rock 'n' roll" reassuring nervous adults and those with financial interests in the music industry (127–128). Rock 'n' roll was variously denounced as "devil's music," a strategy by the NAACP to recruit young whites, or a Communist plot to undermine the morals of youth (125). People also felt that rock 'n' roll was a type of lowbrow music that was frighteningly moving from "the other side of the tracks" into the mainstream (140). Both the music industry and the federal government tried to stem this musical tsunami; in extreme situations, the police would even confiscate offensive recordings (ibid.). Singer Frank Sinatra summarized the attitudes in 1958: "[Rock 'n' roll] fosters almost totally negative and destructive reactions in young people. It smells phony and false. It is sung, played and written for the most part by cretinous goons and by means of its almost imbecilic reiterations and sly—lewd—in fact, dirty—lyrics, and as I said before, it manages to be the martial music of every sideburned delinquent on the face of the earth. This rancid aphrodisiac I deplore."[14]

This incendiary aspect of the highbrow/lowbrow question emerged in the 1958 *Young People's Concerts* fan mail when Mr. and Mrs. Burress asked, "why do we have to listen to such stuff as Elvis etc? and hillbilly—?" and John Kay stated, "I won't mind—and others won't mind—if you don't refer to Elvis Presley, rock 'n' roll, and the like. There's already plenty of that. But I do look forward to everything else." Charlotte M. Leonard revealed the fears engendered by rock 'n' roll, and the image of classical music as the savior of society: "I believe if young people could hear and learn more about classical music they could not help but love it and perhaps they would get away from all this rock and roll and there would be less juvenile delinquency."

Artists in 1950s America easily moved between taste cultures. The new lowbrow art form of rock 'n' roll, however, remained closed off and isolated, a pernicious pariah. While artists could move from Broadway to the classical stage without raising an eyebrow, rock 'n' roll was still considered dangerous territory in 1958 when Bernstein's *Young People's Concerts* began.

The continuing criticism of popular culture repeated four particular fears: it has a negative influence because "it is mass produced by profit-minded entrepreneurs solely for the gratification of a paying audience"; it negatively impacts high culture because it "borrows from high culture, thus debasing it, while luring away many potential creators of high culture, thus depleting its reservoir of talent"; affects audiences negatively because it "at best produces spurious gratifications, and at worst is emotionally harmful to the audience"; and it negatively affects society because it "not only reduces the level of cultural quality—or civilization—of the society, but also encourages totalitarianism by creating a passive audience peculiarly responsive to the techniques of mass persuasion used by demagogues bent on dictatorship" (Gans 1974, 19).

Despite these fears, Bernstein gradually included lowbrow music (such as jazz, rock 'n' roll, and later rock) in his scripts, along with references to lowbrow mass media (television and movies) and lowbrow activities (sports). This eclectic, all-embracing approach could have proven quite dangerous, considering what a pernicious, insidious influence popular culture was considered to be in the mid-twentieth-century. Bernstein had to walk a fine and changing line from the late 1950s and into the 1970s as he integrated examples from the various taste cultures into the programs.

BERNSTEIN'S OWN CULTURAL CONTEXT

Bernstein joyfully embraced anything of quality no matter what the brow level. His solidly lowbrow family background and affinity for lowbrow art and pursuits enabled him to identify with the lowbrows in his audience. He enjoyed touch football, loved movies "of all ranks and persuasions," as well as comedians like Groucho Marx.[15] Bernstein's fondness for radio goes back to his earliest childhood experiences with the piano, picking out songs he had heard on the radio (H. Burton 1994, 10). He adored the blues and folk music of all cultures since he was a child, and his love of jazz (beginning when jazz was still considered lowbrow) resulted in it permeating his works.[16] The adult Bernstein was an avid fan of rock music, even writing and presenting a wonderful 1967 television special for adults called "Inside Pop—The Rock Revolution" that included songs by the Beatles, the Byrds, the Monkees, Bob Dylan, and the Association among others, as well as a personal appearance by Janis Ian.[17]

As he matured, Bernstein embraced the highbrow with the same enthusiasm, which gave him both the knowledge required of a proper highbrow and credibility with highbrows. A highbrow education at Harvard and Curtis certainly prepared him well. Some of his earliest musical experiences (radio, piano lessons) included examples of highbrow music. His brother Burton remembers how the maestro enjoyed a variety of highbrow sports including squash, snow skiing, swimming, and sailing, and his friend and assistant

Gottlieb remembers that Bernstein was skilled in waterskiing and horseback riding.[18] Gottlieb also describes Bernstein's homes having art works complemented by elegant antiques and rugs (Gottlieb 2010, 33, 35; Cott 2013, 29). The maestro moved in the highest levels of society. His career as music director of the Philharmonic (where he wore white tie and tails) would qualify as highbrow musically, culturally, socially, and sartorially (the orchestra performed both highbrow works by composers such as Bartók and upper-middlebrow works by composers such as Brahms). As to his middlebrow qualifications, Bernstein played tennis, loved movies, adored middlebrow music, and engaged in the middlebrow pursuit of teacher-to-middlebrows (*Omnibus*). The maestro obviously adored musicals, not only as a composer but as a friend of, colleague of, and collaborator with Broadway greats Betty Comden and Adolph Green.

As an adult, Bernstein became well-acquainted with the stratification of taste cultures, their accompanying class delineations, and the conflicts that could arise. At the beginning of his career, older conductors and boards of symphony orchestras (who were militant highbrows) seemed to feel that he was "hindered" by his natural affinities for all taste cultures (much like Macdonald's opinions of *Life* magazine). According to Lynes, a highbrow "does not like to be confused" (Lynes 1949a, 21). He is "a serious man who will not tolerate frivolity where the arts are concerned," nor will he tolerate blurring the "distinctions between those who are serious and those who are frivolous" (ibid.). By this definition, Bernstein was frivolous. One of a highbrow's functions was to protect the arts from the "culture-mongers," that is, those who exploit culture for social or business reasons (ibid.).[19] The maestro's love for and success with musicals, coupled with his enjoyment of such lowbrow styles as boogie woogie, was probably partly responsible for his not being given the post of director of the Boston Symphony Orchestra (Secrest 1994, 144). Noted conductor Sergei Koussevitsky's tirade to his young protégé at the opening of the musical *On the Town* in 1944 hammered home a similar theme (H. Burton 1994, 136–137). It had such an effect that Bernstein did not write another show until after Koussevitsky died. The young maestro knew he had to be careful.

Highbrows frowned on frivolity particularly in the arts. Yet "fun," in fact, was an integral part of the maestro's life. People close to him, such as his brother and children, often talk about the role of fun in his life and how he took fun very seriously.[20] For Bernstein, fun had a broad definition that included having a good time with friends, studying, composing, and certainly his "cutthroat" word games (Gottlieb [1962] 2005, xi–xii). Burton notes that "it was fun to him to discover the beauty of Ovid and Keats, to untangle the connections between Shakespeare's history plays and the real-life history of

Plantagenet and Tudor England" (1994, 28). Bernstein described composing his "Hebrew song for mezz. Sop and ork [orchestra]" as fun (61). He gave up conducting operas after a stressful recording session because "Bernstein felt he did not need to do anything if there was no fun involved" (415). He even included an article in *Findings* titled "'Fun' in Art," in which he discussed the importance of fun in the creative arts (1982, 104–106). According to Bernstein, the typical American defined fun as "'a good time,' a party, a relaxation, diversion . . . a hot dog," and he said that artists must help people find those same phenomena in art (105).

Bernstein's love of things from all taste cultures helped him shape programs that made middlebrows and lowbrows feel both challenged and warmly welcomed, while providing highbrows with fresh and interesting presentations. This is one of the reasons the Philharmonic hired him. As Bernstein experimented his way through life, he continued to embrace all taste cultures with equanimity, as seen in the three series discussed below.

THREE SERIES THAT DEMONSTRATE BERNSTEIN'S ABILITY TO REACH ALL "BROWS"

Bernstein's three filmed pedagogical series demonstrate his ability to successfully communicate with all brows. *Omnibus* (from early in his career) was aimed solidly at the middlebrow, *The Unanswered Question: Six Talks at Harvard* (known as the Norton Lectures, from late in his career) was designed for the highbrow, and his *Young People's Concerts* (from the middle years) was created for children (whom Lynes classified as lowbrows) and middlebrow adults.

Bernstein's first television scripts were for the middlebrow series *Omnibus* sponsored by the Ford Foundation (1952–1961); Bernstein's contributions ran from 1954 to 1958.[21] These programs are now recognized as the most successful cultural series in the history of commercial television in the United States, and they provided a model for what later became public television.[22] The Latin word "omnibus" means "for all; for everyone." Each program provided a cultural smorgasbord that ranged from such highbrow offerings as Orson Wells in *King Lear* to lowbrow burlesque with Bert Lahr (who played the Cowardly Lion in the 1939 movie *The Wizard of Oz*). These broadcasts were scheduled in television's "cultural ghetto" on weekend afternoons (as were Bernstein's *Young People's Concerts* at the beginning and end of its run). In writing about *Omnibus*, the Museum of Broadcast Communications offers special tribute to Bernstein, saying that "the most stimulating and original of the electronic teachers was Leonard Bernstein, who single-handedly enlarged the possibilities of musical analysis and performance on television."[23] The tremendous impression Bernstein made is even more remarkable when taken in context; of the 166 episodes of *Omnibus*, he wrote and delivered only ten.

Bernstein's first *Omnibus* program was a turning point for both Bernstein and music education on television.[24] The effusive and universally positive audience reaction to this single program led Robert Saudek (creator, director, and producer of *Omnibus*) to later say, "Thus was born a new Bernstein—television's star teacher" (H. Burton 1994, 241).[25] The maestro transformed music pedagogy through *Omnibus* and his *Young People's Concerts*. Saudek thought so much of Bernstein that after *Omnibus* was cancelled, he produced a series of Leonard Bernstein specials.[26] The press was impressed as well. Both he and the program were praised in *Life*, *Variety*, the *New York Times*, and other periodicals (241). His subsequent appearances on the series received similar accolades (251–253). *Omnibus* was also important for Bernstein politically. Saudek's hiring of Bernstein helped remove the conductor from the blacklist, thereby opening many doors that had been closed due to the Red hysteria (Seldes 2009, 72).

Bernstein's purely highbrow series was *The Unanswered Question*, six lectures Bernstein gave in 1973 as The Charles Eliot Norton Professor of Poetry at Harvard University. This chair had been previously occupied by such eminent artists as Igor Stravinsky, Aaron Copland, E. E. Cummings, and W. H. Auden. Bernstein's love of words and languages led him to be fascinated by Noam Chomsky's linguistic theories, so much so that Chomsky's 1972 book, *Language and Mind*, inspired Bernstein to write the Norton Lectures. As usual, Bernstein's mind saw connections, here between Chomsky's theories and music. Chomsky felt that all languages have a common structure; Bernstein felt that all music must have a commonality as well, which he determined to be tonality.

The Norton Lectures, like much of Bernstein's work, elicited a wide range of critical opinion from excessively effusive to thoughtfully balanced to patently insulting.[27] The negative evaluations came from experts in a specialized discipline who denigrated Bernstein's interdisciplinary approach. Among these, many felt the maestro created a "threatening encroachment on their territory" and reduced the entire series to "mere entertainment or worse, a self-aggrandizing display of quackish intellectualism" (Thomas 2004, 17). Others took the opposite view that his work was creative, opening new interpretations and interdisciplinary insights (ibid.). One point of contention was Bernstein's theories about the overtone series being the basis of a universal musical language that led directly to tonality (23). Nonetheless, the Norton Lectures are still well regarded and continue to stimulate thought among musicologists, linguists, and educators (17).

While the Norton Lectures and *Omnibus* were easy to classify according to taste culture, the task is not so simple with Bernstein's *Young People's Concerts*. They are, rather, something of a hybrid. The intended audience was children, whom Lynes deemed lowbrows. Most of the viewers of his *Young People's Concerts*, however, were adults. Bernstein intentionally crafted the programs for a middlebrow audience, professing that "he is 'very proud' of this [middlebrow] approach if it helps to 'make people feel closer to music'" (Rees 1966, 25). The orchestral repertory ranged from highbrow Bach and modernists to upper-middlebrow Romantic composers such as Berlioz and Brahms, with occasional references to styles which many deemed lowbrow, such as folk, jazz, and rock 'n' roll. Since the series was aimed at children (nominally lowbrows) and they enjoyed many of the same cultural artifacts as lowbrow adults (such as comics, television, movies, sports, and rock 'n' roll), Bernstein could sneak these lowbrow references into the programs with impunity. His *Young People's Concerts* thus invitingly focused on highbrow and upper-middlebrow music for an audience of children and middlebrows that no doubt included some highbrows and lowbrows.

HOW BERNSTEIN TAILORED HIS PRESENTATIONS TO THE PRESUMED BROW OF THE TARGET AUDIENCE

While the structure of individual programs remained essentially the same for all three of these series, subtle differences reveal how Bernstein carefully crafted each script to reach the taste culture of his target audience as effectively as possible. Nevertheless, Bernstein's pedagogical methods remained unchanged. He clearly stated the premise to be discussed, provided explanations with examples, reiterated what was learned, asked rhetorical questions, included incomplete sentences (to add a sense of spontaneity and informality), and made interdisciplinary connections. Sometimes his explanations were so beautifully phrased that they became sheer poetry, as in "What Is Impressionism?" (1 December 1961, 15) when he speaks of "a wavy wisp of a tune in an old church mode" and "you'll hear splashes of foam, all made of the whole-tone scale." He would frequently demonstrate his uncanny gift for expressing the thoughts or fears of his audience, as in "What Is Sonata Form?" (6 November 1964, 17); after he explains the three parts of sonata form (exposition, development, recapitulation), he says, "wow; that's a tough one." He then offers specific help. Bernstein's cultural agenda "to create and recreate a communally engaged audience" is seen throughout all three series, as well as in his other pedagogical talks, such as those at Brandeis University and for the Philharmonic's Thursday Evening concert series (Seldes 2009, 139). The maestro's delivery was consistently "firm, direct, never patronizing or hectoring, folksy enough to win your confidence but with a dash of elevated tone to command your attention" (Clark 1985, 19). The differences between the series lie in three aspects of his presentations: his choice of titles, his use of language (specifically his choice of vocabulary and syntax), and the type of interdisciplinary references he chose for analogies.

The titles he chose for his middlebrow *Omnibus* programs appealingly offered the promise of knowledge without excessive erudition. Bernstein's selection of topics here extols the virtues of music from all three brows. "Introduction to Modern Music" (13 January 1957) and "The Music of J. S. Bach" (31 March 1957) were on highbrow topics; "Beethoven's Fifth Symphony" (14 November 1954) and "What Makes Opera Grand" (23 March 1958) upper middlebrow; "The American Musical Comedy" (7 October 1956) lower middlebrow; and "The World of Jazz" (16 October 1955) lowbrow.[28]

The titles for the first three Norton Lectures were aimed at a highbrow audience with a more comprehensive vocabulary and highly educated interests, and link music with linguistics: "Musical Phonology" (11 January 1973), "Musical Syntax" (18 January 1973), "Musical Semantics" (25 January 1973). Those for the last three Norton Lectures suited a broader range of taste cultures: "The Dangers and Delights of Ambiguity" (8 February 1973), "The Twentieth Century Crisis" (15 February 1973), and "The Poetry of the Earth" (22 February 1973). The contrasting way he discussed modern music for middlebrows and highbrows is revealing: the *Omnibus* title is "Introduction to Modern Music," which implies that the curious audience member need know nothing about the topic, whereas the title of the fifth Norton Lecture is the more intriguing "The Twentieth Century Crisis," which implies that the audience either has some knowledge of the field or is at least interested in an in-depth study of twentieth-century music and its concomitant crises.

The program titles for his *Young People's Concerts* were chosen to appeal to children, but also may have intrigued middle and lowbrows as well. Birthday programs would certainly please the children. Others referred to subjects the young students probably encountered at school, such as "Musical Atoms: A Study of Intervals" (29 November 1965). Bernstein even reached out to youths through the vernacular of hippie drug culture with "Berlioz Takes a Trip" (25 May 1969). Viewers of any age or taste culture would be tempted by the eleven programs whose titles are couched as questions. One title referenced popular culture in a rather tongue-in-cheek way that would amuse both young and old members of the audience; "The Road to Paris"

(18 January 1962) is a word play on the titles of the Bing Crosby/Bob Hope "road pictures," a series of six films (1941–1962) that would have been fondly remembered by his adult audience and known to contemporary young people through television reruns. He even acknowledged those movies at the beginning of the program, saying, "I'll bet a lot of you are mystified by the title of today's program—'The Road to Paris.' What can that be about? A Bob Hope movie?" (2).

Bernstein thoughtfully constructed his scripts with syntax his target audience would find familiar and non-threatening. The syntax of lists delivered to his middlebrow audiences were straightforward, such as his description of the ending to the first movement of Beethoven's Fifth Symphony for *Omnibus* as a "bare, pithy, economical, forthright, direct statement of the greatest possible force" (Bernstein [1959] 2004, 104). For his young audiences, he phrased lists as children do, for instance, with the items separated by "and": "We don't have to know a lot of stuff about sharps and flats and chords and all that business to understand music" ("What Does Music Mean?" 18 January 1958, 39). The charm of this children's syntax is also seen in the way he separates items by "or" when describing the richness of American folk music influences: "whether it's jazz, or square-dance tunes, or cowboy songs, or hillbilly music, or rock 'n' roll, or Cuban mambos, or Mexican huapangos, or Missouri hymn-singing" ("What Is American Music, 1 February 1958, 29).

Bernstein was equally meticulous in his choice of words. In *Omnibus*, Bernstein used a somewhat elevated vocabulary and syntax. Two examples (with my italics) are: "Always probing and rejecting in his dedication to perfection, to the principle of *inevitability*" (Bernstein [1959] 2004, 105), and concerning some people's complaints that jazz is too loud, "Perhaps this objection stems from the *irremediable* situation of what is after all a kind of brass band playing in a room too small for it" (109–110). The maestro incorporates highbrow vocabulary into the Norton Lectures such as "sidereal," "lexical," and "invalid syllogism" (Bernstein 1976, 123–124). This vocabulary, when joined with highbrow syntax, yielded such sentences as: "hasn't everything we've been saying for the last three weeks led us inexorably to the hypothesis that all transformational processes ultimately yield metaphoric results?" (140), and "but Adorno confirms what I've been saying by pointing out, in his Hegelian way, that the Big Split is to be conceived dialectically, or, to use his language, as logical antimonies of the same cultural crisis" (270). In his *Young People's Concerts*, he consciously favors mono-syllabic sentences whenever possible: "And that sounds just fine. What he did was to take the notes in his head and put clothes on them so that they could go out into the world" ("What Is Orchestration?" 8 March 1958, 5). In this example, twenty-nine out of thirty words have one syllable.

Bernstein's contrasting explanations of syncopation in *Omnibus* and his *Young People's Concerts* demonstrate how he tailored his vocabulary and syntax to his audience. In *Omnibus*, he says, "'syncopation,' a word you have certainly heard but maybe were never quite sure of. A good way to understand syncopation might be to think of a heartbeat that goes along steadily and, at a moment of shock, misses a beat. It is that much of a physical reaction. Technically, syncopation means either the removal of an accent where you expect one, or the placing of an accent where you least expect one. In either case, there is the element of surprise and shock. The body responds to this shock, either by compensating for the missing accent or by reacting to the unexpected one" ([1959] 2004, 115–116). For his hybrid *Young People's Concerts* audiences, he says, "the thing that makes jazz rhythm so special is something called syncopation, which means getting an accent where you don't expect one, or getting a strong beat where you expect a weak beat should be" ("What Is American Music?" 18). For the middlebrow adults watching *Omnibus*, Bernstein referenced a familiar physical reaction, provided an intellectual explanation, then acknowledged the "shock" inherent in a syncopated rhythm, all using adult vocabulary; this definition is designed for the intelligent adult ignorant of musical principles. For the children (and others) watching his *Young People's Concerts*, Bernstein described musical expectations disturbed by syncopation employing simple words.

Although most sports were considered lowbrow, cultural straddling allowed Bernstein to incorporate sports analogies in all three series. The relationship of the bases in a baseball diamond is the foundation of his explanation of tonality (tonic is home plate) in both *Omnibus* ("Introduction to Modern Music" [1959] 2004, 192–235) and his *Young People's Concerts* ("What Is Sonata Form?" 18–19). In the Norton Lectures, the maestro mentions lowbrow football as well as the highbrow sports of skiing and golf (1979, 376, 404, 73). In his *Young People's Concerts*, football and baseball make frequent appearances, and boxing is even mentioned twice.[29] Highbrow sports (such as skiing and golf), however, do not appear.

Bernstein's ability to aim references at the target brow can also be seen in the different way he alluded to movies in the three series. Although he rarely references movies in either *Omnibus* or the Norton Lectures, he does so frequently in his *Young People's Concerts*. He was very positive about Hollywood movies in the middlebrow and hybrid series, assuming that his audience enjoyed and respected such films despite the nominally lowbrow nature of the medium. For example in *Omnibus*, Bernstein says, "We have all been privileged to watch Schumann and Brahms and other greats of the silver screen laboring over the keyboard as they search for the right tune"

(Bernstein [1959] 2004, 86). The use of the word "privileged" probably reflects the feeling the average viewer had toward such films. Instead of revering Hollywood's movies on the lives of great composers, one of the film references in the Norton Lectures highlights the problems inherent in these "bio-pics": "you will realize that this music [Debussy's *Prélude à l'après-midi d'un faune*] is not just drowsily improvised, but carefully composed, intentionally designed to produce a specific ambiguous effect—a far cry from the conventional Hollywood idea of the moody composer improvising a vague dream in which anything can happen anywhere at all" (Bernstein 1976, 245). Children and the average lowbrow probably could not care less about the accuracy of a composer's depiction as long as the movie was entertaining; the average middlebrow might care but might also be offended at any suggestion of a problem with a movie he adores. However, the average highbrow would find the maestro's insight fascinating and would not mind having his assumptions challenged.

Although Bernstein refers to lowbrow movie comedians Groucho Marx and the Marx Brothers in the Norton Lectures, *Omnibus*, and his *Young People's Concerts*, his only direct film reference in the Norton Lectures is to Fellini's 1960 award-winning highbrow foreign film *La Dolce Vita*.[30] Most movie allusions in his *Young People's Concerts* are general, such as a reference to a "western thriller" in "*Fidelio*: A Celebration of Life" (29 March 1970, 21). Sometimes they are specific, as when Bernstein uses the theme from the highly esteemed, academy-award-winning 1957 film *The Bridge over the River Kwai* for a musical demonstration of simplicity at the beginning of the series in "What Makes Music Symphonic?" (13 December 1958, 11–12)—which would certainly please his older viewers—and mentioned the popular 1965 Beatles movie *Help!* in "Musical Atoms: A Study of Intervals" and "Forever Beethoven!" (28 January 1968, 7)—which would certainly please his younger viewers.[31]

Bernstein occasionally elevated lowbrow and lower-middlebrow music by showing the parallels between it and upper-middlebrow and highbrow music. His effective method of opening viewers' minds was to relate the new concept or work to a familiar, comfortable concept or work. Robert S. Clark describes Bernstein's pedagogical style for *Omnibus* as being "designed to confront the middlebrow on his own level, without stooping, and to escort him gently, along the path of least resistance, to increased understanding" (Clark 1985, 19). As mentioned previously, highbrows tended to respect lowbrow arts as "a spontaneous expression of folk culture," whereas middlebrows generally avoided lowbrow cultural products (Lynes 1949a, 23). Bernstein, however, made lowbrow music acceptable to his middlebrow audience by showing the connections between lowbrow music and art music. When introducing the *Omnibus* program about jazz, he reveals the parallels between jazz and such respected composers as Haydn and Beethoven: "all music has low-class origins, since it comes from folk music, which is necessarily earthy. After all, Haydn minuets are only a refinement of simple, rustic German dances, and so are Beethoven scherzos. An aria from a Verdi opera can often be traced back to the simplest Neapolitan fisherman" (Bernstein [1959] 2004, 109). Lower-middlebrow musical comedy is shown to have parallels to upper-middlebrow Italian opera and Brahms symphonies: "we anticipate a new musical of Rodgers and Hammerstein or of Frank Loesser with the same excitement and partisan feeling as Milan used to await a new Puccini opera, or Vienna the latest Brahms symphony" (164). By pointing out the similarities, Bernstein suggested that since Haydn, Beethoven, Verdi, Puccini, and Brahms are worthy, such lower status idioms as jazz, folk, and musical theater must be worthy as well.

The maestro had a somewhat stealthy way of educating his viewers while at the same time making them feel learned. In *Omnibus*, he gives an explanation followed by the appropriate highbrow terms, assuming that his middlebrow audience would associate the two: "Mendelssohn fathered the 'elegant' school of conducting, whereas Wagner inspired the 'passionate' school of conducting. Actually both attitudes are necessary, the Apollonian and Dionysian, and neither one is completely satisfactory without the other" (134). Middlebrows who did not know the definition or origin of "Apollonian" and "Dionysian" could feel intelligent for deducing the meaning of the terms. In the highbrow Norton Lectures, however, Bernstein makes esoteric references without explanation, assuming that his educated audience is familiar with such arcane knowledge as: "John Keats' truth-beauty ideal" (Bernstein 1976, 53), "the most intricate word patterns of Henry James" (70), "trochee" and "spondee" (83), and "Lingam and Yoni" (91). This is even true of this somewhat humorous sentence from the Harvard lectures: "I have discovered rhopalism in Beethoven's First Symphony, polysyndeton in *Petruska*, and asyndeton in Bruckner—but fun is fun" (153). Of course, in his *Young People's Concerts*, Bernstein did not count on his young audience having much prior knowledge.[32] He even takes time to explain what the word "suggestion" means at the beginning of "What Is Impressionism?" (3) to ensure that his young audiences would understand.

The world had changed so much by the 1973 Norton Lectures that Bernstein no doubt felt able to include lowbrow references among the highbrow ones, such as the Beatles and their *Revolver* album (Bernstein 1979, 211, 318); the rock group The Kinks (327); and Groucho Marx (365). Nonetheless most lowbrow allusions are found in his *Young People's Concerts*.

BERNSTEIN'S DELICATE HANDLING OF BROW
REFERENCES IN HIS *YOUNG PEOPLE'S CONCERTS*

Bernstein offered a broad range of references in his *Young People's Concerts* that would appeal to not only children (presumably lowbrows) but also adults (presumably middlebrows). A study of the allusions he chose demonstrates, in part, how he successfully reached viewers of all cultural levels.

Bernstein certainly mentioned many items and activities designed to charm children. These were not haphazard but were usually influenced by the age of his own children at the time the script was created.[33] In 1959, he gives *Robinson Crusoe, Alice in Wonderland*, and *Gulliver's Travels* (stories that might have entranced Jamie when she was seven) as examples of a classic, incongruousness, and satire, respectively (no. 5: 29; no. 6: 3–4, 7, 13).[34] Many children's songs were introduced when Jamie and Alexander were little ("Row, Row, Row Your Boat," "Frère Jacques," "Twinkle, Twinkle Little Star," and "Three Blind Mice" as examples of rounds), then reappeared occasionally when appropriate.[35] Bernstein referenced Disney cartoons to explain how music can follow action, a suggestion that would encourage Jamie (and later Alexander) and all children to pay attention to the background music of their favorite cartoons with new relish (no. 6: 25–26; no. 34: 19; 20). Bernstein also mined children's toys for allusions.[36] The maestro compared Bach assembling a fugue to constructing something with an Erector set.[37] The kazoo must have been a Bernstein family favorite, because it received more references than any other single object in the entire series (five shows); the maestro even programmed a kazoo concerto.[38] On twenty occasions, Bernstein also helped young people understand principles of music by comparing musical concepts to subjects that they were studying in school, usually science and math, with several references to space and rockets.[39] In "Musical Atoms: A Study of Intervals," he compared constructing a musical work from individual intervals to matter being constructed of individual atoms (5–7, 24). While the evidence indicates that he initially directed the scripts at Jamie and then gradually included Alexander and Nina as they matured, "Candy" Finkler (of the production crew) felt Bernstein directed them mainly at Jamie (Finkler 1993, 4). The programs did become more complex as Jamie grew up.

Since children enjoy some of the same cultural artifacts as lowbrow adults, Bernstein could include with impunity many items that were otherwise scorned as lowbrow, thereby appealing to lowbrows in the audience without worrying highbrows. Again, many of these choices seem informed by his own children. His references to comics follow the ages of his children: *Mutt and Jeff* demonstrated an incongruous pair of harmonies in the third movement of Prokofiev's Third Symphony when Jamie was six and a half (no.

6: 15); *Dick Tracy* and *Terry and the Pirates* were given as a demonstration of very clear lines visually, such as those found aurally in Stravinsky's "The Story of a Soldier" (*L'histoire du soldat*) when Alexander was ten (no. 33: 35); and Schroeder's playing Beethoven in *Peanuts* references both the great composer and the beloved cartoon when Nina was nearly six (no. 41: 7). Again, sports were mentioned in thirteen programs.[40] Young people would have been familiar with baseball and football from school, and all brows enjoyed watching these games. Although amusement parks and rides were labeled lowbrow, they were a great attraction for children and are mentioned six times in five programs.[41] Jamie remembers how her father loved taking her on roller coasters, and it is easy to imagine the Bernstein family trekking out to Coney Island (Sherman 2010, xi).[42]

The maestro's success in music pedagogy was partly because he enthusiastically shared the fun he found in both listening to and performing music. Certainly, the production crew knew how to have fun (probably one of the reasons they were chosen) and described how much fun it was to work on the series (Finkler 1993; Rodgers, 1993). Fun is so integral to him and his *Young People's Concerts* that his protégé and chosen successor for the series, Michael Tilson Thomas, discusses Bernstein and fun in his introduction to the 2005 edition of selected scripts ([1965] 2005, viii). The many references to "fun" in the scripts no doubt engaged not only his young viewers but his middlebrow and lowbrow adult viewers, while gently reproaching somber highbrows.[43] He points out that many youngsters (such as the young performers) also find classical music fun, and he was encouraged by fan mail to create an entire program called "Humor in Music" (28 February 1959). The essence of this attitude is seen in "Charles Ives: American Pioneer" (23 February 1967, 8): "Now I've always thought that word *fun* was unjustly belittled; it's a wonderful word; and I believe it applies just as much to music as to roller-coaster rides or swimming or movies." All ages and all brows (with few exceptions) found Bernstein's sense of fun infectious and appealing.

The maestro was no doubt pleased to see from the fan mail that many children noticed his message that classical music can be fun. Some liked him, in part, because he looked like he was having fun (Gracie Charboneau, 1958) or was funny (Evalene J. Bill, 1958). Fans who felt there was something wrong with them for finding fun in music were thrilled to see him have fun with it.[44] Ruth Burks (a writing teacher) explained that music appreciation had always been "such a solemn thing" and that "I was about 35 before I knew that one could take pleasure and joy in music" (1958). She then shared, "It had never occurred to me that *music* could be fun!" Bernstein's love of fun must have endeared him not only to children but also to adults who had become disenchanted with the pedantic mantle of seriousness that cloaked traditional music appreciation.

Bernstein made extraordinarily few highbrow non-musical references in his *Young People's Concerts*. While weaving in low and middlebrow cultural artifacts that would please his viewers, Bernstein was obliged to thoughtfully select and limit the number of highbrow artifacts to avoid alienating them. They either might not know to what he was alluding and become intimidated, or might deem the reference as too elitist and stop watching. Those references he did make were carefully chosen to be familiar and/or appealing to all brows. He incorporated poetry by the British poet Keats and the American poet Kenneth Fearing to demonstrate the difference between English as it is spoken in America versus England in "What Is American Music?" The Keats excerpt, with its regular rhythm and rhyme scheme, represents the kind of traditional (highbrow) poetry one might learn in school:

> Bright Star, would I were steadfast as thou art
> Not in lone splendour hung aloft the night,
> And watching, with eternal lids apart,
> Like Nature's patient sleepless Eremite. (22)[45]

The Fearing excerpt has a free structure and incorporates slang, thereby seeming very contemporary and American:

> And wow he died as wow he lived, going whop to the office
> and blooie home to sleep and biff got married
> and bam had children and oof got fired,
> zowie did he live and zowie did he die. (22)

The Fearing was an effective selection. The poet would be known to highbrows as one of the founders of *Partisan Review*, to the upper middlebrows as a frequent contributor to *The New Yorker*, and to lowbrows as the writer of pulp fiction. Even if lowbrows did not know Fearing's work, they would not have been threatened by poetry that included such words as "wow," "whop," "bam," and "zowie."

Bernstein integrated other highbrow references into his *Young People's Concerts* in a similar fashion. Since he had a natural ability to see connections between art forms, Picasso became a logical part of his discussion of Stravinsky's music ("Happy Birthday, Igor Stravinsky," 26 March 1962, 8), and he simply could not talk about Impressionist music without referencing the Impressionist painters Monet and Renoir in "What Is Impressionism?" (3) or Hindemith's *Mathis der Mahler* without mentioning Matias Gruenwald's Isenheim Altarpiece which inspired the composer ("The Genius of

Paul Hindemith," 23 February 1964, 16–28). Although these visual and musical artists were all acknowledged as firmly highbrow, they lacked the exclusivist, elitist atmosphere associated with much of highbrow art; Bernstein knew that viewers anywhere in the United States (even rural areas) would know Stravinsky through Disney's 1941 film *Fantasia* and the artists through reproductions. Highbrow objects, such as a tapestry and a Persian rug, and the highbrow game of chess are mentioned only once, in the program about the opening of Lincoln Center ("The Sound of a Hall," 21 November 1962, 20). Such references were apt since the newly built Lincoln Center was to be the temple of high art in the United States. Other highbrow references (such as the authors Cervantes and Goethe and the philosopher Nietzsche) occur only in connection with particular compositions based on their writings. Bernstein's carefully controlled highbrow references were always appealing and non-threatening.[46]

At one point, the maestro even taunts those highbrows who pompously believed that great art should always be taken very seriously. He teases them for their tendency to look down on anything that is too popular in "A Toast to Vienna in 3/4 Time" (25 December 1967, 7) when he says that a Strauss waltz "is a marvelous invention, so let's not be too snobbish about it."

Musicals are the only purely middlebrow cultural item in Bernstein's *Young People's Concerts*, despite the large, acknowledged audience of middlebrow adults. Bernstein could safely assume that most of his viewers (particularly those abroad or in rural areas) would not be familiar with Broadway musicals (unless they were on film), so rather than frustrate his wide television audience he made vague allusions that would please those in the know. His references to musical theater were rare and so vague that they would only have been recognized by those familiar with the show in question, such as alluding to the production number "Seventy-Six Trombones" from Meredith Willson's 1957 musical *The Music Man* when speaking of the "brilliant and radiant" orchestration in "Enchanted Garden" from Ravel's *Mother Goose Suite* in "Young Performers No. 6" (28 January 1965, 18), or alluding to the 1965 musical *Man of La Mancha* (by Dale Wasserman, Joe Darion, and Mitch Leigh) by calling Don Quixote the "gentleman of la Mancha" in "Fantastic Variations (*Don Quixote*)" (25 December 1968, 5). In the first case, the musical had come out on film and may have been seen by most of his audience no matter where they lived; the second case occurred before the movie came out, so probably only devoted Broadway aficionados would know the show.[47] The one musical mentioned by name, other than his own, is the rock musical *Hair* (see chapter 6). He did perform his own *Candide* overture in "Overtures and Preludes" (8 January 1961, 19), his *Symphonic Dances from West Side Story* in "The Latin American Spirit" (8 March 1963, 21–22), and his Danzón from

Fancy Free in "What Is a Mode?" (23 November 1966, 31). Playing his own works in this international forum was not only acceptable but might lead to increased LP sales.

Although Bernstein could reference the lowbrow medium of television with some impunity since this was a television series, he still had to be cautious. Since the series was considered cultural programming, he had to be careful when talking about other television programs. He alluded only to shows that were appropriate for either children or families; probably he selected from those watched by his own family. Bernstein says that "my little five-year-old daughter Jamie" watched *The Lone Ranger* in "What Does Music Mean?" (3). It is easy to imagine seventeen-year-old Jamie and fourteen-year-old Alexander being avid viewers of *Star Trek*, which is mentioned in "Bach Transmogrified" (27 April 1969, 11), and the Bernstein family watching the variety show *The Ed Sullivan Show* (mentioned in "Young Performers No. 8," 27 January 1967, 18).[48]

Movies, one of those lowbrow things enjoyed by the "oafish classes" (as Sargeant called them), are mentioned in fifteen programs that range throughout the series.[49] If not considered highbrow, his first film reference was safely respected on many levels and aimed at the adults in his audience. As mentioned above, the main theme from *The Bridge over the River Kwai* serves as an example of musical simplicity in "What Makes Music Symphonic?" (11–12). A few months later, he talked about great actors and great comedians (again, relatively safe topics) when discussing "Humor in Music" (7, 22). He moved more firmly into the realm of popular culture with the aforementioned 1962 program "The Road to Paris," then embraced it thoroughly with allusions to the Beatles movie *Help!* in two programs, as mentioned above. When he dissected Richard Strauss's *Also Sprach Zarathustra* in "Thus Spake Richard Strauss" (4 April 1971), he counted on his audience recognizing the piece and did not even mention the pivotal use of the music in *2001: A Space Odyssey*. Only two films are discussed by name in Bernstein's *Young People's Concerts*. The first (*The Bridge over the River Kwai*) came early in the series, as Bernstein was finding his way, and was aimed at adults, and the later references (a few to *Help!*) were aimed at preteens and teenagers struck by Beatlemania.

Highbrows accepted the art form of folk music, although it was considered lowbrow.[50] Bernstein did not hesitate to mention folk music as a positive force whenever it was appropriate, which happens in eleven programs. For instance, folk music is mentioned as a possible source of musical nationalism in "Farewell to Nationalism" (30 November 1964, 2) and "A Tribute to Sibelius" (19 February 1965, 4, 11). Any discussion of Charles Ives's music would be incomplete without mentioning his use of folk tunes, as Bernstein does frequently in "Charles Ives: American Pioneer." The maestro even dedicated an entire program to the concept of classical composers borrowing folk elements in "Folk Music in the Concert Hall" (9 April 1961). Modes were pointed out in Spanish, gypsy, Hebrew, Greek, and Russian (to mention a few) music in "What Is a Mode?"(17, 21, 25). On occasion, Bernstein would mention the parallels between folk and other types of music as part of his continuing crusade for universality in the arts.[51]

Bernstein did his part in the jazz renaissance by mentioning the genre (always in a favorable light) in some eighteen programs, frequently calling it the primary wellspring of much American music.[52] For him, jazz sounds were American sounds. As a result, jazz permeates "What Is American Music?" and "What Is Classical Music?"; the basis for the latter is a comparison between art music and jazz. Bernstein deems jazz a form of folk music, listing it among such folk genres as square-dance tunes, hillbilly music, rock 'n' roll, and Cuban mambos in the quote given earlier from "What Is American Music?" In "What Is Classical Music?" he opens the door to the concept that quality music can be found within jazz and popular music by saying, "Isn't there such a thing as good jazz, or a good pop song?" (1) and "just as many other people think that jazz is also an art—which indeed it is" (3). As in *Omnibus*, he elevated jazz through linking it with highbrow genres. Bernstein did not hesitate to lavish an entire *Young People's Concert* on the genre: "Jazz in the Concert Hall" (11 March 1964); some viewers may have been surprised to see the presence of this lowbrow form in "the concert hall." Bernstein helped to "rehabilitate" jazz by weaving it into his programs in interesting and acceptable ways.

The questions of whether and how to include popular music into his *Young People's Concerts* were thorny ones for Bernstein, since many adults linked popular music with immorality and other ills of society. The awards given to popular songs, such as Grammies, do not carry the panache of an Academy Award, and popular songs were not set by great composers for use in the concert hall, so there was no *Young People's Concert* titled "Pop Songs in the Concert Hall." Bernstein's own experience with the attitudes of highbrows, such as Koussevitzky, to popular music had devastating results. If he were to include rock 'n' roll in his *Young People's Concerts*, Bernstein risked people believing that he was pandering to destructive forces and venal commercial interests. Nonetheless, he mentioned popular music or rock 'n' roll in twenty-one programs.[53] Bernstein did cautiously sneak some popular music in the early programs, usually songs that would more likely appeal to his adult viewers. The drafts indicate that on the very first program, "What Does Music Mean?" Bernstein intended to sing a brief excerpt from the song "All Shook Up" made popular by Elvis Presley, but he did not.[54] No doubt he felt that the time was not ripe for a broadcast by the highbrow New York Philharmonic and their new conductor to include such a lowbrow reference. His specific references to popular music early in the first season rested safely with a nostalgic pop song from 1911, "Alexander's Ragtime Band," and the popular television crooner (probably more favored by adults rather than by children) Perry Como. The first season of his *Young People's Concerts* was a great success, so by the second season Bernstein must have felt freer and began to mix musical styles without prejudice. In the first program of the second season, "What Makes Music Symphonic?" (13 December 1958), he explains what a sequence is, demonstrating the device by using a phrase in Presley's "All Shook Up" (15–16) to create a sequence, and then offers Tchaikovsky's *Romeo and Juliet* as an example of the technique in orchestral music. The popular song "I Can't Give You Anything But Love, Baby" appears in "What Is Classical Music?" (24 January 1959, 6–8), followed by a fallow period with only one popular song reference (to Irving Berlin's classic song "White Christmas" in "The Sound of a Hall," 21 November 1962, 30) between "What Is Classical Music? (24 January 1959) and "Jazz in the Concert Hall (11 March 1964). Things changed suddenly when the Beatles arrived in the United States on 7 February 1964. Nearly half the nation watched the 9 February 1964 American premiere of the Beatles on *The Ed Sullivan Show* in a program that had the largest recorded television audience to date.[55] Bernstein himself was quite taken with the Fab Four, as were many highbrow artists. His daughter Jamie remembers that he was her "co-delighter" in the Beatles (Sherman 2010, xi). He and his children went backstage to meet the quartet during a dress rehearsal for *The Ed Sullivan Show* in 1965. He thought of setting some of John Lennon's poetry to music, and he was not hesitant to tell journalists that he admired the compositions of John Lennon and Paul McCartney (H. Burton 1994, 350–351). Bernstein admitted in a 1966 interview that the pop music of the mid-1960s was much more interesting and adventurous "than anything being written in serious music today."[56] In both *Omnibus* and his *Young People's Concerts*, he sought to convince people to accept lowbrow folk and jazz by relating them to highbrow music; he used a similar method to encourage acceptance of popular music: by treating a Beatles song with the same reverence and clarity of analysis that he treated any other work. Since the season is set in advance, the first opportunity Bernstein had to react to Beatlemania was at the beginning of the eighth season (1964–1965). The maestro must have felt sufficiently secure in his successes by this time to spend a portion of "What Is Sonata Form?" analyzing the Beatles tune "And I Love Her," then comparing its structure with that of the Mozart Sonata in C major (12–13, 18, 20–25). For older viewers, his linking of classical music with rock 'n' roll made the latter more acceptable; for younger viewers the reverse was true. If the Beatles were cool, maybe Mozart was too. The floodgates were now open.

After this show, he talked about the Beatles in five more programs, eventually bringing in references to the Motown singing group Supremes, the Swingle Singers, the Grammy-award winning LP *Switched-On Bach*, and "Aquarius" from the hit rock musical *Hair*.[57] "What Is a Mode?" (23 November 1966) is a tour de force that gives examples of modes in medieval plainchant through rock songs by The Association, The Kinks, and the Beatles, to Debussy, Mussorgsky, and Bernstein. After a performance of the first movement of J. S. Bach's Brandenburg Concerto No. 5 (with solos by concertmaster David Nadien, renowned flutist Julius Baker, and Bernstein on harpsichord), "Bach Transmogrified" (27 April 1969) includes a rock interpretation by the New York Rock and Roll Ensemble. He does warn that "what you're going to hear may astonish you, and out-rage others—but it can't fail to fascinate you" (3A revised). Later, he says "it's going to be fun. And who knows: it may even be beautiful" (25). By the time the series ended in 1972, rock was no longer exiled to the lowbrow ghetto.

Many teenagers in his audience wrote Bernstein enthusiastically thanking him for his support of "their" music in "What Is Sonata Form?" In 1964 Lesley Cowenhoven appreciated his "coming to the defense of us teenagers" and praised him for understanding "our" music, and Donna Seroff thanked him "so very much for believing in us and our music." Kristi Kelly wrote that "what we need in this world is more people who have good taste as you do" (1964). Carol Moody asked Bernstein to repeat the program, so she could record it and mail it to the Beatles (1964). Later, eight-year-old Mark Erlich wrote that Bernstein sang the Beatles song so well that the maestro should "take one of the Beatles place and be one of them" (1966).[58] Where Horowitz (and many others) felt that the maestro "constructs unholy canons" by "irreverently juxtaposing [European masterpieces] with popular tunes," Bernstein's methods and enthusiasm drew in young people who otherwise felt ignored or disenfranchised (Horowitz 2007, 478). Teens gave his shows—and classical music—a chance.

Bernstein lived in a world with clear cultural stratifications. As the son of a Russian immigrant Jew and a lover of movies, sports, and popular music, he knew the lowbrow world. As a graduate of Harvard and the conductor of a major symphony orchestra, he was a part of the highbrow world. As both an aficionado and composer of musicals, he knew part of the middlebrow world, and as a sensitive human being and a born teacher who was hired, in part, to increase audiences by reaching out to middlebrows, he became more familiar with it. His success stemmed partially from his ability to respect the background and abilities of his target audience, no matter what their age or social stratum. His brother Burton recalls how Bernstein agonized over designing the perfect analogy for a script he was to deliver in Berlin (Bernstein and

Haws 2009, 105–109). The maestro wanted to go beyond simple intellectual comprehension and have the Germans intimately and deeply understand his "grander truths of universal interest," so discussions went on for days (105). Bernstein employed any means he could to reach his "students." From his earliest *Young People's Concert*, critics recognized the goal of this conductor/ educator and the fine line he walked. In reviewing the first program, a writer for the *Philadelphia Inquirer* said, "However highbrow Bernstein's purpose, there was nothing highbrow about his approach."[59] As an early postmodernist, the maestro fought preconceived notions by comparing the structure of works by Mozart and the Beatles, by mentioning great painters like Renoir on an equal footing with cartoons like *Mutt and Jeff*, and by demonstrating the use of Dorian mode in a Gregorian chant, the rock 'n' roll song "Along Comes Mary," and Sibelius's Sixth Symphony. Rather than diminishing great art, Bernstein drew in those who may have felt it beyond their understanding.

• 4 •

The Television Pioneer

Origins, Competition, Success

> The great benefit [of television], for me, is the educational value, not only in the pedagogical sense but in the best sense of acquainting people with new stuff they can come to love (which is what I mean by education, rather than having to memorize the conjugation of an irregular verb). Bringing music close to people . . . has always been my lifelong desire and goal even in writing my music. And I think there is nothing that comes near to television for this purpose. This is the best communicative means, and, after all, communication is what television is about.

> —Leonard Bernstein to Humphrey Burton

The television debut of Leonard Bernstein's *Young People's Concerts* was part of a larger "cultural explosion" taking place in 1950s and early-1960s America. Classical music, theater, opera, and ballet permeated the everyday lives of many average Americans, and television played a powerful role in disseminating culture with such programs as *Camera 3, Omnibus, Person to Person, See It Now*, and *Wisdom*. Networks and sponsors were puzzling out the best way to take advantage of the new medium, assisted by the Nielsen ratings system. The time was ripe for broadcasting educational arts programming of award-winning quality—American programming that would eventually be seen internationally.

While Toscanini was the "culture-god" in the first half of the twentieth century, Bernstein assumed that role in the second half. A survey of the various factors surrounding arts programming from television's beginnings through the late 1950s and a brief overview of children's television from 1948 to the 1970s will set the stage for the birth and continuation of his *Young People's Concerts* on CBS. A detailed study of the Nielsen ratings and the various sponsors will track the success or problems the programs had in attracting viewers and corporate sponsorship. The chapter concludes with a look at the role censorship played in the series.

THE IMAGE OF TWO MAESTROS:
TOSCANINI AND BERNSTEIN

The success or failure of a person in the public eye is only partially due to his expertise in his chosen field. Perhaps even more important is how the public perceives that individual—something that has been carefully engineered in the arts ever since P. T. Barnum in the mid-nineteenth century. An innovative American showman and businessman, Barnum heightened enthusiasm for the "Swedish Nightingale," Jenny Lind, by creating ballyhoo both before and after her arrival in the United States.[1] Through similar publicity (in part), Toscanini became the "culture-god" for America in the first half of the twentieth century and Bernstein in the second half.

While both were respected as brilliant musicians and conductors, their image as "culture-gods" was due to a "voracious, multimedia promotional apparatus the likes of which Paganini and Liszt could not have imagined" (Horowitz 1987, 3). The media machine ascertained what would touch the heart of the average American, then deliberately amplified that to achieve the widest appeal while avoiding anything irrelevant or deleterious.

The media fashioned a portrait of Toscanini that matched America's definition of a hero before, during, and shortly after World War II. He was regularly presented as a self-made man (from poverty to success) who courageously risked his life and reputation to fight against Mussolini and Hitler, who was practical and decisive, and who could control the individualists in an orchestra with an iron hand while creating great art that inspired both performers and audiences. A "personality cult of messianic intensity" was created around the Italian conductor (101). The elder maestro, Toscanini, turned to the new medium near the end of his life when he conducted the NBC Symphony in historic television concerts (1948–1952).[2] In contrast, the young maestro, Bernstein, expertly used the new medium at the beginning of his career in *Omnibus*. The mantle of culture-god passed from Toscanini to Bernstein through television. The average music-lover noticed and enthusiastically approved. Mrs. Sonia Bradley wrote Bernstein that "after Toscanini stopped conducting, you filled the vacuum created by his absence, magnificently" (1966).

Bernstein evolved into the "most famous and successful native-born figure in the history of classical music in the USA." Karene Esther Grad

studied the creation of Bernstein's image, noting that Bernstein personi-
fied the popularity of high culture in America during the 1950s and early
1960s (Grad 2006, 12–50). Publicity exploded in earnest after his storybook
debut with the Philharmonic in 1943, when he was suddenly called to
conduct a radio broadcast for an ailing Bruno Walter. Within days of the
performance, he was photographed and interviewed by *Harper's Bazaar*, the
Jewish Day, the *Jewish Forward*, the *Jewish Telegraphic Agency*, *Life*, *Look*,
the *New York Daily News*, the *New York Herald Tribune*, the *New Yorker*,
Newsweek, *Pic*, *Pix*, *PM*, the *Post*, *Time*, and *Vogue* (17). Bernstein became
an American success story. His early life (included, of course, as part of the
publicity furor) revealed that he was, in truth, "an exceptional all-American
kid who got his big break" (20). The media emphasized some of the same
characteristics they had emphasized with Toscanini: both men came from
poor backgrounds and had pulled themselves up by their own bootstraps;
both were, as Jack Gottlieb says, "musician-soldier[s] who performed in
the field during wartime conditions, under threat of military attack" (Gottlieb 2010, 10).[3] But Bernstein added movie star good looks to the formula.
Magazines and newspapers highlighted his sex appeal to such an extent
that teenage girls (and mature women alike) became quite taken by his
handsome, glamorous appearance.[4] Fan clubs sprouted, and Warner Brothers even invited him for a screen test in 1945 (Grad 2006, 18; H. Burton
1994, 142). A 1956 issue of *Time* featured his photograph opposite one of
Elvis Presley in its TV-Radio Report; he was even known as the Presley of
the Podium due to his podium gyrations.[5] Since Americans in the 1950s
were enthusiastic about marriage and parenthood, Bernstein's image had
to incorporate his role as husband and father (Grad 2006, 39–40). Popular
magazines pictured the young maestro with his wife and little children in
front of his house with a white picket fence—the picture of the American
dream (40). By 1958, America perceived Bernstein as a self-made, all-
American boy, who was hardworking, successful, and talented as well as
being a good husband, father, and provider. When Toscanini retired, this
energetic American youth was ready to step into his shoes.

Bernstein was clearly the man to take over the Philharmonic and its
"Young People's Concerts." His engaging charm, innovative handling of the
new medium of television, and unprecedented success on *Omnibus*, linked
with his already proven abilities as a conductor, made Bernstein a perfect
choice. Fortunately, all impediments had been removed by 1956: he was
cleared from the blacklist by his humiliating affidavit (see Seldes 2009, 69,
and Simeone 2013, 299–310), he was no longer barred from television after
Saudek's bold move of hiring him for *Omnibus*, and suspicions about his homosexuality were quieted when he married and had a family. Plus, the media

had crafted an all-American image for him that would appeal to all brows. Seldes opines that, "whereas Toscanini had decades before legitimated New York's coming of age, Bernstein would now personify New York's ascension to the capital of Western culture" (Seldes 2009, 77).

EARLY TELEVISION AND ARTS PROGRAMMING

Although the growth of television was stalled by World War II, the medium exploded shortly after the war and through the 1950s; sales of televisions tripled between 1949 and 1952 alone (Rose 1986, 2). In its first decades, television held great promise for not only entertainment but also enrichment and enlightenment. An objective of highbrows and corporations was to educate the masses (middlebrows and lowbrows), a mission seen in other media since the beginning of the twentieth century. In *Television Magazine*, Sylvester Weaver stated, "to program for the intellectual alone is easy and duplicates other media. To make us all into intellectuals—there is the challenge of television."[6] Cultural programming was a way to achieve this.

The costs of TV programming, however, were nearly ten times that of radio, and very soon clashes emerged between those who sought to produce cultural programming and those who dealt with financial realities (ibid.). Then, as now, sponsors wanted to sell products, and networks wanted the highest viewership possible, allowing them to charge more for advertising. Arts programming, however, attracted a relatively small audience. Consequently, either the sponsor or the network would finance such shows to boost its prestige (ibid.). Low ratings were sometimes unimportant if sponsors were pleased with the shows, but even when sponsors were happy, ratings took precedence in the minds of network executives. Such was the case with the Firestone Tire Company and *The Voice of Firestone* (1949–1963), which featured opera singers in a staid format to great critical praise. NBC, however, felt that the small audience (two to three million) dragged down their Monday evening ratings and demanded a time change, which Firestone refused. The series moved to ABC (1954), was dropped (1959), briefly returned as networks touted their cultural programming (1962), then was finally cancelled (1963).

Television executives want a profile of the average viewer for each series in order to tailor the show to his taste and earn the highest ratings. Since televisions were expensive at first, the earliest TV owners were highbrows—wealthier, better educated city-dwellers who preferred programming that was cultural, clever, or hard news. In 1955, 78 percent of households in cities (50,000 or more) had televisions, while only half of rural households owned one; rural farms averaged only 42 percent (Johnson 2008, 42). As more homes acquired sets, the demographic gradually included more middle- and lowbrows. The brow level of the average viewer dropped. By 1960, 87 percent of all homes had televisions, and by 1970 the figure was up to 96 percent (Comstock and Scharrer 1999, 7). Brilliant news programs such as Edward R. Murrow and Fred W. Friendly's *See It Now* (1951–1956) and clever comedies such as Sid Caesar's *Your Show of Shows* (1950–1954) were cancelled in favor of simpler, more entertaining series with higher Nielsen's.[7] Designed for the lower middlebrow viewer, many of these shows were at first Westerns and game shows, then detective shows, sitcoms, popular dramas, and variety shows with high ratings (Gans 1974, 86–87).

As the market grew in the 1950s, networks began "branding" themselves to carve out a market niche. CBS became known as the "Tiffany" network for its stars (such as Lucille Ball, Jack Benny, and later, Bernstein), quality news programming (by such revered and trusted reporters as Murrow and later Walter Cronkite), and specials (Tchaikovsky's *The Nutcracker*, with choreography by George Balanchine). NBC was known for its "spectaculars" (such as *Richard Rodgers Jubilee Show*, 1951, with Mary Martin, Celeste Holm, and Patrice Munsel). The last of the big three networks to emerge, ABC, sought to serve rural viewers ("plain folks" ignored by the other networks) with a series of westerns and comedies, like *The Real McCoys* (a sitcom about a farm family) (Johnson 2008, 64).

Television executives were confronted by a conundrum. They wanted the prestige of cultural programming but not the low Nielsen's. The solution was to relegate cultural and intellectual shows to unpopular timeslots (such as Sunday mornings and afternoons) in the "cultural ghetto" or what Murrow deemed the "intellectual ghetto."[8] Here, there was little competition, viewership was low, and ads were difficult to sell anyhow, so good ratings were less of an issue (Rose 1986, 5).

In May 1961, FCC Chair Newton Minow gave his famous "Vast Wasteland" speech, encouraging broadcasters to choose diverse programming (including cultural fare) instead of only questing for the highest ratings with violence (such as that seen in Westerns) and popular genres (such as sitcoms) (Minow 1964, 45–69; Barnouw 1970, 196–201). A mini "cultural war" began in the mid-1960s as government agencies and members of Congress launched attacks about the quality of programming with increasing energy (Rose 1986, 8). Advertisers, such as Xerox, IBM, and several oil companies, sponsored token arts specials once or twice a season; AT&T gave more regular support to arts programming with the weekly *The Bell Telephone Hour* (ibid.). The forces of culture versus money continued to put pressure on television, so competition became more ferocious and ratings more important. Networks scheduled arts programming less frequently. By the 1970s, most cultural events were exiled to public broadcasting stations.

CHILDREN'S TELEVISION, 1948–1978

Bernstein's *Young People's Concerts* began life as programming for children, so it is important to understand the context of children's television throughout the run of this arts education series. Both arts programming and children's programming encountered the same issues—costs, reaching viewers, programming, and the like. As people tried to determine which direction the new medium should take, questions surfaced concerning its nature and influence. As early as 1950, Robert Lewis Shayon wrote about the possible effect of television on children in an article appropriately called "The Pied Piper of Video."[9] By 1964, Minow stated that twenty-seven million children under the age of twelve watched each day (1964, 101). In 1976, the Nielsen Television Index reported on the viewing habits of youngsters under eighteen: two- to eleven-year-olds watched an average of 27.6 hours per week and twelve- to seventeen-year-olds 21.9 hours.[10] Everyone was concerned about the "heavy viewing habits of children," from parents, teachers, and medical professionals to various government groups and the broadcasters themselves (Turow 1981, 2).

In *Entertainment, Education, and the Hard Sell,* Joseph Turow thoroughly investigates the four important issues that surrounded children's television from 1948 to 1978: sponsors, scheduling, topics, and the various groups that attempted different levels of control.[11] He suggests that "sponsors and networks used a good portion of the decade [1948–1959] to search for the time period, length, frequency, and kind of programming that would be most efficient for reaching youngsters" (47). Bernstein's fifty-three hour-long *Young People's Concerts* that aired on CBS are included in Turow's study, even though typically only four were telecast each year.

Like the earliest arts programming, the earliest children's shows were sponsored either by networks or corporations. Six out of ten children's programs in 1948–1949 were sustained by the networks, a number that dropped to one in ten by the time Bernstein's *Young People's Concerts* began (1958–1959). Initially, the sponsored programs followed the model of radio, that is, sponsored and controlled by a single advertiser (19). With the success of *Disneyland* in the mid-1950s, both network executives and advertisers began to realize that family programming (that is, programs appealing to both children and adults, as would Bernstein's *Young People's Concerts*) was more cost-effective since it reached a wider audience for each dollar spent (19–20). This resulted in a sharp drop in the number of children's series by the end of the decade (24). By the 1960s, all three networks encouraged advertisers interested in saving money to share sponsorship or "purchase" time on programs (53). Such less-involved support with diminished control gradually became more common. Bernstein's educational series mirrors these trends.

All three networks offered relatively few hours of children's programming per week by 1958. While NBC led in total hours devoted exclusively to children in the 1950s, CBS surpassed the other two networks by the end of the decade (see table 4.1). Throughout both the 1960s and 1970s, CBS consistently maintained a greater commitment to juvenile programming than the other networks (56).

At first, children's series occupied two particular timeslots, Saturday mornings and weekday late afternoons. As costs were "higher than the presumed benefits," however, the networks abandoned late afternoons and turned the so-called children's hour over to local affiliates. By 1958, the networks scheduled 39 percent of children's fare on Saturday mornings; the remainder was scattered throughout the week. Throughout the 1960s, many aired on Saturday mornings, fewer on Saturday afternoons, a smattering on Sunday mornings and afternoons, very few programs Mondays through Fridays (usually in the morning), and only one (Bernstein's *Young People's Concerts*) ever in primetime. Saturday mornings became the overwhelmingly preferred slot for children's series in the 1970s, with between 51 percent (1978) and 69 percent (1970–1971). There was a very practical reason for this. Networks hoped that children would embrace Saturday morning as a single unified "block" to be watched from start to finish rather than as a sequence of unrelated shows; a program isolated from that block was less likely to succeed (82). Gradually, over 86 percent of children's series appeared in one of three slots: Saturday mornings, Saturday afternoons, and Sunday mornings. For example, in 1970–1971, only two juvenile programs aired at other times: *Captain Kangaroo* (which ran Monday through Friday) and Bernstein's *Young People's Concerts*.[12] The maestro's educational series had an unusual history of timeslots for an ostensibly children's program. The first four seasons (1957–1961) aired Saturday or Sunday afternoons, seasons

Table 4.1. Weekly Hours Taken Up by Children's Series, 1948–1959

	1948–49	*1950–51*	*1952–53*	*1954–55*	*1956–57*	*1958–59*
ABC	1.5	13.75	9	10	7.75	8.75
CBS	7	14.5	10.75	14	13	9.5
NBC	9	20.5	19	15.25	13.5	6

Note: The table does not include series scheduled less than once a week.
Source: Turow 1981, 23.

five through ten (1961–1967) during the golden hours of primetime, and the remainder (1967–1972) on Sunday afternoons.

The frequency and duration of juvenile programming stabilized during the 1950s. By 1958, over three-quarters of programs were seen once a week and 7 percent less than once a week (often every other week). With its four programs randomly placed throughout the year, Bernstein's *Young People's Concerts* inaugurated a "new way to schedule children's series on a less than weekly basis" (28). From 1960 through 1969, his *Young People's Concerts* remained a scheduling anomaly: only one other short-lived program was seen less than once a week (*On Your Mark*, 1960–1961), and no other children's series was broadcast during primetime (58–59). While the duration of children's shows were fifteen to thirty to sixty minutes in the 1950s, overwhelmingly most (83 percent) were half an hour by the 1958–1959 season (28). Nonetheless, hour-long shows (like Bernstein's *Young People's Concerts*) maintained a small but steady place in the schedule. After Bernstein left the series, the number of hour-long children's shows increased to a 1970s high of 35 percent in 1978.

The subjects of juvenile series changed over the course of the three decades covered by Turow's study. He lists four main topic areas: fiction, nonfiction, performing activities (including sports), and subject mixture (31). Only one series is listed under "music" for these eleven years, Bernstein's *Young People's Concerts*. Only three of the seven "performing" series in the 1960s were holdovers from the previous decade (65).[13] His *Young People's Concerts* was not only among them, but stood out as the only concert series (77). Broadcasters began looking for new material in the mid-1960s when the supply of older programs dwindled, black-and-white cowboy films became passé, and color was introduced (71). As a result, cheaply produced programs using limited animation techniques (small elements of animation move while the rest remains static) grew to over 80 percent of children's shows overall and 90 percent on Saturday mornings (81). Bernstein's juvenile series was certainly several levels above most (if not all) others in the children's genre— Dorothy D. MacDonald was "bored stiff" with the usual Saturday morning fare, and Mary L. Kiser "disliked" the "junky Saturday television"; both adults then praised Bernstein's shows. Janet Hobbs said "it is a welcome change from the usual Saturday morning run of Mickey Mouse, Captain Midnight, etc.", and David Isen said that his children previously "occupied their Saturday mornings" with Howdy-Doody and such, and then thanks Bernstein for improving "their taste and music appreciation tremendously" (1958).

By the 1970s, only two programs featuring children's concerts were telecast: Bernstein's *Young People's Concerts* until 1972 and later the non-weekly *The CBS Festival of Lively Arts for Young People* (an umbrella title for various types of performances, 1973–1981).[14] The *Young People's Concerts* run by Michael Tilson Thomas (whom Bernstein chose as his successor) were integrated into this series.

The saga of the various groups that attempted to control children's programming and their relative success is complicated and beyond the purview of this book but is explored by Turow (1981). It is sufficient to note that various organizations were involved, such as parent-teacher groups, consumer organizations, academicians, doctors, regulatory bodies, congressional committees, and even the networks themselves. They were most deeply concerned about curbing excessive violence and creating "opportunities for cultural growth as well as for wholesome entertainment" (22). The practical, economic incentive for quality children's programming at least at first was to encourage parents to buy televisions, so both networks and advertisers emulated the "most respectable of children's radio fare" while carefully selecting programming calculated not to offend (37). Minow's famous 1961 speech reinforced this point of view:

> It used to be said there were three great influences on a child: home, school and church. Today, there is a fourth great influence, and you . . . control it. . . . What about your responsibilities? Is there no room in television to teach, to inform, to uplift, to stretch, to enlarge the capacities of our children? . . . Is there no room for reading the great literature of the past, teaching them the great traditions of freedom? There are some fine children's shows, but they are drowned out in the massive doses of cartoons, violence and more violence. (Minow 1964, 54)

Prestige programming came to the fore while Minow was FCC chair, then lost luster when he left in 1963 and pressure decreased considerably (Turow 1981, 51). By the end of the 1960s, a *laissez-faire* atmosphere developed as interest from the public sector faded, letting the commercial needs of networks and their advertisers take center stage (82). By 1967–1968, Bernstein's pedagogical series for youth was back on Sunday afternoons in the cultural ghetto.

From 1958 to 1972 (when Bernstein left), his *Young People's Concerts* retained a unique position. Rather than weekly or bi-weekly, it appeared four times a year (28). It was the only children's concert series (77). Its popularity is confirmed by the fact that it was one of only four children's series to continue through three decades (99).[15] It stands almost entirely alone in offering the best in cultural and prestige programming for children, shining high above the westerns and limited animation shows. It was the only children's program ever offered in primetime. The timeslots and, as we will later see, sponsorship mirror the trends of each decade.

INCEPTION OF BERNSTEIN'S *YOUNG PEOPLE'S CONCERTS*

The Philharmonic at mid-twentieth century was suffering declining audiences and a worsening financial situation. Critic Harold Taubman enumerated the problems and possible solutions in a Sunday essay for the *New York Times* at the end of the 1955–1956 season.[16] He alluded to the "utmost significance" of a "healthy and respected" Philharmonic in the life of New York and the United States. Taubman concluded by saying, "great music has a larger following in America than at any time in the past. The Philharmonic should lead the way in nurturing and increasing this flowering of musical taste."

Barry Seldes recently outlined the views of Taubman and others (Seldes 2009, 72–77). By the mid-1950s, the orchestra needed to find a way out of its financial crisis, attract a young audience by scheduling more new American music, modern works, and semi-classics, and play a central role in establishing New York as a global cultural center (a task made particularly important by the Cold War) (73–74). The federal government and various foundations endeavored to prove to the world that the United States (in part through freedom of expression as seen in the arts) and not the Soviet Union (with its "narrow orthodoxies") could become the world leader after World War II (74). Without realizing it, Taubman provided motivation for televising the Philharmonic's "Young People's Concerts" by saying "the ubiquitous television set has made deep in-roads on attendance at all public entertainments" and mentioning the need to attract younger audiences.

Dating from shortly before Bernstein was hired, a 1956 letter from the Young People's Concert Committee to the Philharmonic's management describes the search for a new talented, charismatic conductor to run the Philharmonic's already existing children's educational series.[17] Previous concerts were led by assistant conductors, but this would be the first time they would be led by an established conductor. The Philharmonic sought someone not only of great ability and repute but also with appeal and charisma to ensure success in the new medium of television (Rose 1992, 131).[18] The committee began the letter by enumerating the strengths and deficiencies of Wilfred Pelletier (current director and presenter of the Young People's Concerts), then requesting assistance in finding a new person(s) to plan and conduct the programs.[19] This new conductor must have the ability to control over 100 instrumentalists, know American music and modern music as well as the European classics, and, very importantly, exude glamour and star power (Seldes 2009, 73–74). The image of the new maestro was crucial. Desirable characteristics were: prestige ("top-flight"), a sound musical background (someone capable of planning the programs well), and availability (someone who lived near or close to New York City); also desired were "good personality, good speech and rapport with children." The letter then states, "An example of a conductor who appears to fill all the above requirements is, we believe, Leonard Bernstein."[20] Five other conductors' names were submitted in a separate paragraph: Frederick Fennell, Howard Mitchell, Robert Shaw, Samuel Antek, and Igor Buketoff.[21] The memo that accompanies this letter approves of approaching Bernstein but notes that the Philharmonic's Managing Director Bruno Zirato "agrees with everything except 'top flight conductor.'"[22]

The idea of creating children's concerts for television was in the air during the cultural explosion, emerging on several fronts simultaneously. The Philharmonic was already considering using this new medium. Carlos Moseley, later president and chairman of the board for the Philharmonic, was director of press and public relations when Bernstein was hired. He reported that Bernstein agreed to run the Philharmonic's "Young People's Concerts" only if they were televised. The young conductor then encouraged William S. Paley, the head of CBS who also ran Columbia Records (the official recording company of the Philharmonic, which already had Bernstein on their roster), to carry the programs on his network.[23] Paley, who already knew Bernstein, was seeking cultural and educational programming, so he welcomed the venture. Although he was not a musician, he knew the value of culture. To Paley, the proper place of Leonard Bernstein and the New York Philharmonic was on his "Tiffany" network. Once Bernstein was appointed co-director of the Philharmonic, he and Paley began discussing the details about airing these educational concerts.[24] Paley knew that Bernstein would be ideal since the young conductor had received such tremendous accolades for his work on *Omnibus* (Rose 1992, 130).[25]

At the same time, producer Roger Englander wanted to translate a series of children's concerts from stage to television. He sought out Richard Lewine, head of CBS's program department, to pitch his idea. Lewine consented to see Englander, not to hear his ideas but instead to interview him for the projected Bernstein-Philharmonic series (130–131). The first season of Bernstein's *Young People's Concerts* was a confluence of ideas that had been fermenting in the minds of the orchestra's management, conductor, head of CBS and Columbia Records, and the man who would be producer/director. The time was right.

NIELSEN RATINGS, SPONSORS, AND BERNSTEIN'S *YOUNG PEOPLE'S CONCERTS*

Programming on commercial television is largely controlled by the complex relationship between Nielsen ratings and sponsorship. The salient issues concern the day and time of broadcast and success in reaching a sponsor's target demographic. The biweekly Nielsen publications supply an overview of the popularity of individual programs and make it possible to compare the success of Bernstein's educational programs with those scheduled opposite them—a task easier then than now, as there were only three primary networks. To place Bernstein's *Young People's Concerts* in the context of its time, we must understand these mechanisms and how they functioned.

The Nielsen rating system provides information about television audiences specifically collected to assist networks in setting advertising rates and deciding which shows should continue or be cancelled. The A. C. Nielsen Company was founded in 1923 by American business executive and market-research engineer Arthur Charles Nielsen (1897–1980), the son of accountants, originally to offer market-research data about products in use in the United States. The Nielsen Company began rating the popularity of radio programs in the 1930s, then of television programs in 1950. The system for television ratings devised by Nielsen Media Research is so efficacious that it is now used to supply audience measurement information around the world. "The Nielsens" were published in biweekly booklets for the use of networks, stations, sponsors, and advertising agencies. The ratings were financed by Nielsen's sales of booklets primarily to the networks, as well as to some enterprising ad agencies.

The sample size and method of collection changed over the years. Nielsen television ratings were initially calculated on a sample market of one thousand homes throughout the United States.[26] At first, viewing information was recorded on "audiometers" installed in sample homes that recorded only the "programming hour" (the time and duration of the show) and the program being watched. The Nielsen booklets also catalogued the sponsors. Later, the data was collected by "set meters" that were hooked directly into telephone lines.

Sponsors want to know that their message is reaching their chosen demographic, which was partly guesswork with the early, less complete Nielsen data. A profound change occurred in the early 1970s when Nielsen began supplying more detailed demographic information collected from Nielsen viewers' diaries, breaking down the viewers according to such factors as age, gender, economic and educational status, and urban or rural location (Barnouw 1978, 70). Then, as now, younger viewers were sought. Eric Barnouw, in *The Sponsor*, declared that "sponsorship became a matching game" in which demographics dominated the buying and selling of programs (71). For instance, although the popular western *Gunsmoke* was considered one of the best dramas on television and received high ratings, the series was cancelled in 1975 after twenty years on the air because the audience was skewing too old and too rural.

Two Nielsen results are the most commonly cited: rating and share. A rating point refers to the percentage of all televisions in the country tuned to the program in question; one point equals one percent. Share, on the other hand, refers to the percentage of televisions *in use* (turned on) that were tuned to the program in question.[27] The number for share will always be the greater of the two. These are usually reported as "rating/share." For example, in a sample size of ten sets, if eight were not turned on and two *were* turned on, and of those two, one was turned to a *Young People's Concert*, the rating would be 10.0 (10 percent) and the share would be 50.0 (50 percent). Nonetheless, ratings are money, so both numbers are important in different ways: "buyers want ratings points," and "TV reps try to sell share."[28]

The program with the highest Nielsen numbers in a timeslot could charge more for advertising than a program with a lower rating, so the Nielsen's led to endless bargaining and prices that fluctuated like those on the stock market (Barnouw 1978, 69). Barnouw explains the economic motivations that ruled television by the early 1970s:

> Everything at the network seemed to revolve around the yes's and no's. A low-rating program had become a menace. Wrong demographics were a menace. To maximize income, these had to be sloughed off. Pressure to this end came from sales executives, who received bonuses based on sales income; from affiliates, whose local sales were likewise affected by ratings and demographics; from stockholders, whose stock prices could reflect ratings fluctuations; from top network executives, whose contracts had stock-options clauses. (73)

Timeslots when more viewers would be watching (that is, primetime) were the most valuable. Primetime (weekday evenings after everyone comes home from work or school and turns on the television) has always had the highest viewership, thereby offering the most appeal for advertisers.[29] Commercials in these slots have always sold for a premium price. At the time of Bernstein's *Young People's Concerts*, primetime programming was controlled by the networks (such as CBS) rather than the local affiliates (Benson, interview).[30] Outside of primetime, any show that had a Nielsen rating of three points or above was marketable (ibid.). Specials, which had little or no Nielsen track record, would be presented to sponsors as part of a package that included more appealing programs (ibid.). Often, the specials would turn out to be bargains once the number of viewers was calculated (Barnouw 1978, 70).

Cultural panache became almost more important to all three networks (ABC, CBS, and NBC) than the Nielsen's after the quiz show scandals of the second half of the 1950s. Television executives began seeking programming that would bring the networks prestige and restore some of their "public service" image (56). They also needed sponsors more interested in prestige than ratings (ibid.). CBS moved to the fore in the cultural battle by announcing that it would search for "the best programming . . . whatever the source," and that the network would schedule only its own productions (when it came to documentaries) (57). In 1958 and 1959, these plans came to fruition with *CBS Reports* and Bernstein's *Young People's Concerts*.

Throughout the 1950s, sponsorship of television programs became the path to financial success as more people abandoned movie theaters and radio in favor of the exciting new medium (46). Barnouw observes that while Bob Hope was a leader on radio for two decades, his ratings slipped from 23.8 in 1949 to 5.4 in 1953 as television took over; on the other hand, when Hazel Bishop lipsticks moved their advertising from radio to television, their earnings shot up from $50,000 a year in 1950 to $4,500,000 in 1952, an amount that only continued to grow as television did (ibid.). In the 1950s, a show would generally have one sponsor (for instance, the *Jack Benny Show* was sponsored by Lucky Strike cigarettes for a time), and their commercials would be woven into the show in addition to being separate events. Even Humphrey Bogart (noted actor famous for *Casablanca* and *The Maltese Falcon*) plugs Lucky Strike cigarettes in the middle of a skit on *The Jack Benny Show* (25 October 1953).[31] As single sponsorship became too expensive, companies would cosponsor a program. Networks executives were happy with this turn of events, as they sought "an increasingly uninhibited exercise of network scheduling power" (Boddy 1993, 161). By the 1970s, networks gained more control, and the connection between sponsor and program became progressively more tenuous, as various sponsors were simply sold commercial slots within a program.

The story of the sponsorship of Bernstein's *Young People's Concerts* is a familiar one for much of arts broadcasting at the time. The first seasons were broadcast as a service by CBS without a sponsor, then one sponsor was found, and eventually two companies shared sponsorship; atypically, the programs returned to a single sponsor, then returned to two before going off the air (see table 4.2).

According to a document titled "*Television Possibilities* in re: *Young People's Concerts*," discussions about the project were opened before a sponsor was found:

Table 4.2. List of Sponsors for Bernstein's Young People's Concerts

Programs	Season	Dates	Sponsor
1–7	1–2	1957–1959	None
8–27	3–7	1959–1964	Shell
28–35	8–9	1964–1966	Bell Telephone (a subsidiary of AT&T)
36–39	10	1966–1967	Bell Telephone and AT&T
40	11	1967	Polaroid
41	11	1968	Eastman-Kodak (28 Jan 1968) / Polaroid (2 Jun 1968 rebroadcast)
42–43	11	1968	Polaroid
44–49	12–13	1968–1970	Polaroid
50–53	14–15	1970–1972	Polaroid and the Kitchens of Sara Lee, a subsidiary of Consolidated Food Corp.

For the sources of this information, see appendix C.

> CBS-TV representatives and Philharmonic management agreed to coop-
> erate in exploring the physical, financial and scheduling problems involved
> in rehearsing and televising four or fewer children's concerts. Based on this
> research, either CBS will take over the entire package and secure commer-
> cial sponsorship, or CBS will cooperate with the Philharmonic in seeking
> support from the Ford Foundation.[32]

Ford never sponsored the programs, and CBS financed the shows for the first
two seasons until a sponsor was found. Copious documents in the Philharmonic archives reveal the great struggles to find a sponsor for the eleventh
season (1967–1968).[33]

The overall Nielsen ratings for Bernstein's *Young People's Concerts* were
surprisingly good and very marketable (Benson, interview).[34] They can be
divided into three groups by broadcast time: early (when the programs were
broadcast on a weekend afternoon), middle (in primetime), and final (back to
weekend afternoons). At the beginning, programs 1 through 15 (1958–1961)
were broadcast on weekends in what was considered a less than desirable
timeslot with slender competition consisting of unrated religious programs
and college sports.[35] The ratings for the first two seasons ranged from a low
of 2.1/9.6 (point/share) for "What Is a Concerto?" (28 March 1959) to a
high of 4.5/16.5 for "What Does Music Mean?" (18 January 1958); these
were high enough to interest a sponsor. For seasons 3 through 5 (in basically
the same timeslot), the ratings improved, ranging from 3.3/16.3 for "Unusual
Instruments of the Past, Present, and Future" (27 March 1960) to 5.6/19.9
for "Who Is Gustav Mahler?" (7 February 1960).

After Minow's famous 1961 "Vast Wasteland" speech and beginning with the fifth season (1961–1962), Bernstein's *Young People's Concerts* were paraded on various weeknights during primetime (usually 7:30–8:30 p.m.) as a badge of the artistic merit found at CBS.[36] The competition was fierce, for example: an episode of the private detective series *77 Sunset Strip* (17.9/30.3 opposite "A Tribute to Teachers," 29 November 1963 that had a rating of 17.7/13.0), the World War II drama series *Twelve O'Clock High* (18.4/35.7 opposite "Musical Atoms: A Study of Intervals," 29 November 1965 with 11.8/19.1), the American Western series *The Virginian* (23.4/41.1 opposite "What Is a Mode?" 23 November 1966 with 17.6/13.8), the historical action-adventure series *Daniel Boone* (27.2/42.6 opposite "Charles Ives: American Pioneer," 23 February 1967 with 5.3/8.3), and *Tarzan* (27.5/45.4 opposite "Young Performers No. 8," 27 January 1967 with 10.5/17.3). It is likely that CBS knew they were going to lose in those particular primetime slots anyhow (since other networks were broadcasting guaranteed blockbusters), so they happily surrendered the time to such a prestigious program (Benson, interview). In primetime, the ratings ranged from a high of 11.8/19.1 (the highest Nielsen's the series ever earned, for "Musical Atoms") to a low of 4.6/12.4 ("The Genius of Paul Hindemith," 23 February 1964), which is still quite a respectable rating.

The problem with broadcasting Bernstein's *Young People's Concerts* in primetime was not that the ratings were poor, but that much more money could have been made with a program that earned even a marginally higher rating. While the Nielsen ratings for the shows were good, they were not good enough for primetime, so the series was moved back to weekends for the eleventh through the fifteenth and final season (programs 40 through 53, 1967–1972), specifically Sunday at 4:30 p.m.[37] Here, the lead-in programs were usually sports (soccer, hockey, football), and the competition was religious programs (usually unrated) and sports (basketball, *American Sportsman*, and golf). While the series was not usually trounced by the opposition the way it was in primetime, the sports programs airing opposite it still had higher ratings (such as an NBA basketball game with 8.7/25.9 opposite "A Toast to Vienna in 3/4 Time," 25 December 1967, with 4.6/15.3). Here, the lowest rating was 2.4/7.7 ("Young Performers No. 9," 31 March 1968, which opposed *American Sportsman* with 18.5/43.1), and the highest was that for the aforementioned "A Toast to Vienna in 3/4 Time."

All in all, the ratings were always worthy, since anything with a rating of three points or higher was considered good—in slots other than primetime, of course (Benson, interview). The lowest rating earned by these Bernstein-Philharmonic programs was a 2.4/7.7 (2,180,000 sets) for "Young Performer No. 9" (on Sunday afternoon) and the highest was 11.8/19.1 (9,850,000 sets) for "Musical Atoms" during primetime (as already noted). The number of sets turned to Bernstein's *Young People's Concerts* in the United States alone ran from a low of just over 2 million to a high of nearly 10 million; these are impressive numbers in light of the fact that in many cases multiple viewers were watching each set.

The fan mail from 1958 alone shows that the Nielsen ratings only begin to reveal the number of viewers. Families often watched together. For example, Bonnie was a twelve-year-old who wrote that she watched with her five- and eleven-year-old sisters and a nine-year-old brother (she does not mention the presence or absence of a parent). Bonnie also mentions that her siblings were "so fascinated by you and your programme that they couldn't even tear themselves away for lunch. And that's no mean feat!" Charles Bain, Mrs. Frederick S. Carr, and many others wrote that they watched with their families as well. Some teachers, students, or youth symphony members wrote indicating that they intended to organize listening groups in schools and homes.[38] The Quincy Symphony Orchestra held "television parties" for the first program.[39] Mrs. Guy Langer, Co-Chairman of Junior Education for the Florida West Coast Symphony Orchestra, indicated that she intended to invite three hundred children from local public schools to view the next program together. Such activities profoundly raised the number of viewers on a single set. The programs had a life after broadcast, even in the 1950s. Both a teacher and a student in 1958 wrote that they had tape-recorded the show (audio only) to play later for their classes and friends.[40]

The international numbers are equally impressive. The concerts were first broadcast internationally starting with the fifth season (1961–1962), beginning with Canada.[41] The Philharmonic Annual Report for 1964 indicated that the series was syndicated in foreign markets on 15 August 1962.[42] According to Burton, "Hungary reported that the *Young People's Concerts* were as popular as 'The Flintstones' and were actually beating 'Bonanza' in the ratings" (1994, 296). A chart dating from 1964 in the Philharmonic archives lists the breadth of viewing abroad: twenty-two countries with a total of 77,211,000 sets, and undoubtedly with several viewers per set.[43] The series was eventually seen in over forty countries. In truth, Leonard Bernstein's *Young People's Concerts* were seen by well over 100 million viewers around the world.

The prestige of sponsoring Leonard Bernstein and the New York Philharmonic in arts education programming emanating from internationally famous concert halls in New York City must not have been enough enticement for sponsors in the beginning. The initial contract that established the relationship between the Philharmonic and CBS stated that CBS "may select or authorize" a sponsor; however, "CBS Television shall not permit the sponsor to make any commercial announcements on the programs which are not in keeping with the dignified nature of the programs and with the reputation of the Society's orchestra."[44] Two seasons passed before a sponsor was found. As a result, CBS Television covered all costs as a public service and cultural experiment while collecting Nielsen's, presumably to assist in finding a sponsor.

By the third season, the programs had proven themselves worthy, and Shell Oil became the sponsor. Since there are no relevant documents, the nature of Shell's target demographic must be deduced. A company selling gasoline was probably courting the family market at that time (Benson, interview). Although the commercials are not currently available for viewing, the title page or closing page of the script frequently reveals some of Shell's attitude.[45] During the third season, the announcer tersely states: "These concerts are brought to you by the Shell Oil Company."[46] By the fourth season someone at Shell realized that these commercials would not only provide visibility for the oil company but would also allow Shell to bask in the reflected glory of Bernstein, the Philharmonic, and Carnegie Hall. A brief memorable tagline was added to build on that association. The programs now open with, "Shell Oil takes you to the newest home of the world's greatest musical events [all scripts that mention Lincoln Center tout the hall in this manner], Philharmonic Hall at New York City's Lincoln Center, for the New York Philharmonic *Young People's Concert* under the musical direction of Leonard Bernstein" and close with "From Philharmonic Hall in Lincoln Center—another New York Philharmonic *Young People's Concert* under the musical direction of Leonard Bernstein has been presented by the Shell Oil Company . . . sign of a better future for you."[47]

When Bell Telephone took over sponsorship in season eight (1964–1965), they continued the practice of linking the prestige of the series to a product. Again, the ad's tagline did not appear until Bell Telephone's second season. The opening and closing was identical to Shell's. By the ninth season, the taglines begin to offer insight into the target market. Bell Telephone directed the ads at the family, adding "the award-winning series" and the tagline "brought to you by The Bell System, providing you and your family with the best in dependable, low cost telephone service." The programs closed with, "The New York Philharmonic *Young People's Concerts* are brought to you by the Bell System, reminding you that someone, somewhere would enjoy hearing your voice by telephone tonight. A long-distance call is the next best thing to being there." At the time, long-distance calls were still a cherished, unique, and somewhat costly experience for most people, as charges were calculated by both the minute and distance. Also home phones were rented not owned, so many had only one; only one person could speak at a time. The tenth season was co-sponsored (not an unusual practice by this time) by AT&T and Bell Telephone, which was a subsidiary of AT&T. Although the ads again allude to the kudos given to the series by opening with, "This award-winning series is brought to you by AT&T and the Bell System Associated Companies," the joys of telephoning loved ones, oddly, was not touted.

AT&T pioneered both sponsored broadcasting and business-sponsored film distribution (Barnouw 1978, 53). They created a questionnaire for viewers and distributed Bernstein's *Young People's Concerts* on film to local schools; later Bell began distributing the films.[48] The programs of the tenth season marketed the films rather than telephone services and products by closing with, "The New York Philharmonic *Young People's Concerts* are brought to you by AT&T and the Bell System Associated Companies, who thank you for being with us tonight. Films of many of these concerts (in this series) are available without charge to schools and other groups. For information, call your local Bell Telephone business office." It seems that the companies were still pursuing the family market.

The first and last page of the scripts for all four programs of the eleventh season (1967–1968) begin and end with a forlorn, "Brought to you by ———," although Polaroid sponsored most of them. Polaroid sponsored or co-sponsored the majority of the programs from the eleventh through the fifteenth, and final, season. Apparently, they trusted their commercials to send their message, as the programs opened and closed with an almost spartan comment: "This special program is being brought to you by the Polaroid Corporation." "Forever Beethoven!" (28 January 1968) was co-sponsored by Eastman-Kodak (which made both film and cameras) and Polaroid (which made instant cameras). The opening and closing pages are missing from the last program of the series.

What motivated a sponsor to underwrite Bernstein's *Young People's Concerts*? It may have been the prestige of the programs, the success the shows had in reaching their target market, or simply a tax write-off. Although the prestige was extraordinarily high, that alone was not enough. Logic might suggest that the corporations financing the series were aiming at the youth market; however, that was not the case despite the emergence of teenagers as a distinct market in the mid-1950s (Gunter and Furnham 1998, 1). Young people are "the major buyers of sweet things and play things" as well as "clothing, consumer electronics, entertainment and hobbies" (2). Only the last four programs were co-sponsored by a purveyor of "sweet things," Sara Lee (frozen baked goods), with Polaroid. A 1964 CBS survey revealed that 83 percent of the viewers were adults.[49] Fan mail from adults confirms that some watched and enjoyed without a young person present.[50] Sponsors accommodated both by targeting "the family." In the 1950s and early 1960s, families often took long car trips on the highway system newly constructed under President Eisenhower's Interstate Highway Act of 1956; both children and parents alike might be inspired to stop at a Shell Oil station as a result of seeing the commercials on these programs. Families whose members were dispersed around the country (as well as teenagers calling friends) would keep in contact by telephoning, "the next best thing to being there." Every parent would want a photographic memory of their child growing up, and Polaroid was famous at the time for its relatively inexpensive "instant film" cameras.

While it may have appeared that sponsors were aiming at the highbrow market by supporting arts education programming, this is doubtful (D. Benson, pers. comm.). Upper-crust individuals were unlikely to be buying their own gasoline or a Polaroid camera. Sponsors were probably not looking for a tax write-off, since "this is a show that actually produced good Nielsen numbers" (ibid.).

The Nielsen ratings of Bernstein's *Young People's Concerts* are more likely a reflection of the broadcast time and competition rather than of the subject or soloists performing. As the program moved from weekends to weekdays, from afternoons to evening and back to afternoons, the ratings remained relatively consistent, indicating a loyal audience that followed the program no matter when it was broadcast.[51] The Nielsen's were good enough to attract major sponsors who wanted to reach the typical American family.

CENSORSHIP

Censorship was a powerful influence in television in the 1950s and into the 1960s, controlling not only who could be hired but also the content of programs. Barnouw has documented the pressure placed on advertisers by "fanatic red-hunters" who engineered successful boycotts during the Red Scare. More than once, sponsors and networks had to surrender to demands that certain individuals not be hired (Barnouw 1978, 48–49). Anyone remotely connected with the blacklist was suspect.

The most famous example of content censorship concerns a script by Rod Serling, the very successful and prolific writer of serious, distinguished television dramas in the 1950s (Presnell and McGee 1998, 11). He was shocked when he read about the acquittal of the murderers of Emmitt Till, a fourteen-year-old African American who was kidnapped and murdered by white men in Mississippi simply for whistling at a white woman.[52] Serling's play on the incident for the Theater Guild was reworked for television, but it was viciously cut and altered by the sponsor under pressure from interest groups such as the Southern White Citizens Council (Barnouw 1978, 50). All references to the South were removed, Till became an unnamed foreigner killed by an all-American boy who was temporarily insane, and so forth.

Serling avoided any future battles with sponsors or networks by switching to writing science fiction after this incident (Presnell and McGee 1998, 12).

On the other hand, some sponsors announced they would stay out of artistic decisions entirely. Alcoa sponsored Murrow and Friendly's newsmagazine and documentary series *See It Now*. The president of Alcoa, Irving W. Wilson, told Murrow and his colleagues, "You do the programs, we'll make the aluminum. Don't tell us how to make the aluminum, and we won't tell you how to make the programs" (Barnouw 1978, 51). They kept their promise, and Murrow was eventually instrumental in ending the reign of Joseph McCarthy and the House Un-American Activities Committee (HUAC). Producers and writers often avoided difficulties by censoring themselves in advance. Vice-President C. Terence Clyne of the McCann-Erickson agency testified to the Attorney General, "Actually there have been very few cases where it has been necessary to exercise a veto, because the producers . . . [and] writers involved are normally pretty well aware of what might not be acceptable."[53]

There is no evidence that the sponsors, the CBS network, or the management of the orchestra ever attempted to censor Bernstein's *Young People's Concerts*.[54] However, Charles S. Dubin was an important director who had been working at CBS for some time when he was chosen to direct the inaugural season of Bernstein's series (Rose 1992, 132). After the first season (1958–1959), he was called before HUAC but refused to testify, pleading the Fifth Amendment twenty-two times. Although he was never cited for contempt, he was blacklisted the next day, removed from Bernstein's production crew, and could not work for three years (ibid.).[55] He later explained that he had no Communist affiliations but felt he should have the right not to testify. Other than the removal of Dubin, I have found no other obvious censorship. Yet the threat was there.

CBS's power is spelled out in the initial contracts and letters. The 17 September 1957 draft of Bernstein's contract for the "Televised Young People's Concerts" clearly stated that the program package and musical compositions had to be submitted to CBS for approval in advance, and that CBS had the ultimate power to demand changes or deletions as late as a hair-raising four days before broadcast.[56] The draft contained what reads as a morals clause with teeth, offering further proof that Bernstein was required to avoid controversy when creating the scripts:

> The Society has also agreed that the persons whose services are regularly furnished by the Society as part of the program package . . . will act at all times with due regard to public morals and conventions, and that if any such person does conduct himself in a manner which shall be an offense involving moral turpitude under federal, state, or local laws, or which

might tend to bring the Society or him into public disrepute, contempt, scandal or ridicule, or which might tend to reflect unfavorably on CBS, the sponsors, if any, or their advertising agencies, if any, or otherwise injure the success of the programs, CBS-TV shall have the right to either require the Society to terminate the series of such persons forthwith and to furnish a substitute, or to terminate the entire agreement.[57]

The letter that established the formal contract between CBS Television and the Philharmonic includes a similar clause.[58] In truth, Bernstein had to control his natural tendency to speak out on social and political issues as well as hide his homosexual inclinations. He became more overtly politically and socially active after he resigned from the Philharmonic and his *Young People's Concerts*. Several factors allowed him a new flamboyance beginning in the mid-1970s. He found a new freedom from the restrictive contracts. The American Psychiatric Association downgraded homosexuality from a sociopathic personality disturbance and neurosis to a "sexual orientation disturbance" in its *Diagnostic and Statistical Manual of Mental Disorders* by 1974[59]; one can only imagine what profound effect this change must have had on Bernstein. Also, Felicia's death in 1978 removed her stabilizing influence in his life (H. Burton 1994, 453). However, during the run of his *Young People's Concerts* Bernstein was careful about his behavior.

The power of the network and sponsors was felt in subtle ways. Each spring or summer in advance of the season, Bernstein would choose subjects for the four programs of the coming season to be submitted to the television network and the sponsor (Rees 1966, 36). While he was not bound by the choices he had made (which could be altered, revised, or substituted with others), Bernstein and the production crew were aware that the network and sponsor were watching. For instance, Bernstein wrote the outline for a script called "Russian Music: Then and Now" that never became a program. Bernstein apparently handled other dangerous topics such as racism and the Vietnam War so subtly and carefully that few, if any, noticed; certainly the sponsor and network did not.

James Lester Rees observed the production crew engaging in self-censorship (48). In "A Birthday Tribute to Shostakovich" (5 January 1966), Bernstein had planned to say "Thank God! He's made it at last," when the trombone enters after the rest of the orchestra toward the end of the first movement of Symphony No. 9. Englander pointed out that the *sponsor* might not appreciate that particular expression, which, after various options were considered, was changed to "Thank goodness" (ibid.). There was no external censorship because the production crew self-censored.

Leonard Bernstein's *Young People's Concerts* won many awards over the fourteen years, but it is challenging to find out exactly which ones. Carlos

Moseley (who held many important positions at the Philharmonic during Bernstein's tenure, including president) somewhat erroneously says, "Emmys and Peabody and Edison awards came to [the series] year after year" (1993). In fact, the shows were nominated for Emmys five times and won four times. Bernstein did win a George Foster Peabody Award from the University of Georgia, but for *Lincoln Presents* in 1958.[60] There is no evidence of any Edison award. The official Leonard Bernstein website offers tantalizing glimpses of Grammys, but *Bernstein Conducts for Young People*, for instance, (which won Best Recording for Children in 1963) has no relationship to the television series.[61] Bernstein's *Young People's Concerts* did win the Sigma Alpha Iota International Music Fraternity Series award six times.[62]

Bernstein's televised *Young People's Concerts* is representative of many trends in arts television from the 1950s through the early 1970s. In its early years, many hoped that this new medium would make the arts more accessible, thereby both educating and uplifting the average person. Newscasters provided hard and insightful news, artists appeared in televised concerts, operas, and plays, and networks participated in these early efforts, even to the extent of producing such shows in the absence of sponsors during the cultural explosion in the late 1950s. Arts broadcasting, however, was extremely expensive, so eventually outside financial backing had to be found. At first, sponsoring corporations probably enjoyed the association of their product with cultural programming, but by the 1960s reaching the largest number of viewers became the priority. In the early 1970s, Nielsen began tracking specific demographics rather than simply tracking the number of viewers, and many wonderful programs with poor demographics were cancelled. Bernstein's *Young People's Concerts* provides a perfect example of all this: the series was first financed by CBS during the blossoming of culture

Table 4.3.   Emmy Nominations and Awards for Bernstein's *Young People's Concerts*

1959	Nominee, Best Public Service Program or Series
1960	Nominee, Outstanding Achievement in the Field of Music
1962	Award, Outstanding Program Achievement in the Field of Children's Programming
1964	Nominee, Outstanding Directorial Achievement in Variety or Music
1964	Nominee, Outstanding Program Achievement in the Field of Music—Children's Programming
1965	Award, Individual Achievements in Entertainment
1965	Award, Outstanding Program Achievements in Entertainment, for "What Is Sonata Form?"
1966	Award, Individual Achievements in Electronic Production, Laurence Schneider, Audio Engineer
1966	Nominee, Outstanding Musical Program

in the United States, in part, to promote its image as the "Tiffany" network; the programs were next sponsored by various corporations to gain prestige and to appeal to the family market. After Minow's 1961 tirade chastising networks for their poor programming, Bernstein's *Young People's Concerts* was broadcast in primetime for six amazing and glorious seasons. The death knell for his *Young People's Concerts* really came when Leonard Bernstein left; none of those who followed him could attract the Nielsen's he did.

The publicity machine for performing artists, begun by P. T. Barnum in the nineteenth century, became even more elaborate and crucial in the twentieth. Both Toscanini's (in the first half of the twentieth century) and Bernstein's (in the second half) already amazing musical abilities were enhanced specifically in America by portrayals of them as self-made, independent men who had elevated themselves from the lower classes through hard work. Both maestros were seen to be the ideal representatives of their times. Through two World Wars, the media reported Toscanini's courageous fight against America's enemies. After World War II, Bernstein as a model husband and family man living in suburban America appeared in newspapers and periodicals, while other aspects of his personality were swept under the carpet. His *Young People's Concerts* certainly contributed to the international image of Bernstein as a gifted maestro and caring father. The interests of everyone connected with the series (from the orchestra to the network, sponsors, advertising agencies, and even Bernstein himself) depended upon sustaining this positive portrait. Shanet says that "Bernstein's TV programs made him the best known musician in America" and that among his programs, "it was the Young People's Concerts that made the most success" (1975, 340–341).

The tenor of the times as well as Bernstein's contract demanded that anything negative or controversial never appear on the screen. While official censorship did exist, generally writers censored themselves in advance, as did Bernstein when he wrote the scripts. Yet as we will see, Bernstein apparently gently and subtly incorporated many potentially incendiary topics into the programs. Whether consciously or unconsciously is unimportant—they are there.

The Pacifist

The Cold War Intrudes

No more war! There just can't be wars anymore!

—Leonard Bernstein quoted in Evelyn Ames, *A Wind from the West: Bernstein and the New York Philharmonic Abroad*

Perhaps music can tell us some surprising things that we cannot learn from books and newspapers.

—Leonard Bernstein in "Leonard Bernstein and the New York Philharmonic in Moscow"

$\mathscr{F}$ear generated by the Cold War permeated life in the mid- to late-twentieth century. Bernstein, the activist, seemed incapable of avoiding controversial issues, yet he was obliged to in his *Young People's Concerts*. Potentially incendiary statements could result in the cancellation of the series and his contract. So to put forth his powerful "artistic voice" on sensitive issues in a nonconfrontational way, there is compelling evidence that Bernstein chose to use the subtle power of suggestion, which, he said, "is often much stronger than a straight order. That's because it's deeper, it's more subtle; those hints can creep into a deeper part of your mind than a simple command can" ("What Is Impressionism," 1 December 1961, 3). During the third season (1960–1961) in the midst of the Cold War and after a successful Philharmonic tour of the USSR, Bernstein proposed an interesting *Young People's Concert* on Russian music, but the script was never written. Instead, we see the Cold War creep into several other programs. He celebrated the life and works of a composer behind the Iron Curtain (Dmitri Shostakovich) and may have addressed issues such as the Cuban Missile Crisis and Vietnam.

The term "Cold War" describes the conflict, sometimes open but often covert, that developed after World War II between the United States and

91

the capitalist Western Bloc and the Soviet Union and the Communist Eastern Bloc. This ongoing clash of primarily political and economic ideologies between the two superpowers lasted from roughly 1946 to the dissolution of the USSR in 1991. Although proxy wars were funded and fought, military action was generally avoided; actual combat was a tool used only to keep allies from defecting, to overthrow them if they had defected, or to prevent them from being conquered, as in Vietnam. The primary tools were propaganda and espionage.

The space race and the arms race reflected the terror, intensity, and competitive nature of the Cold War. The quest to conquer space began in earnest when the Soviet Union launched Sputnik, the first man-made object to orbit the earth, on 4 October 1957. American citizens were dismayed and unnerved that the USSR was first, imagining the military advantages that control of space gave the Communists. The United States rushed to meet the challenge by increasing science education and by launching American satellites. The arms race abjectly terrified everyone throughout the world.[1] The average American was regularly warned that the Soviets could suddenly launch a nuclear attack without warning and were taught how to protect themselves and their families. Even children, the target audience for Bernstein's *Young People's Concerts*, were aware that something scary was happening. They regularly rehearsed "duck and cover" exercises in school in case Soviet bombs rained down.[2]

One tragic manifestation of the Cold War that had a profound influence on the arts was the Red Scare that ran from the late 1940s through the late 1950s. It was widely believed, especially among elected officials, that Soviet Communists had infiltrated the military, government, unions, education system, and entertainment industry of the United States. Thousands of innocents were investigated and questioned by the FBI, the Senate, as well as by private organizations. The most famous examples of this paranoia were Senator Joseph McCarthy's hearings before the Permanent Subcommittee on Investigations of the Government Operations Committee of the U.S. Senate, the activities of House Un-American Activities Committee (HUAC), and the Hollywood Blacklist (see Schrecker 1998). People subpoenaed were expected to explain past actions that made them seem to be Communist sympathizers and to provide the names of "fellow Communists." Anyone who donated money or services or signed a petition for a Communist cause might be called. Simply being named at these hearings could destroy a career, and many were unable to work for years. The first director of Bernstein's *Young People's Concerts*, Charles S. Dubin, was replaced by Englander after only one season because he had been blacklisted (Rose 1992, 132, see chapter 4). Dubin was never rehired for this series.

The McCarthy hearings affected many close to Bernstein. His friends Aaron Copland and Lillian Hellman, like Bernstein, were artists and liberals who regularly lent their names to causes associated with the Communist movement. In 1950, three former FBI agents created the catalogue *Red Channels: The Report of Communist Influence in Radio and Television*, which listed the "un-American" activities of 151 people. *Red Channels* became the bible of the Hollywood Blacklist. Bernstein is listed with seventeen affiliations or actions (*Red Channels* 1950, 16–17), Copland with twenty-one (39–41), and Hellman with thirty (75–77). Copland and Hellman, and later Jerome Robbins (not listed in *Red Channels*), Bernstein's collaborator on *Fancy Free*, *West Side Story*, and *The Dybbuk*, were all called to testify (H. Burton 1994, 220, 229). As Humphrey Burton said, "it was a bad time for liberals" (229). Copland emerged from his HUAC interrogation mostly unscathed but badly shaken. His *Lincoln Portrait* was suddenly pulled from President-Elect Dwight D. Eisenhower's first inaugural program because the composer evidenced Communist sympathies that were considered "more in the interest of an alien ideology than the things representative of Abraham Lincoln,"[3] and shortly after he won a 1949 Academy Award for Original Music Score for *The Heiress*, the Hollywood Blacklist blocked him from writing any more movie scores (Crist and Shirley 2006, 192). When Hellman was compelled to testify, she heroically refused to name names. As a result of HUAC and *Red Channels*, she lost professional opportunities and the income they would have provided (Crist 2006, 490).[4] Although Robbins alienated many by providing the Committee with names, he only listed those already identified (H. Burton 1994, 229).

Bernstein was terrified of being called to testify. In a letter to his brother Burton, he said, "Remember our rehearsed Washington investigation in the Napoleon bar in Boston? Well it came true. Not a subpoena" (Simeone 2013, 309–310). In 1953 the State Department refused to renew his passport. He was obliged to hire an attorney who successfully navigated the red tape created by *Red Channels* and cleared his name, but only after Bernstein signed a "humiliating" affidavit (Seldes 2009, 69–72).[5]

Both Copland's opera *The Tender Land* and Bernstein's operetta *Candide* (book by Hellman) were reactions to the pervasive atmosphere of suspicion (Crist 2006 and 2007, H. Burton 1994, 236). In a *New York Times* article about *Candide* before the premiere, Bernstein asked, "Puritanical snobbery, phony moralism, inquisitorial attacks on the individual, brave-new-world optimism, essential superiority—aren't these all charges leveled against American society by our best thinkers?" (18 November 1956).

Nonetheless, the highest levels of the federal government deemed the arts integral to general welfare and national interests (Grad 2006). The arts were used to promote the American agenda during the Cold War by communicating "the basic concepts of the American way of life or the Western democratic system" to foreign audiences, and by counteracting Soviet propaganda that depicted "our citizens as gum-chewing, insensitive, materialistic barbarians."[6] The result was the founding of the U.S. Information Agency (1953) that created opportunities to learn about American music both in U.S. embassies (by giving concerts, establishing music libraries, and so forth), and on the radio through the Voice of America (which broadcast American music behind the Iron Curtain). The State Department funded international tours of American musicians. The focus was quality classical music, to demonstrate that high culture existed in the United States, and jazz, to show an American art form while repudiating accusations of racism in the states. Modernism was favored, to show the freedom American artists had in contrast with Socialist Realism—Bernstein would have called these styles avant-garde and reactionary respectively. American tonal composers were suspect since tonality was associated with Communism.[7]

Bernstein was a pacifist. In 1948 he was touring Germany and was appalled at the post-war devastation he saw. In a letter to his friend and secretary Helen Coates, he wrote, "God, there's so much beauty and joy—why can't there be some peace?" (box 13). One evening during a tour of Japan, he burst out with, "No more war! There just can't be wars anymore!" (Ames 1970, 153). He was also an activist who firmly believed that artists have a responsibility to shine a light on the ills of society.[8] In the collection *This I Believe*, the maestro, along with many others, including Eleanor Roosevelt, wrote his own "credo" (Bernstein 1982, 137–139). In it he said, "One person fighting for truth can disqualify for me the platitudes of centuries. And one human being who meets with injustice can render invalid the entire system which has dispensed it" (137).

Bernstein's brother Burton remembers that "Lenny, the man of principle was also a 'fierce patriot'" who "worshipped the United States of America in the truest, most honest way" (Bernstein and Haws 2008, 57). But this worship was not blind. He fought against the Cold War and the Vietnam War, both as an American citizen and as an artist. He spoke at two rallies for pacifist presidential candidate Eugene McCarthy in 1968; rallied with over 500,000 demonstrators (including performers and activists) in the later Moratorium to End the War in Vietnam in Washington, DC, on 15 November 1969; and joined Lauren Bacall and others in Riverside Church in New York to read the names of soldiers killed in Vietnam shortly thereafter. He spoke through music as well. Instead of continuing the Philharmonic's 1966 survey of the twentieth-century symphony, Bernstein presented a concert that focused on war, specifically "the horrors of mass murder and bombings; patriotism, pacifism and victory." In his *New York Times* review "Philharmonic Turns to War for Theme of Gripping Concert," Howard Klein reports that after Arnold Schoenberg's *A Survivor from Warsaw*, the audience was "obviously moved" and cheered at the conclusion (14 October 1966). The effect of the entire concert on the audience "was profound." Klein ends with "Mr. Bernstein came up with an adventurous program, one that left the listeners with something to think about." The audience cheered again at the end of the concert. With lyricists Betty Comden and Adolph Green, he wrote the song "So Pretty" for "Broadway for Peace" (a 1968 anti-war fund-raising concert); it was performed in Philharmonic Hall by Barbra Streisand with Bernstein on piano (ibid.).[9] The maestro conducted the Concert for Peace for over 18,000 people at the National Cathedral in Washington, DC, on 19 January 1973, in which Haydn's Mass no. 7 in C (the "Mass in Time of War") was performed (*Washington Post*, 24 June 1973).[10] With Bernstein's visible support, his wife, Felicia, founded "Another Mother for Peace" in 1967, a group that worked to end the Vietnam War (Bernstein and Haws 2008, 50). She even permitted herself to be arrested in a non-violent anti-war protest in 1972. At this time, dissent was seen by many as unpatriotic. Yet as a liberal, Bernstein believed that everyone's opinion should be respected, as seen in this excerpt from his credo: "man cannot have dignity without loving the dignity of his fellow" (Bernstein 1982, 138).

Before performing Ernest Bloch's *Schelomo*, in "The Road to Paris" (18 January 1962), he said,

> One more word before we play; you should know that the name Schelomo, or Solomon, means *peace* in Hebrew—like the famous Hebrew word Scholom; I would like very much—in fact, with all my strength [the following added live] *and I hope all yours too* [end addition]—to dedicate this performance to the coming of peace to all the peoples of our world. (18)

He intentionally chose the phrase "people*s* of *our* world" rather than the more traditional "people of *the* world" in order to inspire feelings of inclusiveness and international unity.

BERNSTEIN IN THE SOVIET UNION

The United States and the USSR arranged cultural exchanges that occasionally became quite tense. One famous example of verbal dueling is the so-called Kitchen Debate that took place on 24 July 1959 in the kitchen of a model suburban house built by the United States at the American National

Exhibition at Sokolniki Park in Moscow. Many capitalistic comforts such as the dishwasher and the washing machine were paraded with exhibitors claiming that anyone in America could afford these luxuries. Seen in newsreels around the world, Vice President Richard Nixon and General Secretary of the Communist Party of the Soviet Union Nikita Khrushchev engaged in a "crackling exchange," during which they argued the merits of capitalism versus Communism; Khrushchev asserted, "the Soviets will overtake America and wave bye-bye."[11]

Shortly thereafter, in the fall of 1959, the Philharmonic went on a Grand Tour of Europe and the Near East, giving fifty concerts within three months in seventeen countries, including a goodwill visit to the Soviet Union (Shanet 1975, 338; H. Burton 1994, 298–312). Burton suggests that this trip was "arguably the most dramatic and eventful in the history of that orchestra" (H. Burton 1994, 298). The tour was a great success even in the USSR. An ovation at a concert in Poland went on for forty minutes (306); audiences at the Moscow concerts became a "cheering, stomping, clapping throng" when demanding an encore of Ives's *The Unanswered Question* (307). Bernstein wrote Copland that they were greeted by screaming, record-breaking crowds (Simeone 2013, 432).

During the tour Bernstein filmed "Ford Motor Company Presents Leonard Bernstein and the New York Philharmonic in Moscow" for American television, which aired in the United States on Sunday, 25 October 1959.[12] Throughout the program he emphasizes the "similarity of our two great peoples, as seen through our music," saying that "Americans and Russians simply love each other's music" and that "somehow we sense a common identity on the deepest level—in that special corner of the heart where music lives and breathes" ("Ford Motor Company Presents," 1959, 2, 4). His most controversial statement was mild: "We are both characteristically candid peoples, even though our political differences don't always allow us to act that way." Otherwise, he expounds on what makes Russians and Americans "so alike in spite of the obvious differences" and tries to "answer that question today at least in part, through music" (3). Scripts for other international programs he filmed at the time ring with the same theme: unity, peace, and brotherhood.[13]

While in Moscow, Bernstein met several prominent Soviet composers, such as Dmitri Kabalevsky and Aram Khachaturian, as well as other notables, including author Boris Pasternak (H. Burton 1994, 306–312). The Philharmonic performed Shostakovich's Seventh Symphony and welcomed the composer onstage. Although Bernstein already knew of the troubles and stifling restrictions creative artists endured in the Soviet Union, meeting

Pasternak put a human face on the issues since he knew how the author had recently suffered due to his government's policies.[14] The image Pasternak created of Soviet Russia in *Dr. Zhivago* was unflattering and had angered the Communist Party. When the book won the Nobel Prize for literature, the Soviet authorities demanded that Pasternak decline the honor, and the author was expelled from the Soviet Writers' Union. Bernstein and his wife, Felicia, actively sought a meeting with the author while they were in Russia. When letters and cables failed, Felicia traveled to the Russian village where Pasternak was living in "disgraced seclusion" to invite him to dinner and the final Philharmonic concert in Moscow. Pasternak's letters from this time demonstrate the fear the author felt in setting up a simple meeting between two great artists (308–310, Simeone 2013, 418–420). Bernstein himself had had some rather mild firsthand experience with the Soviet authorities. He shocked many by breaking Russian tradition and addressing the audience directly during a concert in Moscow; despite the pleasure that the audience took from this, the Cultural Ministry's own newspaper, *Pravda*, denounced Bernstein's actions (H. Burton 1994, 307–308).[15] Eventually, Bernstein was persuaded to respect the wishes of his Russian hosts and cease his podium lectures. Shortly after returning to the United States, Bernstein proposed a *Young People's Concert* on Russian music but the topic was too incendiary for the times.

THE PROGRAM NEVER WRITTEN: LEARNING TO DEAL WITH CONTROVERSY

The draft of Bernstein's contract for the *Young People's Concerts* states that the subjects and pieces had to be submitted to CBS for approval prior to broadcast and that Bernstein himself must avoid anything that would "reflect unfavorably" on the network, the orchestra, the sponsors, the advertising agencies, or even Bernstein himself lest the contract (and the series) be terminated.[16] The first evidence of Bernstein confronting controversial issues comes in the third season (1959–1960) with an outline for a program proposed for 23 January 1960 called "Russian Music—Then and Now" (box/folder 1024/8). He had explored the similarities between the United States and the USSR in the "Leonard Bernstein and the New York Philharmonic in Moscow" program in 1959, so he logically sought to next explore the differences. He intended to expound on, among other things, the political differences between the two countries and "how art is affected by political systems—especially music." An abridged version of the outline compiled from Bernstein's pencil draft and the

typed version is included below so that the reader may see both the noncon-
troversial and potentially controversial elements:

I. Introduction
  a. Since we last met—exciting tour
     Describe Russian attitude toward us on tour and our music in general
     Political diff. betw USA & USSR
     How art is affected by political systems—especially music
  b. Specific reference to Press Club lunch. Pravda editorial
     Explanation in order. This is what I meant.[17]
II. Musical examples
  a. Then (pre-revolution)—Rimsky, Borodin, Glinka
  b. Now (post-revolution)—Prokofiev, Shostakovich, Khachaturian
III. Similarities and Differences
  a. Similarities—Same objectives for both, i.e., Nationalism, Color, Mass
     Appeal
  b. Enlarged Modern Vocabulary
     But enlarged only to a certain degree—not experimental [LB listed
     several pieces to play]
     Nothing wrong with all this. Beautiful music does result. But no real
     progress.
     Personality shines through anyway: Prok #5/ But not free to express.
  c. Experimental Music—examples (twelve tone), play example
     If ten people like it, they have the right to hear it.
     [LB's tendency to proselytize emerges when he added the following to
     the pencil outline] You kids will understand clearly—better than Russ—
     because you're free.
IV. Freedom of choice is essence of democracy—You don't have to like it.
    But some people do, & that's enough reason for playing it.
V. Stravinsky—End with personality who can experiment.
  a. One Russian composer never fitted into old has lived through pre-rev
     and post-rev periods but not in Russia—real Russian experimenter,
     greatest living composer
  b. Three Dances from Petrouchka, Sacre (ibid.)

This outline describes a well-constructed show that promised to be interesting to Americans during the height of the Cold War, particularly some six
months after the Kitchen Debate. Yet the script was never written.[18]

A member of the production crew does not remember this outline, but
shuddered when I recently showed it to him.[19] He said he had forgotten what
an emotionally charged time that had been and stated unequivocally that such

a show would never have been broadcast. This program-never-written must have brought home the need for Bernstein to avoid controversy for the rest of the series.[20] He did not abandon the issues presented by the Cold War but visited them in five later shows. From 1960 on, Bernstein apparently censored himself in advance. Except for this one example, all existing outlines for his *Young People's Concerts* became scripts that were either telecast or performed on tour.[21] Most of the outlines that lightly touch on potentially controversial topics, such as civil rights or Vietnam, only lightly hint at the controversy; on the rare occasions when incendiary ideas appear in the outline, they are removed by the final script.

THE COLD WAR SEEPS INTO BERNSTEIN'S *YOUNG PEOPLE'S CONCERTS*

Without being specific, Bernstein seemed to weave many Cold War issues into his *Young People's Concerts*: a description of an artist's life behind the Iron Curtain (Shostakovich), the Cuban Missile Crisis, and the Vietnam War. For the first two programs, he provided positive images to replace negative ones. For the last, he used music to reach into the hearts and minds of the audience by carefully selecting pieces that he then associated with the right to dissent and the horrors of war. Sensitive, thoughtful viewers would make the connection without realizing that they had.

Although Bernstein could not "take on" the Soviet Union and Communism in his *Young People's Concerts*, he created one program that offered support to a Soviet citizen, Dmitri Shostakovich, while giving audiences a glimpse of the life of an artist living under the stifling oppression of Communism. The Soviet authorities demanded that all composers avoid "formalism" and the "decadent" compositional practices of the West (abstract, atonal, or serial music). Communist composers were required to adhere to Socialist Realism— a generally programmatic, fundamentally tonal idiom employing folk songs. In 1936, Shostakovich's 1932 opera *Lady Macbeth of the Mtensk District* (already performed to great acclaim in Russia and abroad), was reviewed by the official Soviet Party newspaper *Pravda* (Morgan ed. 1998, 127–129). Shostakovich and the "formalism" of this opera were brutally attacked and a new policy of severe artistic repression began. Eventually Shostakovich, Sergei Prokofiev, Aram Khachaturian, and others suffered official censure. Such censure could remove more than a composer's livelihood—Vladmir Ashkenazy relates a story of Shostakovich's water being turned off in his home shortly after this review (Ho and Feofanov 1998, 9).

With a careful, lighthearted program in season nine that highlighted Shostakovich's achievements, Bernstein not only honored the Russian composer but also humanized the Soviet people. International viewers could see that there was more to the USSR than ruthless Communists plotting to overthrow the free world—there were also gentle, accomplished musicians. Since children love birthday parties, a birthday is a perfect occasion for any *Young People's Concert* devoted to a single composer. Copland and Stravinsky had already received such "birthday parties" ("Aaron Copland Birthday Party," 12 February 1961, and "Happy Birthday, Igor Stravinsky," 26 March 1962). Bernstein must have believed that Communist Party officials would find it difficult to object to an innocent children's birthday celebration for Shostakovich, so Bernstein and the Philharmonic celebrated the composer's sixtieth birthday in "A Birthday Tribute to Shostakovich" (5 January 1966). Bernstein chose Shostakovich not only because he liked, programmed, and recorded Shostakovich's compositions but perhaps because he also felt an empathy with him; both composers had been attacked by intellectuals and critics for being traditionalists.[22]

The program opens with the first movement of Shostakovich's Symphony No. 7. Bernstein praises the "*beautiful melody*," which he calls a "*typical Shostakovich sound—broad*, noble, proud, *songful*, rich with feeling" (3, words in italics were ad-libbed), observing that these are not characteristics normally associated with twentieth-century music. He then dedicated the entire program "to him and to his lifelong devotion to his art. May it long continue," offering a "sort of after-dinner speech in Shostakovich's honor":

> I particularly want to do this because, in these days of musical experimentation, with new fads chasing each other in and out of the concert halls, a composer like Shostakovich can be easily put down. After all, he is basically a traditional Russian composer—a true son of Chaikovsky! [*sic*] and no matter how "modern" he *ever* gets, he never loses that tradition; so the music is always, in some way, old-fashioned—*or* at least, what critics and musical intellectuals like to call old-fashioned. But they're forgetting one most important thing: he's a genius—a real, authentic genius. And there aren't too many of those around any more. That's why I want to make this *personal birthday* toast to him. (3–4, the words in italics were ad-libbed)

Bernstein had then planned to show Shostakovich as a loyal Communist, provide a glimpse of the strife that the composer endured at the hands of the Party, and how he tried to work within the system:

> Shostakovich's devotion has not been only to his art, but also to his country, even to the principles of the Revolution in which he grew up. He is an

extremely patriotic man, but he is also an individual, original artist; and that combination has sometimes gotten him into hot water with the people who guide that very revolution to which he is so dedicated. But always Shostakovich has bounced back into favor, either by apologizing, or by slightly changing his style, or perhaps really because the Russians know that he is their greatest composer, and they can't afford to do without him. They simply have to forgive him—and so, they do, which is all to their credit. (5)

All this, however, was cut shortly before the broadcast. In light of this "program-never-written," it seems likely that this passage was cut to avoid controversy—the sentiments expressed in the deleted paragraph might not only worry the children (for a child, being in "hot water" usually means punishment), but they might cause trouble for Shostakovich with the Soviet authorities.

For the most part, the program is politically innocuous and celebrates Shostakovich's sense of humor as it manifests itself in his music. Bernstein, however, briefly interrupts the "fun" at one point to demonstrate to the Communist authorities that Shostakovich was known abroad as a worthy Soviet citizen: he praises Symphonies Seven and Eight—"two whoppers"—as being "very long, very serious, very patriotic [symphonies], and both having grown out of his wartime emotions" (11). The remainder of the program examines the musical jokes Shostakovich wove into Symphony No. 9.

After the concert, Bernstein took the time to send a copy of the film to Shostakovich. Knowing that all the composer's mail would be read by Soviet authorities, he included the following carefully written letter:

> Dear honored Shostakovich:
>   I am happy to be able to send you the film of our recent Young People's television program in honor of your 60th birthday. I hope you like it, and that it brings you some of the affection and esteem which we feel for you. Many happy returns of your birthday.
>
> LB (box/folder 82/35)

It is hard for people in a free country to understand the profound effect that receiving a film and letter like this can have on someone living in a restrictive society, with little or no communication from the outside. Bernstein was careful to honor, praise, and support Shostakovich—to give him news of how respected and liked both he and his compositions were outside of the Soviet Union—without causing conflicts with the Communist Party. The maestro also helped create a positive image of Soviets for viewers in the free world in his ever-present quest for world unity.

THE CUBAN MISSILE CRISIS

The end of 1962 saw one of the major confrontations of the Cold War: the Cuban Missile Crisis. For two weeks, ongoing tensions between the United States, the Soviet Union, and Cuba reached a critical peak, bringing the world closer to nuclear conflagration than ever before or since. This particular conflict between the United States and Cuba began with the Cuban Revolution in 1959 when Fidel Castro overthrew President Fulgencio Batista. The new Cuban socialist regime began expropriating land and businesses, many of which were American-owned. Soviet Premier Khrushchev sought and gained an alliance with Castro, thereby establishing a Soviet presence within ninety miles of Florida, which greatly worried both the U.S. government and average Americans. In 1961 the CIA planned and funded a failed invasion of Cuba by Cuban exiles (referred to now as the Bay of Pigs), and as Cuban-American relations rapidly deteriorated, Cuban-Soviet relations improved. By this time, the two greatest powers in the world had the hydrogen bomb; about a year earlier the Soviets exploded one that was over three thousand times more powerful than the atom bomb dropped on Hiroshima at the end of World War II (Carpenter 1999, 16). On 15 October 1962, reconnaissance photos by an American spy plane showed missile bases being built on Cuban soil. The Soviets would have the capability of launching nuclear missiles from sites not only within the western hemisphere but also incredibly close to the United States. The crisis ended on 28 October when President John F. Kennedy and United Nations Secretary-General U Thant negotiated an agreement with the Soviets for the removal of the missiles in exchange for various concessions.

Since the 1823 Monroe Doctrine, Washington had been seeking political stability in Latin America to keep hostile foreign powers from gaining a foothold in the Western Hemisphere (Smith 1991, 76). The Alliance for Progress, initiated by Kennedy in 1961, was part of the administration's global efforts to contain Communism during the Cold War. The goal was to defeat insurgents on both the social and the military fronts, either through "winning the hearts and minds" (WHAM, as it was called) of the people or through military means. Latin America was considered a vital bulwark in the Cold War.

The Cuban Missile Crisis led the world to believe that nuclear annihilation, the fear of which had already invaded popular and high culture since the end of World War II, could indeed happen. Two films in particular were made after the Cuban Missile Crisis: the 1964 satirical black comedy *Dr. Strangelove, or: How I Stopped Worrying and Learned to Love the Bomb* and the 1964 thriller *Fail-Safe*. In both, an erroneously launched nuclear attack apparently cannot be stopped. Many popular songs also dealt with nuclear attack; two in particular concerned the Cuban Missile Crisis: "Talking Cuban Crisis" by Phil Ochs (1963) and "Red's Dream" by Louisiana Red (1962) (see Titus and Simich 1990, and Wolfe and Akenson 2005). The 1965 two-act opera *Atomtod* ("Atomic Death") by Giacomo Manzoni to a libretto by Emilio Jona takes place inside and outside a number of private nuclear shelters; the plot culminates with the explosion of a nuclear bomb and the subsequent destruction. Even playwrights investigated a potential nuclear Armageddon (see Carpenter 1999).

After 1959, the image of Latin Americans in the minds of many in the United States was that of Castro and his army. Films and photos of him with his huge beard in military fatigues smoking a large Cuban cigar had been in the media since he overthrew Batista's government in January 1959.[23] Newsreels showed Castro planning battles at a crudely assembled wooden table perched on dirt in front of a hut, and addressing large crowds in a way eerily reminiscence of Hitler. Most of Castro's ragtag army looked unkempt and lacked uniforms. Other newsreels showed the people of Havana rioting and destroying buildings and symbols of the previous regime. The missile crisis added to this portrait of abject terror and, for many, anger.

Bernstein had a special affection for Latin America. In 1941, while Bernstein was in Key West composing, a Cuban station "came drifting over his radio. When he heard the Cuban music, he was sold for life."[24] He married the Chilean actress Felicia Montealegre in 1951. In January 1957, Bernstein, Felicia, and Marc Blitzstein went to visit pre-Castro Cuba for a two-week holiday and a pilgrimage to composer Ernesto Lecuona.[25] Over seven weeks in the spring of 1958, Bernstein and the Philharmonic were an "all time smash" on their sold-out tour of twenty-one cities in twelve countries in Central and South America (Simeone 2013, 397–398). Burton points out that Bernstein "had been in deepest sympathy since his first ballet, *Fancy Free*, which has a wonderful Danzón," that "he had fun with the Good Neighbor policy in the 1953 musical *Wonderful Town*, an evocation of the thirties in which the Act One finale is a conga," and that the Old Lady in *Candide* who is so easily assimilated learns to tango within half an hour (H. Burton, e-mail). Michael Tilson Thomas observed that the Latin sound infuses many of Bernstein's early compositions.[26] The plot of Bernstein's 1957 musical *West Side Story* centers on the gang wars between Puerto Ricans and "white" Americans; Cuban dances, such as the mambo and cha-cha, are central to the Caribbean spirit of the show. Burton notes that, "I think LB's strongest sympathies were reserved for Mexico, where he stayed for a lengthy period in the mid-40s and chose as his honeymoon location (Cuernavaca) in 1951. He had first conducted there in 1947 but he knew the Mexican idiom from his friend and mentor Aaron Copland, whose *El Salón México* he transcribed for piano and knew backwards" (ibid.). Outside of the continuing connection to the Latin America spirit through Felicia, Burton also remembers that the housekeeper Julia and various other Latinos were a regular part of the Bernstein family life (ibid.).

The maestro also had close knowledge of the losses some Americans suffered as a result of the Cuban revolution. The new Cuban government had expropriated part of a sugar business owned by David M. Keiser, Chairman of the Philharmonic board from 1956 to 1963 (Shanet 1975, 334). Also, Bernstein openly declared himself a liberal in an op-ed for the *New York Times* titled "I'm a Liberal and Proud of It" (30 October 1988). As a pacifist, he was an active member of the National Committee for a Sane Nuclear Policy (a test-ban organization) and other similar groups.

Bernstein celebrated the educated, elegant, urbane side of Central and South America in "The Latin American Spirit" (8 March 1963), possibly due to the impetus of the Cuban Missile Crisis in October. Since the scripts had to be written weeks in advance of the taping (which could be weeks or months in advance of the broadcast), this was the earliest opportunity he had to address the issue in one of his *Young People's Concerts*.[27] When perusing the program titles, "The Latin American Spirit" stands out as an odd topic. Only two other programs featured geographic regions: "The Road to Paris" (18 January 1962), which studied the accepted and important influence that the French composer Debussy had on other composers (specifically American composer George Gershwin, Swiss American composer Ernest Bloch, and Spanish composer Manuel de Falla), and "A Toast to Vienna" (25 December 1967), which honored the 125th anniversary of both the Vienna Philharmonic and the New York Philharmonic as well as the much-loved Viennese waltz. In the world of music, there is no similar commonly accepted unifying factor to inspire a program called "The Latin American Spirit."

Bernstein must have been inspired by the way President Kennedy used television during the crisis. Rather than contacting Khrushchev through diplomatic channels, Kennedy conducted international diplomacy on television for all the world to see—the first time anyone had taken such an action. The president began his famous 1962 telecast by speaking of the possibility of atomic war. He then pulled the entire international community into the conflict by calling directly upon the chairman "to halt and eliminate this clandestine, reckless, and provocative threat to world peace" and to "abandon this course of world domination and to join in an historic effort to end the perilous arms race and transform the history of man" (Barnouw 1970, 214). Kennedy's gambit worked and the role of television changed irrevocably.

Network news divisions expanded, their budgets rose, and scheduling was often more favorable. A different type of television show was now possible, such as an award-winning film about East Germans escaping to West Germany (217–219). Bernstein, with his awareness of current events and the news, saw the power of television and its increased significance in shaping world opinion. This program is the first time that the maestro consciously or subconsciously reacted to current events in his *Young People's Concerts*, and it may be the first time in any of his television scripts.

Bernstein set the mood by beginning "The Latin American Spirit" with an appealing and lively work, "Batuque," from the Suite *Reisado do pastoreio* by Brazilian nationalist composer Oscar Lorenzo Fernández: "I'm surprised to find you all in your seats. I'd half expected to turn around and see everyone doing the Samba or something, up and down the aisles. This Latin American music is almost irresistible, when it's *good*, like the 'Batuque' we just heard, by the Brazilian composer Fernandez" (3). He wisely begins the program in a very engaging way and without any allusion to Cuba. He reminds the audience that people have enjoyed many styles of Latin American music over the years:

> It has a way of stirring up the blood, not only our North-American blood, but people's blood all over the world. Ever since I can remember there's always been an international craze of some kind for Latin-American dance music, from the old Argentine tango, which swept the world in my childhood, all the way through the rhumba, the samba, the conga, the mambo, the cha-cha, *the* merengue, *the* pachango, right up to the present excitement over something called the Bossa Nova. (3, words in italics were ad-libbed)

Bernstein immediately pulls the audience into the music with an explanation of syncopation. Then, while demonstrating a variety of Latin American percussion instruments, he surreptitiously mentions "what the Cubans call 'claves'" (6). Without being obvious, Bernstein makes the point that Cuba is part of Latin America and part of what he calls "our friends to the south of us" (6). He next points out a kinship between Latin America and many other regions of the world:

> Now actually I'm not crazy about that word "Latin" to describe this kind of music, because it tells only part of the story. When we speak of "*Latin America*" we are, of course, referring to the historical fact that these countries were conquered, settled, and exploited by invaders from Latin countries: like Spain—or, in the case of Brazil, from Portugal. (6)

He observes that, like the United States, Latin American countries are a blending of cultures, and he even manages to weave in support for Native Americans:[28]

> But the Latin-American *spirit* . . . has other ancestors besides the Latin ones, at least as important; and they are first of all the Indians,—the original inhabitants of those countries, and in some cases very strong civilizations in themselves—and secondly, Africans, a tremendously important influence, at least as important as it is in our own country. And it is the mingling of these different ancestors, influences, and heritages, which makes the Latin-American spirit, what it is at any rate in the music. (7)

Without mentioning it directly, he dispels the notion many might have had about the Latin American people—that they are either guerrillas, like Castro's army, or poor illiterates, like the migrant farm workers striking in California in 1962, and that they are only capable of lowbrow/Midcult popular music.[29] He continues, "but we mustn't begin to think that all Latin-American music is only cha-cha dance music—not by a long shot. Our Latin neighbors have produced an impressive number of serious symphonic composers" (8).

Bernstein salves potentially ruffled feathers in the United States while elevating Latin America: "Every single Latin American country, without exception, has produced fine, serious composers, from Mexico to the tip of Chile. But perhaps Mexico and Cuba have been in the lead, possibly because of their closeness to *our* musical centers, or possibly because they have such great international cities of their own" (13). He finally clearly mentions Cuba. He had personally experienced many of those "great international cities" first-hand on tour with the Philharmonic.

He stresses that some fine artists have come from Latin America, such as Silvestre Revueltas, "a sophisticated composer, with a very advanced technique" whose compositions are "controlled by the knowing hand of a real artist" (14). He mentions that Revueltas was "a real artist, who died tragically young," saying "he might have achieved true greatness, if he had lived" (14). If some in the audience had not heard of this composer before, Bernstein suggests that it is not due to mediocre compositions but rather to incorrect assumptions about Latin American composers and Revueltas's early death. The Philharmonic then performs his *Sensamayá*, a piece that blends African, Indian, Cuban, and Mexican styles. By this time, Cuba becomes one thread in the fabric of Latin American music.

Bernstein mentions that "our leading American composer, Aaron Copland" was so fond of Latin America that he honored the region and its people with two works: his "famous" *El Salón México* and *Danzón cubano* (18). He reminds the audience that they heard *El Salón México* two years ago when his

Young People's Concerts celebrated Copland's sixtieth birthday. The maestro characterizes the work as a "musical souvenir of a Mexican visit," then ad-libs a connection between America (specifically New York) and Mexico by likening El Salón México, a dancehall in Mexico City, to "our Roseland," a famous ballroom in the theater district of New York City still in use today (18). Instead of playing this work again, the Philharmonic logically performs Copland's other Latin American work, *Danzón cubano*, what Bernstein called "a souvenir of his [Copland's] Cuban visit" (18); thus, the maestro shared the irrefutable logic behind his choosing a work inspired by Cuba. When introducing this "delightful short piece," Bernstein mentions the "aristocratic" nature of this genre and the "royal bearing and control" of the Cubans as they dance (18–19); no doubt he had seen the Cubans dance when he was there with Felicia and Blitzstein. Having brought Cuba to mind with earlier comments, Bernstein waits until nearly the end of the program to showcase Cuba, and at that, he chooses a Cuban-style piece by a beloved American composer, Copland.

At this point in his outline, Bernstein labels Cuba as the "main center (til [*sic*] recently). Gateway, port, international, Paris of West;" this was, however, excised from the final script (draft, 2). Instead, he lightly mentions the situation with Cuba by saying, "and if we can ever go to Havana again, I hope you'll all get a chance to see a Cuban Danzón in action" (19). The program concludes with another Latin American influenced work by an American composer that the audience would presumably find familiar and enjoy, Bernstein's own *Symphonic Dances from West Side Story*, that he said, "will make you think of Cuba and Mexico" (22).

Is there finite evidence that Bernstein addressed the Cuban Missile Crisis with this script? Not that I have found—but the suggestion is very strong. He understood the use of subtlety. He was an avowed pacifist who used his growing fame to promote peace and unity. This was the first opportunity for such a program after the Crisis. He loved Latin America. A reference to the restrictions on travel to Cuba is excised from the final script. Cuba is gradually mentioned in the program more and more often. He moves from a Latin American nationalistic composition that uses a Cuban percussion instrument ("Batuque" by the Brazilian Fernández), to a work that brings together "native folk-lore elements with the great European musical tradition" (9; *Bachianas Brasileiras* no. 5 by "the great Brazilian" Heitor Villa-Lobos, 8), to one that synthesizes international styles (*Sensamayá* by the Mexican composer Revueltas), to a work by an American composer that celebrates Cuba (*Danzón cubano* by Copland), and finally to another, more familiar work by a different American composer that celebrates a variety of Latin American styles (Bernstein's own *Symphonic Dances from West Side Story*). He delays obvious Cuban references until near the end, and then rather than featuring the work

of a Cuban composer, he chooses two familiar American composers. Fernández and Reveultas are performed only in this one program and Villa-Lobos
briefly in only one other program. The program concludes,

> Which all goes to prove that the word America means much more than
> only the United States—that North America, South America, and Central
> America, [the following words are cut by a margin note] yes, including the
> Caribbean area [end cut] are, or ought to be, a solid united hemisphere.
> But let's not get into politics; let's get into the Latin-American spirit with
> the Mambo from *West Side Story*. (22)

Consciously or unconsciously, this is a carefully crafted program. Even at the
end, after the audience had a presumably pleasant experience enjoying Latin
American music, Bernstein avoids confrontational statements about Cuba,
then closes with his ever-present plea for international unity.

One fan letter (from a Cuban living in Nebraska) praises Bernstein for
this program. Rafael Armada (1963) writes, "unfortunately there is a general
misunderstanding regarding our music.—People think of Latin America
as underdeveloped countries, living in jungles and dancing at the beat of a
drum.—Nothing farest [*sic*] from the truth!" He then thanks Bernstein for
the concert and "spreading our music and for teaching that we are all American, regardless if we are from North, South or Central America!" He found
Bernstein's comment about a "united hemisphere" particularly meaningful.
The maestro made his point and was heard.

As a young man, Bernstein felt that the Latin Americans he met through
Copland at Tanglewood were "Martians, who upon closer acquaintance
turned out to be real, live, gifted, dedicated musicians, not very different from
our own" (Bernstein 1982, 220). Tanglewood taught him that knowledge
can lead to respect and appreciation. So around four months after Americans
feared nuclear conflagration would emanate from Cuba, he demonstrated appreciation for Latin American accomplishments and the similarities between
Latin Americans and Americans—Latin Americans can be sophisticated,
educated, aristocratic individuals and fine artists; like some Americans, they
too have suffered exploitation; they also are a polyglot culture with sophisticated cities. The parallels are clear—they are just like us.

THE VIETNAM WAR

Extending from 1959 through 30 April 1975, the Vietnam War was the
longest and, until recently, the most unpopular war Americans ever fought,

with an incalculable cost in suffering, sorrow, and rancorous national turmoil. Tens of thousands of young men were drafted and sent overseas to prevent South Vietnam from being engulfed by Communism, a goal that eventually failed. In one way or another, the war touched the daily lives of almost every American in the 1960s and into the 1970s. The outcry and protest marches in the United States came from pacifists opposed to war in general and from people who opposed draft policies that exempted college students and graduate students—policies which placed an unfair burden on the poor and working class. Nonviolent protesters were sometimes tear-gassed, and at Kent State University in 1970, even shot by the National Guard. Protesting could be dangerous. The first Moratorium to End the War in Vietnam took place across the United States on 15 October 1969. News of the My Lai Massacre broke on 12 November 1969, bringing protests to a peak. By 20 November, news accounts accompanied by photographs of massacred Vietnamese men, women, and children began to appear in *Time*, *Life*, *Newsweek*, and the Cleveland *Plain Dealer*. Over 58,000 American soldiers died, either in Vietnam or subsequently from injuries or chemical exposure received in Vietnam.[30]

Bernstein must have felt compelled to speak out about the war, but again the controversy surrounding Vietnam demanded he be very circumspect on television. Both programs of the thirteenth season (1969–1970), which took place shortly after the My Lai Massacre, contain references to the war that although veiled, plead for peace and the right of patriots to disagree with the policies of their government.

The maestro sensed that Beethoven's *Fidelio* had "underlying political relevance" to the issues surrounding the war (H. Burton 1994, 388). Therefore, when designing the Philharmonic season and the 1970 Beethoven Festival in Vienna, he chose that opera to honor Beethoven's centennial but also to comment on liberty and the right to dissent; Burton outlines Bernstein's plans for these productions of the opera and describes the links between the performances here and abroad (ibid.). In addition, Bernstein decided to incorporate in his *Young People's Concerts* a televised concert performance of *Fidelio* by Juilliard students both to celebrate the move of the Juilliard School to Lincoln Center and, according to Burton, to offer covert comment on the Vietnam War.[31]

He opens the first program of the fourteenth season, "*Fidelio*: A Celebration of Life" (29 March 1970) by saying that *Fidelio* is "a timeless monument to love, life, and liberty, a celebration of human rights, of freedom to speak out, to dissent. It's a political manifesto against tyranny and oppression, a hymn to the beauty and sanctity of marriage, an exalted affirmation of faith in God as the ultimate human resource" (4). Through offering this opera, the entire program became a tribute to liberty, freedom, and the right to dissent (H. Burton 1994, 388).

Like many, Bernstein had trouble understanding how some people could continue supporting the war after the My Lai Massacre. As mentioned in the epigraph to this chapter, he thought that "perhaps music can tell us some surprising things that we cannot learn from books and newspapers" ("Leonard Bernstein and the New York Philharmonic in Moscow," 1959, 2). This thought may have led Bernstein to believe that music could induce viewers to empathize with those victimized by war. For "The Anatomy of a Symphony Orchestra" (24 May 1970), he chose Ottorino Respighi's *Pines of Rome* to demonstrate the instruments of the orchestra and the variety of sounds possible. When discussing the fourth movement, "Pines of the Appian Way," Bernstein describes the Appian Way as "that great historic road over which passed so many Roman armies, which has seen so many victors and victims, so much glory and cruelty," and suggesting that the "ominous tread" growing incessantly from beginning of the movement to the end represents marching soldiers (38). He describes the opening: "now over these distant marching feet the first sounds we hear are of lamentation—of captured slaves, of Christian martyrs, of massacred children, of all those horrors on which the glory that was Rome was built. Here's one lament: a real heart stab in the muted violins" (39). For the fourth movement of the *Pines of Rome*, Nicholas Slonimsky offers a traditional program: "a march starting in the deep recesses of the somber low region of the instrumental range, and mounting in measured steps to a rousing triumph of militant national pride recalling the glories of the Roman consular army ascending the Capitoline Hill" (Slonimsky 1994, 256).[32] Rather than the ominous tread of soldiers Bernstein describes, Slonimsky writes of a "rousing triumph"; rather than the massacred children and horrors Bernstein describes, Slonimsky writes of "militant national pride recalling . . . glories." A tableau can be crafted for this movement without allusions to cruelty, the ominous tread of soldiers, or the building of a great civilization on massacred children. Bernstein chose his words carefully. Was he alluding to the My Lai Massacre?

The maestro continued his allusions to the horrors of war even in his last *Young People's Concert*, "Holst: *The Planets*" (26 March 1972). Regarding Mars, his outline included "[Holst was] haunted during WWI by German-sounding name" (2) and "juggernaut—grinding, growling machine—inhuman—tanks, gas masks, sleepless, dirty, savage." It seems he then moves in his mind from World War I to the Vietnam War, writing "how can it be that we've reached this point in our solution and still indulge in this savage, senseless murder" (3). In his final script, before playing the movement "Mars," he suggests, "it presents an amazingly realistic picture of war: the racketing of machine guns. The grinding of monstrous tanks, *and the whole horrible jug-gernaut of the war machine*, plus fanfares and marching and screaming and all the rest *of it* [words in italics were ad-libbed]" (9). After the performance, he breaks his usual pattern by speaking against war rather than about the music:

> Now that may be an exciting piece to hear, but it's not exactly *beautiful* music; in fact you might even call it ugly music. But then, what is uglier than war? And this music is not so much an impression of the planet Mars—with its red glow, and its possibility of life—as it is an impression of Mars the god of war, after whom the planet was named. It's an inhuman piece, utterly mechanical, brutal and relentless. Just like war itself, inhuman, brutal, relentless and mindless. (11)

Was he referring to the Vietnam War? Perhaps Bernstein remembered and was inspired by the success of his 1966 anti-war Philharmonic concert. By planting ideas about what an orchestral piece might represent, then performing the work, Bernstein may have hoped to move his listeners toward an understanding of the courage it takes to dissent, how precious human rights are, and the horrors of war.

If my assumptions are correct, the influence of the Cold War can be seen in five of the fifty-three *Young People's Concerts* beginning with program 23, almost seventeen percent of those from program 23 to program 53. Rather than confront public opinion directly, Bernstein may have turned to his skills as a wordsmith to subtly transmit his messages. But this required a delicate balance between disparate goals. For the program on Shostakovich, he simultaneously praises and honors the great composer, avoids conflict with the Communist Party, presents an accurate portrait of the composer's life, and maintains a positive atmosphere for children, while explaining Shostakovich's music. In "The Latin American Spirit," shortly after the negative impressions of Latin America precipitated by the Cuban Missile Crisis, he paints an attractive picture of this region that included great artists, great international cities, and appealing music; he gently and gradually approaches the subject of Cuba while carefully avoiding challenging the audience too much, and again while teaching about music. With the very controversial war in Vietnam, his scripts were different. Rather than replacing negative stereotypes with positive ones, he pleads for peace and the right to dissent—not through words, but through music. Overt statements would be disastrous, and he understood how music can carry a message more effectively than words, on a different, deeper level. To this end, in three programs he selects certain appropriate works, suggests that the music depicts specific images, then performs the works—knowing that the music will intensify the images.

To my knowledge there is no documentation or testimony that Bernstein incorporated the Cold War into the scripts. Yet Bernstein was a vocal pacifist, unafraid to work for peace. Whether he did it intentionally, or it simply was on his mind at the time he wrote the scripts and the thoughts slipped out, the allusions are there. The Cold War was an ever-present danger that permeated the daily lives of the average citizen. It is no wonder such ideas would slide unnoticed into his *Young People's Concerts*. But perhaps after seeing these shows, his viewers began to think about war a little differently.

· *6* ·

The Liberal

Civil Rights, Feminism, and the Counterculture

> I've been appalled . . . at the lack of any artistic voice in the . . .
> crises we've been going through with Vietnam, the Negroes, hu-
> man rights, civil rights (1968).
>
> —Bernstein quoted in John Gruen, *The Private World of*
> *Leonard Bernstein*

> I love my country—so much, in fact, that I am putting all my
> energies into seeing it to a better day, a more tranquil night, a
> shining and limitless future. And I abide by the words of that
> splendid liberal Thomas Jefferson that are inscribed on his
> monument in Washington: "I have sworn upon the altar of God
> eternal hostility against every form of tyranny over the mind of
> man." I, too, am a liberal.
>
> —Bernstein, "I'm a Liberal, and Proud of It," *New York Times*

$\mathscr{B}$ernstein felt that artists have a profound responsibility to use their "artistic voice" to comment on the political and social crises of their time—a
responsibility he honored frequently throughout his life. In his *Young People's
Concerts*, he arguably addressed civil rights and feminism, commented on
hippies, astrology, and psychedelic drug use, and openly lectured on the responsibilities of freedom and democracy. He also offered what he saw as a
solution to many ills of the world—international unity and communication
through the universal language of music.

113

BERNSTEIN SUBTLY WORKING
FOR THE GREATER GOOD

Bernstein was not a reticent individual. His natural tendency was to speak out, especially when he saw injustice or prejudice or learned of the horrors of war. However, his position and contract, as well as concern for those blacklisted during the Red Scare, demanded that he be circumspect in his *Young People's Concerts*. Civil rights and feminism may have simply been on his mind at the time he wrote the scripts discussed below, and any references to such issues were simply chance occurrences. His record as a vocal civil rights activist makes it likely that this self-proclaimed liberal turned to his prodigious skill with words to transmit a subtle message for the greater good while avoiding controversy. He describes his love of words in *Findings*, saying "I have always loved words fully as much as musical notes; I find the same joys of ambiguity, structural surprise, anagrammatic play and grace of phrasing in both. . . . I am not a writer by profession; I have simply written words all my life, for the love of it" (1982, 9). Probably, Bernstein skillfully and subtly used the power of *suggestion* to make points, which he described as "stronger" and that crept into "a deeper part of your mind than a simple command can" ("What Is Impressionism," 1 December 1961, 3). While the sole purpose of his carefully crafted scripts appears to have been music education, the gifted wordsmith probably subtly interwove his points on civil rights and feminism by presenting positive images to counter the narrow, negative images engrained by prejudice.[1]

Civil Rights

After World War II, the issue of civil rights for African Americans moved to the fore, gaining momentum in 1960 with nonviolent sit-ins. The primary objectives of the movement were achieved with the passing of the Civil Rights Act in 1964 and the Voting Rights Act in August 1965. Prejudice inevitably remained, leading to militant protests between 1965 and 1967. On 11 August 1965, five days after the Voting Rights Act was signed, rioting began in the African American neighborhood of Watts in Los Angeles, which left thirty-four dead, around 900 injured, over four thousand arrested, and property damage of more than $35 million (Lytle 2006, 189; Fischer 2006, 124). More than fifteen thousand National Guardsmen were needed to quell the violence. By 1966, race riots exploded in African American sections of Cleveland, Chicago, Atlanta, and thirty-five other cities (Levine 1996, 201). A special commission found that rage over economic conditions was the cause—despite the booming economy, thirty percent of African Americans were unemployed. Leaders of the civil rights movement had previously focused their efforts on the political rights of African Americans in the southern United States; this unrest made it clear that prejudice was not confined to the South. The violence in Watts was used to justify a "white backlash" against civil rights for African Americans (Farber 2001, 254–255). Riots reached a peak when Martin Luther King was assassinated on 4 April 1968.

The image that many held of African Americans evolved during the 1960s and 1970s. In the late 1960s, the image was a poor one that was probably shaped largely by the media: the demeaning 1951–1953 CBS television series *Amos 'n' Andy* (withdrawn in 1965 as a result of pressure from the NAACP) and by newspaper reports and films of the race riots. Portrayals of African Americans became more positive in 1964 when Sidney Poitier became the first African American to win the Academy Award for Best Actor for the 1963 film *Lilies of the Field*, and in 1965 Bill Cosby became the first African American to star in a network television drama, *I Spy*. These stand out as exceptions to the norm of their time by their positive portrayals of African American men.

Bernstein was such an activist for political and social issues that the FBI started a file on him in 1943 that eventually covered nearly 700 pages (Bernstein and Haws 2008, 39). He regularly supported African Americans as they sought equal rights and African American musicians when they met high musical standards. In 1945 he judged musical auditions for the National Negro Congress (39). In 1947 he wrote a *New York Times* article "The Negro in Music: The Problems He Has to Face in Getting a Start," in which he says that he "became interested in the problem of the Negro in music some years back." He calls attention to "the prejudice which exists against the Negro everywhere" and pointed out that the dearth of African Americans in classical music was due to the lack of early training rather than ability (2 November 1947). He tried to help the young black conductor Dean Dixon find a position (Dixon left the United States for a European career in 1949) (37). Bernstein accepted a disabled African American assistant conductor, James DePreist, for the Philharmonic in 1965, and regularly contracted African American soloists (H. Burton 1994, 387–388). During his tenure with the orchestra, the violinist Sanford Allen was the first African American to be hired as a full-time member (in 1962); when a Baltimore restaurant refused to serve Allen, the maestro walked out ("Café Bars Negro, Bernstein Leaves," *New York Times*, 27 May 1962). The number of African American soloists contracted "leaped upward"; at least one African American soloist appeared every single season (Shanet 1975, 347). His well-known support of civil rights issues received a great deal of unwelcome publicity as the result of a meeting organized by his wife, Felicia, to raise money for the American Civil

Liberties Union's defense fund to help imprisoned members of the civil rights group, the Black Panthers (militant African Americans).[2] "Legal outrage" at the unconscionably high bail of $100,000 for the ten led Felicia, an active liberal who founded the women's division of the ACLU New York branch, and her group to raise contributions (H. Burton 1994, 389). Felicia arranged a gathering for discussion and debate at the family's Park Avenue apartment for some ninety people in January 1970. Representatives from both sides of the issue were present. Felicia was following a longstanding tradition, which extends back into the mid-nineteenth century, of New York elite giving fund-raising events for the disadvantaged, described by Thomas Wolfe in *Radical Chic*.[3] Since she served drinks and canapés, some labeled the event a party, which led the press to accuse New York elites of casually dabbling in the problems of the less fortunate. One pundit dubbed this "Radical Chic." *New York Times* Radical Chic articles circulated abroad, leading to international censure of Bernstein and branding the conductor as "a naïve bumbler who hobnobbed with terrorists" (391). Since the Black Panthers were anti-Zionist (Bernstein probably did not know), Jews began booing Bernstein at Philharmonic concerts, and he began receiving hate mail. As the furor continued into June, Bernstein's reputation suffered. The FBI files on the maestro were released in the 1980s and reveal that much of the furor was instigated by FBI operatives and cooperative press contacts. They were attempting to destroy Bernstein's reputation. In a 2008 interview, Jamie Bernstein Thomas "found out through the Freedom of Information Act that all those Jewish Defense League guys, picketing outside our building after Charlotte Curtis wrote her pissy little editorial in the *Times*, were—you guessed it—FBI plants. What an awful time that was."[4] The articles and protests influenced world opinion and made the lives of the entire Bernstein family miserable.

Bernstein featured African American artists in his *Young People's Concerts* several times throughout the series, introducing them with the same warmth as any others.[5] His liberal attitudes and compulsion to speak out against injustice, however, must have impelled him to address civil rights in a 1967 *Young People's Concert* during a critical time in our nation's struggles.[6] The Watts riots the year before might have been simply a unique and unfortunate occurrence during an era of non-violent civil rights protests. However, when there were riots in nearly forty American cities in the summer of 1966, the compassionate pacifist within him must have been moved to counter racial prejudice and violence. Yet he had to be subtle. He perhaps decided to replace negative images of a people with positive images, as he did in "The Latin American Spirit" (8 March 1963). "Alumni Reunion" (19 April 1967) ennobles two accomplished African American performers by presenting their international credentials and lionizing them.

Three young performers were featured, the white cellist Stephen Kates, and two African Americans, soprano Veronica Tyler and soon-to-be-famous pianist André Watts. By this time, both Tyler and Watts had international performing credentials, and since they had performed several times with the Philharmonic, Bernstein was very familiar with their work. His opening re-marks praise all three, saying, "we welcome them back in triumph, as heroes; they have covered themselves with honor, and have added glory to their coun-try's name" ("Alumni Reunion," 5). While introducing Tyler, he remembers that everyone was so "delighted" with her first performance on a "Young Performers" program that she was invited back for a non-Young Performers *Young People's Concert* (10).[7] Bernstein enthusiastically praised her singing in his introduction to her third appearance on these programs: "the sheer beauty of her voice, in addition to her wonderful breath-control, her sense of phras-ing, and her ability to sustain a melodic line through a long, smooth curve" (10). He mentions that her gifts and skill had been recognized at the highest levels: she "triumphantly" won the Tchaikovsky Competition in Moscow and gave a command performance at the White House (10). He then observes that "there is much more to Miss Tyler's vocal gift than just a lovely sound: there is real variety" (10) and describes her "other sound" as "the rich throb and the blazing high notes of the American Negro voice" (11).

The use of the term "Negro" was evidently still acceptable in 1967. It was only in this year that the most influential African American newspaper in the United States, the New York *Amsterdam News*, "announced that the term 'Negro' would no longer be used in its pages."[8] Certainly Bernstein was in the habit of using the word "Negro" when he was in school as it permeates his 1939 Harvard bachelor's thesis, "The Absorption of Race Elements into American Music" in which he discussed the influence of "Negro" music on American music with the greatest respect (Bernstein 1982, 36–99). Here, he opined that "Negro music" was the "universal basis of American composition" (40) and expounded on the "Negro tone color" (51), "Negroid Ornamenta-tion" (51), "Negro scale" (52–62), "Negro voice" (54), and "Negro rhythms" (62–87). This language may have been acceptable in 1939 but was objection-able to some by 1967. His history and support of African Americans through-out his life verifies that he intended only to offer a compliment.

Bernstein's introduction for André Watts in "Alumni Reunion" was even more effusive. He remembers describing Watts's first Young Performers con-cert as "that unforgettable day" that "made us all stand up and cheer" ("Alumni Reunion," 14).[9] He continues by asking, "how many of you were privileged enough to be listening that day? Can you recall the thrilling sensation of being present at the debut of a great artist? It's an extraordinary feeling; somehow you know, after only a few bars of music—even only a phrase—that you are in the presence of royalty, of a musical prince, and that you are living through a historic moment" (14). He then says that Watts is "honoring us today by returning" and welcomes him "with love and with pride" (16). Only twelve years earlier Marian Anderson debuted as the first African American to sing at the Metropolitan Opera, and only ten years earlier she was the first African American to sing the national anthem at a presidential inauguration.[10] As recently as the 1950s, African Americans in the South could not use the same public water fountains and bathrooms as "whites" and were required to sit at the back of the bus, and black adult men were still being called "boy." Here, on national television in 1967, Bernstein is treating two African American performers with unbridled respect. A young black woman is praised for her skill, accomplishments, and the special sound of her "American Negro voice." A young black man is heralded as a musical prince. Bernstein indirectly proved that African Americans could be talented, educated, skilled artists worthy of being welcomed at all levels of society.

Perhaps this program was simply a coincidence not connected to the protests or riots in any way. Nevertheless, civil rights issues must have been on Bernstein's mind at this time. Six days later, Bernstein similarly but less subtly supported civil rights for African Americans in a television program called "Inside Pop: The Rock Revolution." Amidst discussions of the musical attributes of selected rock songs (on recording), a fifteen-year-old Janis Ian appeared and sang her controversial song about interracial romance, "Society's Child." This young person had written a social protest song when she was fourteen and had the courage to perform it in halls as some in the audience screamed "nigger lover."[11] After interviewing Ian, Bernstein acknowledges the controversial nature of the lyrics, mentions that radio stations were banning her song, then calls it a "short social document" in "the spirit of protest" (9, 11). He could have had any number of young rock singers on this program, but Ian was the one he chose. After the program, Ian wrote thanking Bernstein for having her on the show and to let him know that radio stations were apologizing for their timidity. "Society's Child" thereafter became number one in California as stations began playing the song (Simeone 213, 483).

Bernstein's fan mail shows that African Americans thanked Bernstein for his support. After Watts's first appearance on Bernstein's *Young People's Concerts* (Young Performers No. 4, 15 January 1963), Ruth M. Barnwell (an African American teacher) wrote, "it was an indescribable pleasure for me and my classes to watch the debut of a new great star," and "your own description of him as 'a young musical prince' brought forth much comment from my students as well as my colleagues" (1963). When Bernstein called on Watts to replace an ailing Glen Gould at a Philharmonic concert, The Etude Music Club (of the National Association of Negro Musicians) wrote to thank him

(1963). They acknowledged the role Watts's talent played in the maestro's decision, then noted that there had been "great Negro piano talent" but "no conductor of your caliber payed [*sic*] attention to them." After praising Bernstein for his "far sightedness, kindness, and a mind unhampered by artifice and prejudice," the letter concludes, "we're equally proud of you as a distinguished American who has chosen to see further than today."

Feminism

Originating in the West, the feminist movement is now global and may be the most wide-ranging social movement in history. Two events provided the impetus for the activism of the 1960s and 1970s: the President's Commission on the Status of Women formed by President John F. Kennedy in 1961, and (perhaps more significant in terms of popular culture) the publication of Betty Friedan's revolutionary book *The Feminine Mystique* in 1963. After the supposed idyllic suburban life of the 1950s, in which women were restricted to only mothering and housekeeping, Friedan's book revealed that many wives felt themselves unfulfilled and prisoners of this lifestyle. Friedan, a trained psychologist who graduated summa cum laude from Smith College, compiled years of research and interviews into a tome asserting that women were equal to men and therefore deserved equal rights and opportunities.[12] In Friedan's obituary, the *New York Times* called *The Feminine Mystique* "one of the most influential nonfiction books of the 20th century," saying, "rarely has a single book been responsible for such sweeping, tumultuous and continuing social transformation" (5 February 2006).

Even if Bernstein did not read *The Feminine Mystique*, he was probably aware of the book and the feminist movement. When discussing her husband with John Gruen, Felicia Bernstein called him "unbelievably well-read," "a thinker," and "a man with an enormous variety of interests" (Gruen 1968, 100). The maestro mentioned reading book excerpts in the *New York Review of Books*, which was founded in February 1963 (Cott 2013, 88). He demonstrated his familiarity with popular literature when he spoke of Erich Fromm's books on love (Bernstein 1966, 272–273). Presumably, the feminist movement suddenly opened the maestro's eyes to a prejudice he did not know he had.

Although several women harpists had served with the Philharmonic over the years, the first women to receive full-time positions with the Philharmonic were contracted while Bernstein was director: bassist Orin O'Brien in 1966 and cellist Evangeline Benedetti in 1967 (Shanet 1975, 347). Bernstein's growing awareness of feminism can be traced in the scripts for his *Young People's Concerts*. In the second season, he mentions Vivaldi's "strange all-female orchestra" ("What Is a Concerto?" 28 March 1959, 8), and in "Young Performers No. 2" (19 March 1961), he describes the sixteen-year-old cellist Lynn Harrell as looking "more like a football quarterback than a cellist; but when he plays he can make the music as delicate as a girl, or as powerful as a—well—football quarterback" (4). But "Young Performers No. 4" (15 January 1963) seems on the cusp of change: "In the old days . . . young ladies by the thousands studied the piano, as part of good breeding. It was enough if they could play a little piece at a party, which was called a social accomplishment. But our three young ladies today have nothing at all to do with that world; they are serious artists" (7). He redeems himself somewhat by later adding, "It's going to be hard to follow them; I'd be a little bit scared myself" (10).

By the end of 1963, in "Young Performers No. 5" (23 December 1963), Bernstein performed a composition by a woman composer on a *Young People's Concert* for the first and only time—Shulamit Ran's *Capriccio for Piano and Orchestra*. When introducing Ran, he shows how doors had opened for women: "Our next young soloist is . . . a composer, and that is a *very* special case. There aren't many girl-composers around . . . but what's even rarer is to find a 16-year-old composer—male or female—who has reached such an amazing point of professional know-how and of personal expression. But such is the special case of Miss Shulamith [*sic*] Ran" (12). He adds that she is studying at New York's Mannes College of Music and is "fortunate in her teachers: Norman dello Joio for composition, and Nadia Reisenberg for piano" (ibid.). The young woman then performed as pianist in her own concerto with the famed Philharmonic on international television. Bernstein supported feminism by portraying Ran not only as a unique talent and skilled pianist/composer but also as a woman with a mind and a fine education from one of the best music schools.

By the end of the decade, Bernstein invited women into the previously male position of assistant conductor for the Philharmonic. The maestro took pride in introducing Sylvia Caduff in "Young Performers No. 8" (27 January 1967).[13] Noting that there was an "all-male cast," he observes, "we do have one important exception, and that is our conductor. This is really unusual—a female conductor; and what is even more unusual is that she's so good. . . . So all hail the eternal feminine, and let us welcome Sylvia Caduff" (12). By "Young Performers No. 9" (31 March 1968), a woman appearing as a conductor was no longer such an event, and Helen Quach received the same sort of simple accolades as the men: "a very gifted young lady" (21). Bernstein easily welcomed talented women on stage.

His fan mail shows that his viewers, old and young, occasionally opened themselves up to Bernstein, trusting his opinion. Shortly after

Orin O'Brien was hired, Naomi Brami wanted to know why there were no women in the orchestra (1967). Queries even came from men about women's roles. Steelworker Michael Kovack wrote asking "why don't we find, among all the famous and non-famous composers, any women? . . . Women can do almost everything a man can and here we find that women are left out when it comes to composing good music! Have you ever thought about this?" (1964, he must have missed Ran's performance of her own composition). Diane Di Giampaolo writes that her school has been debating "whether a woman is fit to hold any public office" or do jobs traditionally held by men. She then specifically wonders if a woman could "possess the necessary qualifications, and could possibly break through the social barriers" and become a conductor (1963). Catherine P. Cullen was one of several young women who wrote about wanting to become a conductor: "I have not disclosed this ambition to anyone since, because I am a girl, the[y] would probably only laugh" (1964). Lisa Jones had considered her desire to be a conductor futile until she saw the triumphs of Sylvia Caduff and Helen Quach (1967). Bernstein certainly recognized the extraordinary gifts of his protégé Marin Alsop and said he would "put his hand in the fire" for her (Cott 2013, 125). Now a renowned conductor who has broken the glass ceiling in her field, Alsop is director of the Baltimore Symphony Orchestra, principal conductor of the São Paulo State Symphony Orchestra, Brazil, and is the first woman chosen to conduct the Last Night of the Proms in its 118-year history.[14] Bernstein would be profoundly pleased both at his student's successes and in a changed world where her abilities are recognized.

The Americans with Disablities Act was enacted by Congress in 1990, long after Bernstein's *Young People's Concerts* ended. Nonetheless, Bernstein shows his support for disability rights in "Young Performer's No. 7" (22 February 1966). When he introduces "our gifted assistant [conductor] James DePreist," he tells the audience that DePreist was sent to Thailand

> by our State Department to help build a symphony orchestra . . . he was suddenly stricken with polio, and suffered paralysis of both legs. He is still walking with braces; but his courage and stamina are so great as you'll now hear, that this cruel handicap has in no way hurt his conducting. We can all learn a lesson from him. (9–10)

Bernstein has provided us with wonderful evidence—seen internationally—that music and ability are more important than race, sex, or disability. Who knows how many were inspired to emulate the maestro?

Bernstein's firmly held beliefs and actions in other venues lead inexorably to the conclusion that he used the power of suggestion in his *Young*

People's Concerts, as listed below in chronological order. The list includes programs discussed in both chapters 5 and 6:

1. To show a positive side of potential enemies: "Latin American Spirit" (8 March 1963).
2. To celebrate the achievements of an individual living under the control of an enemy and portray a positive side of "the enemy": "A Birthday Tribute to Shostakovich" (5 January 1966).
3. To endorse civil rights: "Alumni Reunion" (19 April 1967).
4. To endorse feminism: "Young Performers No. 5" (23 December 1963), "Young Performers No. 8" (27 January 1967), and "Young Performers No. 9" (31 March 1968).
5. To show that the disabled can be valuable and productive members of society: "Young Performers No. 7" (22 February 1966).

And three veiled commentaries against the Vietnam War:

6. "*Fidelio:* A Celebration of Life" (29 March 1970).
7. "The Anatomy of a Symphony Orchestra" (24 May 1970).
8. "Holst: *The Planets*" (26 March 1972).

Although I have not yet read all the 117 boxes of fan mail, those I have seen contain letters either questioning Bernstein about these issues or thanking him for bringing them to light. And Bernstein was aware of his fan mail (Cott 2013, 71). He must have hoped that these programs would not only teach audiences about music, but also subtly and gently guide them to see the world a little differently, with more empathy and cooperation, and to seek unity and peace.

BERNSTEIN MORE OVERTLY SEEKING TO INFLUENCE THE AUDIENCE

The hippie movement and its culture pervaded the 1960s and most of the 1970s. The "generation gap" allowed Bernstein to share his opinions on this particular subject more openly. Hippies tended to be in their twenties (older than the target audience) and probably either never watched television or never watched seemingly highbrow shows like Bernstein's *Young People's Concerts*. Furthermore, while his *Young People's Concerts* were ostensibly aimed at children, the parents were the ones in control, and many parents in the 1960s feared that their children would be seduced by the hippie lifestyle. While

Bernstein needed to be in touch with and reference hippie culture, many of its tenets frustrated him. He allowed himself to speak out less subtly here, against what he saw as the hippies' lack of logical thinking and against the use of psychedelic drugs, knowing that he could count on near universal support. In two programs, he featured symphonic works that allowed him to weave in his pithy thoughts on astrology and warnings against drugs.

Hippies

Hippies were usually college students in their twenties coming from privileged families in the world's wealthiest nation, who left what they saw as the materialistic world of their parents to find increased self-awareness and a simpler lifestyle more in touch with nature. Their optimistic and open approach to life also involved drug use, free sex, rock 'n' roll, communal living, and a turning away from many traditional values, such as hard work and responsibility. They commonly sought spiritual enlightenment from outside the Judeo-Christian tradition, investigating Eastern religions and astrology. When the Beatles went to India to seek enlightenment through transcendental meditation with the Maharishi Mahesh Yogi in 1968, many hippies followed their example, turning to meditation, Buddhism, or Hinduism. Tribhuwan Kapur interviewed sixty hippies from all over the world between the ages of twenty-one and thirty in India and documented twenty-three countries of origin, from France and Germany to Great Britain and the United States, from Sweden and Norway to Japan and Thailand (Kapur 1981). Bernstein's *Young People's Concerts* were broadcast to forty countries, yet it seems unlikely that hippies would watch this series. Bernstein was probably instead speaking to the impressionable youth not yet swept up in the hippie maelstrom. Adults from middle-class America felt threatened by hippies—understandable since often these rebels were their own children. At the same time, features of hippie life became very "in" and began to monopolize everything from fashions to film. To remain "hip" and reach his young audiences Bernstein had to incorporate references to such a pervasive societal influence while still honoring tradition with all its trappings.

The maestro represented art music and the New York Philharmonic in his *Young People's Concerts*. This obliged him to present a very conservative image both on screen and off. Throughout the series he wears the very traditional attire of a suit (generally dark and single-breasted), dark tie (usually solid, but occasionally a subtle stripe will sneak in), and white shirt, even after the programs were broadcast in color beginning with the tenth season (1966–1967). Some color creeps into his shirts and ties toward the end of the series. When opening the first show televised in color, "What Is a Mode?"

(23 November 1966), Bernstein even jokes that this is "the first season in which all our programs will be seen on television *in color*. Which is why I've got this modishly colorful tie on" (4). He is wearing a black tie with white and gray accent stripes, along with a black, well-tailored single-breasted suit, a black vest with white trim, a white shirt, and a white handkerchief in his pocket—attire that is understated and elegant but comprised entirely of dignified blacks, whites, and grays. Publicity that included pictures of the Bernstein family in front of their house with a white picket fence made Bernstein aware of the role a traditional family played in his public image.[15] Beginning with the first program and occasionally throughout the series, he wove references to his family into the scripts. For instance in the second draft of the first program "What Does Music Mean?" (18 January 1958), Bernstein wrote that "my little girl, Jamie" said "that's the Lone Ranger song" when she heard the opening of the Overture to Gioachino Rossini's *William Tell*. Bernstein later changed "my little girl" to "my little five-year-old daughter" and wrote in the margin "CLEARER, MORE 'FAMILY'" (second draft, 4 revised). In October 1966, Bernstein announced he would leave the Philharmonic when his contract expired in May 1969, and he finally began to feel free (H. Burton 1994, 360).

Bernstein's carefully designed image began to break up very publicly in 1968—he had already left the Philharmonic in his mind by this time—when he allowed himself to be photographed in his jockey shorts while shaving for what many felt was a coffee table book.[16] This tendency exploded after Felicia died. His wife had always been a stabilizing influence, but after her death in 1978, he seemed to "no longer care what he said or whom he shocked" (458). Judith Braun, an actress and friend of Felicia, said that Felicia "served such incredible functions in his life: his morality, his spine. She was a martinet [with] such strict standards about what was acceptable and what was unacceptable" (324). At least until the end of his *Young People's Concerts* in 1972, Bernstein behaved himself like the great maestro. Before 1972, he was an acolyte of tradition and could discuss any aspect of the hippie's lifestyle with impunity, authority, and the approval of parents, sponsors, the CBS network, and the Philharmonic. Bernstein's life after 1972 is beyond the purview of this book.

Bernstein referenced hippie culture to appeal to his young audiences. At the same time, he probably worried about his young viewers, and as the father of three, he certainly must have worried about his own children. While Nina was too young to be caught up in the hippie movement, he might have feared that teenagers Jamie and Alexander would be seduced by the hippie lifestyle.

Astrology is an important theme in the successful 1967 rock musical about hippies, *Hair: The American Tribal Love-Rock Musical* by Gerome Ragni, Galt MacDermot, and James Rado. While the show was controversial for many reasons (such as its nudity and its endorsement of free sex), it won two drama awards, and one song from the show ("Aquarius/Let the Sunshine In") was top on the Billboard list for six weeks and went Platinum.[17] The hippies' spiritual quests and devotion to astrology is evidenced by the lyrics:

> When the Moon is in the Seventh House
> And Jupiter aligns with Mars
> Then peace will guide the planets
> And love will steer the stars.

This occult pseudo-science was an integral part of daily life for many of these young people (Cavan 1972, 183–188).[18] Hippies gave astrological reasons for such problems as simply feeling depressed (184) or incompatibility (185). Eventually, astrology swept the United States in 1968 (perhaps due in part to the popularity of *Hair*) and has remained a part of American culture, as seen by astrology sections in currently available newspapers and magazines.

His outline for this program shows that Bernstein wanted to acknowledge astrology and and reference *Hair*, yet the reverence accorded astrology in the musical (and by society at large) appeared to annoy him. He was an educated, well-rounded man who believed in "learning and reason" and that "rational intelligence" is needed or "our world can no longer survive"; he further believed that "every man of goodwill" must "insist, unflaggingly, at the risk of becoming a repetitive bore . . . on the achievement of a world in which the mind will have triumphed over violence" (Bernstein 1982, 217). The unscientific thinking of astrology apparently bothered Bernstein. In "Holst: *The Planets*" (26 March 1972), the works he chose from the regular Philharmonic subscription series for his final *Young People's Concert* allowed him to speak about outer space and make connections to popular culture. His wry comments about astrology are not in the outline but are in the draft.[19] He offers connections between Holst and hippies (thereby making Holst seem "hip") and between high art and popular art, then debunks astrology by contrasting the science of astronomy with the pseudo-science of astrology:

> Holst wasn't at all interested in astronomy, but in astrology. I'm sure you know the difference. Now we all know that in astronomy the sun is the center of our system, and we all revolve around it; but in astrology the Earth is the center, and everything else revolves around us, including the sun and the moon. So out went Earth as a planet. It's not very scientific but Holst couldn't have cared less about the scientific side of the planets; he was drawn to the mystic side of things, and for him the planets were important as symbols, in relation to the zodiac, to horoscopes, to the

ancient *sort*-of-science known as astrology. I suppose today he would be called a mysticism-freak. (7–8)

Perhaps Bernstein, like Holst, was drawn to the mystic. He was deeply influenced by his Jewish heritage, including the mystical aspects.[20] His first major composition (the *Jeremiah Symphony*) and his big choral works (the *Kaddish Symphony*, the *Chichester Psalms*, and *Mass*) all incorporate settings of Hebrew or Aramaic religious texts. Humphrey Burton calls Bernstein's ballet score *Dybbuk* his "most obvious demonstration of his concern for the mystic aspects of his Jewish blood and faith" (1994, 487). Bernstein's mysticism, however, was only distantly related to the mysticism inherent in astrology.

Bernstein's disdain for astrology continues to emerge throughout the program, sometimes written in the script, sometimes ad-libbed (represented in the following quotations by italics). When providing the background for the movement "Venus," he slips in a slur: "we usually think of Venus as the goddess of love; but astrologers have made her a symbol of peace *by their own special brand of logic*" ("Holst: *The Planets*," 12). For "Uranus," Bernstein alluded to *Hair* and "the Age of Aquarius": "what is so interesting to us in this revolutionary day and age is that Uranus is linked to the sign of Aquarius, and Heaven knows we never stop hearing about how we've entered [Bernstein sings the appropriate melody] the Age of Aquarius. But of course Holst never saw *Hair*, so far as he was concerned, Uranus meant magic to him" (21).

Holst did not write a movement for Pluto, even though the planet was discovered in 1930, while he was still alive. Bernstein works in his final slur against astrology here by drolly pointing out a major flaw in astrological reasoning. "[Pluto] is also the bane of the astrologers' existence, because suddenly there it was in 1930, upsetting all the calculations of centuries, and causing no end of confusion in the world of horoscopes" (24). Now it seems the astrologers were right since Pluto is no longer considered to be a planet. This program concludes in a most unusual way. Both conductor and orchestra improvised a new final movement, calling it "Pluto, the Unpredictable." Bernstein suggests that "we here on stage are going to be just as surprised as you are at the mysterious sounds we will be making" and that "you are about to hear a piece nobody had ever heard, nor will ever hear again" (25). The audience laughed. Punning on the drug culture and the outer space theme of the program, he referred to the upcoming performance as a "spaced-out trip" (25). For the performance of this improvised "Pluto," the maestro made gestures, and the orchestra chaotically tried to represent the gestures in music. Here, in his last *Young People's Concert*, Bernstein referenced popular culture and did not hesitate to offer his opinion, rather more obviously than he had earlier in the series.

Hippies and Drugs

Hippies believed that psychedelic drugs would "expand the mind," thereby providing a path to greater wisdom and enlightenment (Fischer 2006, 304). For example, Charles Reich states "one of the most important means for restoring dulled consciousness is psychedelic drugs" (1970, 258). The issue of drugs permeates Cavan's interviews with hippies (Cavan 1972), so much so that one entire chapter is devoted to how to obtain "grass." During the great rock festival years from 1967 through 1971, rock music and excessive drug use became inextricably linked; substantially more "drugged-out" young people than ever before were seen.[21] The "mecca" for young people seeking drugs was San Francisco's Haight-Ashbury district, but many "restless youngsters" flocked to Greenwich Village and the East Village of Bernstein's beloved New York City as well.[22]

Drugs and addiction were complex issues with Bernstein. Despite being afflicted with asthma from birth, he was addicted to cigarettes.[23] Jack Gottlieb said that "he smoked incessantly" (Gottlieb 2010, 24). Bernstein's nicotine habit was so uncontrollable that when he did a long interview for the BBC and smoking on camera was forbidden, he "was reduced to sucking an empty [Aqua] filter on screen like a baby with a pacifier" (H. Burton 1994, 475). Bernstein's habit is not surprising considering the times. After World War I and during Prohibition, cigarettes gained many of the positive social and cultural attributes formerly attributed to alcohol (e.g., "leisure, pleasure, and sociability") and by the 1920s had become dissociated with other substances "deemed more dangerous and addictive" (Tracy 2004, 386).[24] Despite growing concerns about possible negative effects, cigarettes became central to the social lives of many Americans as "an indicator of social and cultural power, autonomy, and attractiveness" (388). By 1964, over forty percent of Americans smoked (390).[25] Even after the dangers of smoking became known and Felicia died from lung cancer in 1978, Bernstein was unable to stop (H. Burton 1994, 426, 475). He believed, or at least said that he believed, that he was immune to the ill effects of drugs. When Alan Jay Lerner died at sixty-seven of lung cancer in June 1986, people held up signs for Bernstein at Lerner's memorial service that said, "We love you, Lenny. Please stop smoking" (484).

Bernstein also had an "insatiable demand" for prescription drugs, albeit "within reasonable bounds" (475). Gottlieb said that "there were occasions when he had to take an upper to keep going." He was "living on" dexamyl (an amphetamine to elevate mood combined with a barbiturate to counteract its side effects) when preparing for *West Side Story* (Simeone 2013, 370, 382). In the summer of 1968, his children were so bored hearing about the plot of a proposed show and his insomnia that they "took sweet revenge" in a cabaret they wrote for his fiftieth birthday party. In the script, Jamie asked Daddy (portrayed by Alexander) how he slept. When the answer was "TERRIBLE," she asked, "Didn't you take anything?" To which Daddy/Alexander replied, "I took EVERYTHING." To the tune of "Another Opening, Another Show," Jamie (the show's author) listed some seven different drugs he probably tried: Effedrin, Milltown, Placidyl, Noludar, Suponéryl, Seconal, and Nembutal, saying "you wake up groggy and drugged to here" and "after a breakfast of Theragran (a multi-vitamin) and Vitamin C, Daddy ends by taking a pack of Tums" (H. Burton 1994, 374–375). Even his children teased him about his relationship with drugs.

Bernstein also overindulged in alcohol. Fred Begun (Principle Timpanist of the National Symphony Orchestra from 1951 to 1999) remembered that the maestro frequently tippled from the silver flask of Scotch that he always carried (pers. comm.). Michael Tilson Thomas reveals that Scotch and cigarettes were inextricably linked to performing for Bernstein:

> When he got his call he would stand just offstage, saying his mantra, kissing his Koussevitzky cufflinks, taking the final drags of his cigarette. At the last possible second he handed it to a stagehand or cup-bearer and he was on. . . . After the final number, the stagehand and cup-bearer handed him a lighted cigarette and a silver tumbler filled with Scotch the second he got off the stage. A few puffs, a few gulps, and he bounded or staggered on again. (*New York Times*, 21 September 2008)

Throughout most of the nineteenth century, the temperance movement led people to believe that total abstinence from all alcoholic beverages was the only way to avoid dissolution (Holt 2006, 229–230). After Prohibition was repealed in 1933, advertisers began to link public drinking with "images of glamour, wealth, and sophistication."[26]

Bernstein's smoking and drinking were part of the world he inhabited, but he took both to excess and "flaunted his bad habits." In the 6 August 1986 issue of *USA Today*, he said, "I was diagnosed as having emphysema in my mid-20s, and to be dead by the age of 35. Then they said I'd be dead by the age of 45. And 55. Well, I beat the rap. I smoke. I drink. I stay up all night. I screw around. I'm overcommitted on all fronts" (H. Burton 1994, 484). This lifestyle did catch up with him. By the end of his life, he would crumple as he left the stage, then found the energy in Scotch and cigarettes to go back on (Sherman 2010, 114). Bernstein died at seventy-two from a "heart attack brought on by progressive emphysema complicated by a pleural tumor and a series of pulmonary infections"—smoking played a major role in his death (H. Burton 1994, 532).

The question arises as to why Bernstein chose to speak out against drug use when he was an addict himself. Like many smokers of his generation, he felt cigarettes were not really a drug and did not think of himself as an "addict." Prescription drugs were given by a doctor, so they must have been safe and appropriate. Drinking was considered integral to a sophisticated lifestyle. Common knowledge decreed that heroin, opium, cocaine, LSD, marijuana, and such were addictive; these were the drugs of hippies and "real" addicts. Finite evidence that nicotine is addictive did not appear until the U.S. Surgeon General's report on smoking in 1988 (Brodie 2002, 120). To Bernstein, and probably to other smokers and drinkers, true addicts were those repugnant, slovenly, out-of-control people on the streets, not someone like the great maestro who presumably could control his habits if he so desired.

While Bernstein felt himself to be immune to the ill effects of nicotine, prescription drugs, and alcohol, he must have worried about his teenagers being caught by the maelstrom of psychedelic drugs. He was familiar with the impact of drug use on the youth of the world, having seen it firsthand in New York and on his world travels, as well as having kept abreast of the news. Joan Peyser suggests that his son Alexander experimented with drugs, but that may have been only cigarettes (Peyser 1998, 378). Bernstein had found psychiatry helpful, so he sent his son to the psychiatrist Milton Horowitz in the mid-1960s. Peyser reported that, "Alex recalls the single session, in which [Alex] did not open his mouth except to smoke four cigarettes. He was, therefore, not made to go again" (ibid.). His son was only ten by the mid-1960s and evidently already smoking. At least part of Alexander's adolescence was characterized by tension between father and son; he remembered two years during which he and his father did not speak at all (ibid.).[27]

The periodicals of the time were rife with warnings about drugs and drug use by teenagers, as is demonstrated by an examination of various *New York Times* articles in 1968.[28] These include articles about: drug use leading to children being born deformed, a child being murdered by its mother while she was in a drug stupor, minds being destroyed by drugs, drug-induced death, as well as articles about police raiding college campuses and arresting students for violating narcotics laws. In January the *New York Times* ran a five-part series called "The Drug Scene" on the use and abuse of drugs in the United States. The problem was addressed by authorities at the highest levels. President Lyndon Baines Johnson delivered a special message to Congress on the "growing problem of narcotics and dangerous drugs," and a report to the United Nations Narcotics Commission declared that abuse of such drugs had "assumed the proportion of an epidemic" ("Johnson Widens Narcotics Fight," *New York Times*, 8 February 1968). The problem was an international one (Kapur 1981). Some articles offered parents, educators, and others ways of reaching children with the message about the dangers of marijuana and psychedelic drugs.[29] As an avaricious reader and a New Yorker, one can assume that Bernstein saw these articles in the *New York Times*; these specific articles are also representative of similar articles in other periodicals that he might have read.[30]

Bernstein's *Young People's Concert* against drug use was "Berlioz Takes a Trip" (25 May 1969). The program title is a word-play on a voyage and a drug "trip" (in the vernacular of the time), and the only composition on the program is Hector Berlioz's *Symphonie fantastique*. Bernstein's initial motivation for the focus on Berlioz was musical: the 100th anniversary of Berlioz's death. No mention is made in the outline of drugs or trips. However, by the time he wrote the rough pencil draft of the script on 28 December 1968 (Alexander was thirteen), Bernstein's mind had linked the work and its tale of an opium-induced dream with use of psychedelic drugs by teens. The fact that the drug problem was international and that the programs were broadcast internationally may have also been a factor. Whatever his reasoning, Bernstein carefully crafted his message. Rather than emphasizing Berlioz's innovations in orchestration and the compositional technique of the *idée fixe* (as he intended in the outline) or simply retelling Berlioz's program of opium hallucinations—Bernstein took every opportunity to emphasize the horrors of what he called the "first musical description ever made of a drug trip" (4).[31]

As he had done before, perhaps Bernstein hoped to plant ideas about what an orchestral piece might represent and then perform the work, thereby guiding his listeners toward an understanding of the dangers inherent in drug use. In the final script, the word "psychedelic" appears six times. He emphasizes the seamier side of the work, with such phrases as: "portrait of a nervous wreck" (11), "hysterical shrieks" (12), "flipped his lid" (13), "dangerously close to the borderline of insanity" (13), "sick wandering mind" (14 revised), "a desperate soul" (14 revised), "moaning strings . . . soaring to a new climax of hallucination" (14 revised), "the madness takes hold again" (15 revised), "poor drugged lover" (21), "What a nightmare. A marvelous picture of panic and terror" (23, 2nd revised), and "agonized dreamer" (25). Bernstein planned a potent ending for this program. The final sentences of the first draft verify Bernstein's desire to confront this issue: "You take a trip, you wind up screaming at your own funeral. Take a tip from Berlioz: This music is all you need for the wildest trip you can take, to hell and back. With drugs you might make it, but you might not make it back. So let's settle for the music—the last movement of Berlioz's Fantastic Symphony" (15). The final script deletes the first and last sentences but retains the rest (29). The ending as broadcast was less "preachy" but much more powerful. After the performance of "March to the Scaffold," Bernstein says,

Now all this horror builds up into a most brilliant ending—but brilliant or not, I'm sorry to say, [it] leaves our hero still in the clutches of his nightmare. Its brilliance without glory—that's the problem. I can't honestly tell you that we have gone through the fires of hell with our hero and come out nobler and wiser; but that's the way with trips, and Berlioz tells it like it is. Now *there* was an honest man. You take a trip, you wind up screaming at your own funeral. (29)

He then led the Philharmonic in the final movement, "Songe d'une nuit de sabbat." While this is traditionally translated as "Dream of the Witches' Sabbath" (as noted in the script, 30), "Nightmare of the Witches' Sabbath" appears on the television screen as the orchestra begins to play. Perhaps he was trying to warn his son, the youth of America, and the youth of the world against the use of dangerous psychedelic drugs.

BERNSTEIN OPENLY LECTURES HIS AUDIENCE

Hippies had their own concept of freedom. Freedom to "do your own thing" and "drop out" were integral to the hippie credo.[32] While each person "constructs his personal world as he so desires, his actions will never jeopardize the freedom of either himself or others" (Cavan 1972, 67–68). If everyone were able to live life "in accordance with their beliefs concerning individual freedom," the result should be a world "characterized by beauty, harmony, psychic satisfaction, and a spiritual community of all mankind" (107). Anything that prevents individuals from "doing their own thing" was regarded as "a bummer" (149–151). Hippies "dropped out of the mainstream, were uninterested in reforming institutions, rejected political solutions to cultural problems as a waste of time" (Fischer 2006, 308), and deemed politics "a bad trip" (Cavan 1972, 177).

In contrast, Bernstein was a patriotic American who believed in the political system of democracy. So much so that it underlies his contribution to the series *This I Believe*. He noted that man had "built, laboriously and lovingly," through hard work and reason "something we reverently call democracy," that we must believe in "people and in their capacity to change, grow, communicate, and love," and that "all art is a combination of all these powers" and thereby our path to peace (Bernstein 1982, 138). The maestro believed that "my country is the place where all these things I have been speaking of are happening in the most manifest way. America is at the beginning of her greatest period in history—a period of leadership in science, art, and human progress toward the democratic ideal" (139). Many, including Bernstein, could see that the hippies' concept of freedom and apathy toward the operations of government threatened democracy. He decided to use his "bully pulpit" to openly lecture the audience on the advantages and responsibilities of democracy in "Forever Beethoven!" (28 January 1968). He even warns the audience, "Now apropos of this shaping and molding [of the Symphony No. 5 in C minor, Allegro con brio], there is an important thing that needs to be said, and I'm going to try to even at the risk of boring you with a tiny lecture" (11).

Bernstein makes his point through music, as usual. He plays the first five measures of the opening theme of Beethoven's "Eroica" symphony on the piano, chosen specifically to provide an opening for a homily on the nature of freedom. He begins by referring to a biography of Beethoven titled *The Man Who Freed Music*, saying, "freed music from what?" (Schaffler 1929; "Forever Beethoven," 11). After a brief explanation, he points out that *all* great composers freed music *"from the predictable* [Bernstein's emphasis]." This comment could be construed as aligning great composers with hippies in their desire to break away from the restrictions of the past, but he quickly broke that possible link (12). To demonstrate freedom from the predictable, Bernstein plays the E-flat major triadic opening phrase and calls the audience's attention to the "unexpected" D-flat in the fifth measure:[33] "Bang! That D-flat! Surprise: the bondage of the triad is broken. Music is freed. But freed by what? By a D-flat . . . that *one, chosen, limited* note" (12). He then asserts that true freedom does not mean "dropping out," not deciding is a kind of decision, and with freedom comes responsibilities. He continues,

> Now doesn't this tell us something very important about the nature of freedom? Obviously freedom must carry with it the meaning of freedom to limit oneself, and one's material. Freedom is *not* infinite, not boundless liberty, as some hippies like to think—do anything you want, any time, anywhere you want to. No, freedom isn't that. It means being free to make decisions, to determine one's own course. But deciding means choosing; and choosing is impossible without rejection. Can you understand that? You can't *choose* something without rejecting all the other things you haven't chosen. . . . Beethoven chose that one D-Flat, he automatically *un*-chose all the other eleven notes. (13)

An early mimeographed version of the script reveals the extent of Bernstein's frustration with the hippie's concept of freedom, but the following words are removed from the next version of the script:

> In the same way, Determination operates through our will—what we like to call Free Will. But whose will? Hitler's will? A pyromaniac's will? Are these *free* men, because they are free to carry out their impulses, free to satisfy their distorted desires and appetites? No—they are *not* free; just the

opposite—they are victims, *forced* into action by their unconscious motives. They are as unfree as slaves in chains. (5–6)

Bernstein saw how hippies' idea of freedom, if taken to its logical extreme, could end—with Nazis and pyromaniacs. In the final version of the script, he continues,

> So you see, real freedom must contain within itself the freedom to *un-*
> choose, as well as choose, to censor oneself, to limit oneself and that is
> the whole meaning of democracy. The kind of freedom on which we base
> our hopes for a peaceful world—just as it is the meaning of freedom in
> great musical composition. In Beethoven, as in democracy, freedom is a
> discipline, combining the right to choose freely, with the gift of choosing
> wisely. Now do you see what I meant by Beethoven's masterly *shaping* of
> that movement? I hope so! End of lecture. (14 revised)

Like many adults in the 1960s, Bernstein was terrified and appalled by the thought that the future of the nation was in the hands of so many apparently apathetic, "drugged out" youths. This led to the most overt sociopolitical statement he ever allowed into any *Young People's Concerts* script: true freedom requires responsibility and discipline.

INTERNATIONAL UNITY AND COMMUNICATION THROUGH MUSIC

Bernstein's solution to war, and many of the other problems afflicting the world, was to foster international unity through communication—specifically through the common language of music. One particular experience may have led him to this conclusion. In 1958, the State Department sponsored a New York Philharmonic goodwill tour of every country in South America, plus Panama and Mexico. He called the trip "one of the happiest and most exciting trips of my life, especially when I discovered the power of music in establishing friendships and lasting relationships on the widest basis" (Bernstein 1982, 220). The Philharmonic tour coincided with then Vice President Richard M. Nixon's South American tour. When the paths of the conductor and the politician crossed in Ecuador, they exchanged experiences. Where Bernstein encountered "tumultuous receptions; record crowds; cheering, stamping audiences; kisses; roses; embraces," Nixon encountered "unpleasant, distasteful incidents" (ibid.). Bernstein concluded that the difference was in music, that "if we are really serious about communicating with one another, about knowing ourselves through our neighbors—in short, about peaceful civilization—then we can never overestimate the good that comes from artistic communication. When we touch one another through music, we are touching the heart, the mind, and the spirit, all at once" (221).

After World War II Bernstein observed that there was a "new rise of nationalism almost everywhere" (109). He was greatly concerned that this new nationalism could quickly turn to exclusionism. He pleads, "all this at a time when international cooperation and coordination are desperately needed as never before" (ibid.). He felt the United States could lead the world to cooperate: "America—to whom all the world now looks for leadership, in art, in design, in invention, in democratic organization of business methods—has this responsibility. This is a plea for the execution of that responsibility. We can do so much to help our faltering, perplexed, emotion-ridden world. This is not Pollyanna altruism; it is our duty to ourselves, and our own crying need" (110). This theme recurs in his writings and actions. In "Dialogue and . . . " from April 1948, he said, "I have felt for years that if all symptoms of nationalism in the world could be abolished, we might have a start toward living as a human race, instead of as factions. I would love to see all borders and boundaries done away with" (114).

By 1963, Bernstein believed firmly in "those deep, warm ties that arise from artistic communion, and that lead to a fruitful, peaceful life on this earth" (222). The point reappears later in his Harvard lectures when he noted that the commonalities between music of different peoples offer evidence of "a single united human race" (Bernstein 1976, 55). One evening during a tour of Japan, he burst out with, "Everyone in the world should have another language besides his own and if only everyone had the same 'other language' then we could all *communicate* with each other" (Ames 1970, 153). He felt that music was that language.

Bernstein worked for international unity through his composing, conducting, and teaching. For example, *West Side Story* is a reaction to the social unrest in the 1950s, and at the same time, a plea for understanding and unity; *Mass* has a similar message.[34] His reputation as an activist for international harmony made him the obvious choice to lead the 1989 Ode to Freedom concert celebrating the reunification of East and West Germany and the fall of that symbol of the Cold War, the Berlin Wall. The orchestra and chorus were international, coming not only from East and West Germany, but also from the United Kingdom, France, the Soviet Union, and the United States. Bernstein worked for unity even near the end of his life. In 1990, he and Michael Tilson Thomas were music directors of the new Pacific Music Festival with the goals of educating young people and encouraging international unity.[35]

Bernstein fostered a sense of fellowship between nations and universality in his *Young People's Concerts* in a variety of ways: by mentioning the nationality of composers and guests to demonstrate the international nature of the art form, by praising international gatherings and activities in such a way as to make them appealing, by showing how international influences improve a national culture, and by mentioning such institutions as the United Nations. He did this more frequently in Young Performers programs than in the other *Young People's Concerts*. In "Young Performers No. 2" (19 March 1961), he lists the performers' nationalities (Korea, Israel, Greece, United States) and announces "we have quite an international gathering here today—a sort of musical UN" (9). In "Young Performers No. 5" (23 December 1963), Bernstein offers the analogy of soloists and various pieces performed as being like dishes in a dinner party. When introducing the soloists he says, "This season they happen to be all foreign-born—from Italy, Argentina, and Czechoslovakia; so our dinner, I mean our program, is really going to have an international flavor" (8), and later, "Continuing in the international spirit, we have Hungary and Czechoslovakia coming up" (15). He even shares his belief in the superiority of international marriages in "Young Performers No. 4" (15 January 1963). After introducing André Watts, he says,

> that mixed-up name comes from having an American father and a Hungarian mother, who met each other in Nuremberg, Germany, where André's father was stationed with the United States Army. I love that kind of story; I like to believe that international marriages produce [here, in his drafts Bernstein experiments with the best word: superior, highly distinguished, or unusual. He finally selected "highly distinguished."] human beings. (16)

As a patriotic American, he was moved when someone became an American citizen. While introducing the Israeli-born conductor Elyakum Shapira, he mentions that Shapira "as of last Monday is a full American citizen" ("Young Performers No. 2," 19 March 1961, 4). At the same time, he mentions Americans with the same pride, as evidenced by his effusive introductions for Veronica Tyler and André Watts in "Alumni Reunion" (19 April 1967, 10–11, 14–16).

Bernstein also did not hesitate to call the audience's attention to the international in non-Young Performers programs: "The Road to Paris" (18 January 1962) covers the influence that Debussy had on George Gershwin, Ernest Bloch, and Manuel de Falla. Neither did he hesitate to affirm that international connections strengthen rather than diminish life and culture:

> the road to Paris was a heavily traveled one by composers of all nations and races—not only composers with Spanish and Hebrew and American roots, but many others like Villa-Lobos from Brazil, Chavez from Mexico,

Prokofieff and Stravinsky from Russia, Malipiero from Italy, and so on and on. The French spirit has been very contagious in our century, and thank goodness it has; it has greatly enriched our whole musical life. (22)

He describes his ideal in "The Latin American Spirit" (8 March 1963) as those "who have succeeded in preserving the folk flavor of their own countries, while at the same time expanding their music into what we think of as universal art—music that has not only a nationalistic spirit but the spirit of all mankind" (8).

Bernstein wove current events into his *Young People's Concerts* for several reasons: as a politically aware liberal and pacifist, he could not resist suggesting ways to improve the world; his incorporation of current events helped the concerts seem less like an out-of-touch museum, more alive and "in sync" with contemporary society; and he naturally saw links where others saw disparity. He rarely used his *Young People's Concerts* as his personal soapbox, but when he did, he had to be careful. As a consummate teacher, Bernstein knew that the best way to teach is to guide students to make their own discoveries, which will help them to remember better and take the lessons to heart. He also deeply understood the power of music to move the emotions. If my assumptions are correct, he therefore chose three ways to reach into the minds and souls of the audience. To deal with prejudice and unscientific thinking, he subtly proved those notions wrong by providing irrefutable examples to the contrary. To deal with potentially destructive behavior, such as drug use, he used music to help the audience feel what the possible consequences might be. To deal with those who intellectually absorb the news without understanding human costs, he sought to make the news more personal, creating empathy by relating music to some aspect of a news story. In these small ways, Bernstein hoped these concerts would open people's minds and hearts not only musically, but perhaps politically and socially as well.

1   The Bernstein family as they were near the beginning of his New York Philharmonic *Young People's Concerts,* Christmas card (1958–1959).

2   The Bernstein family as they were near the end of his *Young People's Concerts,* Christmas card (1970s).

3 Bernstein with his friend and devoted secretary, Helen Coates, arriving in Cincinnati (January 1946).

4 Bernstein conducting while daughter Jamie enjoys a privileged seat, Philharmonic Hall, later Avery Fisher Hall (1962).

5   A "Young People's Concert" audience in Carnegie Hall (1960).

6   A father and daughter at a "Young People's Concert" in the R.P.I. Field House in Troy, NY (17 February 1962).

7   Enthusiastic young people at a "Young People's Concert," Exhibition Forum, Canada, Vancouver, during a Philharmonic tour (16 August 1960). Photo by Henry Tregillas.

8 Young people surrounding Bernstein (with ever-present cigarette) in the green room after a "Young People's Concert" at Carnegie Hall (1960s).

9 Young autograph seekers surround Bernstein after a "Young People's Concert," Exhibition Forum, Canada, Vancouver, during Philharmonic tour (1960). Photo by Henry Tregillas.

My dear young friends: It is good to be back with you all again for another season of Young People's Concerts here in Philharmonic Hall. These hours have become such an important part of my life that I don't know what I'd do without them. In fact, even next season, a year from now, when I shall be enjoying a whole year composing, and taking a vacation from my conducting duties with the New York Philharmonic -- even then, I will keep these programs going. I shall not take a vacation from you: that's how strongly I feel about these Young People's Concerts.

Now, you may think it strange that I have chosen teachers as the first subject of this new season. After all, aren't these programs always about music? And what have teachers got to do with music? The answer is: everything. The trouble is that we don't always realize how important teachers are. Teaching is probably the noblest profession in the world -- the most unselfish, difficult, and honorable profession. It is also the most unappreciated, underrated, underpaid, neglected and unpraised profession in the world. And so today we are going to praise teachers. Since we are not in a position to pay them higher salaries, we can at least pay them tribute. And the best way I can think of to do this is by paying tribute to some of my own teachers, some of the wonderful men

10   Whimsical drawings of the production crew sketched on a page from Jack Gottlieb's copy of the script for "A Tribute to Teachers" (29 November 1963). Original script in Library of Congress, Leonard Bernstein Collection.

11   A timing chart from the script for "A Tribute to Teachers" showing how meticulous the production crew had to be in timing performances. Original script included in Library of Congress, Leonard Bernstein Collection.

BERNSTEIN

You know, every grown-up can look
back and remember one or two of his
teachers with special affection;
everyone has had at least one teacher
he had a crush on, or one who suddenly
made algebra fascinating, or Egyptian
history, or whatever. But the moment
he thinks about it more deeply he is
bound to realize that there are many
more than one or two how have had a
real, lasting influence on his life.
Out of all the teachers I've had in
my life -- and I'd guess roughly there
have been 60 or 70 -- there are at
least 2 dozen I would want to thank
for the excitement and inspiration they
brought me. Of course we haven't time
for anything like that today; but
I would like to mention a few of the
most important ones, just to give you an
idea of what I mean by a lasting
influence.

(handwritten annotations in margins: was: 20:45 / 19:40 with / IF. 20:05 — CUT / :10 / 20:30 – 21:05 / :20 / 20:23½ / :35 / 20:40 / 20:55 – 21:30 / :45 / 21:05 – 21:40 / 20:55)

(handwritten insert near bottom: can't do — there isn't time; And I can share w/ you my eternal gratitude to them)

(MORE)

12 A page from the script for "A Tribute to Teachers" showing how timing issues influenced cuts in Bernstein's talks. Original script included in Library of Congress, Leonard Bernstein Collection.

(IF NO LAUGH)

40 Now, you see, you didn't laugh out loud.

#14   (IF LAUGH)

30 *12* Now most people don't laugh out loud about
musical jokes. That's one of the things
about musical humor: you laugh inside.

13   An excerpt from the script for "What Is a Concerto?" (24 January 1959) revealing Bernstein's thoroughness in creating the scripts, even planning for different audience responses. Original script included in Library of Congress, Leonard Bernstein Collection.

14   Peter Ustinov dons an eighteenth-century wig (employing the kinds of gimmicks Bernstein shunned) as he rehearses for a "Young People's Concert" at Avery Fisher Hall (May 1970). Photo by Bert Bial.

15   Bernstein maintained a casual demeanor while addressing the audience at a "Young People's Concert" (17 Feb 1961).

16　Bernstein with his sister, Shirley, and brother, Burton, at Martha's Vineyard, Massachusetts (1960).

17 Multiracial group of young musicians for "Young Performers No. 2" (19 March 1961): Veronica Tyler, Lynn Harrell (standing), Jung Ja Kim (seated), and Roger Englander (seated on right).

18   The Bernstein family enjoying the highbrow sport of sailing (1950s).

19   Bernstein enjoying the nominally lowbrow sport of baseball with Seiji Ozawa and others during a Philharmonic tour of Japan and Southern United States (August/September 1970).

20   Bernstein joined by Bolivian Indian musicians from Lake Titicaca during the Latin American Philharmonic tour (15 May 1958).

21   Bernstein addressing television viewers via a CBS camera (1960s). Photo by Bert Bial.

22 An elegant *New York Times* display ad for a televised *Young People's Concert* designed to appeal to a sophisticated market (24 May 1968).

*Polaroid
brings you
Bernstein.*

*The New York Philharmonic
on CBS-TV*

фотоаппарат "Полороид ленд",
Готовый снимок за 60 секунд.

23 Bernstein surrounded by Russians during the Philharmonic tour of the Soviet Union (5 September 1959). The text at the bottom reads "'Polaroid Land' camera, picture ready in 60 seconds."

24 Bernstein's handwritten outline for a never-developed concert, "Russian Music Then and Now," written after the Philharmonic tour of Europe, the USSR, and the Near East (proposed for 23 January 1960). Original script included in Library of Congress, Leonard Bernstein Collection.

25 Bernstein's ever-elegant wife, Felicia, being arrested after participating in a nonviolent "sit-in" in the Capitol Rotunda to protest the U.S. bombing of Cambodia (May 1972).

26 Bernstein conducting a *Young People's Concert* rehearsal with Veronica Tyler, Philharmonic Hall (October 1964). The African American soprano sang in three Young People's Concerts and twelve other Philharmonic concerts.

27 Bernstein and André Watts in rehearsal (1960s). Watts performed a total of twenty-three times with the Philharmonic. Photo by Eugene Cook.

28 The globe-trotting conductor brought his children, Jamie and Alexander, on the Philharmonic tour of Europe and Israel, here in New York preparing to leave for Brussels (22 August 1968).

29 Bernstein and Stravinsky while filming the CBS television program *The Creative Performer* (1960). Also appearing were Eileen Farrell, Glenn Gould, and the New York Philharmonic.

31   Bernstein and his friend Lukas Foss, Carnegie Hall (October 1960).

30   Bernstein with his good friend Aaron Copland during a rehearsal in Philharmonic Hall for the world premiere of Copland's *Connotations* on 22 September 1962.

He writes modern music for people who hate modern music.

Even people who think that listenable music died with Brahms sit still for Aaron Copland. Leonard Bernstein demonstrates why in rousing performances of "Billy the Kid" (excerpts) and the Clarinet Concerto. Produced and directed by Roger Englander.

New York Philharmonic Young People's Concert: A Copland Celebration 4:30 PM CBS②2

32   A display ad for a televised *Young People's Concert* from the *Los Angeles Times*, designed to attract viewers who would avoid anything connected to modern music (27 December 1970).

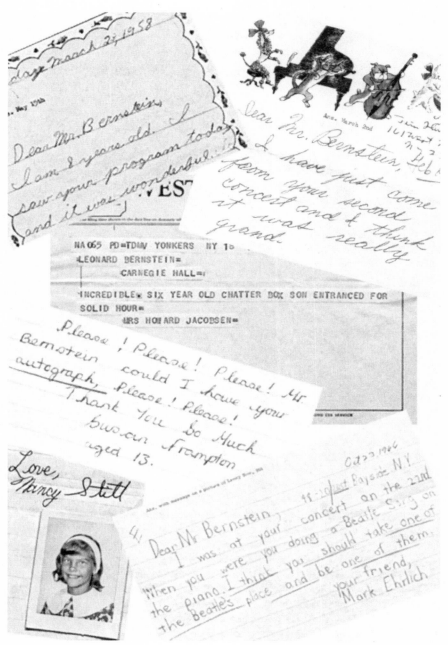

33 A collage of *Young People's Concerts* fan mail addressed to Bernstein from young viewers.

THE BELA BARTOK SOCIETY OF AUSTRALIA

(Registered Society of "The National Art Gallery and Cultural Centre of Victoria")

Canara Street
Victoria
DONCASTER
Telephone: 842-2128

Melbourne, 6 September, 1966

To the Conductor,
NEW YORK PHILHARMONIC ORCHESTRA,
NEW YORK, U.S. AMERICA,

Dear Mr. Bernstein,

One of my daughters directed my attention onto ATVO Television Station that it will be given a Bartok piece on 4th September, 1966, Sunday, at 5 p.m. "Young People Concert".

I attended and I haven't regretted it. You...
...out the Concerto. Your capacities - not only a...
...a Lecturer - was only to marveille; ...
...ll of people, and with peon'

34   Bernstein's fame spread through the world via television and recordings, as seen in this brief collage of international fan mail from adults to the maestro.

35   Charles Schulz's *Peanuts* strip for Sunday, 7 June 1959. Bernstein's *Young People's Concerts* were so popular a year and a half after their debut that Schulz devoted a full Sunday strip on Bernstein.

36   Charles Schulz's *Peanuts* strip from a weekday at the beginning of the tenth season of the *Young People's Concerts* (1 September 1966).

37　Bernstein studying a score, cigarette in hand (1970s).

The Musical Reactionary

Atonality versus Tonality or Composer versus Audience

Everyone says that this is a critical moment in the history of music. I agree, but double in spades: it is a *scary* moment. The famous gulf between composer and audience is not only wider than ever: it has become an ocean. What is more, it has frozen over; and it shows no immediate signs of either narrowing or thawing.

In this role of simple music lover, I confess, freely though unhappily, that at this moment, as of this writing, God forgive me, I have far more pleasure in following the musical adventures of Simon and Garfunkel or of The Association singing "Along Comes Mary" than I have in most of what is being written now by the whole community of "avant-garde" composers.

—Leonard Bernstein, *The Infinite Variety of Music*

The 1960s were not only turbulent culturally, politically, and socially, but musically as well. Throughout the twentieth century, seemingly countless approaches to composition arose, some of which were used as tools and occasionally as weapons. After a cursory survey of the conflict between the tonal and atonal streams of modernism (with their assumed political messages), we look at Bernstein's thoughts on the conflict as seen in his talks and writings, and how he dealt with these influences in his own works. Fellow composers and critics were not hesitant to criticize him and his endeavors. We conclude with a detailed view of how he addressed modernism in his *Young People's Concerts*: the works he scheduled, his explanations of modernist techniques, and his very definite opinions on modernism.

For the public, Bernstein simplified the seemingly countless approaches to composition in the twentieth century by reducing the issues down to two—tonal versus atonal. He described modern music as being "divided into two camps, tonal and atonal, with [Igor] Stravinsky and [Arnold] Schoenberg as the top heap-big chiefs" (Bernstein 1959, 234; see also Bernstein 1976, 270).[1] In his introduction to his 1964 Philharmonic series "The Avant-Garde," Bernstein employed the term "reactionary" for those composers who embraced tonality (Bernstein 2000, CD 9, track 4). Such works use (to some degree) tonality, modality, bitonality, rhythmic regularity, and/or clarity of structure. In the aforementioned Philharmonic series, as well as innumerable writings, he employed the term "avant garde" for those composers who embraced the more experimental approaches to twentieth-century music (see Bernstein 1959, 193; Bernstein 1982, 233). Those works use (to some degree) elements of atonality, serialism, ambiguity, and/or complexity. This discussion will reduce modernism to tonal versus atonal as the maestro did, differentiated by his terms "reactionary" and "avant garde" respectively.

THE CONFLICT BETWEEN REACTIONARY AND AVANT-GARDE MODERNISM

More than ever before, composers in the twentieth century waxed eloquent on their philosophy of music, their approach to composing as found in their own works, and their opinions of both the writings and compositions of other composers.[2] Furthermore, music was wielded as one of the weapons in the cultural arsenal during the Cold War.[3] The following highlights musical factors from the beginning of the twentieth century to the early 1970s that influenced Bernstein and his *Young People's Concerts*.

Music in the early twentieth century remained tonal while expanding on and reinterpreting ideas inherited from the late romantic. As composers continued the search for new ways of writing more expressive music, works became more international in style. At the core of this approach was "unremitting innovation" and an originality that focused more and more on atonality and "pervasive dissonance" (Simms 1999, 2). These composers followed a path shaped by Beethoven and Wagner, believing that they should aim such innovative music at audiences of the future who (they presumed) would be more receptive than contemporary ones (ibid.). Then the overwhelming devastation wrought by World War I led to the most profound changes ever seen in the history of music. Two camps formed by the 1930s. On the one hand, some composers replaced the emotionalism and freedom found in the nineteenth and early-twentieth centuries with a cool objectivity and adherence to rigid forms and principles. Schoenberg's 1934 lecture, *Composition with Twelve Tones*, clarifies: "Form in the arts, and especially in music, aims primarily at comprehensibility. The relaxation which a satisfied listener experiences when he can follow an idea, its development, and the reasons for such development is closely related, psychologically speaking, to a feeling of beauty" (Schoenberg 1941 in Morgan 1998, 86).

Schoenberg equates form with beauty. He continues: "Artistic value demands comprehensibility, not only for intellectual, but also for emotional satisfaction" (ibid.). If an audience did not appreciate a work, he felt it was because they did not understand it. He admits that atonal works "have failed to gain an understanding" but accurately suggests that contemporary judgments "are generally overruled by history" (ibid.).[4] Presumably future listeners would better understand and appreciate such works as they became more accustomed to dissonance, as they had throughout history.

On the other hand, a more democratic attitude led some composers to write a kind of *Gebrauchsmusik* (functional music or music for use) that served the community with approachable music that might incorporate popular styles. By the 1930s, this regionalist-populist approach evolved in the hands of such composers as Aaron Copland and Ralph Vaughan Williams (Simms 1999, 70). Copland and other American composers consciously wrote tonal, accessible, nationalistic music during the Great Depression to lift the spirits of their fellow Americans during a time of great national strife.[5] Around the same time Copland was writing such reactionary works as his ballet *Billy the Kid* (1938), Joseph Stalin began his iron control of composers in the USSR, just prior to the Great Terror (1936–1938). Soviet composers were compelled by the state to abandon any semblance of formalism (or form for its own sake) in music, to embrace the Romantic tradition, and to compose in the state-approved reactionary style known as Socialist Realism. To best serve "the people" Soviet music had to be tonal and melodic.

In 1937 and 1938, German *Entartete Kunst* (degenerate art) and *Entartete Musik* exhibits similarly politicized music under Hitler. Atonal music, jazz, and works by Jewish composers in particular were branded as degenerate. Cultural wares had already become a political weapon for many nations by the 1930s but were not widely wielded in the United States until the Cold War (Dizard 2004, 147).

World War II never really ended. It grew into what was known as the Cold War, which lasted for decades and begat an arms race, a space race, and eventually even an arts race. Some of the political aspects of this conflict are covered in chapter 5, but there were musical ramifications as well. Governments of both the Communist East and the free West began touting their approach to music as representative of the best their political system offered. In the face of restrictive Socialist Realist policies, Western composers declared themselves free for the first time of all influences, whether from royalty, the church, the state, or even audiences. Actively sanctioned by their government, many moved toward a musical aesthetic of dissonance, density, difficulty, and complexity that purported to represent freedom and democracy (Ross 2007, 356).

The resulting aesthetic war eventually pitted composer against composer and occasionally composer against audience. As listeners became more puzzled and distanced from this challenging new music, many composers became obdurate in their quest for innovation at all costs (see Kopp 2006). Attacks between those who espoused different approaches to composition became even more acerbic.

The year 1949 was pivotal in the culture wars, as seen in publications and events that fueled the contentious debates. Theodor Adorno spearheaded attacks on music he deemed retrogressive in his 1949 book *Philosophy of New Music*. Here he stated that Stravinsky's neo-classical preservation of tonality was evidence of Fascism, that Hindemith's adherence to tonal principles was Nazi kitsch, and that "Copland's *Lincoln Portrait* could be found on the gramophone of every Stalinist intellectual" (Adorno 1949, 209 in Ross 2007, 356–357). Adorno further asserted that Schoenberg had pointed the true path into the future and that familiar or conventional aspects of music must be eradicated; since Schoenberg had been denounced by both Hitler and Stalin, his music perforce was as far as possible from their repressive philosophies (Ross 2007, 357). Schoenberg even linked Copland with Stalin by suggesting that both men were suppressing his music (Crist and Shirley 2006, 196–197). René Leibowitz agreed, stating in *Schoenberg and His School* that "our century has produced *only* three musical geniuses of the twentieth century"—Schoenberg and his disciples, Alban Berg and Anton Webern—and that only atonality offered "uncompromising *moral strength*" (Leibowitz 1949, xvi). The Cultural and Scientific Conference for World Peace at the Waldorf-Astoria Hotel in New York held 25 through 27 March 1949 (attended by both Russians and Americans, such as Dmitry Shostakovich, Copland, and Bernstein) brought the propaganda battle between East and West to the fore and severely compromised the reputations of many American reactionaries who attended, Bernstein among them (see Ross 2007, 373–378). Thereafter, any composer who wrote in a tonal, accessible manner was suspected of pandering to commercial interests, colluding with Communists, or lacking individuality and courage.

After 1950, a new generation of musicians swept in bringing new approaches to composition that expanded on the audience-confounding atonal complexities of the recent past. The polarity between the avant-garde and reactionaries grew wider as the former embraced more complicated techniques. Compositional control became even more important to these young musicians, hence serialism of pitch was extended to include dynamics, articulations, rhythms, registers, and other factors, resulting in total serialism. For them, depersonalization and conformity supplanted romanticism and individuality. Concurrently, another branch of compositional thought called chance music developed that was diametrically opposed to such rigid control and instead emphasized freedom. Its champion was John Cage, whose explorations of Eastern philosophies such as Zen Buddhism led him to first seek a kind of internal peace represented musically through silence. His most famous piece is entitled 3'44" in which the soloist sits silently for that length of time. Cage next turned to creating frameworks filled with unplanned sounds that in essence had two goals, that of allowing the performer the freedom to react musically to the inspiration of the moment and allowing the audience to aesthetically be in the present. The 1961 publication of Cage's book *Silence: Lectures and Writings* and his compositions by C. F. Peters brought the composer international fame. His philosophies had a greater impact on twentieth-century music than any other American composer, as chance music (also known as indeterminacy or aleatoric music) became an important facet of modernism in the 1960s. The aural effect for most listeners, however, was strikingly similar to total serialism—seemingly chaotic sounds.

Musical extremes came to represent political extremes. Through the 1950s and 1960s, atonality purported to demonstrate the aesthetic diversity possible when artists were free as in a democracy. Reactionary music, on the other hand, was said to represent the aesthetic repression of composers living under Communism who were forced to write in the state-approved uniform style of Socialist Realism. Nicolas Nabukov, a leader in the avant-garde camp, was at the time in the pay of the CIA and served as general secretary of the Congress for Cultural Freedom from 1951 through 1966.[6] He endeavored to offer balance in the 1952 Masterpieces of the Twentieth Century festival by scheduling tonal works by Benjamin Britten and Virgil Thomson next to avant-garde works by Pierre Boulez, but this attempt led the latter to accuse Nabukov of engineering a "folklore of mediocrity" and to derisively suggest that future festivals could celebrate the "role of the condom in the twentieth-century" (Saunders 1999, 224; Ross 2007, 387).

This statement is very typical of Boulez. The young man became the avatar of the avant-garde through his writings and actions, soon leading like-thinking composers to attack reactionary composers. He incited others to boo, shout, and whistle during performances of Stravinsky's works, turn their backs on pieces by Henri Dutilleux, and walk out on those by Hans Werner Henze (Ross 2007, 361, 362, 392). Boulez eventually even turned against the father of serialism, Schoenberg. In his 1952 obituary for the elder composer, Boulez accused Schoenberg of having composed "a stream of infuriating clichés and formidable stereotypes redolent of the most wearily ostentatious

romanticism" because Schoenberg did not embrace total serialism, that is se-
rializing rhythm, structure, and form as well as pitch (Boulez 1952 in Simms
1999, 149).

Acrimonious statements about those who preferred reactionary music
were directed not only at composers but at audiences as well. In an issue of *La
Revue musicale*, Boulez wrote, "we assert, for our part that any musician who
has not experienced—we do not say understood, but experienced—the necessity of the dodecaphonic language is USELESS."[7] Such vitriolic comments
insulted not only the composers of reactionary music but also demeaned the
audiences who appreciated it. Nabokov, for his part, impugned audiences who
favored tonal music in a letter to Stravinsky. He wrote that Sergei Prokofiev
had "begun to fall into a kind of bourgeois infantilism. And Shostakovich's
Eight Symphony is simply impossible to listen to. Such *merde* is imposed on
the naively stupid, apathetic, and profoundly uncultivated American public by
orchestra conductors . . . who exploit the stupidest emotions of the people in
this cultural desert" (Stravinsky 1982–1985, 376). Those in the avant-garde
camp were acerbic and vocal in their disgust with reactionary music, its composers, and those who enjoyed it.

Some composers intentionally moved from creating beauty (as mentioned by both Bernstein and Schoenberg) to presenting harsh ugliness
with their works. In a conversation with Calvin Tomkins, Cage asserted, "I
am going toward violence rather than tenderness, hell rather than heaven,
ugly rather than beautiful, impure rather than pure—because by doing these
things they become transformed, and we become transformed" (Tomkins
1968, 144). Elliott Carter, another important figure in American modernism through the fifties and sixties, represents a stance taken by many
composers. He abandoned tonal music for complexity and difficulty in the
late forties, declaring, "I decided for once to write a work very interesting
to myself, and so to hell with the public and with the performers too"
(Schiff 1998, 55). Carter could manage this because he was independently
wealthy. Most other avant-garde composers earned a living by finding ref-
uge in universities.

Milton Babbitt believed that composers needed to cloister themselves
in academic ivory towers (that is, the university) in order to conquer what he
called the frontiers of knowledge without distractions (Watkins 1988, 530).
Since laymen could not understand advances in mathematics and theoretical
physics, he opined that it was not surprising they could not understand advances in music (Babbitt 1958 in Simms 1999, 154, 156–157). He elucidated
on the total freedom the composer could have in America in his oft-quoted
article "Who Cares If You Listen?"[8]

I dare suggest that the composer would do himself and his music an immediate and eventual service by total, resolute, and voluntary withdrawal from
this public world to one of private performance and electronic media, with
its very real possibility of complete elimination of the public and social
aspects of musical composition. By so doing the separation between the
domains would be defined beyond any possibility of confusion of categories, and the composer would be free to pursue a private life of professional
achievement, as opposed to a public life of unprofessional compromise and
exhibitionism. (158)

Babbitt listed the assets of this new music, which included increased "efficiency" and reduced redundancy; he felt that the structure of a work should
be "unique to the individual work itself" rather than following preconceived
guidelines. He declared that this would effectively move the principles of
musical composition forward despite the "greater and new demands" on "the
perceptual and conceptual abilities of the listener" (154–155). Composers
had to write elaborate and complex explanations since each avant-garde work
employed a different approach, and these "guidebooks" demonstrated the
scientific nature of their methodology (155). Such prose was often difficult
to follow and although fascinating did not usually enhance the listening experience as the principles were inaudible to the average listener. Later avant-
garde composers were not seeking beauty. They tried instead to trail-blaze
a path for the music of the future through self-expression and innovation,
composing for small audiences of aficionados without concern for pleasing
the mainstream audience.

Freedom was an oft-repeated byword, at Nabokov's festivals as well as
at the Darmstadt Summer Courses for New Music that featured works of
serialists such as Boulez and Karlheinz Stockhausen. Not everyone, however,
felt that serialism and atonality really offered freedom. When Henze attended
Darmstadt as a young composer, he grew frustrated with the unwritten ban
on tonality, and in his memoirs, he wrote in "bitterly mocking terms of
its faddish tendencies" (Ross 2007, 393). Henze observed that "everything
had to be stylized and made abstract" and "discipline was the order of the
day" (ibid.). Audiences would be comprised of experts, while "music-lovers,
music-consumers" were ignored (Henze 1982, 40). When confronted with
"philistines," avant-garde disciples should feel "contempt" and "smug."
Adorno (revered at Darmstadt) asserted that "any encounter with the listeners that was not catastrophic and scandalous would defile the artist" and that
a composer must "write music that would repel, shock, and be the vehicle
for 'unmitigated cruelty'" (41). Henze was one of many composers who were
dismayed and embittered by the avant-garde establishment.

Despite the atonal tsunami, some reactionaries did fight behind the scenes to promote tonality and pull it away from its communist associations, as seen in recent research by Emily Abrams Ansari. Howard Hanson, Thomson, and William Schuman were the three composers on the Music Advisory Panel of the American National Theater and Academy (MAP), which was in charge of selecting performers for international goodwill tours financed by the State Department from 1954 through 1963. It was a requirement that a work by an American composer be heard at every concert. These three men selected performers whose proposed programs consisted of music with three characteristics: American, highbrow, and *tonal* (Ansari 2012b, 41–47). Their demand that only highbrow music be performed resulted in the rejection of any composition with the slightest jazz flavor. Applications including two famous, successful American composers, Bernstein and George Gershwin, were consistently denied, as were Copland's jazz-influenced pieces (Ansari 2012b, 48). MAP was also not interested in providing a broad spectrum selection of American music styles, as evidenced by budgeting that favored classically trained performers (83 percent) (46). Like many, Bernstein found a way to get around these restrictions while supporting American tonal composers. During the Philharmonic tour in Moscow, the maestro and the orchestra were filmed for a television program to be broadcast in the United States. Ansari explains how Bernstein used the event to promote the American tonal style of composing and distance tonality from its communist associations (2012a).

Composers reacted to the avant-garde movement in different ways. Some, like Stravinsky and Carter, abandoned the old ways and wholeheartedly adopted the new. Others, such as Britten, Copland, and Roger Sessions, wove their own modified versions of avant-garde techniques into their more traditional pieces. Béla Bartók designed his own blend of folk and avant-garde. Still others, such as Arthur Honneger and Hindemith, rejected the new style entirely and became vocal advocates for tonality (see Hindemith 1945). Britten generally ignored the polemics (Britten 1964 in Simms 1999, 175–181). Reactionary composers did continue to write in the 1950s and 1960s, developing a conservative style that was an extension of the neoclassicism and populism from the beginning of the century. This more traditional language was particularly popular in the United States with such composers as Samuel Barber, Bernstein, Copland, David Diamond, and Schuman. Simms suggests that their music was "demoted to a secondary status" and typically ignored by the contemporary musical establishment, only gaining attention after the Cold War ended in 1991 (144).

This is the world that surrounded Bernstein. Audiences rejected art music by avant-garde composers who seemed intent on driving them away.

Reactionary composers were suspected by their government of Communist leanings, disdained by critics and their colleagues, but embraced by audiences hungry for "beautiful" music.

BERNSTEIN AS MODERNIST COMPOSER

Bernstein's dedication to tonal, accessible music caused both critics and some of his fellow composers to deride him as a reactionary, yet audiences were drawn to his works while spurning those considered innovative and cutting-edge. He achieved such audience appeal, in part, not by dismissing the hallmarks of the avant-garde (such as atonality, serialism, or extended techniques) but by reserving them for moments that were dramatically appropriate to the angst those sounds created (Laird 2002, 17). These usually involved deep negative emotion (such as anger or stress in *Symphony No. 3: Kaddish* and *Songfest*). James Walter Moore provides an analysis of Bernstein's use of tonality in six of the maestro's compositions, two each from the 1950s, 1960s, and 1970s (1984). Tonality was "an important and omnipresent factor" in Bernstein's music but employed in a non-traditional manner, which Moore describes in detail (161). It did not unify large forms, although it could unify sections or movements. Moore finds no chronological evolution to Bernstein's tonal style (164). In his research guide, Paul R. Laird describes Bernstein's compositional style and how he created such appealing music (Laird 2002, 13–43). The maestro reveled in lyrical melodies yet incorporated attractive disjunct leaps that seem almost pointillistic, such as "Tonight" from *West Side Story* (18–19). His rhythms were vital and incorporated asymmetrical meters or shifting meters such as those favored by the avant-garde; he, however, used them in regular, recognizable patterns, such as in the 7/4 opening of *Chichester Psalms* (22–23). Rather than eschewing popular music, he freely wove in various musical elements from vernacular styles, such as blues, jazz, Latin, Broadway, and rock (32–37). Abstract techniques are reserved for extra-musical reasons such as "conflict, confusion, mysticism, or depression" (Moore 1984, 164). The average music-lover would almost always find something approachable and appealing. In 1970 Bernstein wrote to Jack Gottlieb specifically about his use of twelve-tone rows. Bernstein said that as a composer he employed rows to show hysteria ("Galop" from *Fancy Free*), boredom ("Quiet" from *Candide*), dislocation (*The Age of Anxiety*), blind groping (ditto), dogmaticism (*Mass*), and despair (*Mass*). Bernstein concludes saying, "does this seem to say something about the serial world?" (Gottlieb 2010, 146).

Bernstein's reactionary compositional style in his classical works caused difficulties with the critics. Joan Peyser remembers that "there was a point when everybody was attacking Bernstein because he was such a conservative figure and was writing and conducting only tonal music. [Harold] Schonberg [Bernstein's nemesis at the *New York Times*] was attacking him on this even though he [Schonberg] hated post-Schoenberg work; whatever these guys did they couldn't win" (W. W. Burton 1995, 49). She assumed that Bernstein "always wanted to be seen as *au courant,* to be thought of as avant-garde, even by incorporating some twelve-tone material into his own works." She felt that since "his heart was in tonality" that he should have "stayed in the popular music field" where tonality reigned unquestioned (49–50). In truth, his Broadway shows were enthusiastically received, but his compositions for the concert hall were held to different standards. While some critics gave his works good reviews, others felt that their accessibility diminished their worth. The *Boston Globe* called *Jeremiah* "the best new work of the year," yet Thomson (*Herald Tribune,* 19 February 1944) dismissed *Jeremiah* saying that it had "a certain charm that should give it a temporary popularity" (in H. Burton 1994, 124). Critic Cynthia Jolly praised *Serenade* for "Bernstein's luminous communicative powers and his buoyant musicianship," while the *Herald Tribune* (11 February 1966) rudely belittled *Serenade* as "drab, tawdry and derivative—leaving the listener with the feeling of having spent the time nibbling on a dietetic cotton candy" (in H. Burton 1994, 240, 351). In the *Washington Post* article "Bernstein's Mass: A Reaffirmation of Faith" (9 September 1971), Paul Hume named *Mass* "a rich amalgamation of the theatrical arts" in a "luxuriant fabric" with "power to overwhelm," and "the greatest music Bernstein has ever written." But the more influential review came from Schonberg. He called *Mass* "vulgar trash" amid a few weak compliments in "Bernstein's New Work Reflects His Background on Broadway" (*New York Times,* 9 September 1971). Schonberg continued by dismissing Bernstein as "a composer of skillful lightweight music who can turn out a snappy tune or a sweet-flowing ballad," but who is "thrown for a loss" when writing serious music such as *Jeremiah* and *Kaddish*: "The serious musical content is pretentious and thin." His second review of *Mass* for the *Times* ten days later reported that the work was "a combination of superficiality and pretentiousness, and the greatest mélange of styles since the ladies' magazine recipe for steak fried in peanut butter and marshmallow sauce" (19 September 1971). Positive reviews did not ameliorate the negative effects of such assaults.

Even fellow composers chastised Bernstein for being insufficiently avant-garde. Writing tonal, lyrical music was evidently a mark of being incompetent, too commercial, or painfully old-fashioned to these critics and composers. John Adams, for example, admitted "ragging on" Bernstein about it as a young man (Philip Kennicott, *Washington Post*, 22 June 2010). Although the young student felt that "Boulez's was the wrong way to make art," Adams dutifully tried to "embrace the beast" (Adams 2008, 32). After hearing the *Chichester Psalms*, he wrote Bernstein chiding him about living in the past, disregarding the new compositional methods that favored logic.[9] To his surprise and pleasure, the maestro sent a long and kind reply for Adams's "intelligent letter." He observed that "one writes what one hears *within* one," that he could not "conceive music (my own music) divorced from tonality," and that "the only meaningful thing is the truth of the creative act" (Simeone 2013, 477). Clearly tonality was integral to Bernstein's musical soul.

Schonberg claimed that the barbs from critics had no effect whatsoever on Bernstein: "what difference did an unfavorable review make to him except to bruise his ego?" (Schonberg 1981, 27). The maestro's friend, protégé, and colleague, John Mauceri, revealed that Bernstein was in fact very wounded by the comments of critics and other composers, as confirmed by the Hindemith program discussed in chapter 2 ("Working with Bernstein" at "Leonard Bernstein: Boston to Broadway" symposia at Harvard University, 14 October 2006). Mauceri specified Schonberg's venomous reviews as one of the main reasons Bernstein left New York. He suggested that Schonberg could not understand Bernstein's interpretations and therefore derided them. Eventually, the dreadful reception critics in New York gave Bernstein drove him to flee to Vienna, where he received a warmer welcome (ibid.).

Bernstein took a sabbatical from most of his duties at the Philharmonic during the 1964–1965 season to allow himself time to compose. He joked about being old-fashioned in his post-sabbatical poem published by the *New York Times*. After he "brooded and mused" about "unconventionality," "the death . . . of tonality," "serial strictures, the dearth of romance," and "pieces for nattering, clucking sopranos," he composed the *Chichester Psalms* (Bernstein 1982, 237). He wrote that,

> These psalms are a simple and modest affair,
> Tonal and tuneful and somewhat square,
> Certain to sicken a stout John Cager
> With its tonics and triads in E-flat major.
> But there it stands—the result of my pondering,
> Two long months of avant-garde wandering—
> My youngest child, old-fashioned and sweet.
> And he stands on his own two tonal feet. (ibid.)[10]

Bernstein's compositions suffered a similar fate as did other reactionary works at the time, being demeaned, categorized as middlebrow or popular, therefore secondary, pieces, or simply ignored. By the twenty-first century, compositions like *Mass* and more recently *A Quiet Place* (in a revised version) are finally being rediscovered, performed, and recorded.

BERNSTEIN ON MODERNISM

In his inimitable fashion (and possibly partly in self-defense), Bernstein also expounded on his philosophy of composing and his interpretation of the schism in twentieth-century music.[11] As mentioned earlier, he reduced the seemingly innumerable approaches to composition in the twentieth century to a simple conflict between tonality versus atonality (with Stravinsky and Schoenberg as representatives) for his audiences and readers. He consistently supported tonality and accessibility through his selection of works for the Philharmonic (favoring his fellow reactionaries), through his explanations, and through surreptitious (and perhaps unconscious) negative comments about avant-garde modernism that found their way into his talks and writings. His friend Humphrey Burton notes that Bernstein also "did not appreciate abstract art. For a time he mocked it openly, hanging a painting done by a chimpanzee over his living room fireplace and inviting comments from his friends on his expensive acquisition" (1994, 332).

Bernstein could not ignore such an extremely powerful movement in the world of music, so he did commission, schedule, and talk about modernism and representative pieces.[12] Modernist composers, both reactionary and avant-garde, thanked him for his support.[13] His commissions for the Philharmonic ran the gamut from jazz works by Gunther Schuller to avant-garde by Milton Babbitt.[14] He scheduled for the Philharmonic a two-season survey of the symphony in the twentieth century for 1964–65 and 1965–66.[15] The first season included works by Gustav Mahler, Jean Sibelius, Vaughan Williams, Webern, Prokofiev, Shostakovich, Charles Ives, Copland, Roy Harris, Leo Smit, and Diamond (Ardoin 1965, 37). The second season proposed to cover Schoenberg, Hindemith, Mahler, Schuman, Carter, Albert Roussel, Honegger, and Sessions (ibid.). Most of Bernstein's programming selections were reactionary, with few representing the avant-garde. He also scheduled a series he called "The Search for Nothingness" that examined minimalist music and another called "The Avant-Garde."[16] Of course, the critics, especially Schonberg, acidly complained about both Bernstein's talks and the way the maestro "snugly fitted" avant-garde works by Iannis Xenakis and György Ligeti between more traditional ones by Maurice Ravel and Camille Saint-Saëns to satisfy the conventional tastes of the regular concert-goers. Bernstein must have felt that good programming that would keep the audience in their seats required surrounding an avant-garde work with a more traditional one. Alan Rich quotes his own article from the *Herald Tribune* (n.d.) in which he describes the audience reaction to the Philharmonic performance of Cage's chance piece *Atlas Eclipticalis* during the Avant Garde festival in the winter of 1964 (Bernstein 2000, 85). He suggests that "[Mr. Cage] could have added to the interest by putting bells on the exit doors. . . . They would have drowned out the music." Despite the sniping, the audiences enjoyed Bernstein's programming and explanations. Gottlieb reports that "in his unjustly criticized Thursday evening previews . . . it was patently obvious that audiences savored his urbane talks" (2010, 152). For example, Bernstein was unable to conduct the final avant-garde program entitled "Music of Chance" (featuring works by Cage). Without Bernstein there to lavish his preparatory remarks on the audience, the orchestra "was roundly booed by hundreds of patrons in some of the noisiest scenes ever witnessed at a Philharmonic concert" (H. Burton 1994, 342). With Bernstein's explanations, they gave the avant-garde a chance; without them, they did not.

The maestro supported the top avant-garde composers, worked to understand their pieces, then played them to the best of his abilities. He studied the music as he would one of his beloved puzzles, then relished sharing his insights. His respect for the avant-garde is seen in comments from composers and performers. Peyser incorrectly assumed (as she often did) that "when [Bernstein] performed twelve-tone music it was often with an effort to show how bad it was" (W. W. Burton 1995, 49). However, Orin O'Brien (the first woman hired as a regular member of the New York Philharmonic) remembered that Bernstein would take a contemporary work "apart in front of you until you not only played it better, but understood it better. And eventually he made you love it" (O'Brien 2000, 79). Lukas Foss felt Bernstein understood his avant-garde work *Phorion* almost better than Foss himself, as described later in this chapter. Carter trusted the maestro wanted only the best when performing his *Concerto for Orchestra*—he met with the maestro then sent a long, detailed letter about interpretation (Simeone 2013, 499–501). Cage wrote Bernstein saying how he (Morton Feldman and Earle Brown, as well) admired and respected Bernstein's courage for performing his work despite the hostility many felt, and how grateful he was for the exposure (Simeone 2013, 453). Xenakis said that he was proud and happy that Bernstein included his work in Philharmonic concerts and that the conductor was transforming New York into a center for new music (458). Bernstein understood such music and tried to serve it well in performance.

Even though he lavished great care and effort on performing a work of the avant-garde, Bernstein's natural proclivities caused it to fall from his memory. Occasionally, his assistant Gottlieb and Bernstein would play a guessing game when listening to the classical music radio station in New York, WQXR. Once a modernist orchestral piece was playing, and neither man could even hazard a guess as to the composer or work. Once the music stopped, the announcer said, "You have just heard Elliott Carter's Concerto for Orchestra with the New York Philharmonic, conducted by Leonard Bernstein." After recounting this tale, Gottlieb simply says, "let that sink in and speak for itself" (Gottlieb 2010, 50).

Bernstein's negative opinions of the avant garde sometimes crept into his discourse on television and at concerts. Adams remembered that "Bernstein could not overcome a deep-seated antipathy, an almost gut reaction against it" (Bernstein and Haws 2008, 203). Gunther Schuller chided him for unfairly allowing his negative personal views of the avant-garde to seep into his 1957 *Omnibus*, "Introduction to Modern Music" (Simeone 2013, 357).[17] Although the script presented facts accurately, his slightly sarcastic delivery made his own opinions clear. Peyser reports that when Bernstein was expounding on post-Schoenberg music, "what he did was crazy—he would apologize for it to the audience." She reported that "Gunther Schuller remembered [Bernstein] apologizing in advance to an audience for doing a Stockhausen work. He would say: 'I know you're going to hate this, but you've got to listen to it, it's the right thing to do'" (W. W. Burton 1995, 49). That does not sound like an apology so much as Bernstein sharing his own thoughts. In his outline for the program never written entitled "Russian Music—Then and Now," he says, "if ten people like it, they have the right to hear it" (box/folder 1024/8). Apparently he felt the need to perform it for those ten people (see chapter 5). The ten-CD collection from 2000, entitled *Leonard Bernstein LIVE*, provides the opportunity to actually hear Bernstein addressing the audience of the Philharmonic avant-garde series. In his 1960 introduction to the entire series, he says,

> Some new music has reached the mathematical complexity that staggers the mind, whereas other new music has reverted to a semi-idiotic simplicity where two notes spaced a minute apart can constitute a sonata. For that matter, to the neo-Dada notion of no notes at all [audience chuckles lightly] or in some extreme cases, the notion of dropping a herring down into a tuba and calling it a musical happening or moment or event or conceivably a sonata for herring and tuba [audience laughs]. (Bernstein 2000, CD 9, track 1)

Bernstein got his expected titters and laughs. His disdain is obvious when he introduces the 1964 world première of Xenakis's *Pithoprakta*:

> In the work, each player has his own part, resulting in forty-six different string parts being played at once and all being controlled by a series of

highly advanced mathematical formulae. It's like a piece of gigantic chamber music and of course no human conductor can possibly hear all those
different notes and check on them. Nor, in fact, could Mr. Xenakis himself, I believe, if he were here [audience titters]. Therefore every member
of the orchestra is on the honor system [audience laughs for a long time]
but I trust them [audience laughs again], as must you, as we must all trust
the composer himself. (CD 9, track 4)

He then says, "but quite seriously," but the impression is set in stone.

What arguably worried Bernstein the most about avant-garde music
was the growing gap between composer and listener. As we saw in the first
epigraph to this chapter, Bernstein described the 1960s as not only "a critical moment in the history of music" but "a *scary* moment" (Bernstein 1966,
9). Scary, he said, because there had always been "some relation between
composer and public, a symbiotic interaction that has fed both" in the past.
He added a human element to the tonal versus atonal controversy when he
said that the relationship had changed into almost "composer *versus* public"
(ibid.). Bernstein believed that a composer functions for the sake of society
and, by the 1960s, was dismayed that audiences seemed to no longer anticipate the arrival of new classical works with the delight they once had for a
new Puccini opera or Brahms symphony (Bernstein 1966, 9–10). Popular
music by performers such as Simon and Garfunkel or The Association,
however, did inspire joyful anticipation. He believed that the hope for the
future of music lay not with the atonality that drove most audiences away
but with tonality (10).

Bernstein's most eloquent defense of tonality is possibly in the last two of
his *The Unanswered Question, Six Talks at Harvard*, known as the Norton Lectures (Bernstein 1976, 263–425). Here Bernstein stated that one of the main
questions in both the Ives piece of the same name and in the twentieth century
concerned the future of tonality. In his role as Harvard scholar, Bernstein asked,
"is tonality eternal, immortal? Many have thought so, and some still do. . . . Do
you see how clearly [Ives's *The Unanswered Question*] spells out the dilemma
of the new century?" (269). He admitted that the problem was not quite as
simplistic as tonality versus atonality, since many composers embraced both.
Atonality, he suggested, did not stand alone in total opposition to tonality. He
felt that tonality "haunted" much atonal music since such compositions are constructed from the twelve tones found in a traditional Western scale. Bernstein
then described what he felt were underlying tonal relationships within tone
rows by Schoenberg and, of course, Alban Berg (291–307).[18] Berg's *Wozzeck*
offers, he opined, an excellent demonstration of the tonal-atonal ambiguity and
the use of atonality for dramatic reasons (297–299).

Bernstein declared that atonality should be used when dramatically appropriate, as seen over ten years earlier in "The Genius of Paul Hindemith"

(23 February 1964) during his explanation of the program for the third movement of *Mathis der Mahler*, "the Temptation of St. Anthony." To represent the saint being "plagued and tortured by all kinds of monsters and demons," Hindemith opens the movement with what "sounds almost like a 12-tone row" to represent "this grotesque, scary atmosphere." Bernstein asserts that "it's exactly right in this place, because it describes the feeling of tension and agony with amazing accuracy" (26). The maestro believed that atonality had its place but could not supplant tonality, which he felt was central to human existence and can be neither ignored nor denied (see also Cott 2013, 143).

Bernstein sensed that the music of the future would hold "untold aspects of beauty" (Bernstein 1966, 11). The desire for communication—which he defined as "the tenderness we feel when we recognize and share with another human being a deep, unnamable, elusive emotional shape or shade"—would lead us there (ibid.). All we need to do is to wait for the world to recognize this. "All forms that we have ever known . . . have always been conceived in *tonality*," which he believed was "built into the human organism" (12). "We are still earth creatures, still needful of human warmth and the need to communicate among ourselves," and abandoning tonality would require an unforeseen "fundamental change in our physical laws" (13). When a composer denies pitches "their tonal implications," he leaves "the world of communication" (12). The maestro's reactionary musical attitudes were motivated by his desire to communicate and to contact other human beings.

Communication and people were integral to Bernstein's life. After reading tens of thousands of letters to and from Bernstein, Nigel Simeone chose the title "Ten Thousand Intimate Friends" for his Library of Congress talk about his book of the maestro's letters. On 17 January 1939 the young Bernstein wrote Kenneth Ehrman, "you may remember my chief weakness—my love for people" (Simeone 2013, 27). He formally affirmed this love when he wrote his credo in 1954 for a radio series entitled *This I Believe* (Bernstein 1982, 137–139).[19] He began by stating, "I believe in people. I feel, love, need, and respect people above all else," and ended with, "we must believe in people" (137, 139). Those he performed with cherished that quality. Michael Henoch of the Chicago Symphony Orchestra said that Bernstein loved being surrounded by people so much that he would stay on stage and talk to the musicians on breaks rather than disappear to his dressing room as many conductors did (Sherman 2010, 35).[20]

His friends and colleagues, such as Craig Urquhart (Vice President of Public Relations and Promotion at the Leonard Bernstein Office) and Gottlieb, agree that what the maestro did best was connecting to others. When he spoke to you, he gave you his total attention (Craig Urquhart, "Leonard

Bernstein: Boston to Broadway," Symposium at Harvard University, 14 October 2006; Gottlieb 2010, 19). Urquhart added that teaching is connecting and that he made each student feel confident enough to strive for perfection. At the same symposium, Mauceri said, in essence, that Bernstein made you feel as if you were the center of the universe when he spoke with you; Nina Bernstein gasped when she heard this, perhaps because she felt that Mauceri's assessment was so apt. This was one of the maestro's gifts as a teacher, as recalled by Marin Alsop: "I couldn't be nervous because it was almost as if everyone else faded into the background. He was so focused on me."[21] Few can or could connect with their fellow man as well as Bernstein.

In a 1957 improvised address at the University of Chicago, Bernstein waxed eloquent on communication, love, and connection to others (Bernstein 1966, 265–286). Allowing for his tendency to speak in superlatives, the maestro said that communication is "the most written-about, the most discussed word of the twentieth century" (273). Although Erich Fromm claimed that "love is the only way we can obtain any warmth of communication in the world," Bernstein asserted that we can also communicate through art (ibid.). His approach to composition becomes clear when he says that he always thinks of an audience when he composes: "somewhere in the act of writing there is the sense . . . of the people who are going to hear it. [Many composers, past and present] say that they do not sense an audience" (ibid.). But he thinks differently from his composer friends who "insist that they are going to say their say regardless of whether or not anybody ever hears it or not, they don't care" (ibid.). They declare, "I sit in my ivory tower and write this, anyway" (276). Bernstein could never do that.

Since avant-garde composers were obviously not relating to their fellow man, Bernstein tried to understand what was motivating them. At first he thought they might be seeking beauty. In *The Joy of Music*, Bernstein suggested that both reactionary and avant-garde composers were "engaged in the same struggle for new beauty" (Bernstein 1959, 234). Schoenberg mentioned beauty in the 1930s, but the two composers disagreed on the definition of beauty. As mentioned above, Schoenberg felt that musically "comprehensibility" equaled beauty—that the composer should explain his thoughts, and if the audience did not find beauty, it simply did not understand, and perhaps the audience of the future would (Morgan 1998, 86). Bernstein, however, felt beauty lies in music's ability to connect with, to reach out to the listener (Bernstein 1966, 11). In 1957 Bernstein addressed the issue with some frustration: "have modern composers forgotten beauty? Any modern composer will tell you that his artistic goals are exactly the same as Mozart's or Chaikovsky's [*sic*] were: to write beautiful music" (Bernstein 1959, 195). In "The Genius of Paul Hindemith," Bernstein is livid at the back-handed "appreciations" written on the death of his fellow reactionary composer, which inspired him to become more explicit about his own definition of beauty: "that's really what music is about after all—to be expressive of what's inside us; & when we feel that expression to be true, we call it beautiful. But music critics are a strange bunch of people, & they often forget this simple truth. . . . I still find it hard to take when [critics] get so wound up in their own important words & judgments that they forget what's *really* important in music—beauty" (first pencil draft, 2).[22] That same year, the maestro determined that since avant-garde composers were not seeking expression, they must be relating instead in some way to outer "space rather than his fellow man" (Bernstein 2000, CD 9, tracks 1–2). To put it far more simplistically than he did in his talk, Bernstein felt that the bloodbaths of the World Wars that culminated in the destruction of Hiroshima and Nagasaki by atomic bombs made man realize that he was no longer the center of a Copernican universe but just a life on a speck in space (ibid.). Composers now sought, he concluded, connection with a wider universe as found in space. Perhaps this is one reason why he mentions outer space so often in reference to avant-garde music. He had moved on somewhat by 1973 when he suggested that "all twentieth century composers, however split they are, write what they write out of the same need for newer and greater semantic richness; they are all, whether tonal or nontonal, motivated by the same drive, the power of expressivity, the drive to expand music's metaphorical speech, even if they do so in diametrically opposite ways, and split music apart" (Bernstein 1976, 269–270). He still mentions expressivity, but the search for beauty is gone. Since (in his opinion) man must connect to something, he returned to the idea that perhaps they intended to connect to the greatness of outer space rather than mankind. Apparently, Bernstein was constitutionally unable to understand the motivations behind the avant-garde throughout his life.

Bernstein found justification for avoiding experimental modernism in the words of the people, as seen in fan mail and a letter from his mother. A 1964 *Senior Scholastic* magazine article published several fan letters to him. Among them were two from adults who complained when Bernstein performed modernist music on a *Young People's Concert*: "What a disappointing program you presented last night [on contemporary composers]. As a teacher I have seen pleasure in the faces of children, but not once did I see it last night" [Philadelphia, PA] and "I just turned off your program [devoted to contemporary music] because it sounded like a bunch of screwballs in a snake pit. I'm sorry to make this statement, but if you had played good music written by Bach, Mozart, Beethoven, or Wagner I know it would be so much better. [Tulsa, Okla.].[23] Robert J. Janda wrote a particularly caustic letter after watching "Farewell to Nationalism" (30 November 1964):

> We were amazed and sadly shocked at the degrading sounds you perpetrated in such things as that German junk [Anton Webern's Five Pieces for Orchestra] and particularly the Fourth of July by Charles Ives. Why would you subject tender youngsters of 7 and 8 years, in your audience to such vile sounds—sounds that disturbed us more than any low down, Class 3 murder and rape pictures on television—when there is so much enjoyable music available. We are disappointed that you, to whom one might look for an uplift in music, would stoop to such soul-wrenching musical atrocities. In Wisconsin, we have Hurley, infamous for its strip teasers and prostitutes, degrading in that way. In New York, we have Leonard Bernstein, who prostitutes music, under the guise of culture—degrading in that way. Why would you do such a thing?

Although this letter is a bit extreme, many (among them his mother, Jennie) found the sounds of the avant-garde disturbing:

> Darling Lenny,
>   I must say dear that I am a bit perplexed about our crop of modern composers. Especially the young and serious ones. David Diamond, Lukas Foss and others. They write such *unhealthy* music. It seems that they strive to make us unhappy. Why oh why darling do they do that? I'm sure they could write beautiful music if they wanted too [*sic*] but no they just won't. Music means to uplift in my language and some of there [*sic*] music is anything but. (letter from Jennie Bernstein to Leonard Bernstein, 6 November 1961)

Bernstein knew that many people held opinions similar to his, yet he did program and expound on avant-garde music to good effect. Joan Goldberg was one of many young fans who wrote thanking Bernstein for helping them appreciate avant-garde music: "the selection I liked best was the Fourth of July by Ives. At first I didn't like that kind of music but now I do. You make learning fun and you conduct music better than anyone else" (1 December 1964). Mrs. Frederick S. Carr is a representative adult who wrote to thank Bernstein for his clear explanations of avant-garde music, saying, "I have also grown to appreciate modern American music—something a classically trained person sometimes struggles with" and concluding with "I am so thankful that there are people like you . . . and hope that we will be able to see more and more of you and your orchestra in the future

(1 February 1958). Despite negative reactions, the maestro did open some minds, which made it all worthwhile.

Bernstein tried to understand what might direct a composer toward either the reactionary or avant-garde and so posited seven possible nonmusical influences (Bernstein 1966, 276–280). The list offers insight into his own internal debates as a composer:

1. "Outer-world things" (277): He gave the example of nationalistic tendencies creeping into the compositional process. He did note that composers can shoehorn what they deem nationalistic ideas into their compositions, but he said, "You can always tell whether it has come from an inner place or an outer place. And *the people who can tell best, strangely enough, are not the critics and not the other composers, but the public* [my italics]" (278). Typically and logically, Bernstein turned away from his adversaries to the people, that is, his audience.
2. "Fashionable trend of the time": He suggested that the "great swing away from tonality or toward tonality" might be the result of slavish devotion to a passing fad rather than greater musical values, which has proven to be true (ibid.).
3. "What will the critics [and fellow composers] say?" (ibid.): His article for the *New York Times* after his sabbatical revealed his own awareness of this issue (Bernstein 1982, 230–238).
4. "Society and the dictates of social structures" (Bernstein 1966, 279): His example (which is, as he says, a "very extreme") is from the Soviet Union, where composers were obliged to write in whatever style was deemed acceptable by the Union of Soviet Socialist Composers at the time of composition. This statement and his thoughts on Shostakovich in "A Birthday Tribute to Shostakovich" (5 January 1966) are rare examples of his overtly addressing communism. Perhaps the difficulties he and many others lived through during the Red Scare were in the back of his mind.
5. "Influences from the other arts" (279): He observes that music is "always a little behind the other arts" (280).
6. Commission: Composers here must follow the dictates of the commission, be it for a specific singer or ensemble, and so forth. The amount of time between the commission and the premier can even determine the length of the work (ibid.).
7. "Self-criticism": His specific examples are "Do not do that, it's derivative. . . . Do not do that, it's out of style. . . . Do not do that, it's vulgar." One can almost hear Bernstein addressing himself (ibid.).

By 1962 he also suggested that "contemporary musical matters . . . suffer generally from overopinionatedness" and that "one of today's most fashionable diseases [is] originat-itis," that is, "music that is 'different' for the sake of being different" (Bernstein 1982, 233; Gottlieb 2010, 148).[24] Bernstein was constitutionally unable to embrace formalism and originality for its own sake, so he went his own reactionary way most of the time. He did seem to take solace in the enthusiastic reception audiences gave his music, despite the carping of critics or other composers.

One of the reasons Bernstein gave for retiring as Music Director of the Philharmonic was the lack of exciting new composers. Koussevitzky had "proudly brought forth one Copland symphony after another, Roy Harris, Bill Schuman, Prokofiev, Stravinsky!" Bernstein had been expecting something similar and found it "so terribly disappointing" when it did not happen: "I don't have anybody to champion. Nor do I have any cause to champion—a movement, a group of composers, a school" (Gruen 1968, 28). His Philharmonic and *Young People's Concerts* spanned the years when the hegemony of the avant-garde overwhelmed the world of music. The composers he mentioned to Gruen were all reactionaries, so perhaps it was the lack of new *tonal* composers that he found so disappointing.

MODERNISM IN BERNSTEIN'S
YOUNG PEOPLE'S CONCERTS

Although Bernstein presented entire programs on such musical concepts as melody ("What Is a Melody?" 21 December 1962), intervals ("Musical Atoms: A Study of Intervals," 29 November 1965), modes ("What Is a Mode?" 23 November 1966), development ("What Makes Music Symphonic?" 13 December 1958), sonata form ("What Is Sonata Form?" 6 November 1964), concerto ("What Is a Concerto?" 28 March 1959), instruments ("Unusual Instruments of the Past, Present, and Future," 27 March 1960), orchestration ("The Sound of an Orchestra," 14 December 1965; "The Anatomy of a Symphony Orchestra," 24 May 1970), and such musical trends as impressionism ("What Is Impressionism?" 1 December 1961), nationalism ("Farewell to Nationalism," 30 November 1964), folk music ("Folk Music in the Concert Hall," 9 April 1961), jazz ("Jazz in the Concert Hall," 11 March 1964), and American music ("What Is American Music?" 1 February 1958), and even acoustics ("The Sound of a Hall," 21 November 1962), there was no single *Young People's Concert* devoted solely to techniques of twentieth-century composition. He did not, however, neglect the topic in other venues. In *Omnibus*, he presented "Introduction to Modern Music," and, as mentioned earlier, he performed surveys of the twentieth-century symphony, minimalism, aleatoric music, and the avant-garde with the Philharmonic. Since the avant-garde was such a force in the musical world, however, Bernstein felt obliged to occasionally include it in his *Young People's Concerts*, which he did by incorporating individual works.

The repertory of the Philharmonic was the guiding force behind the pieces chosen for Bernstein's *Young People's Concerts*. Within the perimeters set forth in chapter 2, he would logically have to select works for these programs that he thought the television audience (both young and old) would enjoy, that he could discuss in an engaging manner, that would work well on the small screen (Roger Englander's concern), and that would showcase the Philharmonic. Seemingly, this would eliminate chance music and electronic music, but both were performed (see below).

Bernstein's polarized and polarizing approach to modernism as seen in his *Young People's Concerts* is revealed by the modernist repertory he scheduled and by the comments he made when discussing the pieces.[25] As seen in appendix F, Bernstein lavishly programmed reactionary works and chose extraordinarily few avant-garde pieces.[26] In the span of fourteen years, he performed over one hundred works by forty-five reactionary composers. Labeling different movements of the same work or song cycle as one performance, ten were repeated once, sometimes only briefly but still enough to remind the audience of the piece and its composer. Four works were performed three times: Copland's *Music for the Theatre*, Richard Strauss's *Rosenkavalier Suite*, Gershwin's *Rhapsody in Blue*, and Prokofiev's *Classical Symphony*. Gershwin's *An American in Paris* received four performances (more than any other single work), varying in length from forty seconds to about eleven and a half minutes. Several reactionary composers were kept in the public eye by appearing on four or more programs: Stravinsky (four), Hindemith (four), Richard Strauss (five), Prokofiev (six), Gershwin (seven), and Ravel (seven). Copland received the most lavish attention with fourteen performances of thirteen works on nine programs. Bernstein's selections for his *Young People's Concerts* show that he believed Copland and Gershwin represented American music at its best. On the other hand, only thirteen works by eight avant-garde composers or teams were chosen, distributed among only six programs. None of the works were repeated, and, excluding Ives, only one composer (Webern, well known for his compositions being extraordinarily brief) reappeared.

When he did perform one of the more challenging works, Bernstein offers his sense of historical perspective. After an excerpt from Nono's *Incontri* in "Farewell to Nationalism," he states, "I don't want you to get the idea that *all* new music sounds like this, or sounds exactly alike. It's just . . . the general trend these days. . . . And I'm not saying that this is either good or bad; it's just a fact of history" (5–6). Bernstein seemed to phlegmatically accept that avant-garde modernism was considered "right and normal" and part of the "general trend these days" as a "fact of history." He pricks the bubble of those who think they invented atonality in the twentieth century in "Liszt and the Devil" (13 February 1972). He points out that the composer uses all twelve tones of the chromatic scale in succession in the keyless opening theme of the *Faust Symphony*: "in other words, Liszt, that daring, brash romantic pioneer, had written the first really *atonal* music a century before atonal music became the thing to write" (10). He shares his idea that atonality was nothing new, just a passing fad.

Specifically in his *Young People's Concerts*, the maestro suggests that young people—who were not so set in their tastes—might be more open to the avant-garde. The thought recurs in several scripts. In Toronto, he notes that "a lot of people, especially grown-ups, get all upset at the idea of hearing modern music. . . . But not you young ones. I find that young people are more open-minded about music; all you care about it whether it's good or bad, whether it's fun to listen to or not—and not how old or new it is" ("Young People's Concert—Toronto, Modern Music from All Over" (2). He wrote similar sentiments in the outline for the never-written program "Russian Music—Then and Now" and in "Young Performers No. 5" (23 December 1963, 13). Even in the first program when he plays Webern's *Six Pieces*, he says, "But I know that *very often* young people can understand *this kind of music* better than older people" then afterward asks "what did you think of it? Pretty special, isn't it? Was it ugly, or funny, or pretty?" ("What Does Music Mean?" 40–41 revised, the words in italics were ad-libbed).[27] Evidently Stravinsky agreed. When asking Stravinsky to participate in a *Young People's Concert* celebrating his birthday in 1962, Bernstein wrote "perhaps you could say a word of greeting to the young people (who, as you have said, understand your music better than anyone!)" (Simeone 2013, 443).

The maestro's reactionary leanings subtly colored his talks. He rarely presented technical explanations without adding his own impressions. First, Bernstein usually added his subjective comments. His discussion of Mozart in "What Is Sonata Form?" is rather typical of his enthusiastic presentations. Bernstein is effusive as he tells the audience to "just sit back and enjoy this glorious first movement of Mozart's Jupiter Symphony" (page labeled "4&5"), then later says, "now that we've had the pure pleasure of hearing that divine Mozart, let's get to work and find out why that music gives us such pleasure" (8), following with "how can we explain the immense popularity and growth of sonata-form over 200 years? What makes it so satisfying, so complete?"

(10). The maestro creates such an attractive picture, using such words as "enjoy," "glorious," "pure pleasure," and "divine," that the audience begins to crave the answers to the questions he has posed. His impressions even slipped into probably the most objective program of this series, "Musical Atoms: A Study of Intervals." Here Bernstein generally restricts himself to facts (5 to page labeled 16–17) until he begins to discuss the specific work he has chosen, as an example, Brahms Fourth Symphony, first movement. Subjectivity creeps in when he introduces the work as "one of the great classics of all time" (14) and Brahms as "a great master," then says that it is "astonishing" how from a single interval and its inversion (16–17) Brahms created "the beautiful main theme" (18). Then the Philharmonic performs "this magnificent, dramatic movement" (21). He clinically explained intervals then rhapsodizes about Brahms and the work. Bernstein did not hesitate to add his editorial comments to the scripts.

His explanations often incorporate appealing analogies. For instance, when discussing the last movement of Mozart's "Jupiter" symphony (no. 41) in "What Makes Music Symphonic?" he likens development to a seed growing into a flower then into a fruit tree (2–6), saying, "see if you can follow the fascinating life of these four notes as they blossom out into an entire piece" (3). He makes his topic engaging with such words as "fascinating" and a nature analogy.

Lastly, Bernstein tends to describe things in emotionally dramatic terms when the opportunity presents itself, rather than providing cold, logical explanations. For example in "What Is Sonata Form?" he discusses the polarity of tonic and dominant by saying, "If I play a tonic and a dominant chord . . . what do you feel? . . . You feel a desperate urge to get back to the tonic, don't you?" and by later asserting that "the tonic is like a magnet. . . . That's where the drama, the tension lies" (19–20).[28] He calls Mozart "a magician" who "begins to lure us away from the tonic" (20). With Bernstein, nearly every statement is accompanied by ideas or adjectives that are linguistically or dramatically charged.

Bernstein was very aware of the emotional effect of music, particularly on children. Before performing some avant-garde works, he prepared his young audience for the strange sounds, letting them know what to expect and how to behave. The tape recorder used in the Concerted Piece for Tape Recorder and Orchestra by Otto Luening and Vladimir Ussachevsky is grouped with instruments of the future in "Unusual Instruments of the Past, Present, and Future" (24–29). The maestro does take a moment to describe the two ways of creating "weird new sounds" on a tape recorder (by manipulating recorded sounds and by creating artificial sounds) and describes the music as "a very hard scientific business" adding "I've heard a lot of the sounds and they're really new and exciting" (26). His introduction is rather neutral until he is about to play the piece, when he cautions "we're actually going to play for you a whole piece using this strange instrument . . . I warn you: it's really way out *and it's also pretty scary, but don't be frightened by it because it's only music. Also it may make you want to talk or whisper or yell because it's so peculiar but please don't because after all, it is music even if it is way out*" [words in italics are ad-libbed] (27). Even in the first program, "What Does Music Mean?" Bernstein warns the children to behave even though Anton Webern's *Six Pieces* may sound strange to them: "[Webern] writes music that's so special in its sounds, that some people don't understand it at all and just call it crazy, modern music. . . .*You see if you even sneeze or cough you're liable to miss it, it's so delicate and so deep inside that you mustn't even breathe while it's going on*" [words in italics are ad-libbed] (40–41 revised). If his adult audience had a difficult time sitting through such pieces, certainly the young might get frightened or restive.

Despite the absence of an entire program dedicated to modernism, Bernstein nevertheless lightly touched on some hallmark modernist compositional techniques. Usually these would be introduced in connection with a reactionary piece or composer, hence, many times accompanied by neutral or positive comments. "Unusual Instruments of Present, Past, and Future" is a festival of "unusual new sounds," "unusual old sounds," and "the unusual instruments that make them" (3)—in other words, extended techniques. He describes Villa-Lobos's reactionary work, *The Little Train*, as a "charming little piece" (3), then explains that the "peculiar noises are really caused by the regular instruments of the orchestra playing in peculiar ways" (8), such as flutter-tonguing (6), playing in extreme ranges (6), and glissandos (7).[29] The maestro wedges chance music into the program "Holst: *The Planets*" (26 March 1972). Since Holst did not write a movement for Pluto (which had not yet been discovered), the Philharmonic improvises a "Pluto-piece" (25). Bernstein introduces it without mentioning chance music or providing insight into the aleatoric practices. While he offers no subjective statements on the technique or the result, he does play up the once-in-a-lifetime aspect of a chance performance. Insofar as rhythmic complexity, Bernstein points out the regular use of the asymmetrical meter of 5/8 (in neutral terms) in the "Dance" movement of Copland's *Music for the Theatre* in "Aaron Copland Birthday Party" (12 February 1961, 12). The maestro obviously enjoys discussing bitonality and whole tone scales, for instance, in the works of Gershwin and de Falla in "The Road to Paris" (18 January 1962, 6, 16–17, 20). Bitonality is revisited again in "Happy Birthday, Igor Stravinsky" (26 March 1962); after he pays "tribute, with all our respect and admiration and devotion, to the greatest composer in the world today" (3), he calls attention to the famous use of bitonality in *Petrushka* by ad-libbing, "isn't that wonderful?"

(18). His mention of a twelve-tone row in Liszt's *Faust Symphony* in "Liszt and the Devil" is very brief, neutral, and without any real explanation (9–10). These statements about avant-garde techniques in reactionary works by Villa-Lobos, faux-Holst, Copland, Gershwin, de Falla, and Stravinsky are either couched in neutral terms or accompanied by positive statements.

Occasionally, Bernstein's negative attitude toward the avant-garde is subtly present, as in "Happy Birthday, Igor Stravinsky." Here, the maestro rhapsodizes about Stravinsky's music twice, when speaking of his early nationalist ballets and when discussing the bitonality in *Petrushka*. He briefly mentions Stravinsky's switch to serial composition:

> Since the beginning of our century there has been a new kind of music developing in the world, sometimes called atonal music, sometimes twelve-tone music, or serial music. Now Stravinsky had always represented the exact opposite of this kind of music; but lo and behold, in the last ten years he has fooled the bull again [as suddenly as a bullfighter swishes his cape] and begun to write his own kind of serial music, or atonal music, or whatever you want to call it. Listen to these bars from his latest ballet called *Agon*. Now that's really a switch. In fact, Stravinsky has now become the world leader of this kind of music. (7)

By describing atonality as "whatever you want to call it," by playing only a brief excerpt, Bernstein avoids the need to explain Stravinsky's approach. He subtly expresses his sorrow at Stravinsky's abandonment of tonality, although he later bemoans Stravinsky's "defection . . . to the enemy camp" in the Norton Lectures (Bernstein 1976, 419).

Bernstein likes to voice the thoughts he imagines his viewers are having, so when he plays avant-garde works he makes frequent allusions to "crazy modern music," "spooky effect," "nightmare," and "indigestion."[30] He acknowledges the importance of avant-garde scores in film when he links outer space sounds and "movie music." Such analogies make sense. Bebe Baron composed a score for the 1956 science fiction movie *Forbidden Planet* that for the first time used only electronic music. Experimental modernist Girogy Ligeti composed some of the music for the 1968 science fiction film *2001: A Space Odyssey*. Sections of Bernard Herrmann's music for Alfred Hitchcock's 1960 film *Psycho* used extended techniques to embody "crazy" and "nightmare." These are just a few of many such films. His aforementioned opinion that avant-garde composers were connecting to space is evident when he alludes to "Mars," and "outer space," or makes statements like, "I feel as though I've been on a space ship somewhere around the moon—don't you? That music really takes us into the future" in "Unusual Instruments of the Past, Present, and Future" (29). Before the Moog synthesizer plays "the bizarre version of the Bach fugue [in G minor]" in "Bach Transmogrified" (27 April 1969), ad-libbing, he teases, "Hello Hal!" (referring to the murderous computer in *2001: A Space Odyssey*), then follows his script, "prepare decompression chambers. Force field operative. All systems go. And, blast off!" (11 revised). He apparently does not take avant-garde modernism seriously.

Bernstein's point of view can be clearly seen by comparing the comments he made about various pieces in "Aaron Copland Birthday Party" with those he made about the last avant-garde piece performed on the series, *Phorion* by Lukas Foss in "Bach Transmogrified." The long-standing profound relationship between Bernstein and Copland is well known.[31] The fondness and respect Bernstein felt for Copland and his music is clear throughout this script. To engender a similar affection for Copland in his audience, Bernstein's selections move from a more avant-garde/dissonant work through a quirky, fun work, to a beautiful one, ending with "one of his very friendliest compositions" ("Aaron Copland Birthday Party, 24). The program "Bach Transmogrified" does not permit Bernstein to do the same for Foss, since only *Phorion* fits his plan for the program.

Bernstein begins the Copland program with appealing nature analogies, encouraging his listeners to love Copland's more approachable pieces and give the more difficult ones a chance:

> [Copland's] music is full of variety, like a flower-garden. There are big juicy white flowers, and little thorny ones, and great majestic bushes, and then tiny shy little buds—all kinds. But perhaps the main difference in his music is between the big white ones—which are so easy to see and appreciate and even love . . . and those thorny ones that are not so easy to see and love right off the bat, and are sort of tricky to handle, especially at first touch. Although some of Copland's greatest compositions are thorny ones, I don't see why we shouldn't play some of them too, especially for this audience of young people; your minds are wide-open to everything, new or old. Besides, these thorny pieces aren't really so frightening once you know a little about them. (5–6)

He beautifully prepares the audience to not be prejudiced against Copland's "thorny" compositions and reiterates the thought that that young people (not yet so set in their tastes) might be accepting of dissonance and the avant-garde.

Copland had corresponded with Bernstein about the works to present in this birthday celebration. Copland wondered how to show what he referred to as his "'tougher' side" (Simeone 2013, 431). The maestro's garden analogy was an effective device. To help his audience understand and perhaps even enjoy Copland's "thorny" use of dissonance, Bernstein provides a dramatic basis for "Dogmatic" from *Statements* by suggesting that the "rocky, thorny sounds" represent the "hard-boiled idea" of being dogmatic (6). He suggests to his viewers that they should "feel like iron, stubborn and dogmatic, and see if this little piece doesn't completely satisfy that emotion" (9). He guides them if not into accepting, at least into understanding the possible dramatic motivation behind Copland's use of dissonance. This is very in keeping with Bernstein's own use of dissonance and atonality.

When performing "Dogmatic," Bernstein revisits his views on atonality. Beforehand, he says, "don't forget that this is modern music, music of our time; and we are living in some pretty rocky times. Besides, music changes and grows all through history, like all ideas; and what used to be considered right and normal is very different from what's right and normal these days" (7). After "Dogmatic," Bernstein links Copland to the modernists who militantly ignore their audiences by saying: "Don't clap. You're not supposed to. It's as if Aaron Copland were saying, 'This is what I have to say, and I don't care if you agree with me or not'" (11). Yet by offering a dramatic reason for the dissonance in "Dogmatic," he implies that Copland *was* thinking of his audience. He immediately reassures the viewers about his dear friend: "That's one side of Aaron Copland . . . the rest of his pieces on this program are much friendlier ones" (11).

Next, Bernstein parades the more appealing side of Copland. He begins by pointing out Copland's fun use of dissonance in conjunction with *Music for the Theatre*, saying, "did you also hear those funny little notes that were also going on? . . . [They were] on purpose wrong notes that make you want to laugh" (13). Copland's "beautiful and famous score" for the film *Our Town* follows, which he says is "so real, so quiet, so deeply felt" (16, 17). Next are Copland's settings of "Simple Gifts" and "I Bought Me a Cat." Bernstein notes that, "Copland has arranged them with his special style and orchestration and with such a personal understanding and love for them that they seem to come out as brand-new pieces by him. I don't know how he does it: it's part of the magic that goes on in this wonderful garden we're in today. . . . [They] come out like little homey, familiar daisies or dandelions" (21). The program concludes with "one of [Copland's] very friendliest compositions," *El Salón México* (24), thereby providing a complete picture. Through the appealing analogy of a garden, Copland's thorny works have their place, and the more accessible works by this "magician" are praised as "funny," "beautiful," and "friendly."

Bernstein's talk on Lukas Foss's *Phorion* for "Bach Transmogrified" (27 April 1969) presents quite a contrasting picture. Bernstein and Foss were longtime friends, having met at Curtis in 1939 (and taken many of the same classes), so the strength and longevity of their friendship resembles that between Bernstein and Copland (H. Burton 1994, 63). Like Bernstein, Foss became a noted composer (his works were performed by the Philharmonic some twenty-one times from 1945 to 2003, eleven of those during Bernstein's tenure), pianist (he often performed in his own works with the Philharmonic), and conductor (he was considered as a replacement for Bernstein at the Philharmonic) (xii. See also many of their letters in Simeone 2013).[32] Bernstein scheduled works by Foss for his first season with the Philharmonic, and Foss conducted the Philharmonic in the world premiere of Bernstein's *Symphonic Dances from West Side Story* (H. Burton 1994, 291, 320). Bernstein was probably pleased by his friend's early compositions, since Foss's early period (1944–1960) was predominantly neo-classical and eclectic, with aspects of American populism. But by 1960, Foss's compositional approach had changed. He abandoned tonality and clear, fixed forms, choosing instead serialism and indeterminacy often written in graphic notation. Bernstein felt lost in 1967 when he was preparing to conduct the world première of his friend's new composition, *Phorion*. The piece was disturbingly avant-garde and employed many new techniques: themes from Bach's Partita in E major were fragmented and distorted; chance techniques were included along with the non-musical sound of a soda bottle breaking; extended techniques appear when the cellos are instructed to stop bowing notes but only finger them with the left hand (thereby producing only the sound of their fingers tapping on the strings). According to Humphrey Burton, Foss remembers Bernstein calling him at 11 p.m. the night before the first rehearsal, stating, "I don't understand your music any more. It's gotten so violent. Would you please come over and explain it to me" (364). The two friends pored over the score, and by 2 a.m. Bernstein was explaining the piece to Foss. The maestro took great pains (with twenty pages of notes) to explain *Phorion* to the orchestra, who became enthused to perform it. Unfortunately, the audience made their opinion known with a "round of boos" (ibid.). This is the only truly avant-garde work Bernstein talked about at length in his *Young People's Concerts*. Again, Bernstein's choice of compositions supported a friend.

Bernstein begins his talk on *Phorion* in "Bach Transmogrified" by saying that this work "may make your hair stand on end" ("Bach Transmogrified," 13). To demonstrate the model on which *Phorion* is based, concertmaster David Nadien plays an excerpt from the Praeludium of Bach's E major Partita, which Bernstein interrupts saying, "I hate to stop that beautiful playing" (15). The maestro manages to compliment both Bach and Nadien's performance with these few words. He then describes Foss as "one of our best-known and most talented composers . . . who for some years has been experimenting with various new wrinkles in the world of the so-called avant-garde, the way-out fringes of contemporary music" (15). Bernstein's word choice immediately begins to create some apprehension; there are no positive words, and those

that he uses have unfortunate associations. He continues similarly: "Mr. Foss
. . . has taken this well-loved and world-famous piece of violin music, and
has made . . . a whole new modern piece of his own. . . . But the way he puts
these notes together is something else" (15). After an unprecedented three
script pages of explanation (chance music, extended techniques, breaking of
the soda bottle, and so forth) he introduces the performance:

> And by the end of the piece, with everyone going at once for all they're
> worth, Bach has been turned into a bloody battlefield of noise. It's cer-
> tainly not Bach any more, and you may not even think it winds up being
> music in its usual sense, but whatever it is, it's an intensely personal expres-
> sion by a dedicated, talented composer who adores Bach, as I happen to
> know. So if it seems to you to be *murdering* Bach, it may be really that he
> is expressing something about our century that can be expressed only by
> committing this kind of violence on the music of the past. This *Phorion*
> can amaze us and amuse us . . . but it can also tell us something awfully
> important if we listen with our minds as well as our ears. (19)

It would be very difficult to listen with an open mind after this introduction.

The works on "Aaron Copland Birthday Party" are mostly reactionary
but include a respectable visit to the avant-garde for dramatic reasons. Bernstein feels his dear friend Copland has written music ranging from "thorny"
to "beautiful" that is "deeply felt." On the other hand, his good friend Foss
created, he says, an avant-garde work that is not music "in the usual sense"
and that committed "violence" to Bach by "murdering his music" in a "bloody
battlefield of noise," yet the maestro suggests we should be "amazed" and
"amused." Foss is a musical murderer and writes works that must be listened
to with the mind. Try as he might to the contrary, Bernstein's proclivities
seeped through.

Bernstein's acknowledged opposition to avant-garde techniques was not
due to lack of understanding or ignorance. He always sought understanding.
In 1959 he wrote Copland that "I don't think I really understand the direction [of music] any more (or the purpose); & I long to talk to you & have
you explain it to me, & reassure me that new music is just as exciting as it
was when you showed me all about it 20 years ago" (Simeone 2013, 422). As
a mature musician, he studied the pieces carefully, explained them in great
detail to the performers (and sometimes to the composers), performed them
with the same dedication he gave to nineteenth-century standards, and incorporated many of the techniques into his own compositions. He knew avant-
garde modernism well and appreciated it, in its place. Gottlieb confirms the
maestro's leanings in his book *Working with Bernstein*: "in general, LB was
not sympathetic to the twelve-tone school. Between 1958 and 1971, he did

program six works of the Second Viennese School [for the Philharmonic]" (Gottlieb 2010, 145). Bernstein knew how negatively audiences (and even his mother) reacted to works in this vein; he was probably aware of their letters, he watched them storm out of concerts in which such works were performed, and no doubt, many people made their opinion known to him verbally. In his *Omnibus* presentation, "Introduction to Modern Music," he acknowledged that "we do have a certain amount of so-called *avant garde* music in our modern art which does try to shock and be original for originality's sake" (Bernstein 1959, 193). The maestro was not entirely opposed to avant-garde modernism. He believed that there was nothing wrong with shocking the listener, as long as it is done for dramatic reasons. But he was a powerful and dedicated advocate for tonality—through his writings, his talks, and his own compositions. His understanding of the human need to communicate helped him believe that atonality would never, in the final analysis, supplant tonality. He felt that avant-garde works, although intellectually fascinating in their structure, cannot reach into the hearts of audiences seeking emotional fulfillment in music.

Bernstein viewed the changing fads with phlegmatic amusement. In his preparatory remarks at the beginning of the Philharmonic's 1964 series "The Avant-Garde," he pokes fun at the necessity of being "new": "Of course, since [the works that will be performed] were not written five minutes ago they may already be passé [audience titters] and not indicative at all of what is really new. The Xenakis piece, for example, was written way back in 1956 which makes it practically pre-historic from the avant-garde point of view" (Bernstein 2000, CD9, track 1). He notes that by the mid-1960s, even works that had been heralded by the avant-garde and the ivory towers of academia began to seem "old-fashioned," suggesting that "electronic music, serialism, chance music . . . have already acquired the musty odor of academicism." While the pundits searched for the future of music in esoteric techniques, "tonal music," he said, "lies in abeyance, dormant," or in other words, tonality was ready to again spring forth (Bernstein 1966, 10). He summarized the problems of the avant-garde as he saw them after his sabbatical, saying, "consider the avant-garde, with its short-lived fads and in-groups, its chic efficiency, its cavalier attitude toward communication with a public" (Bernstein 1982, 233). For Bernstein, innovation for the sake of innovation, detailed, intricate compositional techniques requiring extended explanations, and intentionally ignoring the desires of the public were a betrayal of artistic integrity. Formalism, or form for its own sake, he found pointless. He also bemoaned the fact that "the only area where there is to be found unabashed vitality, the fun of invention, the feeling of fresh air" is in popular music (Bernstein 1962, 10).

Bernstein apparently thought that young people, who were less entrenched in the Romantic classics, might understand and accept avant-garde modernist music better than the older generation. Furthermore, an adult wrote that "it would do no good to tell me that I do not understand the new stuff, because I do not understand the old stuff either" (Marc Heiman, 1964). Nonetheless, he rarely programmed such works for his *Young People's Concerts*, in part because he appreciated the fact that his audiences were "hungry for musical joys," a joy that the avant-garde did not satisfy (Bernstein 1966, 11). Through the efforts of reactionary composers, the maestro knew that, as Ross said in *The Rest Is Noise*, "in twentieth-century music, through all the darkness, guilt, misery, and oblivion, the rain of beauty never ended" (Ross 2007, 410). Bernstein preferred works from that "rain of beauty," actively seeking, programming, discussing, and performing them over avant-garde innovation whenever he could. In the face of profound opposition from his government, critics, and other composers, Bernstein remained devoted to tonality and reactionary works throughout his entire life.

· 8 ·

The Advocate for American Music

Search for an American Identity

I don't think there's anyone in this hall, or anywhere in the country watching this program, or anyone in the civilized world for that matter who wouldn't know right away that that music we just played is American music. It's got "America" written all over it—not just in the title, which is, you know, *An American in Paris*, and not just because the composer, Gershwin, was American, but it's in the music itself: it *sounds* American, *smells* American—makes you *feel* American when you hear it.

—Leonard Bernstein, "What Is American Music?"
(1 February 1958)

From its very beginnings in the nineteenth century, the New York Philharmonic declared that one of its missions was to support American composers and performers. That support was lukewarm until Bernstein came on the scene. As the first music director who was American born, American educated, and who from his earliest years loved American music in all its guises, the young conductor was the perfect advocate for indigenous classical music. However, before a conductor can champion American music, he must first define it—a task which Bernstein essentially completed while he was a student at Harvard. After a brief glimpse at the endeavors of the orchestra and conductor on behalf of American composers and performers, we will see the evolution of the maestro's definition of American music. His programming and comments on American music in his *Young People's Concerts* reveal the path and nature of his support of American music—how it became more expansive while remaining basically unchanged, and how it began with great enthusiasm and ebbed by the 1970s.

BERNSTEIN AND THE PHILHARMONIC
AS ADVOCATES FOR AMERICAN MUSIC

An integral part of the Philharmonic's mission almost from its founding in 1842 was the campaign to encourage American music, which reached its zenith under Bernstein.[1] By the fourth season (1846–1847) a bylaw added to the orchestra's constitution formalized the mission by requiring one American composition be performed each season.[2] The Philharmonic, however, did not firmly commit to American music until Bernstein became music director.[3] As Howard Shanet wrote, just the act of hiring an American-born and American-trained musician was a "sign of America's musical maturity"—"not that it could *produce* a musician capable of filling this important post (it had long been able to do so) but that it had finally developed the self-confidence and security to *offer* its most honored musical position to a native son" (Shanet 1975, 327).[4]

For most of his life, Bernstein was an indefatigable champion of American music. He was drawn to it as early as his Harvard years when it was the subject of his senior thesis. He kept his eye open for American works, as evidenced by his complaint to Copland in 1950 that there hadn't been "a real exciting American premiere in years" (Simeone 2013, 279). His natural affinities made him a gifted interpreter of American music. Shanet observed that the maestro "had an unmatched 'feel' for the syncopations and other rhythmic and metric complications of the nationalist style of George Gershwin, Aaron Copland, and Roy Harris," as well as the next generation (Marc Blitzstein, David Diamond, Irving Fine, and William Schuman), "including the jazz and popular-music elements" (Shanet 1975, 358). As a result of the goals of both Bernstein and the management of the Philharmonic, just under one-third of the works he conducted for the Philharmonic were by American composers, and American music in the overall Philharmonic repertory (including that of guest conductors) increased from 5 percent (the typical rate in the early 1950s) to 15 percent (in the 1960s) annually.[5] His advocacy of American music at the Philharmonic began in his first season as music director, as seen in his plan for the season: "The over all [*sic*] point of my eighteen weeks is a general survey of American Music from the earliest generation of American composers to the present. This does not mean that any one program will be made up entirely of American music, but rather that this music is featured or emphasized as the consistent factor running through my programs."[6] Although Bernstein mentioned few composers, his design was already shaped.[7]

In his role as educator, writer, and lecturer, however, Bernstein apparently saw little need to speak out on behalf of American composers. Bernstein probably felt that audiences would come to accept and even welcome American music into their hearts if he programmed American works and gave them exciting performances. Perhaps he again chose the subtle path that he followed with many political and social issues.

BERNSTEIN'S CONCEPTION OF AMERICAN MUSIC

Without doubt, Bernstein's most extensive writing on the subject of American music dates back to his years as a student at Harvard and his 1939 senior thesis, "Harvard Bachelor's Thesis: The Absorption of Race Elements into American Music" (Bernstein 1982, 36–99). The few other writings on this subject are scripts (which add little to his original theories, hence are not covered here).[8] He also comments on American music in a number of his *Young People's Concerts* as discussed below.

Joseph Horowitz states that the subtext of Bernstein's *Young People's Concerts* was "a relentless self-inquiry asking, again and again, 'What is American Music?'" (Horowitz 2007, 477). In fact, Geoffrey Block's comprehensive study (entitled "Bernstein's Senior Thesis at Harvard: The Roots of a Lifelong Search to Discover an American Identity") reveals that Bernstein defined American music for himself while in college (Block 2008, 52–66). Block shows how this definition was probably informed by Copland, shaped his own life as a composer, and changed little as he grew from student to an internationally renowned representative of American music. A brief outline of Bernstein's thesis and Block's work follows.

Bernstein's Harvard thesis is in two parts. Part one is in three sections that cover "The Problem of Nationalism in American Music," "The Periods of Pre-Nationalism," and "Nationalism: First Stage." Bernstein begins by suggesting that nationalism must not be "arbitrarily inflicted upon music; it must be organic," then continues by describing what he felt was integral to the development of a national style: "material" (referring to the superficial use of indigenous folk music) and "spiritual" (referring to the fact that the spirit of the folk music infuses the material) (Bernstein 1982, 37). He suggests that three problems prevent the United States from evolving its own national style: the lack of an aboriginal race (he dismissed the Native American culture as "almost negligible"), the heterogeneous balance of races, and the excessive youth of the nation. The most profound problem faced by any composer attempting to sound American is the lack of musical material that the majority of Americans hold in common (38–39). Two styles, he feels, had sufficient universality to offer hope: the music of the colonists of New England and jazz. Since jazz permeates American culture more deeply, he concludes that jazz was "the ultimate common denominator" (40). Bernstein offers a short history of American classical music in the section titled "The Periods of Pre-Nationalism." American music in what would later become the United States fell under the sway of European musical practices from the earliest Puritan days. European influence began to wane at the beginning of the twentieth century as composers intentionally sought and incorporated what they deemed American material into their compositions. The result was materially but not spiritually American, as found in the works of composers such as Edward MacDowell. In "Nationalism: First Stage," Bernstein relates the story of Antonín Dvořák's visit to America and his suggestions that composers turn to Indian (Native American) and "Negro" music for their nationalist material (as a young student in the late 1930s, Bernstein uses commonly accepted terms of the day).[9] After a brief analysis, he dismisses Dvořák's New World Symphony as lacking true American spirit. Henry F. Gilbert, on the other hand, had a "profound feeling for the Negro folk art," as seen in his *The Dance in the Place Congo* (45–46). The young student lavishes several pages on this work and lists several other Gilbert compositions as further examples.

Part two moves into the twentieth century with "Nationalism, Second State, and the Negroes"; "The Negro Scale"; "Negro Rhythms"; "The Integration of New England and Negro Strains"; and "The Tempering Force." Jazz immediately enters the discussion when Bernstein asserts that it "has certainly been the most powerful, even if not the most permanent, influence upon American music" (50). He suggests that American music entered the second stage of development when jazz "entered the mind and spirit of America" and that any "sensitive creator" cannot escape its influence (ibid.). The section on what he calls the Negro scale (what is now known as the blues scale) demonstrates how dependence on this scale restricted composers to tonality and nineteenth-century methods.[10] Gershwin (despite his "sheer genius") was a victim of such self-imposed limitations, dooming him to conservatism (54–55). Copland used the blues scale in a similar manner in his Piano Concerto of 1926. Since Copland was "very sensitive to American jazz," he was gradually able to organically "reconcile the scale with his own advanced style," a necessary step in the evolution of a natural, spontaneous-sounding, true American music (57). The most extensive section of Bernstein's thesis covers "Negro Rhythms." Bernstein elaborates on characteristic rhythmic "distortions" and offers what he felt were examples of more organic American works by Roger Sessions and, again, Copland (62–87). The young Harvard student states, "the development [of Negro rhythms] has advanced so far that the rhythms have practically lost all their Negro quality, and have become something typically and wholly American" (63). As Block observes, Bernstein "regarded African-American rhythm as the indispensable starting point on the road to an authentic, modern, and assimilated American style," but only when such rhythms lose their African American connections (Block 2008, 57). Bernstein concludes that American music owes a great debt to African Americans "not only for the popularly acknowledged gift of jazz, but for the impetus which jazz has given to America's art music." Influences are primarily seen in melodic and rhythmic patterns, but also in timbre and counterpoint. Gershwin was the first to freely weave jazz into his symphonic works. As composers became more evolved, "this initial use—especially of the rhythms—[grew] into a new style, which might be called the first tangible indigenous style that can be identified in American music" (Bernstein 1982, 87).

In the penultimate section, "The Integration of New England and Negro Strains," Bernstein discusses "the only other strain that can be said to have reached any universality at all," that is music from New England (87). He explains how Roy Harris, Charles Ives, and Sessions "combined certain features of the Negro [style]" with that of their native New England largely through "a personal and genuine use of the Negro rhythms" (87, 95). As Block says, "to Bernstein's ear the result is a universal American music that does not create direct audible associations with either African-American rhythm or jazz" (Block 2008, 60). This lack of connection to its African American origins is vital both to Copland (in his writings about jazz) and to Bernstein in his Harvard thesis (Copland 1927, 9–14). Neither man even mentions leading contemporary African American jazz musicians. Block observes, "for Copland and Bernstein, jazz was a practice and a style to make use of but of little value in and of itself. Both men made sharp distinctions between vernacular and cultivated traditions and neither composer considered jazz as the cultural equivalent of serious (that is, art) music" (Block 2008, 61).

In the concluding section of his Harvard thesis, "The Tempering Force," Bernstein describes how the use of jazz elements had finally moved from material to spiritual. He suggests three influences that shape a "composer's particular, personal Americanism": African American (as the "only really universal racial influence in America"), in some cases New England (as "the sociological backbone of the country"), and the composer's "own heritage, unconsciously or not" (Bernstein 1982, 99).[11]

Block makes an excellent case for the profound influence that Bernstein's mentor and dear friend Copland had on the young student and his Harvard thesis. Block describes how Bernstein wrote to Copland with his ideas and how the elder composer in his letters helped shape them by sharing his experience and insights with Bernstein (for some of their relevant correspondences, see Simeone 2013, 24, 25–26). He also reveals how Copland may have introduced Bernstein to the music of Ives, that Copland's ideas are woven through Bernstein's thesis, and that Copland's compositions frequently served as models. Bernstein heralds Copland's 1929 *Variations* as the turning point from material to spiritual Americanism in music.[12] Block's article tracks Bernstein's theories on Americanism through the maestro's scripts and books throughout his life and concludes that his opinions changed little over the course of time.[13] Bernstein's openness toward music of all brow levels is integral to his concept of American music.

The reception of symphonic works colored by jazz was problematic. During the Cold War in the 1950s and early 1960s, such compositions were considered middlebrow and were rejected for government-sponsored cultural export (Ansari 2012b, 41, 42, 47–49).[14] Under President Dwight Eisenhower (1953–1961), the American National Theater and Academy (ANTA) housed the advisory committees for music, dance, and theater for the Cultural Presentations Program, while the State Department was in charge of financing and travel arrangements (41–42). Although the music committee did arrange for a few jazz performers to tour, the lion's share of the funding went to classical ensembles that had to submit their proposed repertory in advance. Works by Copland, Gershwin, and Bernstein were among those rejected (46–47). A symphonic work with jazz influences was not considered to properly represent the full weight of America's contributions to classical music. Reviewers also questioned the validity of including popular styles in the classical repertory. For instance Howard Taubman of the *New York Times* criticized Bernstein's *Serenade* saying, "Mr. Bernstein writes jazz with a flair, but does it really belong in the musical context of this piece?" ("Bernstein Serenade Played: Composer Conducts It at Carnegie Hall," 19 April 1956). Such adverse reactions did not change Bernstein's convictions about what makes music sound American.

AMERICAN MUSIC IN THE *YOUNG PEOPLE'S CONCERTS*

Bernstein's *Young People's Concerts* spanned his middle years. The programming and prose show his dedication to his image of American music, which remained essentially the same yet became more inclusive, and his advocacy for selected American composers.

Bernstein's vision of American music crystallized between his student years and his appointment as music director of the Philharmonic, as found in his two most extensive explorations of the subject: his 1939 Harvard thesis and one of his *Young People's Concerts* from nineteen years later entitled "What Is American Music?" A comparison of the two shows the evolution of Bernstein's ideas over nearly twenty years and reveals a more complete picture of the mature Bernstein's definition of American music.

Bernstein's description of the stages in the development of American music in "What Is American Music" is nearly identical to his Harvard thesis. Since the earlier work is much more extensive and written as an undergraduate thesis, it includes far more detail and examples than his later broadcast for young people—the time constraints of television demanded brevity.[15] To help his young audience understand the stages more readily, he compares each step to a grade in school, all the way from kindergarten through college. American classical composers graduated to high school when jazz influences first appeared (as with Gershwin and Copland), then graduated to college when those influences became so well-integrated that their jazz origins were no longer obvious (as with Copland and others).

Both writings describe the same problems, motivations, and catalysts. The concert includes examples from the same composers (omitting only Ives) and many of the same pieces, as seen in table 8.1. The proportion of each presentation devoted to the composers is also nearly identical. The discussion of Harris was abridged probably due to time restrictions. Despite his having lavished so many pages on Ives's *Concord Sonata* in his Harvard thesis, for unknown reasons this American composer was not included. Perhaps Ives was cut to save time, or there was trouble obtaining permissions, or perhaps the challenging nature of the orchestral works led Bernstein (early in his tenure) to decide that either the orchestra or his young audience was not prepared for such pieces, or, more likely, Bernstein decided to focus on Americans who were actively composing at the time of broadcast (Ives died in 1954). In both documents, Bernstein asserts that American music began with Gilbert and MacDowell, was inspired by Dvořák's teaching and *New World Symphony,* exploded with Gershwin when jazz arrived, and reached adulthood in the hands of Copland. The young Harvard student was not restricted by musical medium in selecting works for his examples, whereas the professional conductor had to largely restrict himself to works that would showcase the Philharmonic. Hence, Copland's 1930 Piano Variations, listed as the turning point in the Harvard thesis, was replaced by the 1946 Symphony No. 3, and Harris's a cappella *A Song for Occupations* was replaced by his Symphony No. 3. When speaking of American music almost twenty years later, Bernstein updated his selections by adding newer works by American composers Morton Gould, Schuman, Virgil Thomson, and Thompson. The only work added that had been composed before 1939 was a symphony by Randall Thompson. The lion's share of both Bernstein's thesis and "What Is American Music?" went to Gershwin and Copland.

Two changes are evident in Bernstein's thinking between 1939 and 1958. First, his concept of American music had become broader and more inclusive.

Table 8.1. Comparison of American Compositions Found in Bernstein's Harvard Thesis and "What Is American Music?"

Composer	Work	Harvard (1939)	YPC (1958)
Gilbert	The Dance in Place Congo (1922)	X	X (1:25 min.)
	Comedy Overture on Negro Themes (1912)	X	
	Humoresque on Negro Minstrel Tunes (1913)	X	
MacDowell	Suite No. 2 "Indian" (1897)	X	X (1:25)
Chadwick	Melpomene (1887)	X	X (1:15)
Gershwin	Rhapsody in Blue (1926)	X (4pp)	X (1:20)
	An American in Paris (1928)*	X	X (7:35)
	Piano Concerto (1925)	X	
	Of Thee I Sing, "Wintergreen for President" (1932)	X	
Copland	Ukelele Serenade (1928)	X	
	Music for the Theatre (1925)	X	X (2:15)
	Piano Concerto (1926)	X (4, 7 pp)	
	Piano Variations (1930)	X (3 pp)	
	Billy the Kid (1938)	X	X (1:05)
	Symphony No. 3 (1946)		X (9:00)
Sessions	Piano Sonata (1928)	X	
	Three Chorale Preludes (1927)	X	X (0:25)
	Symphony in E Minor (1927)	X	
Harris	A Song for Occupations (1934)	X (4 pp)	
	Piano Quintet (1936)	X	
	Concerto for Piano, Clarinet, and String Quartet (1936)	X	
	Symphony No. 3 (1938)		X (0:40)
Ives	Concord Sonata (1938)	X (4.5 pp)	
Gould	Interplay (1945)		X (0:10)
Schuman	American Festival Overture (1939)		X (1:10)
V. Thomson	Mother of Us All (1947)		X (1:00)
R. Thompson	Second Symphony (1931)		X (1:10)

The order of composers comes from Bernstein's Harvard thesis. The publication or première dates of the compositions are given in parenthesis; the Ives date is the first known performance. All excerpts are discussed in one page or less unless otherwise indicated. The list of American compositions appearing on "What Is American Music?" comes from box/folder 990/03; this document lists every excerpt from a few seconds to extended performances with the copyright information. All Young People's Concerts excerpts are for orchestra except the Sessions Three Chorale Preludes, which is for organ.

* Gershwin's An American in Paris has a long history with the New York Philharmonic. The world premiere was given by The Philharmonic-Symphony Society of New York (the official name of the New York Philharmonic) in Carnegie Hall under Walter Damrosch on 13 Dec 1928. "Carnegie Hall 120th Anniversary Concert with Alan Gilbert and the New York Philharmonic," Great Performances, 5 May 2011.

For the younger Bernstein, three streams created the river of American music: jazz (the most important factor), music from New England, and the personal influences of each composer. While those streams recur in "What Is American Music?" the elder Bernstein adds subjective characteristics to his definition of American music, such as optimism (as represented Schuman's works), ruggedness (Harris), loneliness (Copland), and sentimentality (Thomson), yet offers little explanation of the compositional techniques involved. The maestro probably thought that such subjective guides would be welcomed by children and his middle- and lowbrow audiences, and this change is musically insubstantial. Second, Bernstein's attitude toward jazz musicians changed. In his thesis, jazz composers and performers remained anonymous (both Bernstein and Copland did not feel that jazz artists were the equal of classical artists), whereas in "What Is American Music?" he admiringly names specific performers such as Stan Kenton and Louis Armstrong.

Bernstein's devotion to presenting American music effectively can be seen in the number of musical examples he chose for "What Is American Music?" Usually the number of selections on his *Young People's Concerts* varied from one work (such as "*The Second Hurricane* by Copland," 24 April 1960 or Berlioz's *Symphonie Fantastique* in "Berlioz Takes a Trip," 25 May 1969), to several (such as five for "Happy Birthday, Igor Stravinsky!" and six for "A Toast to Vienna in 3/4 Time," 25 December 1967). Rarely a topic would demand as many as seventeen ("What Is a Mode?" 23 November 1966) or eighteen excerpts ("Humor in Music," 28 February 1959). "What Is American Music?" has by far the most—a lavish twenty-four musical excerpts.

Most fan mail praising Bernstein for his enthusiastic support of American music arrived in 1958 in response to "What Is American Music?"[16] Many writers acknowledged the neglect American composers had suffered. H. Proctor wrote, "it is about time that American symphonic composers should be given their proper place in the repertoire. To me it is *incredible* that it required 40 years for such a work as Ive's [*sic*] 2nd Symphony to be played." Richard F. Dobson said, "I was deeply moved to see your enthusiasm for the music of our native composers [on the second *Young People's Concert*] of which you are one of the greatest." Dobson felt sure that since Bernstein was succeeding Mitropoulos "much badly neglected American music" will appear on his programs, saying "this is, indeed, happy news to my listening circle which cherish [*sic*] anything written by a Copland, Harris, Barber, or Riegger." V. J. Gregory acknowledged the poor reputation of American symphonic compositions when he wrote, "I take this means of saluting a brave man." He felt that many, "I suspect, have criticized you severely for introducing the works of American composers to the public through the Philharmonic. . . . I hope and pray that you are strong enough to defy critics. . . . If we are to have a distinctive American music, it is necessary to give musical creators an opportunity to develop." Even the average music-lover was in sympathy with Bernstein's mission regarding American music.

The mature Bernstein's definition of American music resounds through his *Young People's Concerts*. His comments on it can be divided into two categories: sharing his criteria that define American music as found in specific works or offering a simple marker (such as pointing out that a composer is American).[17] Since he equated jazz with American music, any tally should include programs that mention jazz.[18] He addressed either or both in twenty-three programs yet did not champion American music in nearly half of the fifty-three *Young People's Concerts*.[19] Extensive investigations only appear in eight. It is worth noting their titles: "What Is American Music?"; "What Is Classical Music?" (1 February 1958); "Aaron Copland Birthday Party" (12 February 1961); "The Road to Paris" (18 January 1962); "Jazz in the Concert Hall" (11 March 1964); "Farewell to Nationalism" (30 November 1964); "Charles Ives: American Pioneer" (23 February 1967); and "A Copland Celebration" (27 December 1970).

Other than Copland and Gershwin (discussed below), most of the American composers mentioned in "What Is American Music?" appear only in that program or one additional program.[20] Bernstein did, however, touch on other American composers throughout his *Young People's Concerts*.

Jazz permeates the latter portion of "What Is American Music?" as mentioned above. "What Is Classical Music?" begins with a lengthy, amusing, and enthusiastic comparison of the jazz and classical approach to performance. "Jazz in the Concert Hall" showcases the works of Larry Austin, Gunther Schuller, and, of course, Copland, but Austin and Schuller were restricted to only this program. The maestro, society, and/or the genre had grown enough that he now mentions African American jazz greats Miles Davis and Thelonius Monk (19, but deleted due to time constraints) as well as the Newport Jazz Festival (2). As usual, Bernstein uses positive comments when he connects jazz with an American sound. Jazz references range from a simple quick identification (such as Mixolydian sounding "jazzy" in "What Is a Mode?" 23 November 1966, 37), to longer reminders of his definition of American music: "you could always spot American music by its jazziness" ("Farewell to Nationalism," 6).

As mentioned in chapter 7, Bernstein reduced the plethora of approaches to twentieth-century composition down to two, atonal and tonal, which he referred to as avant-garde and reactionary. Bernstein does play four American avant-garde composers in his *Young People's Concerts*, but he makes little note of any American qualities. Avant-garde music was an international phenomenon not identified with any particular nation, so Bernstein's neglect is understandable. In his mind, all these avant-garde works were cosmopolitan and exhibited no American characteristics, despite the composers' country of birth. When the Philharmonic performs *Concerted Piece for Tape Recorder and Orchestra* by Americans Otto Luening and Vladimir Ussachevsky in "Unusual Instruments of the Past, Present, and Future" (27 March 1960, 27), America is not even mentioned in Bernstein's wry introduction. Bernstein might mention a composer's nationality without noting any American flavor to the work. Milton Babbitt is labeled "a gifted American" in "Farewell to Nationalism" (5) when the maestro performs an excerpt from his *Composition for Twelve Instruments* as an example of music that does not sound nationalistic. Bernstein calls Lukas Foss (who had been a reactionary) "one of our best-known and most talented composers" in "Bach Transmogrified" (27 April 1969, 15) before proceeding with his negatively slanted introduction to the performance of Foss's avant-garde work *Phorion*.[21] For Bernstein, being composed by an American is not enough to make avant-garde music American music. However, the maestro probably had other reasons for excluding the American avant-garde in any discussion of American music—it did not align with his theory of American music, plus he simply did not feel empathic toward the avant-garde.

Bernstein is uncharacteristically reticent when talking about his own music. Not once does he comment on the American sound of his own works, or go into any depth despite performing them in three different programs. Granted, these works are stylistically either more international (the Overture to *Candide* in "Overtures and Preludes," 8 January 1961) or Latin American (*Symphonic Dances from West Side Story* in "The Latin American Spirit," 8 March 1963, and "Danzón" from *Fancy Free* in "What Is a Mode?") than American by his own definition.

Bernstein's preference for reactionary American composers as well as his attachment to and respect for Copland is seen in his programming selections. Only two Americans are featured among the seventeen programs devoted to a single composer: Ives (one program) and Copland (three programs).[22] In total, Bernstein performed thirteen of Copland's works (eighteen different movements) on nine different programs.[23] The maestro lavished more air time on Copland than any other composer. Mozart was next, then Beethoven.[24] Another of Bernstein's favorite American composers, George Gershwin, had three works performed on seven programs, but again, no program devoted to him alone.[25] Among American composers, only Ives and Copland were so honored.

Ives's reputation grew throughout the twentieth century. By his centenary in 1974, he was internationally acknowledged as both the first to create distinctively American art music and a free thinker who anticipated almost every avant-garde technique that appeared later in the century. He was also a multi-faceted composer who wrote both appealing reactionary music and what Bernstein might call thorny modernist works. As mentioned above, Copland may have introduced Bernstein to this pioneering American composer (Block 2008, 58–59). Both Copland and Bernstein probably appreciated Ives's ability to compose equally well in both the conservative and avant-garde style (long before the concept of avant-garde existed). Ives must have made a deep lifelong impression on Bernstein, since he named his six Norton Lectures at Harvard after Ives's *The Unanswered Question*. No matter how Bernstein first encountered Ives, he was aware of the composer's innovative American sound as far back as his Harvard years, when he obtained a score of the *Concord Sonata*, and discussed the piece in his thesis. He touted Ives for his use of traditional American tunes in "Folk Music in the Concert Hall" (9 April 1961), in which the featured work was the finale of Symphony No. 2, and again later in "Charles Ives: American Pioneer," which included five Ives compositions.[26] Despite Bernstein's obvious reverence for Ives, neither his name nor his music appears in any other program.

Two themes concerning Ives recur in these two programs: his Americanness and his sense of fun (offered as a motivation for Ives's thorny sounds). In "Folk Music in the Concert Hall," Bernstein describes Ives as "a salty old Yankee" who was a "first-class composer—perhaps the first great composer in American history . . . one of the first American composers to use folk songs and folk dances in his concert music. It was his way of being American to take marching tunes and hymns and patriotic songs and popular country music and develop them all together into big symphonic pieces" (20–21). By 1967 in "Charles Ives: American Pioneer," the maestro firmly announces that Ives was our "first great American composer" (33). He then points out Ives's use of American tunes and describes how the composer represented Americana in his music (9), mentioning the "cozy [*sic*], home-town, old-fashioned ditties" he wove into works like *Washington's Birthday* (11). A complete portrait of the composer had to include his more challenging compositions. Bernstein opens "Charles Ives: American Pioneer" not with words but with one of the composer's more avant-garde sounding works, *The Gong on the Hook and Ladder, or Firemen's Parade on Main Street*, then tells his audience,

> Don't clap. I want to ask you a question: If you heard that rather bizarre piece of music without knowing its title or its composer, what would you say it was? Something by a composer from outer space? Or by a child? Or something the orchestra is making up as it goes along? No; you're too smart for that; but I'll bet you dollars to doughnuts you'd say it was something modern—in fact very modern, probably one of those wild musical experiments that the bright, new, young composers are making these days. (5)

He points out that Ives wrote this modern-sounding piece at the beginning of the century, years before the "big modern experiments by Arnold Schoenberg or Stravinsky" (5). Bernstein paints a picture of Ives-as-visionary by saying that he was "both a genius and a pioneer—two kinds of people who always seem to have a touch of madness—and it's a good kind of madness. Think of our Early American pioneers: weren't they just a bit mad to go trekking westward across a wild continent. . . . Well, Ives was very much like them. He was an adventurer, too—a musical pioneer" (7). Ives, the American composer, adventurer, and genius, is linked with true American pioneers.

The stage is now set for a discussion of his more challenging compositions with fun as the motivation. Bernstein felt fun was such an important part of this program that this single word jumps off the page of his outline—it's larger than all the other words, and in a very large box surrounded by lots of space. Bernstein continues, "once you get the idea of how important *fun* was in Ives' mind, then you begin to hear his music with new ears. And you understand why that *Firemen's Parade* we just played is so freakish; for instance, why there are so many different rhythms going on in the orchestra at the same time, so that it sounds all mixed up. Why? Because it's fun" (8). To Bernstein, fun seemed one of the valid reasons to employ avant-garde techniques—so much so that he mentions "fun" in this script several times (7, 8, 9, 10, 11, 12, 20, 25). Fun (as he defined it) was incredibly vital to Bernstein, and attributing Ives's quirkier compositions to a sense of fun must have pleased the maestro.[27] Furthermore, he appreciated Ives's "wild musical experiments" because the composer used those "mixed up" techniques for a dramatic purpose. He understood that frame of mind and approved—complexity for the sake of complexity as found in many avant-garde works made no sense to him. Another quote from the program makes his stance clear:

> If you're trying to make a musical picture of a Fireman's Parade down Main Street, and you've got a gong banging away on the big shiny red fire engine, what better way is there to show the noise and confusion and general hilarity than to have all these different rhythms going on at once? And it's not just the rhythms. What about those notes—those howling dissonances? They're also part of the fun, of the general hilarious goings-on. And this spirit of fun also explains why, amidst all the confusion, there suddenly emerges that innocent and plaintive old tune, "My Darlin' Clementine." (9)

All in all, Bernstein respected Ives and honored him with so much screen time probably because the composer intentionally used American tunes innovatively modified, and the avant-garde moments in Ives's music all had a dramatic basis. The maestro's outline for this program offers an insight into this innovative American composer. According to Bernstein, Ives "pretended not to care about not being performed but danced a jig . . . at [a] broadcast of [the] 2nd symphony" (box/folder 111/4).

Some viewers appreciated Bernstein's explanations of Ives and his music. Along with the letters mentioned in chapter 7 (Joan Goldberg, 1964, and Mrs. Frederick S. Carr, 1958), Jeanne Ellen Christensen wrote thanking him for the Ives program (1967): "because of your explanations, I now have a better understanding and a deeper appreciation for Charles Ives and his music. His music had always seemed strange and not altogether pleasant. Now, however, it is a pleasure to listen to and a challenge to figure out what themes and musical phrases he is teasing his listeners with." The fan mail helped Bernstein know that his message was getting through.

Aaron Copland was special to Bernstein both personally and professionally. Copland immediately became a vital part of Bernstein's life when they met while the latter was a student at Harvard.[28] The two men connected on many levels. They both were composer-conductors, loved jazz, enjoyed music with a lyrical simplicity, believed in reaching out to others through teaching and through writing accessible music, experimented with avant-garde techniques for dramatic purposes, sought to write a true American opera, advocated for American music, were homosexuals, and were liberals who suffered under the Red Scare.[29] Bernstein's deep abiding affection and respect is evident in his introduction to "Aaron Copland Birthday Party":

> Today, we're going to have a 60th birthday party for another composer, our own loved and admired Aaron Copland, and this time we're going to meet him in person later in the program. When you do meet him, I think the first thing about him that will strike you is his youthfulness—not only the youthfulness of his face, but also of his smile, of his conducting vigor, of his almost boyish personality, and especially of his spirit. It's almost impossible to list for you all the things Mr. Copland has done for the young during his lifetime: the dozens of young composers he has rooted for and brought success to; the even more dozens whom he has taught at Tanglewood and at Harvard and other places; and most of all, the many pieces he has written mainly to be performed by young people. (2)

The maestro deeply respected Copland as a trailblazer who helped shape American music. Both men seemed to agree wholeheartedly with the concept of an American nationalistic style in which American influences (such as jazz, folk-tunes, and hymn-tunes) and twentieth-century innovation are inextricably blended. Any time Copland is mentioned, Bernstein makes comments such as, "one thing [all his pieces] have in common is American-ness" ("Aaron Copland Birthday Party," 11). Bernstein describes how Copland was in the forefront of those who wove jazz sounds into their music: "now the first of these American-roots pieces we're going to hear is a dance from a piece he wrote way back in 1925 [*Music for Theatre*, "Dance"] . . . when he was first making experiments in using jazz in symphonic music" ("Jazz in the Concert Hall," 18, 11–12). He also highlights Copland's use of American hymn-tunes:

> In 1940 Copland wrote a beautiful and famous score for a movie called "Our Town" . . . if it makes you think of church, and hymn-tunes from long ago, well—you're thinking right, because that's just what he meant. This another side of America, another root, far from the noisy big city we heard about before: this is the simple rural American life that is such an important part of our country. Copland has often painted that side of America for us in his music—as in his famous ballet, *Appalachian Spring*, or in his opera *The Tender Land*; but perhaps in this little piece from the film "Our Town" he has painted it best of all, because it seems so real, so quiet, and so deeply felt. ("Aaron Copland Birthday Party," 16–17)

In addition, he lauds the way Copland transformed folk-songs by making use of cowboy songs without actually quoting them. "Rather, he transforms them by some magic into his own music. That's why I call it a masterpiece; it's a model of how to use folk-music in a symphonic way without just making high-powered arrangements of the tunes" ("A Copland Celebration," 15).

The maestro also praises Copland's ability to create a musical representation of the American West in one of the first *Young People's Concerts* as well as in one of the last. In "What Is American Music?" he says, "there's a kind of loneliness to be found in a lot of American music that's different from other kinds of loneliness. You find it in the way the notes are spaced out very far apart, like the wide open spaces that our huge country is full of. [An excerpt from *Billy the Kid* is performed.] Did you feel that wide-open feeling? That's really American, too" (26–27). Twelve years later, his salute is stronger, more assured, and poetically American in "A Copland Celebration": "I have always considered his ballet *Billy the Kid* a masterpiece of stage-music; it's not only rousing but also tender; and in its opening and closing pages it even has a majesty and grandeur as wide as the prairie, as lofty as the Rockies" (13).

Bernstein's appealing descriptions of Copland's music encouraged everyone to look forward to hearing it. Before performing *An Outdoor Overture* in "Aaron Copland Birthday Party," he says, "I think you'll understand immediately why he called it 'outdoor' when you hear those athletic marchy rhythms, and those long melodies filled with fresh air and light" (3). Later in the same program he says,

> Now that's what you call an *outdoor* overture—it really gets your blood circulating, like a brisk walk in the woods. And it's very typical of Copland—that easy, fresh style, so open-hearted and frank . . . his music is full of variety,

like a flower-garden. There are big juicy white flowers, and little thorny ones, and great majestic bushes, and then tiny shy little buds—all kinds. (5)

He continues the floral analogy and describes the "big white ones" as "so easy to see and appreciate and even love" (ibid.). Some may have felt that creating such attractive reactionary music did not require the high level of craftsmanship that avant-garde modernists demanded of themselves. Bernstein addresses this issue directly when introducing Copland's Concerto for Clarinet and String Orchestra:

> [Copland's musical language is] simple—but so special, so sophisticated, every note chosen with immense care, so that no matter how simple the music is it is always as fresh as new bread. When Copland first wrote this Concerto back in 1948, and he played it for me on the piano, I became very conscious of this highly selective note picking. I remember his playing the ravishing opening theme and when he came to this note [LB plays theme stopping on that note] this E-flat in the bass, I involuntarily went "*umb*" with delight and Copland said: "That's the note that costs." And that's the whole point about Copland. His notes *are* expensive—not just lots of notes a dime a dozen. ("A Copland Celebration," 9–10)

While pointing out the beauty in his compositions with homey analogies, the maestro hints that Copland writes with the same attention to detail exhibited by the avant-garde composers (as seen in their elaborate explanations of compositional techniques that accompany their works).

Several times in the course of his *Young People's Concerts*, Bernstein tells the international audience that they should hold Copland dear as well, in part by focusing on Copland as teacher: "I take tremendous personal pleasure in welcoming to this podium a great composer, a dear person, a true friend to youth, one who has guided and encouraged so many young people; including myself when I was just starting out. My thanks, our thanks, the thanks of all musicians and music-lovers all over the world. Happy birthday, Aaron Copland!" ("Aaron Copland Birthday Party," 25). Three years later he focused on Copland as pioneer: "Of course, today, Mr. Copland is America's leading composer, loved, admired, and respected by the whole world of music, including you all . . . [he was] a young pioneer of American music" ("Jazz in the Concert Hall," 18). By 1970 (near the end of his *Young People's Concerts*), Bernstein shares the insights that time gave him: "Copland has often been called the 'Dean of American Composers'—whatever that means. I suppose it means that he's the oldest, but he isn't the oldest: he's just unique. He has led American music through paths both pleasant and thorny for half a century, and he has never ceased fighting for the cause of new music, especially new American music" ("A Copland Celebration," 5).

Copland was honored in Bernstein's *Young People's Concerts* with eighteen performances of thirteen works on nine programs, but he was important to the series in other ways as well. He appeared as a guest performer or conductor on three programs (more than any other single performer), and he even took Bernstein's role in an untelevised *Young People's Concert* on 1 November 1969.[30] For Bernstein, Copland wrote beautiful music and was the model American composer. He used his *Young People's Concerts* in part as a forum to celebrate Copland while spreading his name and his music throughout the world.

When Bernstein was asked by the *Parkersburg* [Virginia] *News* about American music, he quoted Copland, who had told him, "sit down and write what comes into your head; if it's good it will be American."[31] In truth, that was not enough for Bernstein. For him, the sound of American music included either the urban sounds of jazz, the rural sounds of traditional folk-tunes, hymn-tunes, or marches, or works like Copland's that somehow musically portray the wide open spaces of the American West, colored by twentieth-century compositional techniques. Bernstein exhibited great warmth and pride when a composer wrote true American music (according to his definition).

We can now see that Horowitz's suggestion that the subtext of Bernstein's *Young People's Concerts* was "a relentless self-inquiry asking, again and again, 'What is American music?'" is flawed (Horowitz 2007, 477). While American composers, American music, and/or jazz appears in twenty-four programs (over 45 percent), he only expounds on the topics in 15 percent of the programs. Bernstein had shaped his concept of American music for himself in his Harvard thesis, a concept that essentially did not change but became more inclusive throughout his life. Although he promoted American music or composers in nearly half of his *Young People's Concerts*, he did not make a conscious effort to promote all American composers with equal zeal. His comments ranged from nothing more than a quick allusion to jazz or a composer's nationality to entire programs that celebrated American composers and the American-ness of their music.

When the opportunity presented itself, he did act as a powerful advocate for American composers and American music. Bernstein, however, felt a void that he expressed to John Gruen:

> When I think back on the years of Koussevitzky, who proudly brought forth one Copland symphony after another, Roy Harris, Bill Schuman, Prokofiev, Stravinsky! He had all those glorious pieces. That period is over. When I came to the Philharmonic, I was expecting something like that to happen, and I find it so terribly disappointing that it hasn't—not really. I

don't have anybody to champion. Nor do I have any cause to champion—a movement, a group of composers, a school. (Gruen 1968, 28)

Other than in his survey of American music in program 2, Bernstein championed the works of only two American composers no longer living (Ives and Gershwin) and very few that were still practicing:[32]

- Luening-Ussachevsky ("Unusual Instruments of Present, Past, and Future," 27 March 1960)
- Gian Carlo Menotti ("Young Performers No. 2," 18 March 1961)
- Walter Piston ("A Tribute to Teachers," 29 November 1963)
- Schuller and Austin ("Jazz in the Concert Hall," 11 March 1964)
- Foss ("Bach Transmogrified," 27 April 1969)
- Copland (many programs, as noted above)

Except for Copland, only one work by each of these composers appeared on Bernstein's *Young People's Concerts*, so it can hardly be said that he championed them. His negative comments as he introduced the works by Luening-Ussachevsky and Foss make it clear he was not endorsing their current works.[33] Table 8.2 shows that his efforts to champion American music declined throughout the series. He began by supporting American (generally reactionary) composers with great hope. He gradually lost his enthusiasm as what he considered to be appealing American works became more scarce, then finally wilted into simply supporting Aaron Copland.

Table 8.2. Chronological List of *Young People's Concerts*, Indicating Those That Mention American Music and/or Jazz

Program Title	Program Number	Broadcast Date
What Does Music Mean?	1	18 January 1958
What Is American Music?	2**++(many composers)	1 February 1958
What Is Orchestration?	3+	8 March 1958
What Makes Music Symphonic?	4+	13 December 1958
What Is Classical Music?	5 ++	24 January 1959
Humor in Music	6* Copland	28 February 1959
What Is a Concerto?	7	28 March 1959
Who Is Gustav Mahler?	8	7 February 1960
Young Performers No. 1	9	6 March 1960
Unusual Instruments of Present, Past, and Future	10*+Luening-Ussachevsky	27 March 1960
The Second Hurricane by Copland	11*Copland	24 April 1960
Overtures and Preludes	12*Bernstein	8 January 1961
Aaron Copland Birthday Party	13**++Copland	12 February 1961
Young Performers No. 2	14*Menotti	19 March 1961
Folk Music in the Concert Hall	15*+Ives	9 April 1961
What Is Impressionism?	16+	1 December 1961
The Road to Paris	17**+Gershwin	18 January 1962
Happy Birthday, Igor Stravinsky	18	26 March 1962
Young Performers No. 3	19	13 April 1962
The Sound of a Hall	20*Copland	21 November 1962
What Is a Melody?	21+	21 December 1962
Young Performers No. 4	22	15 January 1963
The Latin American Spirit	23*+Bernstein/Copland	8 March 1963
A Tribute to Teachers	24*+Piston	29 November 1963
Young Performers No. 5	25	23 December 1963
The Genius of Paul Hindemith	26	23 February 1964

(continued)

Table 8.2. (Continued)

Program Title	Program Number	Broadcast Date
Jazz in the Concert Hall	27**++Schuller / Copland / Austin	11 March 1964
What Is Sonata Form?	28	6 November 1964
Farewell to Nationalism	29**+Ives/Babbitt	30 November 1964
Young Performers No. 6	30	28 January 1965
A Tribute to Sibelius	31	19 February 1965
Musical Atoms: A Study of Intervals	32	29 November 1965
The Sound of an Orchestra	33*Gershwin/Copland	14 December 1965
A Birthday Tribute to Shostakovich	34	5 January 1966
Young Performers No. 7	35+	22 February 1966
What Is a Mode?	36*+Bernstein	23 November 1966
Young Performers No. 8	37	27 January 1967
Charles Ives: American Pioneer	38**Ives	23 February 1967
Alumni Reunion	39*Gershwin	19 April 1967
A Toast to Vienna in 3/4 Time	40	25 December 1967
Forever Beethoven!	41	28 January 1968
Young Performers No. 9	42+	31 March 1968
Quiz-Concert: How Musical Are You?	43	26 May 1968
Fantastic Variations (Don Quixote)	44	25 December 1968
Bach Transmogrified	45*Foss	27 April 1969
Berlioz Takes a Trip	46	25 May 1969
Two Ballet Birds	47	14 September 1969
Fidelio: A Celebration of Life	48	29 March 1970
The Anatomy of a Symphony Orchestra	49	24 May 1970
A Copland Celebration	50**+Copland	27 December 1970
Thus Spake Richard Strauss	51	4 April 1971
Liszt and the Devil	52	13 February 1972
Holst: The Planets	53	26 March 1972

* indicates a brief mention of American music or performance of a work by American.
** indicates extensive talk about American music.
+ indicates a brief mention of jazz.
++ indicates an extensive talk about jazz.
If a composer's work is performed in the program, his name is given after the program number.

Epilogue

> As you listen to these exalted final pages [from Strauss's *Don Quixote*]—try to keep in the back of your mind that there are two ways to think about all this. One way is that life is absurd to start with; that only a madman goes out and tries to change the world, to fight for good and against evil. The other way is that life is indeed absurd to start with and that it can be given meaning only if you live it for your ideals, visions and poetic truths, and despite all the skepticism of all the Sancho Panza[s] in the world, saddle up whatever worn-out horse you've got and go after those visions. Take your pick.
>
> —Leonard Bernstein, "Fantastic Variations (*Don Quixote*)," (25 December 1968)

Leonard Bernstein's *Young People's Concerts* have always been considered a portrait of Bernstein's incredible success as an educator and conductor (with a few examples of Bernstein as a performer). They are recognized for changing the way music appreciation is taught, for championing many fine young artists at the beginning of their careers, and for turning two generations of viewers into music lovers, but for nothing more. This is not surprising since none of the viewers I spoke with ever noticed anything other than music pedagogy in the series.[1] Seen from a different point of view, the series is both a portrait of troubled times and a kind of biography of the man, Leonard Bernstein: the contexts that influenced him; his growing courage to confront some of the important political, social, and cultural issues of his day; his interaction with and influence upon the canons of his day; and, importantly, Bernstein as an early postmodernist. All of this is found in the non-pedagogical aspects of this sterling arts education series.

189

Like most Americans, Bernstein was distressed by the world situation, so much so that worries about the Cold War, civil rights, and so forth crop up in his letters—from "vomiting over the European situation" in 1939, probably due to the actions of Hitler and Mussolini (Simeone 2013, 29), through fretting over "race riots, Vietnam . . . and the increasing horror in the world from Cairo to Memphis Tenn" (484).[2] Unlike most Americans though, he had a forum that he could use to address the inevitable negative assumptions about some of the nations involved and their people. "Lenny paid a price for his open-mouthed activism, but that never deterred him from being a warrior for what he felt was right" (Bernstein and Haws 2008, 56). With "A Birthday Tribute to Shostakovich" (5 January 1966), he showed the world that Communists are people, too (while avoiding clearly negative statements about the Soviet Union), brought Shostakovich's name to the lips of international viewers, and might have increased the Russian composer's income.[3] Those who thought Latin America was populated by ignorant, violent, crude, uneducated reprobates certainly had to change their opinion after seeing his portrayal of the educated, cultured side of the region in "The Latin American Spirit" (8 March 1963). The maestro's pacifist ideologies are seen as what could be described as his understated proselytizing against the Vietnam War in "*Fidelio: A Celebration of Life*" (29 March 1970), "The Anatomy of a Symphony Orchestra" (24 May 1970), and "Holst: *The Planets*" (26 March 1972).

Bernstein had a long history of supporting civil rights before his *Young People's Concerts*. He readily included African Americans in his broadcasts with the same fanfare he gave other talented performers. When the racial strife of the mid-sixties threatened to tear the country apart, Bernstein very pointedly presented African Americans with great honor and respect (while including irrefutable evidence of their accomplishments) in "Alumni Reunion" (19 April 1967). The maestro, however, seemed oblivious to women's rights until the feminist movement brought them to his attention. He boldly scheduled a disabled conductor, briefly related the story of his illness, then switched to his excellent musical abilities ("Young Performers No. 7," 22 February 1966). Fighting for the rights of an oppressed minority was in accord with his personal philosophy. His treating African Americans like treasures, women as equals, and the disabled as important contributors to society must have helped change some people's attitudes. He understood how an appearance on an internationally televised *Young Peoples Concert* could help someone's career. Once people saw the famous maestro giving opportunities to African Americans and women, they might be inspired to do the same.

As the father of three (and as an empathic individual who probably felt like a father to the children of the world), he intentionally and subtly reached out to at-risk teens who might have been seduced by the drug culture of the time when he preached against hallucinogenic drug use in "Berlioz Takes a

Trip" (25 May 1969). His altruism is in contrast with his blindness about his own addictions to alcohol, prescription drugs, and cigarettes; he was not alone in this since in the 1960s society at large was only beginning to acknowledge the addictive nature of these legal, socially acceptable drugs. Nonetheless, Bernstein's personal shortcomings are not evident in his *Young People's Concerts*. His sense of responsibility as a citizen of the United States is proudly displayed when he openly lectured teens who believed in "hanging loose" and "doing your own thing" on the obligations of living in a democracy in "Forever Beethoven!" (28 January 1968). The result, however, may not have been as significant as he had hoped because the target of his homilies—hippies—was not watching. Adolescents sliding down the slippery slope of hallucinogenics and the counterculture were not the type to turn to an arts education program. It is more likely that he hoped wavering teens would be swayed.

Bernstein's desire to teach and help mankind led to one of his most heartfelt missions, international unity. His constant, joyful embrace of performers and composers from around the world must have encouraged his audiences to be less xenophobic. It would have been nearly impossible for someone who saw people from various countries being introduced so enthusiastically, interacting so warmly, and working together to create such beautiful music to remain suspicious of foreigners. He cared so much about his fellow man that he encouraged mankind toward peace and harmony.

The question arises, did Bernstein consciously incorporate these issues in the scripts for his *Young People's Concerts* or was this simply coincidence? Were the scripts he wrote shortly after the Cuban Missile Crisis, the My Lai Massacre, and race riots in cities unconnected to those events? There is no doubt that his first and most important goal was to teach about music, but too many events coincide for this to be unintentional. Furthermore, Bernstein himself gives the answer in the script for "Inside Pop—The Rock Revolution" (25 April 1967)—a show broadcast six days after "Alumni Reunion" and a few months after race riots in many cities in America. Any rock performer would have been thrilled to appear live on Bernstein's program, but he chose Janice Ian. She sang her tragic song "Society's Child" about society censuring interracial love—a song so controversial that it was banned by many radio stations and elicited shouts of "nigger lover" from some audiences. After interviewing Ian, Bernstein reflects:

> It would seem that the kids of our pop generation have a lot to say. Actually what Janis has written is a short social document: not a satire, not a protest— just a picture of a social trap. Of course, underneath it *is* the spirit of protest, which underlies so many of these pop songs. The implication is, and strongly, that this is not at all the way things ought to be. . . . In fact, the message in the lyrics of most of these songs *is* delivered by implication. This is one of our teenagers' strongest weapons: it amounts almost to a private language. But this use of implication produces another effect as well: something bordering

on poetry. Many of the lyrics, in their oblique allusions and "way-out" meta-phors are beginning to sound like real poems. And protected by this armor of poetry, our young lyricists can say just about anything they care to. And they do care. They care about civil rights, about sexual freedom, and peace; they talk about alienation, mysticism, drugs. ("Inside Pop—The Rock Revolution," 25 April 1967, 11–12)

All these issues, however, are outside the realm of music. Bernstein also en-deavored to change four facets of the musical canons. He actively sought to increase the acceptance of certain composers not previously in the canon, as well as foster tonality, American music, and the aesthetic position of what to-day we call postmodernism. This series was one of the venues through which he helped shape opinions about and increase the visibility of not only Latin American composers but also Dimitri Shostakovich, Charles Ives, Gustav Mahler, and Aaron Copland.[4] However, the time, energy, and attention he invested on tonality, American music, and postmodernism changed during the course of the series.

Bernstein's support of tonality is well known. The composers and works he championed were reactionary (incorporating to some degree tonality, melody, regularity, clarity, and so forth) and reserved avant-garde concepts (incorporating serialism, atonality, ambiguity, and complex structures) for the representation of stressful or tumultuous moments rather than for an intel-lectual appreciation of form and structure. Eighty-eight percent of the 112 twentieth-century works that were performed on his *Young People's Concerts* were reactionary. Bernstein's most immoderate comments surfaced whenever he discussed purely avant-garde music, ranging from pointedly neutral to sarcastic and painfully insulting. Again, his attitudes did not alter with time, but his expression of them did. His early comments were not overtly criti-cal, just a bit flippant. Bernstein did later discuss a few avant-garde works by Copland and Ives at some length, but always to explain what he saw as the dramatic purpose behind the avant-garde techniques—to his mind, the only acceptable reason to employ these techniques. By the time he performed the last avant-garde piece on his *Young People's Concerts* (Lukas Foss's *Phorion* in "Bach Transmogrified," 27 April 1969), Bernstein was openly hostile. He could not understand why his friend abandoned reactionary music to com-pose a work he felt was "murdering Bach" (19). If his deprecating remarks did not convert members of his audience to his way of thinking, those who hated the avant-garde found affirmation from the maestro. Late in his life Bernstein observed that during the time of his *Young People's Concerts* many thought tonality was dead—only avant-garde works were worthy—but "the return to tonality seems to be coming true" (Cott 2013, 128).

Supporting American performers and composers was an important mission for both Bernstein and the Philharmonic. He was hired, in part, because he was an American and because his interpretations of American music were engaging and insightful. He took his mission to heart. The proportion of American musicians in the orchestra increased to seventy-eight percent by 1969 (Shanet 1975, 347–348). His first season as music director of the Philharmonic included a survey of American music in his *Young People's Concert*, "What Is American Music?" (1 February 1958). Slightly under one-third of the works he conducted for the Philharmonic were by American composers (347). As Sedgwick Clark says, "his fellow American composers never had a greater champion" (Sedgwick 2007, 26). As time passed, though, he found few American composers who met his standards, so he was left showcasing primarily Copland, Gershwin, Ives, himself, and a few others. A lack of worthy (American or otherwise) new works was actually a factor in his decision to retire from the orchestra.

Arguably one of Bernstein's greatest influences was his anticipation of postmodernism. This term can have many definitions, and Jonathan D. Kramer endeavors to enumerate them as they relate to music in his essay "The Nature and Origins of Musical Postmodernism" (Kramer 2002, 13–26).[5] Of the sixteen characteristics he postulates, several are found in Bernstein's *Young People's Concerts*. The maestro certainly considered music "not as autonomous but as relevant to cultural, social, and political contexts" (16). Wherever relevant, he called attention to "quotations of or references to music of many traditions and cultures" and programmed "pluralism and eclecticism" as much as possible. The maestro certainly challenged the "barriers between 'high' and 'low' styles" and questioned "the mutual exclusivity of elitist and populist values" at every opportunity. If my assumptions about Bernstein's intentions are accurate, he hints to listeners that "multiple meanings" can be found in the works he performed.

Bernstein's *Young People's Concerts* reflect the changing attitudes toward popular culture and the dying reverence for high culture in the late twentieth century. He could include some lowbrow elements in the series since children are nominally lowbrows. Yet at first the maestro had to be cautious about weaving lowbrow culture into the programs for many reasons (see chapter 3). Later, he boldly included them. Throughout the series, he treated jazz, musical theater, and folk music with the same reverence as classical music. In "A Birthday Tribute to Shostakovich" (24), he mentions that Shostakovich included "what used to be called Salon Music—that is, music not so much for the concert hall as for hotel-lobbies and old-fashioned restaurants, or maybe for a private, elegant tea-party" in his Symphony no.9. The maestro even teases highbrows and their pompous derision of waltzes in "A Toast to Vienna in 3/4 Time" (25 December

1967, 7). People now would be surprised to find that when Bernstein's *Young People's Concerts* began, symphonies (as well as operas) were considered upper middlebrow rather than pure highbrow. Allusions to popular music were an insignificant part of the programs until the Beatles burst on the scene in 1964. At his first opportunity, the maestro analyzed a Beatles song and a Mozart sonata with the same loving attention to detail in "What Is Sonata Form?" (6 November 1964); Bernstein, Mozart, and the Beatles were sufficiently famous that such a comparison was possible. From then on, he incorporated popular music whenever he felt it was warranted. In the later programs, he occasionally makes classical music "cool" by noting how rock musicians accept it, such as in "Forever Beethoven!" (28 January 1968, 6). Furthermore, the composers he chose to champion were known for enthusiastically incorporating folk and popular elements into some of their classical works. Bernstein's postmodern inclusiveness in his compositions is well known; his *Young People's Concerts* show that this inclusiveness was central to his choice of repertory as well. His attitude never changed. Society changed around him, allowing him to reveal his love of all styles.

Sometimes his *Young People's Concerts* offer a glimpse of the inner Bernstein. His vexation with illogical behavior oozed out in his disparaging remarks about astrology in "Holst: *The Planets*" (26 March 1972, 20–21). "The Genius of Paul Hindemith" (23 February 1964) was motivated by an emotional explosion fired by his anger with the unfavorable reception of reactionary composers (in particular, Hindemith and himself) by critics and avant-garde composers. The explosion was mitigated by the time it reached the small screen (particularly since his contract demanded that there be nothing controversial on the programs) but nonetheless colored the final broadcast.

The maestro was not an eccentric musician who lived only for his art; his abilities as a good businessman (and his self-interest) benefitted not only himself but also the Philharmonic, its players, and living composers whose works were performed. He successfully negotiated with network president William S. Paley regarding producing and televising the series on CBS, thereby increasing the exposure (and income) of the Philharmonic and its conductor. He also served the orchestra's management and members well by using his *Young People's Concerts* rehearsal time in a cost-effective way, linking it to the subscription series or recording sessions. He probably increased LP sales by frequently scheduling pieces available on LP for television performance. Bernstein knew how to manage money, generate profits, and bring performers and composers into the public eye.

The deep impression these programs made on the average viewer can be gleaned from the fan mail. Craig Urguhart remembered that Bernstein "loved his fans and he knew how important they were to him because it takes them to make music too" (Sherman 2010, 53), and there is every indication that he read his fan mail (Cott 2013, 71). The preceding chapters are peppered with letters from fans commenting on specific programs. His admirers also offered high praise along with more general comments. Harold S. Walker, a sergeant in the U.S. Army stationed in Tacoma, Washington, reported that "your TV programs are our only source of a better understanding of the finer things in life" (1967). David Arnold wrote, "It is with love that you serve the children of American through T.V." (1958). In 1958, Armin Beck wrote to the National Education Association noting that Bernstein's "excellent" teaching had profound influence on the children and adults of America and recommended that he be made an honorary life member. There are many such letters of praise from both teachers and students. That same year, Miss Evalene J. Bill praised the maestro for the "perfectly wonderful thing you are doing for *all* America."

The Bernstein that many now know is the older maestro after he left the Philharmonic. In those last years of his life, Bernstein became more flamboyant and gave his tendency to excess free rein. For his *Young People's Concerts* though, he had to be very disciplined, remaining within TV strictures by keeping within time constraints, avoiding controversial topics and language in the scripts, keeping his audiences, sponsors, and the network pleased by carefully selecting interesting topics and pieces, giving lively, lucid presentations, and so forth. This was, however, not an anomaly. In his early and middle years, the maestro was successful in many and various endeavors that required such discipline and restraint, such as composing, touring, writing and making various television presentations, and managing his career. The dramatic change occurred between 1975 and 1976. The incidents and causes for this change are described by Humphrey Burton in his biography *Leonard Bernstein* and relate to his wife Felicia's cancer and Bernstein "coming out" as a homosexual. In December 1976, Bernstein ended speculation about his sexuality and marriage as he described to a Philharmonic audience the strife Shostakovich endured defiantly fighting the tyranny of the Soviet political machine while composing his Fourteenth Symphony. Within his fifteen-minute talk that prefaced the performance, Bernstein added:

> Studying this work, I came to realize that as death approaches [Bernstein was fifty-eight at the time] an artist must cast off everything that may be restraining him and create in complete freedom. I decided that I had to do this for myself, to live the rest of my life as I want. (H. Burton 1994, 438)

After Felicia died in 1978, what remained of her stabilizing influence was gone; he no longer cared what he said or "whom he shocked" (458). Bernstein was a far more disciplined individual during the years of his *Young People's Concerts*.

The series itself is still very much alive. Twenty-five of the fifty-three programs were selected, remastered, and made available first in VHS format and later as DVDs. Now all fifty-three programs are available on DVD. Joseph Horowitz bemoaned the unsuccessful attempts to rebroadcast the programs in the United States in his 1992 *New York Times* article, "Is Bernstein Passé on Television? Only in America," as Germany and Japan enthusiastically rebroadcast them. Finally in 2002, the cable channel Trio began broadcasting the remastered programs, with new introductions by guest hosts Joshua Bell, Whoopi Goldberg, and John Lithgow.[6]

Bernstein's contribution to music is still honored by a flood of new publications on everything from *West Side Story* (Simeone 2009, Wells 2011) to a survey of his influence in *Leonard Bernstein, American Original: How a Modern Renaissance Man Transformed Music and the World during His New York Philharmonic Years, 1943–1976* (Bernstein and Haws 2008) and a fascinating new collection of his letters (Simeone 2013). Bernstein was featured on the cover of a recent issue of *BBC Music Magazine* that bore the headline, "Why he was the greatest musician of modern times, composer, conductor, teacher: how he mastered all three."[7] Sedgwick Clark (editor of *Musical America*, who was also the author of one of the several Bernstein articles in the issue) did not know Bernstein personally but grew up watching the *Young People's Concerts* and said, as many have, "Bernstein changed my life."[8] Another author in the *BBC* magazine encomium, writer and broadcaster Edward Seckerson, wrote, "I only met Bernstein once; the most satisfying hour of my career."[9] Such comments are pervasive, coming from both professional musicians, who feel Bernstein gave their life focus, and non-musicians, who simply gained a lifelong love of classical music from Bernstein's talks. Brian G. Rose confirms this:

> Through their national network exposure, the *Young People's Concerts* helped initiate an entire generation into the wonders of music making, and there are many young conductors today who credit the series for changing the course of their lives. (Rose 1992, 7)

This was true not only for young conductors, but also for young performers and music teachers. Professionals and amateurs alike, viewers of Bernstein's *Young People's Concerts* often work to pass on their love of music, if only by purchasing DVDs of the programs for their children and grandchildren.

Many of the musicians Bernstein touched realize their responsibility to carry on the maestro's legacy. His friend and former assistant Craig Urquhart (Vice President for Public Relations and Promotion for the Leonard Bernstein Office) was inspired by Bernstein's young performers programs to establish The Craig Urquhart Agency, dedicated to assisting musicians and organizations in the arts. Marin Alsop discovered that she wanted to be a conductor when her father took her to one of Bernstein's *Young People's Concerts* in New York; she eventually studied under Bernstein, becoming one of his protégés.[10] Alsop not only keeps Bernstein's legacy alive by performing his works (such as the 2009 productions of *Mass* in Baltimore and the District of Columbia), but also through such activities as the ten-month Bernstein festival called "The Bernstein Project" at the Southbank Centre in London. She realizes the importance of supporting young musicians by sponsoring the Taki Concordia Conducting Fellowship for young women conductors (http://www.takiconcordia.org), and she supports education, the disadvantaged, and the next generation. Her "OrchKids" outreach program is a "year-round during and after school music program designed to create social change and nurture promising futures for youth in Baltimore City neighbourhoods" and is offered "in collaboration with several community partners, including Baltimore City Public Schools; OrchKids provides music education, instruments, academic instruction, meals, as well as performance and mentorship opportunities at no cost." Bernstein was so proud of her that he said he would "put his hand in the fire" for her (Cott 2013, 125).

Anthony Tommasini titled a July 1998 article for the *New York Times* "When Bernstein Saw the Future." Although this article focused only on the maestro's *The Unanswered Question: Six Talks at Harvard* known as the Norton Lectures (and his projections regarding the future of avant-garde modernism versus tonality), Bernstein also made accurate predictions regarding the future of classical music in his *Young People's Concerts*. He opined that audiences would gravitate toward tonal music and pull away from purely avant-garde music unless it represented life's stressful moments. He knew that classical music could be energized by incorporating popular elements as well as elements from different times and different cultures. The maestro also advanced the concept of integrating context into music appreciation:

> That's really the best and most exciting way to know history: not just by studying about dates and battles and who was king of what in which century, but by coming close to the *art* of history—by looking at the pictures people painted in any certain period of history, or reading the poems they wrote, and hearing the music *they* heard. Then we can almost put ourselves in their place, and pretend we're living in those long-ago days; then we can really understand history—which is not just a dull subject in school, but an exciting way of knowing about what happened in our world before we were living in it. ("Unusual Instruments of the Past, Present, and Future," 27 March 1960, 19)

His prescient comments even described the plight of performing musicians in a technological age when he projected that one hundred years from now "who knows: maybe it will be all tape-music, which would put an awful lot of good musicians out of work. But luckily we don't have that problem yet" ("Unusual Instruments of the Past, Present, and Future," 29). Bernstein knew these auguries might come to pass in the twenty-first century.

Bernstein would be pleased to see that accessibility and the new approach to tonality are drawing audiences to orchestral concerts in the twenty-first century. Music Director Robert Spano and the Atlanta Symphony Orchestra founded and are successfully nurturing the Atlanta School of Composers who write tonal music with "a primacy of melody" that is influenced by world music and/or popular music; concertgoers buy more tickets for these concerts than for other classical music events.[11] John Corigliano's 2003 Concerto for Violin and Orchestra (drawn from the music he composed for the film *The Red Violin*) is the most performed concerto composed in the last quarter century.[12] Some conductors now tout their support of appealing works; for instance Alsop is now "hailed as one of the world's leading conductors for her artistic vision and commitment to accessibility in classical music."[13] Musical eclecticism is no longer such a pejorative term. Composer John Zorn easily ignores boundaries between genres, finding inspiration from such varied sources as John Cage, Carl W. Stalling (who composed and arranged for animated cartoons), the grindcore rock band Napalm Death (which blends elements of hardcore punk and death metal), and American jazz innovator Ornette Coleman. Bernstein would approve.

Joseph Horowitz confirmed the hope these new trends offer classical music by changing the subtitle of his book *Classical Music in America* from *A History of Its Rise and Fall* (for the 2005 edition) to simply *A History* (for the 2007 paperback edition). Horowitz subsequently discovered that jazz influences were no longer considered a threat in classical music (what he deemed the "jazz threat") and that the musical landscape had changed, as evidenced by Gershwin's and Ives's recent admission to the "rarified precincts of American classical music" (543). At this "post-classical" moment, according to Horowitz, music is at "a threshold at once frustrating and exhilarating" (548). Horowitz quotes Bernstein's Norton Lectures when the maestro asked "whither music?" noting that Bernstein "came up empty" (541). The answer, Horowitz feels, lies in popular music and music of non-Western cultures that have "refreshed classical music in our time." Bernstein did not come up empty. In his own way, he helped make that happen by opening minds.

In "A Tribute to Teachers" (29 November 1963), we find Leonard Bernstein's goal for his *Young People's Concerts* embraced more than just teaching:

> it is in that spirit that we play [Brahms Academic Festival Overture]; to honor . . . all the great teachers on earth who work so hard to give young people a world that is a better, richer, and more civilized place. (25)

Appendix A

Young People's Concerts' *Program Numbers, Titles, and Dates with Chapter References and Possible Motivations for Topic*

This appendix offers an overview of the series by listing the program number, title of the *Young People's Concerts*, broadcast date, chapter(s) with a study of that particular program, and a possible motivation that likely guided Bernstein to his choice of topic. The abbreviation LB refers to Leonard Bernstein, NYP to the New York Philharmonic, and YPC to his *Young People's Concerts*.

No. 1: "What Does Music Mean?" 18 January 1958, chapter 1.
No. 2: "What Is American Music?" 1 February 1958, chapter 8, LB's Harvard thesis, LB supporting American music.
No. 3: "What Is Orchestration?" 8 March 1958.
No. 4: "What Makes Music Symphonic?" 13 December 1958, later seen in talk given in Berlin during 1960 NYP tour.[1]
No. 5: "What Is Classical Music?" 24 January 1959.
No. 6: "Humor in Music," 28 February 1959, chapter 2, audience request.
No. 7: "What Is a Concerto?" 28 March 1959.
No. 8: "Who Is Gustav Mahler?" 7 February 1960, LB's effort as Mahler advocate to change canon.
No. 9: "Young Performers No. 1," 6 March 1960, encouraging young performers.
No. 10: "Unusual Instruments of the Past, Present, and Future," 27 March 1960, support of modernism.
No. 11: "*Second Hurricane* by Copland," 24 April 1960, chapter 8, friendship, past Philharmonic YPCs, American music.
No. 12: "Overtures and Preludes," 8 January 1961, chapter 2, LB's own childhood.

No. 13: "Aaron Copland Birthday Party," 12 February 1961, chapters 7 and 8, LB's friendship with Copland, American music.

No. 14: "Young Performers No. 2," 19 March 1961, chapter 6, encouraging youngsters and supporting international unity.

No. 15: "Folk Music in the Concert Hall," 9 April 1961, chapter 3, LB's own interests.

No. 16: "What Is Impressionism?" 1 December 1961.

No. 17: "The Road to Paris," 18 January 1962, chapter 3, importance of international influences, reference to Hope-Crosby "road" films.

No. 18: "Happy Birthday, Igor Stravinsky," 26 March 1962, chapter 8, composer's birthday, support of modernism.

No. 19: "Young Performers No.3," 13 April 1962, encouraging young performers.

No. 20: "The Sound of a Hall," 21 November 1962, chapter 2, opening of Lincoln Center.

No. 21: "What Is a Melody?" 21 December 1962.

No. 22: "Young Performers No. 4," 15 January 1963, chapter 6, encouraging youngsters and supporting international unity.

No. 23: "The Latin American Spirit," 8 March 1963, chapter 5, Cuban Missile Crisis.

No. 24: "A Tribute to Teachers," 29 November 1963, chapter 1, honoring LB's own teachers and the profession of teaching.

No. 25: "Young Performers No. 5," 23 December 1963, chapter 6, encouraging youngsters and supporting international unity.

No. 26: "The Genius of Paul Hindemith," 23 February 1964, chapter 2, Hindemith's death, obits, and published "appreciations."

No. 27: "Jazz in the Concert Hall," 11 March 1964, chapter 8, LB's love of jazz, incorporation of "lowbrow" art of jazz, LB's Harvard thesis, *Omnibus* program on jazz.

No. 28: "What Is Sonata Form?" 6 November 1964.

No. 29: "Farewell to Nationalism," 30 November 1964, chapter 3, LB's own attitudes, postmodernist links between lowbrow (folk, and the like) and highbrow art.

No. 30: "Young Performers No. 6," 28 January 1965, chapter 6, encouraging youngsters and supporting international unity.

No. 31: "A Tribute to Sibelius," 19 February 1965, Sibelius's 100th birthday, honored by United States.

No. 32: "Musical Atoms: A Study of Intervals," 29 November 1965, link between music and science.

No. 33: "The Sound of an Orchestra," 14 December 1965.

No. 34: "A Birthday Tribute to Shostakovich," 5 January 1966, chapters 1 and 5, composer's birthday, Cold War, support of reactionary modernists.

No. 35: "Young Performers No. 7," 22 February 1966, encouraging young performers.

No. 36: "What Is a Mode?" 23 November 1966, Jamie Bernstein's suggestion.

No. 37: "Young Performers No. 8," 27 January 1967, encouraging youngsters.

No. 38: "Charles Ives: American Pioneer," 23 February 1967, chapters 2 and 8, release of new Philharmonic Ives LPs, support of Ives and American music.

No. 39: "Alumni Reunion," 19 April 1967, chapter 6, civil rights for African Americans.

No. 40: "A Toast to Vienna in 3/4 Time," 25 December 1967, birthdays of Vienna Philharmonic Orchestra and New York Philharmonic, waltzes at Christmas.

No. 41: "Forever Beethoven!" 28 January 1968, chapter 6, Vietnam War, meaning of democracy.

No. 42: "Young Performers No. 9," 31 March 1968, encouraging young performers.

No. 43: "Quiz-Concert: How Musical Are You?" 26 May 1968, old quiz show on radio, past Philharmonic YPCs.

No. 44: "Fantastic Variations (*Don Quixote*)," 25 December 1968, nostalgia for LB's NYP debut.

No. 45: "Bach Transmogrified," 27 April 1969, chapter 3, *Omnibus* on Bach, popular LP of J. S. Bach pieces performed on Moog synthesizer, "Switched-On Bach," LB's friendship with Lukas Foss.

No. 46: "Berlioz Takes a Trip," 25 May 1969, chapter 6, hippies, drugs, and counterculture.

No. 47: "Two Ballet Birds," 14 September 1969.

No. 48: "*Fidelio*: A Celebration of Life," 29 March 1970, chapter 5, Beethoven centennial and Vietnam War.

No. 49: "The Anatomy of a Symphony Orchestra," 24 May 1970, chapter 5, Vietnam War, My Lai Massacre.

No. 50: "A Copland Celebration," 27 December 1970, chapter 8, LB's friendship with Copland, composer's birthday, support of American music and modernism.

No. 51: "Thus Spake Richard Strauss," 4 April 1971, chapter 3, the movie *2001* (not mentioned in program).

No. 52: "Liszt and the Devil," 13 February 1972, Philharmonic Liszt festival.

No. 53: "Holst: *The Planets*," 26 March 1972, chapters 5 and 6, pacifism, hippies, and astrology, Philharmonic season, support of reactionary modernism.

Appendix B

Alphabetical List of
Bernstein's Young People's Concerts

Program Title	Program Number	Broadcast Date
Aaron Copland Birthday Party	13	12 February 1961
Alumni Reunion	39	19 April 1967
The Anatomy of a Symphony Orchestra	49	24 May 1970
Bach Transmogrified	45	27 April 1969
Berlioz Takes a Trip	46	25 May 1969
A Birthday Tribute to Shostakovich	34	5 January 1966
Charles Ives: American Pioneer	38	23 February 1967
A Copland Celebration	50	27 December 1970
Fantastic Variations *(Don Quixote)*	44	25 December 1968
Farewell to Nationalism	29	30 November 1964
Fidelio: A Celebration of Life	48	29 March 1970
Folk Music in the Concert Hall	15	9 April 1961
Forever Beethoven!	41	28 January 1968
The Genius of Paul Hindemith	26	23 February 1964
Happy Birthday, Igor Stravinsky	18	26 March 1962
Holst: *The Planets*	53	26 March 1972
Humor in Music	6	28 February 1959
Jazz in the Concert Hall	27	11 March 1964
The Latin American Spirit	23	8 March 1963
Liszt and the Devil	52	13 February 1972
Musical Atoms: A Study of Intervals	32	29 November 1965
Overtures and Preludes	12	8 January 1961
Quiz-Concert: How Musical Are You?	43	26 May 1968
The Road to Paris	17	18 January 1962
The Second Hurricane by Copland	11	24 April 1960
The Sound of a Hall	20	21 November 1962
The Sound of an Orchestra	33	14 December 1965

(continued)

Program Title	Program Number	Broadcast Date
Thus Spake Richard Strauss	51	4 April 1971
A Toast to Vienna in 3/4 Time	40	25 December 1967
A Tribute to Sibelius	31	19 February 1965
A Tribute to Teachers	24	29 November 1963
Two Ballet Birds	47	14 September 1969
Unusual Instruments of the Past, Present, and Future	10	27 March 1960
What Does Music Mean?	1	18 January 1958
What Is a Concerto?	7	28 March 1959
What Is a Melody?	21	21 December 1962
What Is a Mode?	36	23 November 1966
What Is American Music?	2	1 February 1958
What Is Classical Music?	5	24 January 1959
What Is Impressionism?	16	1 December 1961
What Is Orchestration?	3	8 March 1958
What Is Sonata Form?	28	6 November 1964
What Makes Music Symphonic?	4	13 December 1958
Who Is Gustav Mahler?	8	7 February 1960
Young Performers No. 1	9	6 March 1960
Young Performers No. 2	14	19 March 1961
Young Performers No. 3	19	13 April 1962
Young Performers No. 4	22	15 January 1963
Young Performers No. 5	25	23 December 1963
Young Performers No. 6	30	28 January 1965
Young Performers No. 7	35	22 February 1966
Young Performers No. 8	37	27 January 1967
Young Performers No. 9	42	31 March 1968

Appendix C

Production and Broadcast Information for Bernstein's Young People's Concerts

$\mathcal{T}$he televised *Young People's Concerts* were broadcast and produced by the CBS Television Network. The production data for each show is given below, organized chronologically and broken down by seasons. Programs were broadcast live until separate taping and airing dates are given. All times are Eastern Standard Time. This information comes from the title page of the individual script for each program unless otherwise noted. The sponsor is never given on the title page, but is usually listed on either the opening or closing page of each script. When the sponsor is not listed in the script, the information comes from either the Nielsen ratings or advertisements in *New York Times* as indicated. When the *New York Times* television listings provided a different broadcast time from that provided by the script, both times are given. The members of the production crew changed over the run, except that Leonard Bernstein wrote all programs, and Roger Englander produced all programs as well as directing no's. 4–53. Full names for the other production crew members are listed the first time their name appears, and their initials on subsequent programs.

KINESCOPE FILM

First Season, 1957–1958, remote from Carnegie Hall

Program 1: "What Does Music Mean?" Aired: Saturday, 18 January 1958, 12:00–1:00 p.m. [Sponsor: None listed]. Director: Charles S. Dubin; assistant to the producer: Mary Rodgers; production assistant: Elizabeth (Candy) Finkler; executive producer: Richard Lewine.

Program 2: "What Is American Music?" Saturday, 1 February 1958, 12:00–1:00 p.m. Production crew: CD, MR, EF, RL.

Program 3: "What Is Orchestration?" Saturday, 8 March 1958, 12:00–1:00 p.m. Production crew: CD, MR, EF, RL.

Second Season, 1958–1959

Program 4: "What Makes Music Symphonic?" Saturday, 13 December 1958, 12:00–1:00 p.m. [Program not televised due to CBS strike]. Production crew: MR, EF, Richard Lewine's title changed to director of special programs.

Program 5: "What Is Classical Music?" Saturday, 24 January 1959, 12:00–1:00 p.m. Production crew: MR, EF, RL.

Program 6: "Humor in Music." Saturday, 28 February 1959, 12:00–1:00 p.m. Production crew: MR, EF, RL. Added to production crew: assistant to Mr. Bernstein: Jack Gottlieb; music consultant: David Oppenheim; production assistant: Ronald Liss.

Program 7: "What Is a Concerto?" Saturday, 28 March 1959, 12:00–1:00 p.m. Production crew: MR, JG, DO, R. Liss, RL.

BLACK AND WHITE 2-INCH
QUADRUPLEX VIDEO TAPE[1]

Third Season, 1959–1960, VTR remote from Carnegie Hall

Program 8: "Who Is Gustav Mahler?" Sunday, 7 February 1960, 1:00–2:00 p.m. [Sponsor: Shell, from Nielsen]. Production crew: MR, RL, Marc Brugnoni replaced Finkler as production assistant.

Program 9: "Young Performers No. 1." Sunday, 6 March 1960, 1:00–2:00 p.m. [Sponsor: Shell, from Nielsen]. Production crew: MR, EF, RL. Teleprompter used.

Program 10: "Unusual Instruments of the Past, Present, and Future." Taped: [Saturday], 26 March 1960, 12:00–1:00 p.m. Aired: Sunday, 27 March 1960, 1:00–2:00 p.m. Sponsor: Shell Oil Company. Production crew: MR, RL. Production assistants: EF, Joan Pilkington.

Program 11: "*Second Hurricane* by Copland." Taped: [Saturday], 23 April, 1960, 12:00–1:00 p.m. Aired: Sunday, 24 April 1960, 1:00–2:00 p.m. Sponsor: Shell. Production crew: MR, EF, RL.

Fourth Season, 1960–1961

Program 12: "Overtures and Preludes." Taped: [Saturday], 22 October 1960, 12:00–1:00 p.m. Aired: Sunday, 8 January 1961, 4:00–5:00 p.m. Sponsor: Shell. Production crew: MR, RL, production assistant: James Bernard.

Program 13: "Aaron Copland Birthday Party." Taped: 12 November 1960, 12:00–1:00 p.m. Aired: Sunday, 12 February 1961, 4:00–5:00 p.m. Sponsor: Shell. Production crew: MR, JG, JB, RL.

Program 14: "Young Performers No. 2." Taped: Saturday, 18 March 1961, 12:00–1:00 p.m. Aired: Sunday, 19 March 1961, 4:00 p.m.–5:00 p.m. Sponsor: Shell. Production crew: MR, JP, RL.

Program 15: "Folk Music in the Concert Hall." Taped: Saturday, 8 April 1961, 12:00–1:00 p.m. Aired: Sunday, 9 April 1961, 3:00–4:00 p.m. Sponsor: Shell. Production crew: MR, JP, RL.

Fifth Season, 1961–1962

Program 16: "What Is Impressionism?" Taped: Saturday, 14 October 1961, 12:00–1:00 p.m. Aired: Friday, 1 December 1961, 7:30–8:30 p.m. Sponsor: Shell. Production crew: MR, production assistant: Anthony Wolff.

Program 17: "The Road to Paris." Taped: Saturday, 11 November 1961, 12:00–1:00 p.m. Aired: Thursday, 18 January 1962, 7:30–8:30 p.m. Sponsor: Shell. Production crew: MR, AW.

Program 18: "Happy Birthday, Igor Stravinsky."[2] Taped: Saturday, 24 March 1962, 12:00–1:00 p.m. Aired: Monday, 26 March 1962, 7:30–8:30 p.m. Sponsor: Shell. Production crew: MR, production assistant: Lewis Lloyd.

Program 19: "Young Performers No. 3." Taped: Saturday, 7 April 1962, 12:00–1:00 p.m. Aired: Friday, 14 [corrected to 13 in pencil] April 1962, 7:30–8:30 p.m. Sponsor: Shell. Production crew: MR, LL.

Sixth Season, 1962–1963, VTR Remote from Philharmonic Hall, Lincoln Center

Program 20: The Sound of a Hall." Preview: Sunday, 30 September 1962, 3:00–4:00 p.m. Taped: Saturday, 13 October 1962, 12:00–1:00 p.m. Aired: Wednesday, 21 November 1962, 7:30–8:30 p.m. Sponsor: Shell. Production crew: MR, EF.

Program 21: "What Is a Melody?" Taped: Saturday, 3 November 1962, 12:00–1:00 p.m. Aired: Friday, 21 December 1962, 7:30–8:30 p.m. Sponsor: Shell. Production crew: MR, EF.

Program 22: "Young Performers No. 4." Taped: Saturday, 12 January 1963, 12:00–1:00 p.m. Aired: Tuesday, 15 January 1963, 7:30–8:30 p.m. Sponsor: Shell. Production crew: MR, EF.

Program 23: "The Latin American Spirit." Taped: Saturday, 9 February 1963, 12:00–1:00 p.m. Aired: Friday, 8 March 1963, 7:30–8:30 p.m. Sponsor: Shell. Production crew: EF, production assistant: Tirandaz S. Irani.

Seventh Season, 1963–1964

Program 24: "A Tribute to Teachers." Taped: Saturday, 2 November 1963, 12:00–1:00 p.m. Aired: Friday, 29 November 1963, 7:30–8:30 p.m. Sponsor: Shell. Production crew: assistants to the producer: RM, EF, production assistant: Robert Livingston.

Program 25: "Young Performers No. 5." Taped: Saturday, 23 November 1963, 12:00–1:00 p.m. Aired: Monday, 23 December 1963, 7:30–8:30 p.m. Sponsor: Shell. Production crew: RM, EF, RL.

Program 26: "The Genius of Paul Hindemith." Taped: Saturday, 25 January 1964, 12:00–1:00 p.m. Aired: Sunday, 23 February 1964, 5:00–6:00 p.m. Sponsor: Shell. Production crew: RM, EF, RL.

Program 27: "Jazz in the Concert Hall." Taped: Saturday, 8 February 1964, 12:00–1:00 p.m. Aired: Wednesday, 11 March 1964, 7:30–8:30 p.m. Sponsor: Shell. Production crew: RM, EF, RL.

Eighth Season, 1964–1965

Program 28: "What Is Sonata Form?" Taped: Saturday, 17 October 1964, 2:30–3:30 p.m. Aired: Friday, 6 November 1964, 7:30–8:30 p.m. Sponsor: Bell Telephone System. Production crew: MR, EF, assistant to the director: John Corigliano Jr., production assistant: Patricia Jordan.

Program 29: "Farewell to Nationalism." Taped: Saturday, 21 November 1964, 2:35–3:35 p.m. Aired: Monday, 30 November 1964, 7:30–8:30 p.m. Sponsor: Bell Telephone. Production crew: MR, EF, PJ.

Program 30: "Young Performers No. 6." Taped: Saturday, 23 January 1965, 2:35–3:35 p.m. Aired: Thursday, 28 January 1965, 8:00:10–8:58:54 p.m. [*sic*]. Sponsor: Bell Telephone. Production crew: MR, EF, PJ, JG, assistant to the director: John Corigliano Jr.

Program 31: "A Tribute to Sibelius." Taped: Saturday, 13 February 1965, 2:35–3:35 p.m. Aired: Friday, 19 February 1965, 7:30:10–8:28:54 p.m. [*sic*]. Sponsor: Bell Telephone. Production crew: MR, EF, JC, PJ, JG.

Ninth Season, 1965–1966

Program 32: "Musical Atoms: A Study of Intervals." Taped: Saturday, 23 October 1965, 2:35–3:35 p.m. Aired: Monday, 29 November 1965, 7:30–8:30 p.m. Sponsor: Bell Telephone. Production crew: MR, EF, JC, PJ, JG.

Program 33: "The Sound of an Orchestra." Taped: Saturday, 20 November 1965, 2:35–3:35 p.m. Aired: Tuesday, 14 December 1965, 7:30–8:30 p.m. Sponsor: Bell Telephone. Production crew: MR, EF, JC, PJ, JG.

Program 34: "A Birthday Tribute to Shostakovich." Taped: Saturday, 18 December 1965, 2:35–3:35 p.m. Aired: Wednesday, 5 January 1966, 7:30–8:30 p.m. Sponsor: Bell Telephone. Production crew: MR, EF, JC, PJ, JG.

Program 35: "Young Performers No. 7." Taped: Saturday, 19 February 1966, 2:35–3:35 p.m. Aired: Tuesday, 22 February 1966, 7:30–8:30 p.m. Sponsor: Bell Telephone. Production crew: MR, EF, JC, PJ, JG.

TWO-INCH QUAD TAPE IN COLOR

Tenth Season, 1966–1967

Program 36: "What Is a Mode?" Taped: Saturday, 22 October 1966, 2:35–3:35 p.m. Aired: Wednesday, 23 November 1966, 7:30–8:30 p.m. Sponsors: AT&T and Bell System Associated Companies. Production crew: MR, JC, associate producer: CF, production assistant: David Kent, assistant to Mr. Bernstein: Robert B. Browne.

Program 37: "Young Performers No. 8." Taped: Saturday, 17 December 1966, 2:35–3:35 p.m. Aired: Friday, 27 January 1967, 7:30–8:30 p.m. Sponsors: AT&T and Bell System. Production crew: EF, MR, JC, DK, RB.

Program 38: "Charles Ives: American Pioneer." Taped: Saturday, 21 January 1967, 2:35–3:35 p.m. Aired: Thursday, 23 February 1967, 7:30–8:30 p.m. Sponsors: AT&T and Bell System. Production crew: EF, MR, JC, DK.

Program 39: "Alumni Reunion." Taped: Saturday, 25 February 1967, 2:35–3:35 p.m. Aired: Wednesday, 19 April 1967, 7:30–8:30 p.m. Sponsors: AT&T and Bell System. Production crew: EF, MR, JC, DK, JG.

Eleventh Season, 1967–1968

Program 40: "A Toast to Vienna in 3/4 Time." Taped: Saturday, 28 October 1967, 2:35–3:35 p.m. Aired: Monday, 25 December 1967, 5–6 p.m. [Sponsor: Polaroid Corporation, from Nielsen]. Production crew: EF, MR, JC, JG, production assistant: Ann Blumenthal.

Program 41: "Forever Beethoven!" Taped: Saturday, 6 January 1968, 2:35–3:35 p.m. Aired: Sunday, 28 January 1968, 4:30–5:30 p.m. [Sponsor: Eastman-Kodak, from Nielsen]. [Program not broadcast in full due to "overlong hockey game."] Repeated: 2 June 1968[3] [Sponsor: Polaroid, from Nielsen]. Production crew: EF, MR, JC, AB, JG.

Program 42: "Young Performers No. 9." Taped: Saturday, 27 January 1968, 2:35–3:35 p.m. Aired: Sunday, 31 March 1968 [listed in Nielsen as 24 Marth], 4:30–5:30 p.m. [Sponsor: Polaroid Corporation?]. Production crew: EF, MR, JC, AB, JG.

Program 43: "Quiz-Concert: How Musical Are You?" Taped: Saturday, 24 February 1968, 2:35–3:35 p.m. Aired: Sunday, 12 May 1968, 4:30–5:30 p.m. Production crew: EF, MR, JC, AB, JG.

Twelfth Season, 1968–1969

Program 44: "Fantastic Variations *(Don Quixote)*." Taped: Saturday, 26 October 1968, 2:35–3:35 p.m. Aired: Wednesday, 25 December 1968, 5:00–6:00 p.m. Listed in Display Ad, *New York Times*, 24 December 1968 as 5:30–6:30 p.m. Sponsor: Polaroid. Production crew: EF, MR, JC, AB, JG.

Program 45: "Bach Transmogrified." Taped: Saturday, 8 February 1969, 2:35–3:35 p.m. Scheduled for: Sunday, 30 March 1969, 4:00–5:00 p.m. but preempted. Aired: Sunday, 27 April 1969, 4:30–5:30 p.m. [time from "Television This Week," *New York Times*, 27 April 1969]. Sponsor: Polaroid. Production crew: EF, MR, JC, AB, JG.

Program 46: "Berlioz Takes a Trip." Taped: Saturday, 11 January 1969, 2:35–3:35 p.m. Aired: Sunday, 25 May 1969, 4:30–5:30 p.m. Sponsor: Polaroid. Production crew: EF, MR, JC, AB, JG.

Program 47: "Two Ballet Birds." Taped: Saturday, 19 April 1969, 2:35–3:35 p.m. Aired: Sunday, 14 September 1969, 4:30–5:30 p.m. Sponsor: Polaroid. Production crew: EF, MR, JC, AB, JG.

Thirteenth Season, 1969–1970: Bernstein Became Laureate Conductor

Program 48: "*Fidelio*: A Celebration of Life." Taped: Saturday, 10 January 1970, 2:35–3:35 p.m. Aired: Sunday, 29 March 1970, 4:30–5:30 p.m. Sponsor: Polaroid. Production crew: EF, MR, JC, AB, JG.

Program 49: "The Anatomy of an Orchestra." Taped: Saturday, 14 February 1970, 2:35–3:35 p.m. Aired: Sunday, 24 May 1970, 5:00–6:00 p.m. Sponsor: Polaroid. Production crew: EF, MR, JC, AB, JG.

Fourteenth Season, 1970–1971

Program 50: "A Copland Celebration." Taped: Saturday, 26 September 1970, 2:35–3:35 p.m. Aired: Sunday, 27 December 1970, 4:30–5:30 p.m. Listed in "Television This Week," *New York Times,* 27 December 1970 as 5:00–6:00 p.m. Sponsor: Polaroid Corporation, the Kitchens of Sara Lee, a subsidiary of Consolidated Food Corp.[4] Production crew: EF, MR, JC, AB.

Program 51: "Thus Spake Richard Strauss." Taped: Saturday, 24 October 1970, 2:35–3:35 p.m. Aired: Sunday, 4 April 1971, 5:00–6:00 p.m. Sponsor: Polaroid, the Kitchens of Sara Lee. Production crew: EF, MR, JC, AB.

Fifteenth Season, 1971–1972

Program 52: "Liszt and the Devil." Taped: Saturday, 14 November 1971, 2:35–3:35 p.m. Aired: Sunday, 13 February 1972, 4:30–5:30 p.m. Sponsor: Polaroid, the Kitchens of Sara Lee. Production crew: JC, AB, associate producer: Jim Gately, assistants to the producer: JC, Mary Ahern, production assistant: AB.

Program 53: "Holst: *The Planets*." Taped: Saturday, 18 December 1971, 2:35-3:35 p.m. Aired: Sunday, 26 March 1972, 4:30–5:30 p.m. Sponsor: Polaroid, the Kitchens of Sara Lee. Production crew: Jim G., JC, AB.

Appendix D

Young Performers on
Bernstein's Young People's Concerts

$\mathcal{T}$he information in this appendix has been compiled from a document in box/folder 990/03 and the script for each program. "[ncog]" indicates that no "country of origin" is given.

Young Performers No. 1, 6 March 1960, Program No. 9

1. **Daniel Bomb**, age 15, from Israel, cello, Dvořák's Concert for Cello and Orchestra in B minor, I. Conductor: **Kenneth Schermerhorn**, from Schenectady, NY.
2. **Barry Finclair**, age 14, from New York, NY, violin, Wieniawski's Concerto for Orchestra in D minor, no. 2, finale. Conductor: **Stefan Mengelberg** from Germany (now U.S. citizen).
3. **Alexandra Wager**, age 9, [ncog], narrator, Prokofieff's *Peter and Wolf.* Conductor: **Leonard Bernstein**.

Young Performers No. 2, 19 March 1961, Program No. 14

4. **Lynn Harrell**, age 16, from United States, cello, Dvořák's Concerto in B minor, op. 104, finale. Conductor: **Elyakum Shapira** from Israel.
5. **Jung Ja Kim**, age 16, from Korea, piano, Chopin's Concerto no. 1 in E minor, op. 11, II. Conductor: **Russell Stanger**, from Boston, MA.
6. **Veronica Tyler**, age 22, from United States, lyric soprano, Puccini's "Addio" from *La Boheme* and Menotti's "Lucy's Aria" from *The Telephone*. Conductor: **Gregory Millar** from United States (Greek parents).
7. **Henry Chapin**, age 12, from New York, NY, narrator, Britten's *Young Person's Guide to the Orchestra.* Conductor: **Leonard Bernstein**.

Young Performers No. 3, 13 April 1962, Program No. 19

    8. **Seiji Ozawa**, age 26, from Japan, conducted Mozart's Overture to *The Marriage of Figaro.*

    9. **Gary Karr**, age 20, from United States, double bass, Bloch-Antonini's *Prayer.* Conductor: **Maurice Peress**, age 32, [ncog].

   10. **Gary Karr**, double bass, Paganini-Reinshagen's Fantasy on a Theme from Rossini's *Israel in Egypt.* Conductor: **John Canarina**, age 27, [ncog].

   11. **Ruth and Naomi Segal**, age 21, [ncog], duo-piano; **Paula Robison**, age 20, flute and piccolo, [ncog]; **Paul Green**, age 13, [ncog], clarinet; **Tony Cirone**, age 20, xylophone, [ncog]; **Gary Karr,** double bass; **David Hopper**, age 14, [ncog], glockenspiel; Saint-Saens: *The Carnival of the Animals.* Conductor: **Leonard Bernstein.**

Young Performers No. 4, 15 January 1963, Program No. 22

   12. **Joan Wiener**, age 14, from Arlington, VA, piano, Mozart's Concerto for Piano and Orchestra in A major, K. 488, Allegro. Conductor: **Yuri Krasnopolsky**, United States.

   13. **Claudia Hoca**, age 12, from Buffalo, NY, piano, Mozart's Concerto for Piano and Orchestra in A major, K. 488, Andante. Conductor: **Zoltan Rozsnyai**, from Hungary.

   14. **Pamela Paul**, age 13, from New York, NY, piano, Mozart's Concerto for Piano and Orchestra in A major, K. 488, Presto. Conductor: **Serge Fournier**, from France.

   15. **André Watts**, age 16, from Philadelphia, PA, piano, Liszt's Concerto No.1 for Piano and Orchestra in E-flat major. Conductor: **Leonard Bernstein.**

Young Performers No. 5, 23 December 1963, Program No. 25

   16. **Heidi Lehwalder**, age 14, from Seattle, WA, harp, Handel's Concerto for Harp and Orchestra in B-flat major, op.4, no. 6, I. Conductor: **Leonard Bernstein.**

   17. **Heidi Lehwalder**, age 14, from Seattle, WA, harp; **Amos Eisenberg**, age 24, from Israel, flute; **Weldon Berry Jr.**, age 16, from TX, clarinet; Ravel's Introduction and Allegro for Harp, Flute, Clarinet, and Strings. Conductor: **Claudio Abbado**, from Italy.

   18. **Shulamith [*sic*] Ran**, age 16, from Israel, piano and composer, Ran's Capriccio for Piano and Orchestra (World Premier). Conductor: **Leonard Bernstein.**

19. Stephen Edward Kates, age 20, New York, NY, cello, Bartók's Rhapsody No. 1 for Cello and Orchestra, II. Conductor: **Zdenek Kosler**, Czechoslovakia.

20. Stephen Edward Kates, age 20, New York, NY, cello, Rossini's Overture to *William Tell*. Conductor: **Leonard Bernstein**.

Young Performers No. 6, 28 January 1965, Program No. 30

21. Patricia Michaelian, age 15, from San Francisco, CA, piano, Mozart's Concerto no. 20 in D minor, I. Conductor: **Leonard Bernstein**.

22. James Oliver Buswell, IV, age 18, from Wheaton, IL, violin, Mendelssohn's Concerto in E minor, op. 64, I. Conductor: **Leonard Bernstein**.

23. [No young performers], Ravel's *Ma Mère l'oye* (*Mother Goose Suite*), complete. Conductor: **Leonard Bernstein**.

Young Performers No. 7, 22 February 1966, Program No. 35

24. Paul Schoenfield, age 19, from Detroit, MI, piano, Mussorgsky's *Pictures at an Exhibition*, Promenade, Gnomus. Followed by Ravel's orchestration conducted by: **James DePreist**, Philadelphia, PA.

25. Stephanie Sebastian, age 19, from Hollywood, CA, piano, *Mussorgsky's Pictures at an Exhibition*, Promenade, The Old Castle. Followed by Ravel's orchestration conducted by: **Jacques Houtman** from Nirocourt, France.

26. David Oei, age 15, from Hong Kong, piano, *Mussorgsky's Pictures at an Exhibition*, Promenade, Tuileries, Promenade, Ballet of Chicks in their Shells. Followed by Ravel's orchestration conducted by: **Edo de Waart**, from Amsterdam, Netherlands.

27. Horacio Gutierrez, age 17, from Havannah, Cuba, piano, Mussorgsky's *Pictures at an Exhibition*, The Great Gate at Kiev. Followed by Ravel's orchestration conducted by: **Leonard Bernstein**.

Young Performers No. 8, 27 January 1967, Program No. 37

28. Mark Salkind, age 13, from San Francisco, CA, oboe; **Donald Green**, age 20, from New York, NY, cello; **Elmar Oliveira**, age 16, from Waterbury, CT, violin; **Fred Alston**, age 19, from Philadelphia, PA, bassoon, Haydn's Symphonia Concertante, Op. 84. 1st mvt. Conductor: **Juan Pablo Izquierdo** from Chile; 2nd and 3rd mvts by **Sylvia Caduff**, from Switzerland.

29. Stephen Dominko, age 19, from Trumbull, CT, accordion, Chopin's Concerto No. 2 in F minor, Finale. Conductor: **Sylvia Caduff**, from Switzerland.

30. George Reid, age 21, New York, NY, bass, Mozart's "In Diesen Heiligen Hallen" from *The Magic Flute*. Conductor: **Juan Pablo Izquierdo**, from Chile.

31. Young Uck Kim, age 19, from Korea, violin, Saint-Saëns's Concerto for Violin and Orchestra in B minor, I. Conductor: **Leonard Bernstein**.

Young Performers No. 9, 31 March 1968, Program No. 42

32. Lawrence Foster, age 14, from Chicago, IL, cello, Saint-Saëns's Concerto in A minor for Cello and Orchestra. Conductor: **Alois Springer**, from Germany.

33. Martin and Steven Vann, age 17, from FL, piano, Weber's Piano Pieces for Four Hands, Allegro in A minor, Turandot March, March in G minor.

34. Hindemith: Symphonic Metamorphosis on Themes of Carl Maria von Weber. Each movement of the Weber immediately precedes the Hindemith movement on which it is based. Allegro and March. Conductor: **Leonard Bernstein**; Turandot March Conductor: **Helen Quach** (of Chinese parentage, born in Saigon, South Vietnam).

Appendix E

Existing Nielsen Ratings for Bernstein's Young People's Concerts

The first column in the table at the end of this appendix lists the number of each program in the series; the second column provides the date of broadcast formatted as month/day/year. "Total Audience, # Homes" records the highest number of homes with a television tuned to a *Young People's Concert*, given in thousands (3,188 means 3,188,000). "Total Audience Rating" states that number as a percentage of the total number of homes that owned a television. "Average # Homes" records the average number of homes tuned to a *Young People's Concert*, also given in thousands. "Average Audience Rating" states that number as a percentage. "Audience Share" refers to the percentage of televisions tuned to a *Young People's Concert*. The difference between rating and share is that a rating reflects the percentage of the total population of televisions tuned to a particular program while share reflects the percentage of televisions actually in use.

When three numbers are given in the "Average Audience Rating" and "Audience Share" columns, the first is the total, the second is for the first half hour, and the third is for the second half hour. In a few cases, the first number reflects the total, and four numbers separated by backslashes reflect the ratings for each quarter-hour. A few numbers will put the Nielsen ratings given here in perspective. The United States Census placed the total population of the United States in 1950 as 150,697,361, in 1960 as 179,323,175, and in 1970 as 203,211,926.[1] The number of households with televisions in 1950 was 3,880,000, in 1958 was 41,920,000, in 1960 was 45,750,000, and in 1970 was 59,550,000.[2]

The source for the Nielsen ratings from 1 January 1958 through 18 January 1962 is found in NYpa, 019-04-23 and from 3 November 1964 through 19 February 1965 is NYpa, 019-14-01. All other ratings come directly from the biweekly publication *National Nielsen TV Ratings* (Chicago: A. C. Nielsen). When no Nielsen rating is entered, no rating was published; such weeks are called "black weeks" and often coincide with holidays. Of the shows with no ratings, four are in the eighth season (1964–65) when CBS and the Philharmonic were having trouble finding a sponsor. An asterisk (*) next to the program number indicates there was no sponsor.

Program	Date	Total Audience # Homes	Total Audience Rating	Average # Homes	Average Audience Rating	Audience Share
1*	1/18/58	3,188	7.5	1,913	4.5	16.5
2*	2/1/58	3,018	7.1	1,743	4.1	15.1
3*	3/8/58	2,593	6.1	1,445	3.4	15.2
4*	12/13/58	2,306	5.3	1,479	3.4	14.8
5*	1/24/59	2,948	6.7	1,628	3.7	15.7
6*	2/28/59	2,200	5.0	1,056	2.4	11.1
7*	3/28/59	1,760	4.0	924	2.1	9.6
8	2/7/60	3,706	8.2	2,079	4.6	16.2
Nielsen		3,706	10.1	2,079	5.6	19.9
9	3/6/60	3,616	8.0	2,260	5.0	16.2
Nielsen		3,616	9.6	2,260	6.0	19.4
10	3/27/60	2,034	4.5	1,266	2.8	13.8
Nielsen		2,034	5.3	1,266	3.3	16.3
11	4/24/60			Black Week		
12	1/8/61	5,206	11.1	3,049	6.5	19.3
13	2/12/61	3,893	8.3	2,298	4.9	16.8
14	3/19/61	4,690	10.0	3,095	6.6	21.6
15	4/9/61	2,767	5.9	1,735	3.7	14.3
16	12/1/61	6,332	13.5	3,471	7.4	12.9
17	1/18/62	6,076	12.4	3,773	7.7	12.5
18	3/26/62	7,938	16.2	4,606	9.4	16.6
19	4/13/62	7,007	14.3	4,410	9.0	16.2
20	11/21/62	5,876	11.8	3,884	7.8	14.1
21	12/21/62	7,370	14.8	4,333	8.7	15.2
22	1/15/63	8,466	17.0	5,777	11.6	18.7
23	3/8/63	6,374	12.8	3,735	7.5	13.0

(continued)

Program	Date	Total Audience # Homes	Total Audience Rating	Average # Homes	Average Audience Rating	Audience Share
24 by quarter hr	11/29/63	5,950	11.6	3,950	7.7	13.0
					9.7/7.5/6.7/6.8	
25	12/23/63			Black Week		
26 by quarter hr	2/23/64	3,800	7.4	2,360	4.6	12.4
					4.6/4.3/4.8/4.6	
27 by quarter hr	3/11/64	4,980	9.7	2,770	5.4	8.9
					6.9/5.4/4.7/4.5	
28	11/6/64				6.3	10.9
29	11/30/64				10.2	16.0
30	1/28/65				9.6	14.1
31	2/19/65				8.2	13.3
32 by quarter hr	11/29/65	9,850	18.3	6,350	11.8	19.1
					13.7/12.3/10.4/10.6	
33	12/14/65	6,890	12.8	4,520	8.4	14.1
34	1/5/66	7,690	14.3	4,900	9.1	14.7
35 by quarter hr	2/22/66	7,750	14.4	5,000	9.3	14.5
					10.5/8.8/8.5/9.4	
36 by half hr	11/23/66	7,470	13.6	4,170	7.6	13.8
					7.6/7.6	14.1/13.5
37 by half hr	1/27/67	8,560	15.6	5,760	10.5	17.3
					10.3/10.6	17.4/17.1
38 by half hr	2/23/67	5,160	9.4	2,910	5.3	8.3
					5.8/4.8	9.3/7.3
39	4/19/67			Black Week		
40 by half hr	12/25/67	4,650	8.3	2,580	4.6	15.3
					4.4/4.9	15.2/15.7

41	1/28/68	4,090	7.3	2,580	4.6	11.5
41 rebroadcast	6/2/68	2,630	4.7	1,570	2.8	10.8
					2.9/2.8	11.4/10.5
42	3/31/68	2,180	3.9	1,340	2.4	7.7
					2.3/2.5	7.5/7.8
43 by half hr	5/26/68			Black Week		
44	12/25/68			Black Week		
45	4/27/69			Black Week		
46 by half hr	5/25/69				3.3	12
					3.7/3.0	14/11
47 by half hr	9/14/69				4.6	15
					5.0/4.2	16/13
48 by half hr	3/29/70	5,090	8.7	2,570	4.4	13
					4.6/4.3	14/12
49 by half hr	5/24/70	3,280	5.6	1,520	2.6	9
					2.6/2.5	9/8
50	12/27/70			Black Week		
51 by half hr	4/4/71				3.4	11
					3.6/3.2	12/10
52 by half hr	2/13/72	4,350	7.0	2,300	3.7	8
					3.6/3.8	8/6
53 by half hr	3/26/72	4,100	6.6	2,240	3.6	11
					4.1/3.1	13/9

Appendix F

Twentieth-Century Works in Bernstein's Young People's Concerts

*T*he following is a list of composers and pieces Bernstein performed with the Philharmonic, however briefly, in his *Young People's Concerts* (including repeat performances) with the program number (no.). While all of the works in this appendix premiered in the twentieth century, some were actually composed in the late nineteenth century. Timings are included (as "minutes:seconds") to show the degree to which Bernstein focused on specific works. Some pieces are brief excerpts, lasting only a few seconds; others are longer excerpts, Bernstein expounding at some length about the work or composer or both. All information comes from the charts recording the date broadcast, composer, work performed, publication information, and timing for each work in each program found in box/folder 990/03. Reactionary works employ (to some degree) elements of tonality, modality, bitonality, rhythmic regularity, and clarity of structure. Avant-garde works employ (to some degree) atonality, serialism, ambiguity, and complexity. Popular music is not included. "NT" indicates that the relevant document states "no record of timing."

REACTIONARY WORKS

Austin, Larry. Improvisations for Orchestra and Jazz Soloists (no. 27, **12:05**).

Bartók, Béla. Concerto for Orchestra, V, VI (no. 7, **13:35**); Music for Strings, Percussion, and Celeste (no. 15, **NT**); Rhapsody no. 1 for Cello and Orchestra, II (no. 25, **6:00**).

Bernstein, Leonard. Overture to *Candide* (no. 12, **4:02**); Symphonic Dances from *West Side Story*, Danzón (no. 23, **7:19**); *Fancy Free* (no. 36, **2:25**).

Bloch, Ernest. *Schelomo* (no. 17, **15:27**).

Bloch, Ernest and Alfredo Antonini (arr.). *Prayer* (no. 19, **4:45**).

Britten, Benjamin. *Young Person's Guide to the Orchestra*, "Tug of War" (no. 14, **17:00**).

Bucci, Valentino. Concerto for a Singing Instrument, III (no. 10, **4:20**).

Canteloube, Joseph (arr.). *Songs of the Auvergne*, "L'Antoueno," "Lo Fiolaire," "Malurous Qu'O Uno Fenno" (no. 15, **7:40**).

Chávez, Carlos. *Sinfonía India* (no. 15, **11:15**).

Copland, Aaron. *Music for the Theatre* (no. 2, **2:15**; "Burlesque," no. 6, **3:20**; "Dance," no. 13, **3:05**); *Billy the Kid Suite* (no. 2, **1:05**; various, no. 52, **14:55**); Symphony no. 3 (no. 2, **9:00**); *Second Hurricane* (no. 11, **37:00**); *Outdoor Overture* (no. 13, **8:32**); *Statements for Orchestra*, "Dogmatic" (no. 13, **1:37**); *Music for the Movies, Our Town*, "Grover's Corners" (no. 13, **2:47**); *Rodeo*, "Hoe-Down" (no. 13, **3:13**); *Old American Songs* ("Boatman's Dance," "Bought Me a Cat," no. 13, **4:08**; "The Little Horses," no. 20, **2:30**); *El Salón* México (no. 13, **10:40**); *Danzón cubano* (no. 23, **10:30**); Concerto for Piano and Orchestra (no. 27, **15:20**); *Rodeo*, "Hoedown" (no. 33, **3:13**); Concerto for Clarinet and Orchestra (no. 52, **16:20**).

De Falla, Manuel. *The Three-Cornered Hat Suite* (no. 17, **7:31**; no. 29, **4:20**).

Debussy, Claude. *Prelude to the Afternoon of a Faun* (no. 3, **0:30**; no. 12, **9:59**); *La Mer* (no. 16, **27:07**); *Ibéria*, II, Finale (no. 33, **5:23**); *Nocturnes*, Fêtes, no. 36, **5:36**).

Fernandez, Oscar Lorenzo. *Reisado Do Pastoreio Suite*, "Batuque" (no. 23, **3:30**).

Gershwin, George. *An American in Paris* (no. 2, **7:35**; no. 6, **0:40**; no. 17, **11:28**; no. 33, **1:00**); *Rhapsody in Blue* (no. 2, **1:20**; no. 3, **0:50**; no. 4, **0:15**); *Porgy and Bess*, "My Man's Gone Now" (no. 39, **3:40**).

Gilbert, Henry F. *The Dance in Place Congo* (no. 2, **1:25**).

Gliére, Reyngol'd Moritsevich. *The Red Poppy* (no. 29, **3:20**).

Goodman, Saul. *Canon for Percussion* (no. 3, **0:30**).

Gould, Morton. *Interplay* (no. 2, **0:10**).

Harris, Roy. Symphony no. 3 (no. 2, **0:40**).

Hindemith, Paul. *Kleine Kammermusik* for Wind Quintet (no. 3, **0:15**; no. 26, I, **3:00**); Concert Music for Strings and Brass, op. 50 (no. 21, **3:35**); String Quartet no. 3, op. 22 (no. 26, **0:30**); Symphony: *Mathis der Maler* (no. 26, NT, but is the featured work); *Symphonic Metamorphosis after Themes of Carl Maria von Weber* (no. 42, **16:00**).

Ives, Charles. Symphony no. 2, Finale (no. 15, **8:25**); *The Circus Band* (no. 38, **3:00**).

Kodály, Zoltán. *Háry János* (no. 6, **0:10**).

Mahler, Gustav. Symphony no. 1, III (no. 6, **1:55**); Symphony no. 4, I, II, Finale (no. 8, **11:25**); *Das Lied von der Erde* ("Of Youth," "Farewell," no. 8, **12:05**); Symphony no. 2, II, III, V (no. 8, **3:00**); *Des Knaben Wunderhorn* ("St. Anthony's Sermon to the Fishes," no. 8, **1:05**; "Rheinlegendchen," "St. Anthony's Sermon to the Fishes," "Verlorne Müh'," no. 40, **9:50**).

Menotti, Gian Carlo. *The Telephone*, "Hello, Hello" (no. 14, **3:25**).

Piston, Walter. Suite from *The Incredible Flutist* (no. 6, **0:35**; no. 24, **16:00**).

Prokofiev, Sergei. Symphony no. 1 "Classical" (no. 6, I, III, **5:20**; no. 28, IV, **4:00**; no. 43, I, **4:00**); *Peter and the Wolf* (no. 3, **0:07**; no. 9, **21:55**); *Lieutenant Kijé* Suite (no. 36, **0:25**).

Puccini, Giacomo. *La Bohème* ("Mimi's Farewell," no. 14, **2:50**; "Mi Chiamano Mimi," no. 39, **4:25**).

Ran, Shulamit. Concerto for Piano and Orchestra (no. 25, **7:15**).

Ravel, Maurice. *La Valse* (no. 1, **8:55**); *Rapsodie espanole* (no. 2, **0:15**); Introduction and Allegro for Harp, Flute, Clarinet, and Strings (no. 3, **0:20**; no. 25, **10:00**); *Bolero* (no. 3, **13:00**); *Daphnis et Chloé Suite* (no. 15, **NT**; no. 16, **4:04**); *Ma Mère l'oye Suite* (no. 30, **15:28**).

Respighi, Ottorino. *The Pines of Rome* (no. 49, **20:00**).

Revueltas, Silvestre. *Sensamayá* (no. 23, **5:57**).

Schuller, Gunther. *Journey into Jazz* (no. 27, **18:00**).

Schuman, William. *American Festival Overture* (no. 2, **1:10**); Symphony for Strings (no. 3, **0:45**).

Sessions, Roger. Chorale Prelude for Organ (no. 2, **0:25**).

Shostakovich, Dmitry. *The Golden Age* (no. 6, **2:20**); Symphony no. 7, I (no. 34, **0:47**); Symphony no. 9 (no. 34, **25:03**).

Sibelius, Jan. Fifth Symphony (no. 4, **0:20**); *Finlandia* (no. 31, **8:00**); Concerto for Violin and Orchestra in D (no. 31, **14:45**); Symphony no. 2 (no. 31, **19:10**); Symphony no. 6, I (no. 36, **0:39**); Symphony no. 4, II (no. 36, **0:13**).

Strauss, Richard. *Der Rosenkavalier Suite* (no. 6, **0:50**; no. 40, **6:35**; no. 43, **0:20**); *Don Quixote* (no. 1, **4:05**; no. 44, **24:38**).

Stravinsky, Igor. Symphony for Wind Instruments (no. 3, **0:15**); *L'Histoire du Soldat* (no. 3, **0:50**); *Greeting Prelude* (no. 18, **0:55**); *Le sacre du printemps* (no. 18, **0:15**); Concerto "Dumbarton Oaks" (no. 18, **0:21**); *Agon* (no. 18, **0:15**); *Petrouchka* (no. 18, **18:55**); *L'Histoire du Soldat*, "The Royal March" (no. 33, **2:42**); *Firebird Suite* (3 mvts) (no. 47, **20:33**).

Thompson, Randall. Symphony no. 2 (no. 2, **1:10**); Symphony no. 2, scherzo (no. 24, **5:45**).

Thomson, Virgil. *The Mother of Us All* (no. 2, **1:00**).

Vaughan Williams, Ralph. *Fantasia on a Theme by Thomas Tallis* (no. 3, **0:50**); Symphony no. 4, finale (no. 32, **8:15**).

Villa-Lobos, Heitor. *Bachianas Brasileiras* no. 2, Toccata, "The Little Train of Caipira" (no. 10, **3:15**); *Bachianas Brasileiras* no. 5 (no. 23, **11:32**).

Walton, William and Edith Sitwell. "Tango-Pasodoble" from *Façade* (no. 20, **1:30**).

White, Paul. *Mosquito Dance* (no. 6, **0:30**).

Weill, Kurt. *Three Penny Opera*, "Moritat" (no. 21, **0:08**).

AVANT-GARDE WORKS

Babbitt, Milton. Composition for 12 Instruments (no. 29, **0:30**).

Foss, Lukas. *Phorion* (no. 45, **5:58**).

Ives, Charles. "Fourth of July" from *Holiday Symphony* (no. 29, **5:20**); *The Gong on the Hook and Ladder* (no. 38, **4:00**); *Holiday Symphony*, "Washington's Birthday" (no. 38, **9:00**); "Lincoln, the Great Commoner" (no. 38, **3:15**); *The Unanswered Question* (no. 38, **5:30**).

Luening, Otto and Vladimir Ussachevsky. Concerted Piece for Tape Recorder and Orchestra (no. 10, **8:00**).

Mayazumi, Toshiro. Pieces for Prepared Piano and Strings (no. 29, **0:10**).

Nono, Luigi. *Incontri* (no. 29, **0:20**).

Sessions, Roger. Chorale Prelude for Organ (no. 2, **0:25**).

Webern, Anton. *Six Pieces* (no. 1, **0:55**); *Five Pieces for Orchestra* (complete) (no. 29, **0:45**).

Appendix G

American Music in Bernstein's Young People's Concerts

The following is a list of pieces for chamber or symphony orchestra by American composers performed in Bernstein's *Young People's Concerts* with the program number (no.) and timing. Timings are included to show the degree to which Bernstein focused on specific works. Some pieces are brief excerpts, lasting only a few seconds. Others are longer excerpts, with Bernstein expounding at some length about the work or composer or both. All information comes from the charts recording the date broadcast, composer, work performed, publication information, and timing for each program found in box/folder 990/03.

> **Austin, Larry.** Improvisations for Orchestra and Jazz Soloists (no. 27, **12:05**).
> **Babbitt, Milton.** Composition for 12 Instruments (no. 29, **0:30**).
> **Bernstein, Leonard.** Overture to *Candide* (no. 12, **4:02**); Symphonic Dances from *West Side Story* (no. 23, **7:19**); *Fancy Free* (no. 36, **2:25**).
> **Chadwick, George Whitefield.** *Melpomene* (no. 2, **1:15**).
> **Copland, Aaron.** *Music for the Theatre* (no. 2, **2:15**; "Burlesque," no. 6, **3:20**; "Dance," no. 13, **3:05**); *Billy the Kid Suite* (no. 2, **1:05**; various, no. 52, **14:55**); Symphony no. 3 (no. 2, **9:00**); *Second Hurricane* (no. 11, **37:00**); *Outdoor Overture* (no. 13, **8:32**); *Statements for Orchestra*, "Dogmatic" (no. 13, **1:37**); *Music for the Movies, Our Town*, "Grover's Corners" (no. 13, **2:47**); *Rodeo*, "Hoe-Down" (no. 13, **3:13**); *Old American Songs* ("Boatman's Dance," "Bought Me a Cat," no. 13, **4:08**; "The Little Horses," no. 20, **2:30**); *El Salón* México (no. 13, **10:40**); *Danzón cubano* (no. 23, **10:30**); Concerto for Piano and Orchestra

227

(no. 27, **15:20**); *Rodeo*, "Hoedown" (no. 33, **3:13**); Concerto for Clarinet and Orchestra (no. 52, **16:20**).

Foss, Lukas. *Phorion* (no. 45, **5:58**).

Gershwin, George. *An American in Paris* (no. 2, **7:35**; no. 6, **0:40**; no. 17, **11:28**; no. 33, **1:00**); *Rhapsody in Blue* (no. 2, **1:20**; no. 3, **0:50**; no. 4, **0:15**); *Porgy and Bess*, "My Man's Gone Now" (no. 39, **3:40**).

Gilbert, Henry F. *The Dance in Place Congo* (no. 2, **1:25**).

Goodman, Saul. *Canon for Percussion* (no. 3, **0:30**).

Gould, Morton. *Interplay* (no. 2, **0:10**).

Harris, Roy. Symphony No. 3 (no. 2, **0:40**).

Ives, Charles. Symphony No. 2, IV (no. 15, **8:25**); *Holiday Symphony*, "Fourth of July" (no. 29, **5:20**); *The Circus Band* (no. 38, **3:00**); *The Gong on the Hook and Ladder* (no. 38, **4:00**); *Holiday Symphony*, "Washington's Birthday" (no. 38, **9:00**); "Lincoln, the Great Commoner" (no. 38, **3:15**); *The Unanswered Question* (no. 38, **5:30**).

Luening, Otto and Vladimir Ussachevsky. *Concerted Piece for Tape Recorder and Orchestra* (no. 10, **8:00**).

MacDowell, Edward. *Indian Suite* (no. 2, **1:25**).

Mayazumi, Toshiro. Pieces for Prepared Piano and Strings (no. 29, **0:10**).

Menotti, Gian Carlo. *The Telephone*, "Hello, Hello" (no. 14, **3:25**).

Piston, Walter. Suite from *The Incredible Flutist* (no. 6, **0:35**; no. 24, **16:00**).

Schuman, William. *American Festival Overture* (no. 2, **1:10**); Symphony for Strings (no. 3, **0:45**).

Schuller, Gunther. *Journey into Jazz* (no. 27, **18:00**).

Sessions, Roger. Chorale Prelude for Organ (no. 2, **0:25**).

Thompson, Randall. Symphony no. 2 (no. 2, **1:10**; no. 24, **5:45**).

Thomson, Virgil. *The Mother of Us All* (no. 2, **1:00**).

White, Paul. *Mosquito Dance* (no. 6, **0:30**).

Appendix H

Young People's Concerts
without Bernstein, 1958–1972

$\mathcal{L}$eonard Bernstein was not the only conductor presenting untelevised Young People's Concerts for the New York Philharmonic during his tenure. Many conductors prepared and delivered the programs, as listed below. These programs may have served as auditions for his successor after Bernstein announced in October 1966 that he would allow his contract as music director of the Philharmonic to lapse as of the 1969–1970 season. The maestro eventually handed the reins to Michael Tilson Thomas. The first table in this appendix was compiled from The New York Philharmonic Performance History Search site at http://history.nyphil.org/nypwcpub/dbweb.asp?ac=a1 (accessed 18 April 2014). After Bernstein announced his retirement as music director of the Philharmonic, others occasionally ran the televised *Young People's Concerts*. Perhaps these performances also served as auditions for Bernstein's replacement. The second table comes from boxfolder/911/07.

Conductor	Date(s)
Thomas Schippers	12 February 1958, 1 November 1958
Dimitri Mitropoulos	12 March 1958
Howard Shanet	21 November 1959
Izler Soloman	16 May 1961, 17 May 1961, 8 May 1962
Andre Kostalanetz	26 March 1963, 30 March 1963, 22 March 1968, 11 March 1969, 26 December 1971
Lukas Foss	14 April 1964, 23 March 1963, 25 March 1966
William Steinburg	15 November 1964, 23 March 1966, 25 March 1966
Josef Krips	25 February 1965
Seiji Ozawa	13 March 1965, 28 February 1969, 24 October 1969
Lorin Maazel	2 April 1965, 18 November 1966, 20 April 1970, 1 May 1970
William Steinberg	23 November 1966, 10 February 1967, 8 April 1967
Alfred Wallenstein	2 December 1967, 5 December 1967
Colin Davis	21 November 1968
Aaron Copland	1 November 1969
Claudio Abbado	13 March 1970
Peter Ustinov	5 May 1970
Aldo Ceccato	9 November 1970
Daniel Barenboim	11 January 1971
Dean Dixon	23 January 1971
Michael Tilson Thomas	5 November 1971
Stanislaw Skrowaczewski	2 April 1971
Yehudi Menuin	27 March 1971
Philippe Bender	26 February 1971

Conductor	Taped	Aired	Title
Aaron Copland	1 November 1969	28 December 1969	"Music for the Movies"
Peter Ustinov (Assistant Conductor: Alfredo Bonavera)	9 May 1970	20 September 1970	"Words and Music"
Dean Dixon	23 January 1971	23 May 1971	"Participation Concert"
Yehudi Menuin	27 March 1971	26 September 1971	"Concerto for Orchestra"
Dean Dixon	18 March 1972	7 May 1972	"Bruckner, the 4th B?"
Michael Tilson Thomas	22 April 1972	24 September 1972	"Patterns of Threes"

Notes

PREFACE

1. The Leonard Bernstein Office is in charge of information about Bernstein, licensing the use of his artistic products as well as the well-presented and well-researched official Leonard Bernstein website, accessed 11 March 2014, http://www.leonardbernstein.com. The fall 1993 issue of *prelude, fugue & riffs* announced that selected *Young People's Concerts* were available on VHS tapes and honored the series with several articles by producer/director Roger Englander, production crew members Elizabeth (Candy) Finkler and Mary Rodgers Guettel, as well as Philharmonic president Carlos Moseley.

2. Peyser's biography is problematic. She emphasized the seamier side of Bernstein's life, frequently adding unfounded assumptions as to Bernstein's motivations. Burton warns that it "is marred by many inaccuracies, a biased approach and inane psycho-babble." When Peyser interviewed the Bernstein children, "the siblings were wooed, as Jamie put it, like Hansel and Gretel being trapped by the wicked witch." Bernstein "made a solemn promise to my children on my knees" to never read it (H. Burton 1994, 491).

3. Gottlieb's "The Art of Shooting an Orchestra" (2010, 312–317) delves into how a television director interprets the music with his camera work.

4. Gelleny erroneously concludes that Bernstein's comments on women in music "introduce more uncertainties regarding how far Bernstein agreed with or was willing to support feminist causes in the *Young People's Concerts*" (Gelleny 1991, 103–104). The apparent inconsistencies are rather the result of Bernstein's growth. Early in the series, he spouted the commonly accepted attitudes before feminism and, gradually, enthusiastically endorsed feminism. See chapter 6.

5. *Journal of the Society for American Music* 3/1 (February 2009), Special Issue on Leonard Bernstein in Boston, documents the results of a team-research seminar on Bernstein's early years titled "Before *West Side Story*: Leonard Bernstein's Jewish Boston" given at Harvard University in the spring of 2006.

6. For a brief history of the collection, see Library of Congress, Leonard Bernstein Collection, accessed 11 March 2014, http://memory.loc.gov/ammem/collections/bernstein/lbabout.html.

7. There are 117 boxes spanning 1938–1990. Horowitz says: "Our general policy with significant quantities of fan mail at the time we acquired the collection was to select a representative sampling. In the case of the Bernstein Collection, we decided to retain all the fan mail, because it was so complete, so many letters had his responses written on them (either in his own hand or by Helen Coates), and, while clearly a majority were insignificant, collectively they painted a picture of several significant issues related to American musical life, culture, and the times during which they were written" (M. Horowitz, pers. comm.). The existence of this rare fan mail collection is due to Coates's foresight in saving and filing the letters, and the Library of Congress choosing to retain them.

8. Gottlieb explains that Bernstein marked scores with red pencil for directives to the librarians (to copy those markings into the parts) and with blue pencil for "*aides-mémoire*" for himself (2010, 109).

9. In 1942 Bernstein worked for the New York publisher Harms, Inc., under the pseudonym Lenny Amber, thus the name Amberson Enterprises for his company.

10. Some programs are digitized and can be seen anytime. Others are on tape and reservations for viewing should be made in advance.

INTRODUCTION

1. Marin Alsop, "Revisiting Bernstein's Immodest 'Mass'," NPR Music, last modified 27 September 2008, http://www.npr.org/templates/story/story.php?storyId=94965140, accessed 15 April 2014.

2. An excellent brief overview of the issues surrounding Jews immigrating to the United States from Russia comes from Fitchburg State University by Ethan Forbes, Suzanne Lauer, Kathleen Koonz, and Pam Sweeney, "A Resource Guide for Teachers: Russian Jewish Immigration 1880–1920," accessed May 8, 2014, http://www.fitchburgstate.edu/uploads/files/TeachingAmericanHistory/RussianJews.pdf. The link includes a brief history, resources, and an annotated bibliography. See also Sachar 1992.

3. Bernstein's son, Alexander Serge Bernstein, is named after Koussevitzky, showing the depth of the relationship between the two conductors.

4. A valuable source on Bernstein and television is the exhibition catalogue, Museum of Broadcasting 1985.

5. Jamie Bernstein, "Leonard Bernstein: A Born Teacher," Leonard Bernstein's official website, accessed 8 May 2014, http://www.leonardbernstein.com/educator.htm.

6. Tributes to Bernstein the teacher appear in the interviews with his protégé, conductor, and friend John Mauceri, protégé and conductor Justin Brown, Carol Lawrence (the first Maria in *West Side Story*) in W. W. Burton 1995. Bernstein's pro-

tégés Marin Alsop and Michael Tilson Thomas often praise their mentor's teaching abilities and seek to emulate him.

7. The most comprehensive catalogue of Bernstein's work is Gottlieb 1998.

8. Alexander's and Nina's biographies are found on the Press Room page of Leonard Bernstein's official website, accessed 8 May 2014, http://www.leonard bernstein.com/press.htm. Jamie's biography is from Opus 3 Artists, accessed May 8, 2014, http://www.opus3artists.com/artists/jamie-bernstein. The "brilliant and innovative" musician and composer Mark Blitzstein was Jamie's godfather, and her two siblings were named after characters in Blitzstein's works for stage: "Alexander" appeared in *Regina*, and "Nina" was the heroine in *Ruben, Ruben* (Simeone 2013, 268).

9. The Leonard Bernstein Center for Learning was founded in April 1992 shortly after Bernstein's death. The Artful Learning system has expanded from five to more than forty schools around the country with strong results. "Artful Learning," accessed 15 April 2014, http://www.leonardbernstein.com/artful_learning.htm.

CHAPTER 1

1. Occasionally a member of the orchestra's management attended as well.

2. Some of the Committee's minutes are in the archives at NYpa, but they are not well organized. From the gaps in dates, it is clear that many are missing. Women have played an important role in cultivating the arts and making them available to the general public in the United States. See Locke and Barr 1997.

3. Appendix H lists the dates and presenters.

4. Michael Tilson Thomas became Bernstein's successor for this series at the maestro's recommendation.

5. US-NYpa, 019-14-12. Letter from Anne Straus and Constance Carden, Co-Chairmen, Young People's Concerts Committee to George E. Judd Jr., 19 March 1959. They reported that at the first three programs, many children were between three and five years old and were not only bewildered (therefore restless) but distracting to older children and adults nearby. A resolution was passed that children under six should not be admitted to the concerts.

6. Letter from Carlos Moseley of the New York Philharmonic to Mrs. Elaine A. Fry of the United States Information Agency, in response to a request on how to organize young people's concerts for Mrs. Lily Caballero de Cueto, the wife of the Minister of Education of Peru, 7 September 1966 (NYpa, 020-02-04). In a document that predates Moseley's letter, "Program Planning for Philharmonic Young People's Concerts," n.d. [1950s?], 1 (NYpa, 019-03-23), the age is given as eight through early teens. Carlos Moseley was a guiding force for the Philharmonic during the years of Bernstein's tenure as director. When Bernstein became music director in 1957, Moseley was director of press and public relations for the Philharmonic; he became associate managing director in 1959, managing director in 1961, paid president in 1970, and chairman of the board in 1983. His contributions to both the Philharmonic

and the Metropolitan Opera were so respected that a new mobile, perfectly tuned, outdoor performing shell was named the Carlos Moseley Music Pavilion in his honor. Bernstein and Moseley became good friends through their long association with the Philharmonic, and Moseley was one of the few individuals interviewed by the Leonard Bernstein Office for their feature issue on Bernstein's *Young People's Concerts*. In his administrative capacity, he is the sender or recipient of many correspondences and memos relating to the programs.

7. Finkler noticed that Bernstein wrote the scripts with Jamie in mind (1993).

8. Val Adams, "Young People's Concerts Are for Young in Heart," *New York Times*, 30 August 1964.

9. For instance, A. Sheshroff (?) declared she was fifty-two years old and wanted to thank Bernstein "for the enjoyment you have given me" (1958).

10. "Young People's Concerts Are Young at Heart." CBS made this statement while announcing a new sponsor for the next season, Bell Telephone. CBS probably intended to prove to Bell that the advertising should be aimed at adults rather than at children. The article does not state how CBS obtained their information. At this time, the Nielsen reports did not break down the figures demographically.

11. Rozen excluded the nine Young Performers programs as well as "A Tribute to Teachers" (29 November 1963) and "Alumni Reunion" (19 April 1967) for being non-pedagogical (Rozen 1998, 80–81).

12. At first, encores were performed but not filmed. Encores ceased in 1961. See memo from Carlos Moseley to Mr. Leonard Bernstein, re: YPC—Bonus Works, 25 October 1961 (NYpa, 019-03-31) in which the Young People's Concerts Committee suggested that "the bonus work" be discontinued. They felt that "confusion and anticlimax set in, chauffeurs don't know how long they can park, etc." This is a comment on the affluence and influence of some of the attendees but not of the television audience. John Christian MacInnis incorrectly states that part of "What Is Impressionism?" (1 December 1961) "was not televised due to the constraints of time. Bernstein's script ended after a selection from Ravel's *Daphnis and Chloe*, but the Carnegie Hall audience was treated to Debussy's *Saxophone Rhapsody*." The Debussy was an encore for the live audience (MacInnis 2009, 24).

13. Except for program 29 (scheduled for 2:30–3:30 p.m.) according to the title pages of the scripts.

14. Bernstein greets the new Canadian viewers in "What Is Impressionism?" saying, "a special hello to our new friends up north in Canada," then incorporates the first international reference in a *Young People's Concert* script. He makes the analogy personal by talking about trying to explain the beauty of the sea to someone in land-locked Winnipeg (2–3).

15. "Edward R. Murrow, RTNDA [Radio-Television News Directors Association] Convention, Chicago, 15 October 1958" at "Television's Hidden Agenda," Ron Kaufman, ed. http://www.turnoffyourtv.com/commentary/hiddenagenda/murrow.html. Two Christmas programs were scheduled on weekdays: "A Toast to Vienna in 3/4 Time" (Monday, 25 December 1967 at 5:00–6:00 p.m.) and "Fantastic Variations (*Don Quixote*)" (Wednesday, 25 December 1968, 5:00–6:00 p.m.).

16. Handwritten on the cover page of "Unusual Instruments of the Past, Present, and Future" (27 March 1960) is the comment, "First time teleprompter used, therefore *may* be *some* inaccuracies—(check with JG [Jack Gottlieb] script.)."

17. The information regarding video technology comes from Richard Wandel, associate archivist emeritus at the New York Philharmonic (pers.comm.). A CBS-generated list of all the programs in the series accompanied a letter from John Walker to Harry Kraut, Amberson Productions, n.d., (box/folder 924/2); according to CBS, "Overtures and Preludes" (8 January 1961) was the first program in black and white on two-inch videotape.

18. Only twenty-five of the fifty-three programs were transferred to VHS for a variety of reasons. For instance, sales projections determined that some programs, such as the Young Performers programs, would not sell many copies and would therefore not be cost effective. The Amberson Business Papers in the Leonard Bernstein Collection (box 924) document the search for master copies of all the films, the categorization of the programs, contracts with Handmade Video for transfer from one format to another, and contracts with Unitel for distribution.

19. The most useful single source for documenting the editing process by the production crew is Rees (1966), who observed conferences for the preparation of the script for "A Birthday Tribute to Shostakovich" and interviewed Bernstein, Englander, Helen Coates, Jack Gottlieb, and others.

20. Notes exist for seventeen programs: No's. 1, 3, 10, 15, 20, 21, 23, 28, 32, 33, 36, 38, 42, 43, 46, 52, and 53. Outlines exist for ten programs: No's. 1, 3, 4, 21, 23, 28, 32, 34, 36, and 40. Sometimes it is difficult to tell the difference between an outline and notes.

21. "So the Young May Feel," *Newsweek*, 2 March 1959, 83. He once tried dictating to his friend Mary Rodgers, but abandoned it after eleven pages. See "What Is Classical Music?" (24 January 1959, box/folder 105/6).

22. In "Aaron Copland Birthday Party" (12 February 1961), the final script states that William Warfield will sing "Simple Gifts," but he actually performed "A Boatman's Dance" (written in the margin). That marginalia is in the script at the Leonard Bernstein Office but not in the copy at the Library of Congress.

23. First drafts exist for all programs.

24. Alan Branigan, "New Approach: Bernstein Aims Music at Kids on Adult Level," *Newark News*, 9 February 1958. Scrapbook 24.

25. Walter H. Stern, "Music on the Air," *Musical Leader*, 2 February 1958. Ibid.

26. John White, "Leonard Bernstein Sun Nearing Zenith," *Times Dispatch*, 26 January 1958. Scrapbook 24.

27. Ronald Eyer, "Are Those Concerts Still Concerts?" *New York Times*, 22 January 1967.

28. On self-censorship see later in this chapter and chapter 4. Bernstein's handling of sensitive political and social issues is covered in chapters 5 and 6.

29. For more on this program, see chapter 5.

30. Letter Moseley to Fry, 7 September 1966 (NYpa, 020-02-04). Moseley states, "Mr. Bernstein himself, in consultation with a small staff of his own, determines the themes and composition[s] for each program." For a list of the personnel who worked on each show, see appendix C.

31. For more about Dubin, see chapter 5.

32. For more on Englander, see chapters 2 and 4.

33. For the technical aspects of producing a *Young People's Concert*, see Englander 1993.

34. For Rodger's biography, see the Rodgers and Hammerstein official website, accessed 8 May 2014, http://www.rnh.com/bio/146/Rodgers-Mary. She was an award-winning author of several novels for young people, including her 1972 book *Freaky Friday*; she wrote screenplays for both the 1977 and 2003 movie adaptations. Rodger's married name was Guettel. Her son, Adam Guettel, is the Tony award-winning composer. Her father was on the board of the Philharmonic when Harold Taubman wrote his assessment for the *New York Times* of the troubles plaguing the orchestra (29 April 1956).

35. An entry in Bernstein's 1957 datebook on Friday 13 December is, "6:45 Rodgers for dinner & Steve & Mary." Box 322.

36. For Corigliano's biography, see "C250 Celebrates Columbians Ahead of Their Time," accessed 8 May 2014, http://c250.columbia.edu/c250_celebrates/remarkable_columbians/john_corigliano.html.

37. Gottlieb 1964. Gottlieb's studies under Bernstein are mentioned in H. Burton 1994, 240. For more about Gottlieb's personal and professional relationship with Bernstein, see Gottlieb 2010.

38. For Gottlieb's biography, see "The Milken Archive: American Jewish Music," accessed 8 May 2014, http://www.milkenarchive.org/people/view/all/509/Gottlieb,+Jack. Gottlieb was also a noted scholar, a composer (whose works have been performed by such orchestras as the Chicago Symphony Orchestra and the Detroit Symphony), a professor at the School of Sacred Music at Hebrew Union College-Jewish Institute of Religion in New York, and publications director of Amberson Enterprises (which manages the Bernstein legacy).

39. Upon winning, Rodgers received a congratulatory letter from Bernstein: "My dear little Miss Rodgers: I am happy to inform you that you have won the contest for the best word to replace 'classical'. Your magnificent choice of EXACT will ring down through the centuries, and no doubt enter Webster's 567th edition, if only as a footnote. Congratulations; and please accept the enclosed gift as a token of our esteem and gratitude for your fine thinking. Faithfully yours, Leonard Bernstein" (Rodgers 1993). She never cashed Bernstein's enclosed check for $50.

40. This explains the duplicate scripts with similar notes in different hands in the Library of Congress and the occasional discrepancies between those at the Library of Congress and the Leonard Bernstein Office.

41. Bernstein's handling of controversy in these programs is covered in chapters 4 and 5.

42. Burton Bernstein accompanied the maestro when the Philharmonic performed in Berlin in 1960. He wrote his "personal account of one of the more famous Philharmonic tours abroad" for *Esquire* magazine in 1961. An abridged version of this article appears in Bernstein and Haws 2009, 102–115.

43. See chapter 5.

44. Eyer, "Are Those Concerts Still Concerts?"

45. "Fidelio: A Celebration of Life" (29 March 1970) is one exception to this plan. It opens with: "This special program is being brought to you by Polaroid Corporation, and it will be presented without interruption. Once the concert has begun, there will

be no commercials. Polaroid will have a message only at the beginning and at the end of the program." This was so unusual for the time that they made the statement three different ways. A fan letter from eleven-year-old Jonathan Kleefield, 18 January 1958 (shortly after the first televised *Young People's Concert*) demonstrates that members of the live audience were "annoyed" by "the invasion of television." He primarily complained that "a man kept waving signs to 'speed up'. Why can't you just keep on playing at the right speed even if the television audience misses a part of the piece?" No doubt the signs were to let Bernstein know that he was behind and should accommodate as he saw fit, either to increase the tempo of the piece or cut some of the coming talk.

46. Frequently the copies of scripts from the Leonard Bernstein Office (LBO) have these markings, but the copies at the Library of Congress (LoC) do not. For example, the pages of the script for "A Tribute to Teachers" from the LBO are dominated by many scribbled timings that track prose and possible cuts, but the copy in LoC folder 02 copy has only the timings of pieces that were typed onto the pages. Compare Figures 1.2 and 1.3 with those online or in Bernstein 1982, 191, 193.

47. By 1964, the waiting list for tickets for Bernstein's *Young People's Concerts* had some 4100 names (Letter to Miss Constance Keene, 24 April 1964, NYpa, 019-04-01). Bernstein, Englander, CBS, and the Philharmonic management decided that there would be a "double YPC series" (memo from Carlos Moseley to Leonard Bernstein, 28 April 1964, NYpa, 019-04-01). This would require no additional labor with only a slight increase in cost, while doubling the number of people who could attend. The cost increase was offset by selling tickets to the "Preview Concert" (letter from Carlos Moseley to Alfred Manuti, President of Local 802, American Federation of Musicians, 20 May 1964, NYpa, 019-04-01).

48. Box/folder 110/2, last page of draft labeled "1st Draft Very Rough" (first typed draft) of "Musical Atoms: A Study of Intervals" (29 November 1965).

49. Caleen Jennings, interviewed by the author, American University, 2 July 2007. Everyone I interviewed thought that Bernstein was speaking off the cuff.

50. Memo from William L. Weissel to Carlos Moseley, "Subject LB—YPC Concerts," 22 November 1965, NYpa, 019-04-13. Weissel was the assistant manager of the Philharmonic from 1962 to 1977. He also served as executive secretary to the Board of Directors from 1970 to 1977.

51. "So the Young May Feel."

CHAPTER 2

1. NYpa, 019-03-24, 15 August [1957] "General Idea for the Entire Series." This became the outline for the first program, "What Does Music Mean?" (18 January 1958), rather than for the entire first year of the series.

2. "*Young People's Concerts* Overview" at the official Leonard Bernstein website, accessed May 8, 2014, http://www.leonardbernstein.com/ypc.htm. While the Philharmonic performing repertory (1942–1971) can be researched in Shanet 1975, the

238   *Notes*

New York Philharmonic Archives website is the most current (includes archive files, programs, newspaper articles, and firsthand accounts), accessed 8 May 2014, http://archives.nyphil.org. For recordings see North 2006.

3. Several memos in NYpa, box 019-04-11, track changes for the eighth, ninth, and tenth seasons. Here, either no information was given, or the subjects were selected for all programs at the beginning of the season, and the order or specific title might change ("Motives and Intervals" became "Measuring Music" and finally the more science-oriented "Musical Atoms: A Study of Intervals," and "Shostakovich—The Russian Tradition" became "Shostakovich and His Musical Heritage" and finally the more appealing—and less intimidating—title "A Birthday Tribute to Shostakovich").

4. In a memo from Carlos Moseley to Amyas Ames, re: Young People's Concerts 1964–1965 Season, 29 January 1964, NYpa, 019-04-01 memo, Moseley observes that if there were no *Young People's Concerts* while Bernstein was on sabbatical the orchestra would have no income from either television work or recordings, making contract negotiations more difficult. Clearly the contracts for the orchestra offered an attractive financial package that included symphony concerts, tours, recordings, and television appearances.

5. For his master's thesis, James Lester Rees interviewed Bernstein in New York in December 1965 and January 1966 (1966, 2).

6. Rhea Sykes's (Director of Education Services for PBS) classification comes from a memo from Paul de Hueck to Harry J. Kraut, 23 July 1975, box/folder 923/8. Nikolaus H. Kloiber of Unitel wrote Harry Kraut of Amberson Productions, 17 May 1989, box/folder 924/3. The PBS plan for broadcasting the series fell through due to lack of funding. Unitel distributed the selected programs internationally on VHS, then later on DVD. The PBS and Unitel stories are found in boxes 923 and 924.

7. "Musical Atoms: A Study of Intervals" (29 November 1965) represents "technical musical concepts"; "The Sound of an Orchestra" (14 December 1965) "the symphony orchestra, or music in general"; "A Birthday Tribute to Shostakovich" (5 January 1966) "composers"; and "Young Performers No. 7" (22 February 1966) "young performers."

8. Box/folder 1024/12. From Wladimir Lakond, Director of Southern Music Publishing Co, Inc. in New York City to Leonard Bernstein, 5 August 1957. Lakond offers five suggestions for the *Young People's Concerts*: Gail (Thompson) Kubik's *Gerald McBoing Boing*; Bernard Rogers's *Leaves from the Tale of Pinocchio*; Hungarian Rudolf Maros's Sinfonietta No. 1; a suite by Belá Bartok; Czech Jaromir Weinberger's *The Bird's Opera*. For the latter, Lakond includes a synopsis, with a list of the characters, scenes, instruments needed, and the length (thirty minutes).

9. Four works aimed at young people were performed: Prokofiev's *Peter and the Wolf* in "Young Performers No. 1" (6 March 1960), Britten's *The Young Person's Guide to the Orchestra* in "Young Performers No. 2" (19 March 1961), Saint-Saëns's *Carnival of the Animals* in "Young Performers No. 3" (13 April 1962), and Ravel's Mother Goose Suite in "Young Performers No. 6" (28 January 1965). The young performers for the Prokofiev and the Britten were narrators. Young musicians performed the solos in the Saint-Saëns, and no young performers appeared in the Ravel. None of these were on the Philharmonic season at the time, but pieces performed on young performers programs needed to cater to their abilities and repertory.

10. Memo from Clara Simons to Helen Coates, re: Guest Artist re Young People's Concerts, 13 June 1958, NYpa, 019-03-05. The letter does not survive, so we do not know whether he was suggesting a topic, work, or guest appearance.

11. Memo from Carlos Moseley to Leonard Bernstein, re: Dalcroze School of Music, 8 November 1963, NYpa, 019-04-06. The head of the Dalcroze School visited Moseley personally to discuss the possibilities. The three composers were in the repertory.

12. AT&T cosponsored the televised *Young People's Concerts* for only the 1966–1967 season but distributed selected concerts on film for some years. CBS Films Inc. sent the survey results to Bernstein, 26 July 1966, see NYpa, 020-02-02 and box/folder 1024/7. A letter from Wallace Magill of N. W. Ayer & Son, Inc. to Helen Coates, 3 August 1966 (ibid.) indicates that the AT&T questionnaire went out to approximately 775 teachers around the United States who wished to show films of the programs at their schools. Magill reported that "instruments of the orchestra" was high on the list of desirable subjects and, through Coates, encouraged Bernstein to consider such a program. "The Sound of an Orchestra" (which covered the different sounds instruments could make) had just been broadcast on 14 December 1965. The survey probably predated this concert.

13. The member of the production crew wishes to remain anonymous.

14. Memo from Joan Bohime to Carlos Moseley, Subject: YPC—possibility of *L'enfant et les sortilèges*, 5 September 1962, NYpa, 019-04-23, includes a list of soloists and orchestration required. Two documents follow the September memo. NYpa, 019-94-16, from Adolph Vogel to Joan Bonime, 21 November 1962, Mme. Jourvenel about permitting a concert performance; NYpa, 019-04-16, from René Dommange to Roger Englander, 25 April 1963, in which Mme. Colette de Jourvenel (daughter and heir) decided not to permit her mother's work to be performed by marionettes.

15. From a member of the production crew who wishes to remain anonymous. Bernstein's acrostic for Sondheim opens with he is "a maker and solver of puzzles," lists a few, and praises him (Simeone 2013, 441). Bernstein's love of games is well known. He had even appeared some half-dozen times on a radio quiz show called "Information Please" by 1951. See H. Burton 1994, 134.

16. Copland's *The Second Hurricane* was adored by Bernstein's immediate family. In July 1960 he wrote Copland that Felicia loved it, and Jamie and Alexander "sing it marvelously by the yard" (Simeone 2013, 429).

17. "A Resume of Children's Concert Activities, The Philharmonic-Symphony Society of N.Y." NYpa, 019-03-23, beginning of 1952–1953 season.

18. Under the famed Ernest Schelling (who established and ran the children's concerts from 1924–1939), the youth programs of later years were divided into Elementary and Advanced series. Schelling's youth concerts are discussed in Shanet 1975, 240–244. The lantern slides are described on 242. For more information on Schelling, see Hill 1970.

19. The nine young performers' concerts were titled and advertised as such. Bernstein used young singers from the Juilliard School rather than professionals as the soloists in "*Fidelio*: A Celebration of Life" (29 March 1970), which caused some controversy. "Alumni Reunion" (19 April 1967) reintroduces three young performers who became professionals.

20. Memo from Roger Englander to Leonard Bernstein, 5 January [1960], box/folder 1024/8.

21. Other similar documents can be found in boxes 393 and 1024.

22. H. Burton 1994, 314, mentions the survey of the concerto. For more on Bernstein and Mahler, see page 2000.

23. Wendy Carlos studied composition with Otto Luening and Vladimir Ussachevsky at Columbia University (one of their compositions appeared on "Unusual Instruments of the Past, Present, and Future" [27 March 1960]) and advised Robert Moog about the synthesizer.

24. Although purists "blasted" the recording, *Switched-On Bach* became the number-one-selling classical album for ninety-four weeks and remained on the charts for 310 weeks. As of 1972, only one other classical album had ever sold more copies—Van Cliburn's recording of Tchaikovsky's First Piano Concerto (O'Neil 1993, 154). In 1970, *Switched-On Bach* won Grammys for: Classical Album of the Year (159); Best Classical Performance, instrumental soloist(s) (with or without orchestra) (160); and Best Engineered Recording Classical (161). The information about the album "going platinum" comes from Wendy Carlos's official website, accessed 8 May 2014, http://www.wendycarlos.com/+sobox.html. For an album to earn platinum status, it must sell at least one million units.

25. Folk music appears in programs no. 2: 3, 5, 9, 10–14, 17, 27, 29; no. 4: 6–10; no. 5: 1, 2, 8; no. 13: 19; no. 15: entire program; no. 19: 29, 31; no. 23: 7, 8, 9, 13, 14; no. 29: 2; no. 34: 28; no. 36: 17, 21, 25, no. 40: 11, 25.

26. This information came from a member of the production crew who wishes to remain anonymous.

27. The documents in the Library of Congress folder include: handwritten draft; mimeographed script; inserts/revisions; loose sheets handwritten by Bernstein expressing sorrow on the death of John F. Kennedy and Paul Hindemith; typed final script; music ms paper with some musical notation; music cues; the Philharmonic program 1963–1964 with this *Young People's Concert*; the obituary and Harold Schonberg's "appreciation" entitled "Musical Logician" from the *New York Times*, Monday, 30 December 1963.

28. For more on Bernstein's self-censorship, see chapters 4, 5, and 6.

29. Bernstein possibly felt Hindemith was a kindred spirit; both composers chose tonality over atonality and suffered for it. Many sentiments found in this script also appear in his Thursday Evening Preview Script for 2 January 1964 in which he also addressed Hindemith's death.

30. H. Burton 1994 offers many instances of Bernstein's trouble with critics, especially Schonberg. For more, see chapter 7.

31. *Herald Tribune*, February 11, 1966, quoted in H. Burton 1994, 321. The quote about fencing comes from Winthrop Sargeant, the *New Yorker*, 17 April 1961, quoted in H. Burton 1994, 321. In retrospect, members of the Philharmonic felt his movements always served art and energized them, drawing better performances from them. Plus, it thrilled audiences while showing them what to listen for in the music (Sherman 2010, 108, 122). Even when Bernstein was a student at Tanglewood, his mentor Serge Koussevitzky told him that he "liked the rehearsal today, but insisted

that I looked like un moulin qui va avec le vent" or a windmill that moves with the wind (Simeone 2013, 77).

32. Harold Schonberg, "Music: Avant-Garde at Philharmonic: Bernstein Conducts 14 Minutes of the New," *New York Times*, 3 January 1964.

33. *Herald Tribune*, 11 February 1966, quoted in H. Burton 1994, 351.

34. The positive comments come from *Philadelphia Inquirer*, 20 January 1958 and *Chicago News*, 21 January 1958. The negative comments come from Seymour Raven, "Some Thoughts on TV Concert," *Chicago Tribune*, 2 February 1958, and from the *New York Herald Tribune*, 19 January 1958. These articles are pasted in the Bernstein scrapbooks, which are on microfilm in the Leonard Bernstein Collection, reel 15, volume 24, item 29. Occasionally, the title and/or author are missing from the scrapbook. Two fans leapt to Bernstein's defense after they read the review in the *NY Herald Tribune*. On 20 January 1958, Richard Rodda wrote George Judd, the assistant manager of the Philharmonic, to say that, "It was hard for us to conceive that a person could have seen the show and paid any attention to the proceedings and still come up with a review of the type that appeared in yesterday's paper" and that, "I felt compelled to write telling you of our complete enjoyment in the program." On 19 January 1958, Phyllis L. Lauritzen wrote Bernstein directly to say that the review was "absolutely unfair, unwarranted, irrational and stupid."

35. NYpa, 019-04-16, 7 October 1963, memo titled "YPC Program Plans–As of Today." The program scheduled 2 November is listed without title, but the subject is given as "a salute to the profession of teaching," followed by a description of Bernstein's plans; this program was delayed until the fall. 23 November is listed as "Young Performers" and 25 January as "No program ideas proposed as yet." 8 February lacks a title, but the subject is given as "Way-out" music followed by ideas: "Xenakis or Ligeti, chance piece, tape piece, improvisation work, Webern cantata."

36. In the introduction to a collection of his Sunday essays, Schonberg stated that Bernstein's unfavorable reviews had little effect on either the conductor or his career: "Critics don't make careers. Artists make careers. A bad review in the *Times* may set a career back for a season or two. That is about all. . . . For years, as an example, Leonard Bernstein could not get a favorable review in the *Times* or the *Herald Tribune*. What difference did an unfavorable review make to him except to bruise his ego?" (Schonberg 1981, 27).

37. Bernstein eventually wrote his parents that it is "better to forgive, and if possible, forget" Nazi atrocities (Simeone 2013, 479).

38. On 14 October 2006, John Mauceri spoke at the "Working with Bernstein" session, part of the "Leonard Bernstein: Boston to Broadway" festival at Harvard University. He said that Schonberg was one of the main reasons Bernstein left New York and the Philharmonic, then asked the scholars in the audience to research the effect of negative criticism on composers. He knew that Bernstein had been profoundly upset by critics' attacks and suggested Bernstein as an example of the effect bad reviews can have on a composer.

39. The Prokofiev was recorded on 16 February 1960 and released the same year; the Saint-Saëns was recorded on 9 April 1962 and released in 1992 (North 2006, 123 and 144 respectively).

40. Only three pieces are proposed for "What Makes Music Symphonic?" (13 December 1958). For an example of "purely musical meanings," the maestro listed Webern, Beethoven, Bach, and Brahms, and finally chose Webern for the first show, "What Does Music Mean?" Thirty-nine composers are listed as possibilities for "Folk Music in the Concert Hall" (9 April 1961). Outlines exist for fifteen programs: No's. 1, 3, 4, 10, 15, 21, 23, 28, 32, 33, 34, 36, 40, 43, and 46.

41. "Bits" of other works were also performed, albeit briefly.

42. In 1945 former Philharmonic conductor Artur Rodzinski noticed the same problem. He wrote to Goddard Lieberson that any recording had to be "made as close as possible" to the rehearsals for a regular series performance. Unusual numbers are "entirely forgotten by the orchestra" if they are not immediately recorded. He offered as evidence that "the very easy Bizet Symphony" had to be postponed "continuously because with every week it was more and more forgotten" (North 2006, xix).

43. Twenty-nine of the fifty-three broadcasts were associated with forty-seven recording sessions. Both a subscription series concert coupled with a *Young People's Concert* served as preparation for thirty-three recording sessions. The only preparation for eight recording sessions was a *Young People's Concert*: "Charles Ives: American Pioneer" (23 February 1967), "Two Ballet Birds" (14 September 1969), and young performers programs (3 March 1960; 19 March 1961; 15 January 1963; 23 December 1963; and 28 December 1965).

44. No recordings were made shortly before or after programs no's. 2, 3, 4, 10, 13, 14, 18, 26, 28, 33, 35, 36, 37, 39, 41, 43, 45, 46, 47, 48, and 49, as well as after Bernstein was made Laureate Conductor, no's. 50, 52, and 53.

45. The four that did not were: "Young Performers Concerts Numbers 8 and 9" (27 January 1967 and 31 March 1968, respectively), "Alumni Reunion," and "Quiz-Concert: How Musical Are You?" (26 May 1968). The works for the first three of these were no doubt chosen from the limited repertory of the young performers, and the quiz program was a special case.

46. A study of the correlation between Bernstein's television performances and comments and the sales of LPs would give valuable information on the influence of the programs in this regard.

47. "Dear Dr. Bernstein . . . : A Look at Leonard Bernstein's 'Young People's Concerts' Mail" was the cover story from *Senior Scholastic* magazine, 2 December 1964, 6 (Detroit, Michigan) in NYpa, 019-04-01.

48. The context for "The Latin American Spirit" is discussed in depth in chapter 5.

49. Bernstein conducted the Philharmonic in the world première of the Second Symphony on 22, 23, 24 February 1951. The Ives was sandwiched between Mozart and Copland's *Scherzino Mexicano*. New York Philharmonic archives website, accessed 8 May 2014, http://archives.nyphil.org.

50. *Fireman's Holiday* and *Circus Band* were released in 1972 (North 2006, 191).

51. The recording session for *The Unanswered Question* was 17 April 1964 (ibid., 349).

52. Six of these programs are based on only one work, and two are based on two works: "Berlioz Takes a Trip" (25 May 1969) is based on *Symphonie fantastique*; "Fidelio: A Celebration of Life" (29 March 1970) on Beethoven's opera; "The Anatomy

of a Symphony Orchestra" (24 May 1970) on Respighi's *The Pines of Rome*; "Thus Spake Richard Strauss" (4 April 1971) on *Also sprach Zarathustra*; "Liszt and the Devil" (13 February 1972) on the *Faust Symphony*; "Holst: *The Planets*" (26 March 1972) on only this work; "Two Ballet Birds" (14 September 1969) on *Swan Lake* by Tchaikovsky and the *Firebird Suite* by Stravinsky; and "A Copland Celebration" (27 December 1970) on the Concerto for Clarinet and Orchestra with excerpts from the Suite from *Billy the Kid*.

53. Memo from Mrs. Simons and Joan Bonime to Messrs. Bernstein and Englander, 27 February 1961, re: YPC repertoires, NYpa, 019-03-25. This document offers three pieces that Jung Ja Kim was prepared to play, with the note, "Her teacher is most anxious for her to do the Mendelssohn. She has performed it three times with orchestra." The note about Lynn Harrell and his pieces is similar. Veronica Tyler offered nine arias. The memo concludes with "All of the soloists, as well as their respective teachers are very anxious to know what is selected so as to begin working as soon as possible." The procedural form is in NYpa, 019-04-06.

54. NYpa, 019-04-03.

55. Memo from Clara Simons to Larry Steiner, 12 January 1965, re: Checks due, NYpa, 019-04-03. The memo notes that soloists Patricia Michaelian and James Oliver Buswell IV (already represented by Columbia Artists Management, Inc.) were paid $225 and $200 respectively. A 14 February 1966 form from Accounts Payable indicates that the amount had been increased; Stephanie Sebastian received $400. NYpa, 019-04-02. Letters to various performers are also found in NYpa, 019-04-02.

56. See also chapter 6 regarding the connection between Watts and African American issues.

57. See the advertisement for "The Bell System Leonard Bernstein Concert Films," NYpa 020-02-02.

58. Margaret Dean R. Akin, Mrs. Richard Deschamps among others (1958).

59. Leonard Bernstein's official website, accessed 8 May 2014, http://www.leonard bernstein.com/ypc.htm.

CHAPTER 3

1. Many recent sources describe these debates. Among the most important are: Bourdieu 1984, Cullen 2002, Gans 1974, Grant 1998, Kammen 1999, Levine 1988, Rubin 1992, and Travis 2002. For sources contemporaneous with Bernstein's *Young People's Concerts*, see note 4.

2. Two dictionaries were consulted: Oxford English Dictionary Online, http://www.oed.com/, and the Merriam-Webster Online Dictionary, http://www.m-w.com/, accessed 13 May 2014. According to the OED, the term "highbrow" first appeared in 1884, "lowbrow" in 1906, and "middlebrow" in 1928. The debate over definitions, functions, and purposes became more active in the 1930s after all three terms appeared.

3. Talmudic scholars (such as Bernstein's father) were highly educated, but in a specialized way.

4. Five primary sources provide the basis for the discussion of the various brows from 1950s through the early 1970s: Lynes 1949a and 1949b, Sargeant 1949, Macdonald 1960a and 1960b, and Gans 1974. Russell Lynes's tongue-in-cheek writings popularized the terms. Fitting one's personal preferences into these descriptions became a parlor game. Both were based on his observations of society rather than scientific methodology and were written to entertain *Harper*'s upper middlebrow and *Life*'s lower middlebrow readers (as classified by 1949b). Lynes 1949b was followed by an irreverent parody by Winthrop Sargeant (1949). Eleven years later, Dwight Macdonald published what scholar Joan Shelley Rubin calls the most famous critique of middlebrow culture: "Masscult and Midcult" for the highbrow periodical *Partisan Review* (MacDonald 1960a and 1960b; Rubin 1992, xiv). Macdonald's scathing and dismissive comments on middlebrow culture were also based solely on his impressions. He focused on middlebrow (or "Midcult") and popular ("Masscult," as distinct from folk) cultures. He intended to spark controversy while entertaining his highbrow audience. Whereas Lynes supported the middlebrow, Macdonald lauded the noble highbrow, while making acrimonious comments about middlebrow and popular culture. Sociologist Herbert J. Gans's valuable scientific study clearly describes the taste cultures and delineates items that defined them in the 1960s and early 1970s (1974). He defended "popular culture [deemed lowbrow by Lynes, Macdonald, and others] against some of its attackers" and was in the vanguard of research into popular culture (vii). Scholars before 1960 only studied cultural products created without concern for financial gain (by unpaid folk or by "serious" artists "who apparently do not think about earning a living" [viii]). Gans hoped to change this anti-commercial bias, saying that "all people have a right to the culture they prefer" (vii). Lynes and Gans divided American society into four "taste cultures": high, upper-middle, lower-middle, and low; Gans added a quasi-folk low classification not relevant here.

5. Lynes declared highbrows came from the intellectuals, "the thinkers of global thoughts" (1949a, 19).

6. The best survey of the twentieth-century highbrow/lowbrow issue in the United States is Halle 2007. An overview of sources is found in Rubin 1992, xi–xvi.

7. Dating from the early 1950s through the early 1960s, rock 'n' roll is the progenitor of rock music. Early performers include Bill Haley and His Comets, Buddy Holly, and the Dominos; some songs from the British Invasion in the early 1960s are also considered to be rock 'n' roll, such as many early Beatles songs. The term is still popular as evidenced by The Rock and Roll Hall of Fame. See Garofalo 2002, and Wald 2009. On Presley as a rock 'n' roll star, see Garofalo 2002, 115–116.

8. *Life* apparently regularly drew parallels between different types of items and activities. Another issue had a photo essay titled "Ballplayers and ballerinas have a lot in common." Pictures of a ballerina were set alongside athletes (baseball, basketball, and jai lai) showing the similarity of movement, for instance, *sur le point* mirroring a baseball player preparing to throw a ball (11 April 1949, 22–24).

9. Joseph Horowitz examines reactions to classical music (and commercial manipulation of those reactions) from the nineteenth to the late-twentieth centuries in American culture, society, and music criticism on the substrate of a biography of Toscanini (Horowitz 1987).

10. Lopes documents the upgrade in social and cultural status that occurred during the modern "jazz renaissance" of the 1950s and 1960s (2002). See also Davenport 2009.

11. For example Milhaud (*La création du monde*, 1923) in France, Hindemith (*Suite '1922'*, 1922) and Krenek (*Jonny spielt auf*, 1927) in Germany, and Copland (*Music for the Theatre*, 1925) in the United States.

12. Dizzy Gillespie, "Jazz Is Too Good for Americans," *Esquire* (June 1957), 55, quoted in Lopes 2002, 1.

13. Alvin Toffler, "A Quantity of Culture," *Fortune*, 64 (November 1961), 124–27 and "The Culture Business," *Newsweek* 60 (3 December 1962), 62, as quoted in Grad 2006, 2.

14. Russell Sanjek, "The War on Rock," *Downbeat Music '72 Yearbook* (Chicago: Maher Publications, 1972), 18, quoted in Garofalo 2002, 143.

15. Comment about Bernstein enjoying touch football comes from The Leonard Bernstein Office, accessed 8 May 2014, http://www. leonardbernstein.com/person. htm, and about movies is from Bernstein and Haws 2009, 8.

16. Bernstein said, "I have always been a folk-music fan, ever since I can remember—any kind: Hindu, Swahili, hillbilly" (1982, 221). He describes folk music from Spain, Greece, Bulgaria, and India with great enthusiasm (Cott 2013, 134, 136–139). At the *Leonard Bernstein: Boston to Broadway* Symposium, 13 October 2006, his son Alexander remembered Bernstein saying that he had played with Miles Davis once; the maestro said that Davis found him terrible at jazz improvisation. Jack Gottlieb included a chapter on Bernstein's popular influences (2004). Lars Helgert investigates Bernstein's use of jazz in selected compositions (2008).

17. Bernstein opens "Inside Pop—The Rock Revolution" with two questions: "why do adults resent it so?" and "why do *I* like it" (1). Presumably if the famous conductor likes rock, perhaps the audience should give it a chance. He does say that he only likes about 5 percent of the repertory, but finds that fascinating. Through carefully chosen recordings he demonstrates arbitrary but interesting changes of meter and key, polyphony, modes, unequal phrases, and stylistic eclecticism, among other things. By the 1980s Bernstein was quite disappointed by rock music "because any asshole can do it" (Cott 2013, 132). He blamed the record companies and their focusing solely on making money from kids for the decline (133).

18. Burton Bernstein's comment comes from The Leonard Bernstein Office, accessed 8 May 2014, http://www.leonardbernstein.com/person.htm, Gottlieb (2010, 62). I am taking the liberty of deeming these sports highbrow due to the expense involved.

19. Lynes suggested that some highbrows "in ardent good faith expend themselves in endeavor to widen the circle of those who can enjoy the arts in their purest forms" and that they try to "make the arts exciting and important to the public." Unfortunately, he also says that they do this "without a great deal of hope" and the knowledge that "most of their labors are wasted" (Lynes 1949a, 21). This was certainly not true for Bernstein.

20. The family spoke of Bernstein's love of fun at the symposium *Leonard Bernstein: Boston to Broadway* held at Harvard University, 12–14 October 2006. His daughter Jamie also mentions her father's ideas of fun in "Leonard Bernstein: A Born Teacher," Leonard Bernstein Office, accessed 8 May 2014, http://www.leonardbernstein.com/educator.htm.

21. *Omnibus* was first televised on CBS (1952–1956), moved to ABC (1956–1957), then ended on NBC (1957–1961). Museum of Broadcast Communications, accessed 9 July 2014, http://www.museum.tv/eotv/omnibus.htm. For more on *Omnibus*, see also Bernstein (1959) 2004, Henderson 1988, Museum of Broadcasting 1985, as well as Rose 1986 and 1992.

22. Ibid.

23. Ibid.

24. Bernstein's experiences surrounding *Omnibus* are documented in H. Burton 1994.

25. Shortly after the broadcast, Saudek wrote Bernstein that they rarely had so much mail on a program and that every telegram was "wildly enthusiastic." Robert Saudek to Leonard Bernstein, 24 November 1954. See Leonard Bernstein Office, accessed 17 March 2014, http://www.leonardbernstein.com/omnibus_letters.htm.

26. *The Current*, "Saudek's *Omnibus*," accessed 14 March 2014, http://www.current.org/wp-content/themes/current/archive-site/coop/coopomni.html.

27. Naomi Thomas's 2004 thesis on Bernstein's *The Unanswered Question* includes a comparative study of the critical reception of these Norton Lectures that summarizes thirteen sources ranging from newspapers, letters to the editor of the *New York Times*, and book and record reviews to biographies and scholarly articles (16–25). See also: The Leonard Bernstein Office, Norton Lectures, http://www.leonardbernstein.com/norton.htm, accessed 14 March 2014; H. Burton 1994, and Anthony Tommasini, "When Bernstein Saw the Future," *New York Times*, 22 July 1998.

28. The scripts for these programs plus "The Art of Conducting" (4 December 1955) are found in Bernstein ([1959] 2004, 85–315). The unpublished *Omnibus* scripts are: "The Role of the University in American Life" (about Harvard University, 25 March 1956), "Bernstein: A Musical Travelogue" (about Israel, 1 December 1957), and "A Midwinter Night's Dream" (about Lincoln Center, 1 January 1961).

29. Football: program no. 1: 38 revised; no. 7: 4; no. 14: 4; no. 42: 23; no. 45: 3A (specifically to Joe Namath, football player). Baseball: no. 3: 27; no. 9: 11; no. 28: 19; no. 32: 13; no. 37: 3; no. 43: 27. Boxing: no. 12: 15; no. 23: 5. Bernstein also mentioned the following: Olympic pole vault champion (no. 7: 4); foot racing (no. 21: 9); target practice (no. 21: 9); and swimming (no. 38: 8).

30. Slapstick lowbrow comedians, the Marx brothers are mentioned in "Humor in Music" (28 February 1959, 6), and Groucho Marx is mentioned in the Norton Lectures (Bernstein 1976, 365). Gans 1974 labels foreign films as highbrow (78), and *La Dolce Vita* is mentioned twice in the Norton Lectures (Bernstein 1976, 315, 318).

31. The 1957 film won seven Academy Awards as well as twenty-three other awards.

32. Children at that time were more knowledgeable about classical music than they are now. In his introduction to the most recent edition of Bernstein's *Young People's Concerts*, Michael Tilson Thomas says, "Sadly, Bernstein's assumptions about the range of knowledge and experience of his young listeners cannot be taken as much for granted today as when he made these shows" (Thomas [1962] 2005, viii).

33. Jamie was born 8 September 1952, Alexander on 7 July 1955, and Nina on 28 February 1962.

34. Lewis Carroll's *Alice in Wonderland* was a Bernstein family favorite, so much so that Bernstein's children placed a copy in his casket (Cott 2013, 153, 165). When Bernstein cabled Felicia about the brilliant Washington, D.C., opening of *West Side Story*, she was thrilled by the "frabgeous [*sic*]" news (Simeone 2013, 372). The word "frabjous" appears in *Alice* and is attributed to Carroll.

35. "Row, Row, Row Your Boat" appears in no. 4: 19; "Twinkle, Twinkle Little Star" or "Ah, vous dirais-je maman" in no. 5:1, no. 19: 30, and no. 28: 11; "Frère Jacques" in no. 4: 19–20; no. 6: 15, 18; and "Three Blind Mice in 4: 19; no. 19: 29. "The Farmer in the Dell" is in no. 49: 21.

36. The Flexible Flyer snow sled is mentioned in no. 20: 5, and building blocks in no. 32: 18.

37. No. 5: 15, 17, 19. See also no. 3: 34 revised.

38. The kazoo is mentioned in no. 1: 17, 18, 19A, ad libbed on 21 revised; no. 3: 34 revised; no. 5: 6, 13, 15, 19; no. 7: 17; no. 9: 3; no. 10: 29–30, which includes Mark Bucci's (b. 1924), *Concerto for a Singing Instrument*, III: "Tug of War" (originally scored for violin and string orchestra) in "Unusual Instruments of the Past, Present, and Future."

39. School subjects were mentioned in programs: no. 1: 4 revised, 6, 7, 10; no. 3: 25; no. 4: 5–6, 33; no. 5: 2; no. 7: 6; no. 10: 29; no. 20: 4; no. 21: 6, 9; no. 22: 2; no. 28: 20; no. 32: 5–6, 8–9, 24, 25; no. 45: 3A revised; no. 49: 5; no. 53: 16, program about astronomy.

40. See endnote 29.

41. No. 5: 13–14, 21; no. 13: 13; no. 16: 2; no. 34: 17; no. 38: 8.

42. Jamie Bernstein Thomas, "Leonard Bernstein Was Their Daddy Too," *Bernstein LIVE* (New York: The Philharmonic-Society of New York, 2000), 8.

43. Bernstein mentions fun or jokes in programs no. 3: 5; no. 5: many; no. 6: many; no. 9: 2; no. 10: 29; no. 12: 19; no. 13: 13; no. 24: 10; no. 25: 2; no. 26: 15; no. 38: many; no. 44: 4 revised; no. 45: 25; no. 53, 4, 5.

44. Critic Anne Midgette bemoans the reputation classical music still has in the twenty-first century as "good for us, but a little dull" in "Make It Short, Sweet and Fun," *Washington Post*, 25 April 2010. She suggests specific performances for the White House, saying that "there's no better way to send a signal about the benefits of classical music than to show Obama having fun listening to it." The quest for fun in classical music continues.

45. This poem was a favorite of Bernstein's. He recited the entire poem by memory to Jonathan Cott in the famous last interview (Cott 2013, 130).

46. In programs nos. 44: 5, 6A; no. 52: 4–5; and no. 51: 6 respectively. See other references in programs no. 5: 12, 29; no. 8: 33; no. 17: 9; no. 27: 3; no. 33: 35.

47. The film of *The Music Man* was released in 1962 and of *Man of La Mancha* in 1972.

48. In addition to these television shows, Bernstein mentions: *Superman* (no. 1: 17, 19A revised); *Dragnet* (no. 1: 42 revised–43 revised; no. 43: 30, 31); *The Flintstones* (no. 19: 9); *The Lone Ranger* (no. 25: 19); *Secret Agent* (no. 36: 19); *Ed Sullivan* (no. 37: 18); *Huntley-Brinkley Report* (no. 43: 29, 31); and general comments (no. 3: 7; no. 5: 7; no. 43: 29, 31; no. 49: 3; no. 51: 4 revised; no. 53: 18).

49. Movies are mentioned in programs no. 4: 11; no. 6: 7, 22, 24; no. 10: 25; no. 12: 4–5; no. 13: 16; no. 16: 9; no. 17: 2; no. 20: 12; no. 21: 9; no. 32: 2; no. 38: 8; no. 40: 12; no. 41: 7; no.44: 14, 18; no.45: 10; no. 48: 21; no. 49: 5; no. 51: 4 revised, 21; no. 53: 4.

50. Bernstein's love of folk music is explored in chapter 2.

51. See also no. 2: many; no. 4: 6–10; no. 5: 1, 2, 8; no. 13: 19; no. 15, 9; no. 19: 29, 31; no. 23: 7, 8, 9, 13; no. 29: 2; no. 31: 4, 11, 18; no. 40: 11, 25.

52. Jazz is mentioned in programs no. 2: many; no. 3: 9; no. 4: 12; no. 5: 1, 3, 6–7, 8; no. 10: 24; no. 13: many; no. 15: 9; no. 16: 14; no. 17: 5–6; no. 21: 4; no. 23: 18; no. 24: 9–10; no. 27: many; no. 29: 6; no. 35: 15; no. 36: 37; no. 42: 20, 21; no. 50: 9.

53. Popular music or rock 'n' roll are mentioned in programs no. 1: 5; no. 2: 15, 20, 28; no. 3: 34 revised; no. 4: 10, 11, 15–16; no. 5: many; no. 16: 9; no. 20: 30; no. 27: 19; no. 28: 12–13; no. 32: 2, 13, 14; no. 33: 12; no. 34: 24; no. 36: 5, 15, 20, 30; no. 37: 18; no. 40: 7; no. 41: 7; no. 43: 28; no. 44: 21; no. 45: 3A revised, 11 revised, 25; no. 46: 4; no. 53, 21.

54. First pencil draft on yellow-lined paper, 16.

55. Allan Kozinn, "Critic's Notebook: They Came, They Sang, They Conquered," *New York Times*, 6 February 2004.

56. *Milwaukee Journal*, 22 June 1966, quoted in H. Burton 1994, 351. Bernstein makes a similar statement in an introduction (1966, 10).

57. According to Jamie, Bernstein adored the Beatles, the Rolling Stones, the Supremes, and the Kinks. *The Legacy of Leonard Bernstein*, interview with Jamie Bernstein by Joan Baum, Education Update Online, accessed 8 May 2014, http://www.educationupdate.com/archives/2008/OCT/html/mad-interview.html. Horowitz incorrectly reports that the music of the folk-pop duo Simon and Garfunkel were cited on Bernstein's *Young People's Concerts* (2007, 478).

58. Probably Mark had the wrong month in mind and meant November, referring to Bernstein's singing of the Beatles song "Norwegian Wood" in "What Is a Mode?" (23 November 1966, 30).

59. *Philadelphia Inquirer*, 20 Jan. 1958. No title or author is given in Bernstein's scrapbook for 11 January 1958–31 March 1958, reel 15, volume 24, item 29.

CHAPTER 4

1. On Jenny Lind, see Shulz 1962 and Ware and Lockard 1980. Joseph Horowitz thoroughly studies the evolution of ballyhoo (Horowitz 1987, 18–22).

2. These broadcasts are available on DVD as *Arturo Toscanini, NBC Symphony Orchestra, The Television Concerts—1948–52,* volumes 1–5, NBC Enterprises, 1987; remastering by Testament, 2005.

3. Regarding the media's reporting of Toscanini's experiences with the wars in Europe, see Horowitz 1993, 81–83, 177–180.

4. In a letter dated 3 November 1958, Tully Plesser wrote that when he and a lady friend attended a Philharmonic concert, she "developed a sudden attack of Bernsteini-

tis." He continues, "the symptoms are varied, and include long periods of podium staring, audible sights and involuntary gestures similar to those of a conductor." He suggests that meeting Bernstein after a concert might "snap her out of her present state." There are several such letters from star-struck fans.

5. *Life*, 18 October 1956, 58, quoted in Grad 2006, 52.

6. Sylvester (Pat) L. Weaver Jr., "Enlightenment through Exposure," *Television Magazine* (January 1952), 31, quoted in Rose 1986, 2.

7. Larry Gelbart (one of Sid Caesar's writers) discusses the series cancellation in *Make 'Em Laugh: The Funny Business of America* (2009), Season 1, Episode 6: "Sock It to Me?: Satire and Parody," Original Air Date, 28 January 2009. The award-winning comedy writer was best known for developing the landmark TV series *MASH*, co-writing the book for the 1962 hit Broadway musical *A Funny Thing Happened on the Way to the Forum*, and the 1982 movie comedy *Tootsie*. Gelbart said: "When Caesar's Hour was in flower, there were not a lot of television sets in use. They were . . . bought by people who made a lot of money and tended to be educated, so we had a very sophisticated audience. As the price of sets went down, so did the I.Q. of the watchers and we were finally knocked off the air by Lawrence Welk [a musical variety show aimed at rural audiences]."

8. Edward R. Murrow's speech to the Radio-Television News Directors Association in Chicago, 15 October 1958, accessed 26 July 2014, http://www.turnoffyourtv. com/commentary/hiddenagenda/murrow.html.

9. Robert Lewis Shayon, "The Pied Piper of Video," *Saturday Review of Literature* 33 (25 November 1950), 9.

10. Quoted in Comstock 1978, 92.

11. Turow focused on programs intended for children as defined by network publicity releases and the National Nielsen Television Index Reports (Turow 1981, 6). Anthony Michael Maltese (1967) offers another survey of children's television. Although Maltese covers some of the same information, he focuses more on a survey of the programs classified by network (with a description of plot, costs, sponsors, broadcast times, and so forth) during those years.

12. Captain Kangaroo offered to appear on the *Young People's Concerts*. See chapter 2.

13. The seven were *Howdy Doody*, Bernstein's *Young People's Concerts*, *The Paul Winchell Show*, *Lunch with Soupy Sales*, *Magic Land of Alakazam*, *On Your Mark*, and *Video Village Junior*.

14. This anthology (airing one to five times a year) offered such diverse programming as: "HMS Pinafore" (23 November 1973), "[noted dancer Alvin] Ailey Celebrates Ellington" (28 November 1974), "Henry Winkler [portrayed Fonzie in the sitcom *Happy Days*] Meets Shakespeare" (20 March 1977), and "What's a Museum for, Anyway?" (5 February 1978).

15. The others were *Captain Kangaroo* (a mixture of fiction, nonfiction, and performing activities), and the two cartoons *Heckle and Jeckle* and *Woody Woodpecker*.

16. Harold Taubman, "The Philharmonic—What's Wrong with It and Why," *New York Times* (29 April 1956), 139. The article breaks down the problems according to: orchestra, conductors, soloists, programs, board, management, and public. For more on Taubman's article and its effects, see Shanet 1975, 323–327. One complaint

addressed the sparseness of works by living composers; the critic recommended many specific composers for consideration, Bernstein among them. He also suggested that the Philharmonic repertory include "all schools and trends" of twentieth-century music, including commissioning works by American composers.

17. NYpa, 019-03-40. Letter from Lelia M. Wardwell and Anne H. Straus, Co-Chairmen, Young People's Concerts Committee to Mssrs. Judson, Zirato, and Judd, 31 May 1956.

18. Memo from George E. Judd Jr. to Mr. John J. Totten, Subject: Young People's Concerts—1957–1958, 17 May 1957, specifically states that the Philharmonic was investigating televising the next season's "Young People's Concerts." Bernstein participated in these discussions, according to the minutes of a meeting on 2 May 1957 at the Philharmonic. See Minutes by CBS, 1957–1958 Season, *Television Possibilities* in re: *Young People's Concerts*, NYpa, 019-03-01.

19. They mentioned the possibility of one person organizing the concerts and another conducting them.

20. The people involved probably saw Bernstein's successful television debut on *Omnibus* on 14 November 1954.

21. At the time of this memo, Frederick Fennell taught and directed ensembles at the Eastman School of Music, had recorded with Mercury Records, received many awards, and guest conducted many major orchestras. Howard Mitchell was the director of the National Symphony Orchestra, engineering what critic Ted Libbey called the nadir of the orchestra (Libbey 1995, 42). Robert Shaw was associate conductor under Szell of the Cleveland Orchestra, founder of the Robert Shaw Chorale (which toured internationally and made recordings), and later became music director of the Atlanta Symphony Orchestra; he was arguably the most noted choral conductor in the United States. Samuel Antek had played under Toscanini in the NBC Symphony Orchestra and was director of New Jersey Symphony Orchestra; he unfortunately died in 1958. Igor Buketoff taught at Butler University and Columbia, had been music director of the Chautauqua Opera Association, conducted the Philharmonic's Young People's Concerts (1948–1953), and guest conducted the Philadelphia Orchestra.

22. Memo, sender, receiver, and date unknown, re: Bernstein and YPC, NYpa, 019-03-40.

23. Carlos Moseley, "Leonard Bernstein as Music Director," *Bernstein LIVE* (New York: The Philharmonic-Symphony Society of New York, 2000), 16.

24. Minutes re: 1957–58 Season, *Television Possibilities* in re: *Young People's Concerts*, 2 May 1957, NYpa, 019-03-01.

25. For more on *Omnibus*, see chapter 3.

26. In the early twenty-first century, the sample size was 25,000. See "Nielsen, Home Measurement, Television," accessed 30 May 2010, http://en-us.nielsen.com/tab/measurement/tv_research (site discontinued).

27. *National Nielsen TV Ratings, Second Report for January 1962 (Two Weeks Ending January 21, 1962)*, (A. C. Nielsen Co., 1962), 7. See also Media Literacy Clearing House, Math in the Media, accessed 8 May 2014, http://www.frankwbaker.com/ratingshare.htm. I am grateful to David Benson for his clarifications.

28. David Benson, interview by the author, Bethesda, Maryland, 19 August 2009. Benson worked for various affiliates and used Nielsen ratings to sell commercial time to businesses and advertisers. Benson earned a master's degree in Radio, Television, and Film from the University of Maryland College Park, Maryland, (1981), and worked for several different radio and television stations, 1970–1997, from Virginia and North Carolina to New York.

29. Primetime was determined by the Primetime Access Rule (PTAR) enacted by the Federal Communications Commission (FCC) to limit the number of hours a network could dictate which programs its local affiliates broadcast. At first, primetime ran from 7 to 10, then 7 to 11, then 8 to 11 EST.

30. The Philharmonic wrote local orchestras suggesting that they influence their local affiliate to carry Bernstein's *Young People's Concerts,* evidently to good effect. See documents in NYpa, 019-03-07.

31. "Internet Archives of Classic Television," accessed 8 May 2014, https://archive.org/details/Jack_Benny_10_25_1953.

32. Minutes by CBS, 1957–1958 Season, *Television Possibilities* in re: *Young People's Concerts,* NYpa, folder 019-03-01.

33. NYpa, those in folders 019-04-01 and more importantly 020-11-26.

34. The available Nielsen ratings for the series are found in appendix E.

35. The days, dates, and times of all broadcasts are detailed in appendix C. Scheduling an appealing timeslot was a challenge. In a letter to Floyd D. Blair, the orchestra's president, from Dorothy G. Sinnett, 26 January 1955, Sinnett bemoans the inconvenient time of the orchestra's radio broadcast and suggests a better slot when the family would be able to listen. Accessed 2 September 2013, http://archives.nyphil.org/ ID: 009-11-06.

36. This was part of a general increase in "public service" programming after Minow's speech. Such programs were defined as "programs which are primarily informational and educational in nature in contrast to regular programs which are primarily entertainment." According to Minow 1964, 68–69, the A. C. Nielsen Media Research Division recorded the number of public service programs as: 1959: 94; 1960: 109; 1961: 151; 1962: 152; 1963: 179. Minow's address apparently had an effect on the industry's conscience.

37. Two Christmas programs were broadcast slightly later in the afternoon on Christmas Day: "A Toast to Vienna in 3/4 Time" (25 December 1967 at 5:30–6:30 p.m.) and "Fantastic Variations (*Don Quixote*)" (25 December 1968, 5:00–6:00 p.m.).

38. Letter from George E. Judd to "Friends," January 1959, NYp, 019-03-07.

39. Memo from Clara Simons to Roger Englander, re: Response to Jan. 18 Young People's Telecast, 24 January 1958, NYpa, 019-03-01.

40. The teacher was Jim Sewery, and the student signed "Cichillo."

41. Bernstein greets the new Canadian viewers in "What Is Impressionism?" (1 December 1961): "It feels great to be back with all my good young friends in this hall, and all over the country; and I'd like to say a specially warm hello to our new friends up North in Canada." This is the live version, which is warmer than the one in the script (2). As the show progresses, he continues to incorporate references to Canada.

42. Confidential Annual Report for the Year Ending May 31, 1964, NYpa, box containing original annual reports 1950–1959, 60/61, 1975. The report also notes that tapes of the series were made available to "non-television, non-theatrical, non-paying audiences (such as schools, colleges, hospitals, etc.)" in the spring of 1964.

43. No title, nd. NYpa, 019-04-01. The document is accompanied by others dating from 1964 and is a chart listing "Number of Television Sets" and "Type of Broadcast," that is, commercial, limited commercial, non-commercial.

44. NYpa, 019-03-24, letter from CBS Television to Mr. Bruno Zirato Sr., The Philharmonic Symphony Society, 10 June 1957, 4.

45. The programs on DVDs lack the commercials, and the films at the Library of Congress have commercials on only one program.

46. "Unusual Instruments of the Past, Present, and Future" (27 March 1960), the page after page 31 lacks a number.

47. The opening quote is from the script for program 20 (the opening page is missing for programs 10–19), and the closing quote is from the final page of the scripts for programs 13–19. Many scripts are missing the opening or closing page.

48. The AT&T survey results are found in box/folder 1024/7 and NYpa, 020-02-02. For more about films of this series in schools, see box/folder 923/8, 990/3, and NYpa 020-02-02. Evidently the "McGraw-Hill Text-Films New Product Information [1965?]" announcement found in box/folder 990/3 was submitted to Bernstein for his approval. He wrote in the margin, "these summaries are accurate but succeed in making the shows sound dull in the extreme. But I don't know what to suggest to avoid this. LB." He was still fighting the boredom and lack of fun that accompanied most music education. NYpa 020-02-02 has an advertisement for "The Bell System Leonard Bernstein Concert Films . . . A Teacher's Classroom Guide" that "contains information to help the teacher use the films as effectively as possible." The booklet supplies teaching materials for "What Is Sonata Form?" "Young Performers 1966 [No. 6]," "A Tribute to Sibelius," "Musical Atoms," "The Sound of an Orchestra," "A Birthday Tribute to Shostakovich," and "Young Performers 1966 [No. 7]." Although thirty-five programs had been broadcast by 1966, Bell distributed only seven. Since two Young Performers programs were included, these must have had great value to teachers and young students. By 1975, AT&T, McGraw Hill, and B.F.A. Educational Media had taken over distributing the films, and Viacom was in charge of the international broadcast syndication market; see box/folder 923/8.

49. Also Val Adams, "Young People's Concerts Are for Young in Heart," *New York Times*, 30 August 1964. Adams asked "just who watches the Young People's Concerts" when CBS announced the new sponsor for the next season, Bell Telephone. The network provided the ratings to show that the advertising should be aimed at adults rather than at children. Their figures indicated that of the 83 percent adult viewers, 37 percent of viewers were men, 46 percent women; of the remaining 17 percent, 6 percent were teens, and 11 percent children. The article does not state how CBS obtained their information; at this time, the Nielsen ratings did not break down their figures demographically.

50. In 1958, the following adults wrote specifically praising Bernstein's *Young People's Concerts*: H. F. Anderson, David Arnold, Mrs. Frank W. Adams, Mr. and

Mrs. C. Burress, Mrs. Philip Berg, Ruth R. Burks, Ruth and John Cusack, and many others. Dr. Erwin Krauzs wrote to say his eighty-eight-year-old patient enjoyed the program.

51. David Benson, email to author, 20 December 2009.

52. The saga of Serling's difficulties with this script is documented in many sources. See Presnell and McGee 1998, 11–12; Zicree 1989, 14–15; and Barnouw 1978, 49–51.

53. *Report of the Attorney General to the President, Dec. 30, 1959*, quoted in *Television Network Program Procurement* 1963, 372.

54. A member of the production crew who wishes to remain anonymous asserted that no one (not the sponsors, the CBS network, nor the management of the orchestra) ever attempted to censor Bernstein's *Young People's Concerts*.

55. Dubin is listed in the scripts as director for all three shows in the first season (18 January 1958, 1 February 1958, and 8 March 1958). Englander erroneously states that Dubin was removed after the first show rather than after the first season (Rose 1992, 132).

56. Memo from Bruno Zirato to Leonard Bernstein, *Suggested Draft of Letter-Contract*—re: *Leonard Bernstein* and Televised *Young People's Concerts*, 17 September 1957, NYpa, 019-03-24, 2.

57. Memo from Zirato to Bernstein, 3–4.

58. Letter from CBS Television to Mr. Bruno Zirato, The Philharmonic Symphony Society, 10 June 1957, NYpa, 019-03-24, 9.

59. Bernstein began his "process of self-exploration" after leaving college with psychoanalyst Marketa Morris, whom he called "Frau" (Simeone 2013, xiv–xv), and had regular visits with other psychiatrists throughout his life (H. Burton 1994, 108–109, 436). It is safe to assume that such a questioning, well-read individual would be familiar with psychiatric tools and diagnoses. The bible of the psychiatric field (the *Diagnostic and Statistical Manual* published by the American Psychiatric Association) was the main reference source for clinicians, researchers, psychiatric drug regulation agencies, health insurance and pharmaceutical companies, the legal system, and policy makers.

60. My thanks to University of Georgia archivist Mary Miller for this information.

61. The official Leonard Bernstein website, accessed 8 May 2014, http://www.leonardbernstein.com/honors.htm.

62. In 1959, 1960, 1964, 1965, 1966, and 1967. The "Leonard Bernstein and the New York Philharmonic" series won in 1961, 1962, and 1963. This means the maestro had won the "Series Award" with various projects for nine consecutive years. My thanks go to Ruth Sieber Johnson, executive director of Sigma Alpha Iota International Music Fraternity for this information.

CHAPTER 5

1. One example is the satirical book *The Mouse That Roared* by Irish author Leonard Wibberly (1955), in which small nations worry that the superpowers will blow up

the entire world. Through a bumbling series of events, Grand Fenwick (the world's tiniest nation) forces the superpowers to disarm. The book was made into a film starring Peter Sellers in 1959. Other artistic reactions are found below.

2. A frightening 1951 civil defense film, *Duck and Cover* (produced in cooperation with the Federal Civil Defense Administration and in consultation with the Safety Commission of the National Education Association) was distributed to schools. To cheery music (presumably to make the idea of an atomic bomb falling anytime or anyplace less frightening to children), Bert the Turtle learns to duck and cover when an atomic bomb explodes. See Internet Archive, accessed 8 May 2014, https://archive.org/details/DuckandC1951.

3. Crist 2005, 197, from Fred E. Busbey, "Aaron Copland and the Inaugural Concert," January 16, 1953, 83rd Congress, 1st sess., *Congressional Record*, 99, pt. 9, Appendix 169. Copland's experience with the anti-Communist hysteria is described in: DeLapp 1997, Copland and Perlis 1999, and Pollack 1999.

4. See Hellman's distorted memoir of the mid-twentieth century *Red Scare* (1976).

5. The story is fleshed out in Crist 2006, 493–495, and H. Burton 1994, 231. The complete affidavit, Simeone's investigation of Bernstein's FBI files, and Bernstein's letters about the incident to his brother and David Diamond are in Simeone 2013, 299–311. Regarding Bernstein's symphony, *The Age of Anxiety* and McCarthyism, see Gentry 2011.

6. The first quote comes from U.S. Congress, Senate. Public Buildings. *National Cultural Center*—Senate, 1958, 24, quoted in Grad 2006, 117; the second from U.S. Congress, House, *Federal Grants to Fine Arts Programs and Projects. Hearings before a Special Subcommittee of the Committee on Education and Labor on H.R.* 452, 5136, 5330, 5397, 7106, 7185, 7192, 7383, 7433, 7533, 7953, 8047, 9111, 83rd Cong., 2d Sess. 1954, quoted in Grad 2006, 112.

7. See Ansari 2010, 2011, 2012a, and 2012b.

8. "I've been appalled . . . at the lack of any artistic voice in the . . . crises we've been going through with Vietnam, the Negroes, human rights, civil rights." Bernstein quoted in Gruen 1968, 150–151.

9. Paul Boyer offers a wonderful article titled "Leonard Bernstein: Humanitarian and Social Activist" in Bernstein and Haws 2008, 35–53.

10. The number in attendance comes from Linton Weeks, "At Washington Cathedral, Pop Music, Politics and Prayers for Peace," *Washington Post*, 17 October 2007, accessed 8 May 2014, http://www.washingtonpost.com/wp-dyn/content/article/2007/10/16/AR2007101602498.html.

11. Excerpts from the newsreel by Universal-International News from 27 July 1959 titled *Nixon in U.S.S.R.: Opening U.S. Fair, Clashes with Mr. K* was seen on YouTube, 8 May 2014, http://www.youtube.com/watch?v=PIJ1S9wAGbA.

12. I would like to thank Marie Carter of the Leonard Bernstein Office for guiding me to and supplying this script. Emily Abrams Ansari delivered an insightful paper ("Leonard Bernstein and the New York Philharmonic in Moscow") on Cold War diplomacy and the politics of tonal music at the 2012 New Orleans meeting of the American Musicological Society.

13. See also "Ford Motor Company Presents Leonard Bernstein and the New York Philharmonic in Berlin," air date: 24 November 1960, and "Ford Motor Company Presents Leonard Bernstein and the New York Philharmonic in Japan," air date: 6 February 1962. My thanks go again to Marie Carter for guiding me to and supplying these scripts.

14. Bernstein mentions in his 1953 affidavit that he learned to share his mentor Koussevitzky's strong antipathy for the Soviets and listed the many times he spoke out "against the inhibitions imposed upon creative artists . . . under the Soviet regime" (Simeone 2013, 307).

15. Bernstein wrote a speech for the National Press Club explaining the altercation with the Soviet press from his point of view. Rather than delivering his written speech, Bernstein spoke extemporaneously; the intended speech is reproduced in Bernstein 1982, 153–163.

16. Memo from Bruno Zirato to Leonard Bernstein, *Suggested Draft of Letter-Contract*—re: *Leonard Bernstein* and Televised Young People's Concerts, 17 September 1957, US-NYpa, 019-03-24, 3–4. See chapter 4.

17. Bernstein refers here to his being censured by the Soviet government for speaking directly to the audience from the podium.

18. The script is not at either the Library of Congress or the New York Philharmonic Archives.

19. The member of the production crew wishes to remain anonymous.

20. Bernstein must have felt safe making several negative comments about Russian imperialism in Finland in "A Tribute to Sibelius" (19 February 1965), since those events happened in the nineteenth century.

21. During tours the Philharmonic often gave youth concerts that were not filmed for broadcast. One such program was "Modern Music from All Over" (13 May 1961, Toronto tour, box/folder 107/4).

22. Before "A Birthday Tribute to Shostakovich," the Philharmonic recorded two of his piano concertos and four of his symphonies (North 2006, 353).

23. Several contemporary newsreels of the Cuban revolution, Castro, and the Cuban Missile Crisis can be seen on YouTube.com, including the Universal International News newsreel *Fidel Castro Triumphs! 1959-01-05*, *Rally for Castro, One Million Roar "Si" to Cuban Executions, 1959-01-22*, and *Kennedy Addresses the Nation on the Cuban Missile Crisis*, accessed 8 May 2014.

24. Bernstein's eldest daughter, Jamie Bernstein Thomas, recounted this story to Michael Tilson Thomas in *Great Performances: Carnegie Hall Opening Night 2008*, PBS, 29 October 2008. Tilson Thomas opened the program by welcoming the audience to this "birthday bash" for Bernstein. This program was an unofficial part of the festival "Bernstein: The Best of All Possible Worlds," commemorating the 90th anniversary of his birth and featuring fifty events throughout New York City, presented by Carnegie Hall and the New York Philharmonic 24 September–13 December 2008. Bernstein's music was also the cornerstone of the 2008–2009 season of the Baltimore Symphony Orchestra, Marin Alsop, Music Director.

25. About Bernstein's trip to Cuba, see H. Burton 1994, 266–268. The information about Lecuona comes from Humphrey Burton, e-mail message to author, 2 April 2009.

Both Bernstein and Blitzstein were depressed following the failures of their productions of *Candide* and *Reuben Reuben* respectively. During this vacation, Bernstein made decisions that shaped his life, choosing to focus on his career as a conductor rather than as a composer. Bernstein had been enjoying Lecuona's music for most of his life; he and his friend Mildred Spiegel had been playing duets and two piano pieces by this Cuban composer, among others, since they were fourteen and sixteen years old respectively (20).

26. *Great Performances*, 29 October 2008. Tilson Thomas specifically mentioned "You Got Me, Baby" from *On the Town*, *West Side Story*, and all the early symphonic pieces, saying, "It's just a flavor that's always there."

27. Programs 20 through 23 comprise the sixth season. Program 20 predates the Cuban Missile Crisis. Program 21 was taped on 3 November, too soon after the missile crisis. Program 22 featured young performers and was probably set at the beginning of the season. See appendix C.

28. For a brief discussion of the Native American activist movement referred to as "red power," see Fischer 2006, 354–359, which also includes a comprehensive bibliography, and Lytle 2006, 269–288.

29. Galvanized by the successes achieved by African Americans regarding social issues, Latinos (who experienced similar obstructions) began seeking equality and political power in the 1960s. On 30 September 1962, César Chavez and others formed the labor union called National Farm Workers Association to fight for civil rights for Latino domestic migratory farm workers. These poor, unskilled, illiterate itinerants had no voice and were excluded from the social advances afforded to African Americans. See the web site for the United Farm Workers of America, accessed 8 May 2014, http://www.ufw.org/_page.php?menu=research&inc=research_history.html. The impression that the average American had of Latin Americans in the early 1960s was not a good one.

30. See Vietnam Veterans Memorial Wall, accessed 8 May 2014, http://thewall-usa.com/summary.asp.

31. The contentious debate surrounding Bernstein's somewhat controversial casting decision is documented by H. Burton 1994, 388.

32. A search of scores of *Pini di Roma* at the Library of Congress turned up no prose program by Respighi. Slonimsky continues "and, by historic association, the successful march on Rome of Benito Mussolini's Fascist legions."

CHAPTER 6

1. Boyer surveys Bernstein's actions on behalf of African Americans and women in "Leonard Bernstein: Humanitarian and Social Activist," in Bernstein and Haws 2008, 35–53.

2. In 1969 twenty-one Black Panthers were awaiting trial on charges of plotting to plant bombs in various populous locations and murder policemen. Many felt they were being denied fair legal treatment. See H. Burton 1994, 389–393.

3. For a detailed account of the party from Wolfe's point of view, see Wolfe 1970, 3–94, and from Bernstein's point of view, see Cott 2013, 85–86. See also the website for the Leonard Bernstein Office, "The Panther 21 Fundraiser and 'Radical Chic'" by Kate Chisholm, with contributions from Jamie Bernstein, accessed 26 June 2014, http://www.leonardbernstein.com/person_radical_chic.htm.

4. Jamie Bernstein Thomas, "SFist interviews Jamie Bernstein," accessed 8 May 2014, http://sfist.com/2008/02/06/sfist_interview_12.php. For more on Bernstein's troubles with the FBI, see Seldes 2009.

5. Reri Grist in "Who Is Gustav Mahler?" (7 February 1960), William Warfield in "Aaron Copland Birthday Party" (12 February 1961), Veronica Tyler in "Young Performers No. 2" (19 March 1961), André Watts in "Young Performers No. 4" (15 January 1963), Weldon Berry Jr. in "Young Performers No. 5" (23 December 1963), James de Priest in "Young Performers No. 7" (22 February 1966), Simon Estes in "Charles Ives: American Pioneer" (23 February 1967), and the five-member jazz band in "Jazz in the Concert Hall" (11 March 1964).

6. The complexities of creating and scheduling the programs meant that there was always a delay between a political event and a *Young People's Concert* related to that event. Scripts had to be ready four to six weeks in advance of the taping, and programs were taped several weeks in advance of the broadcast (see appendix C). The first and second programs of the tenth season, "What Is a Mode?" (taped 22 October 1966, broadcast 23 November 1966) and "Young Performers No. 8" (taped 17 December 1966, broadcast 27 January 1967), were probably already in place by the late summer. Bernstein needed to focus on Ives in the third program, "Charles Ives: American Pioneer" (23 February 1967), to coincide with the Philharmonic subscription series and release of a Bernstein/Philharmonic LP of Ives. The earliest Bernstein could have commented on civil rights was the final concert of the season, "Alumni Reunion." There may also have been other obligations on the soloists' calendars.

7. Tyler appeared on "Young Performers No. 2" (19 March 1961) when she was twenty-two and again on "What Is Sonata Form?" (6 November 1964). She also performed on several summer Promenade concerts and a subscription concert before "Alumni Reunion."

8. For information about the *Amsterdam News,* see Farber 2001, 337.

9. Watts was sixteen when he appeared in "Young Performers No. 4" (15 January 1963).

10. Anderson's Metropolitan Opera debut was 8 January 1955, and Eisenhower's Second Inauguration was 10 January 1957 (Collier-Thomas 2000, 20 and 58).

11. See the excerpt from her biography about the performance "Society's Child" in the Janis Ian Reading Room, accessed 1 April 2014, http://www.janisian.com/reading/autobiographyhb.php.

12. Brief surveys of the feminist movement with bibliographies can be found in Fischer 2006, 336–344 and in Lytle 2006, 269–282.

13. Ms. Caduff later guest conducted the Berlin, Munich, and Royal Philharmonics and was the first woman to become a music director in Europe (at Solingen, Germany, 1977–86).

14. *The Telegraph*, 28 July 2013, accessed 8 May 2014, http://www.telegraph.co.uk/culture/music/proms/10207749/Ill-beat-my-injury-in-time-for-Rule-Britannia.html.

15. *Life*, 18 October 1956, 58, quoted in Grad 2006, 64.

16. Gruen 1968, with photographs by Ken Heyman. A contemporaneous review from Atlanta, Georgia, says that the photos were "embarrassingly banal"; Burton, however, calls them "remarkable for their tenderness and intimacy" (1994, 377). Burton also suggests that the book "falls between the two schools of biography and coffee-table gossip" (378).

17. In 1968, *Hair* won the Drama Desk Award and the Vernon Rice-Drama Desk Award. The song "Aquarius/Let the Sunshine In" is actually a medley of two songs, "Aquarius" and "Let the Sunshine In."

18. Sherri Cavan lived in the Haight-Ashbury district of San Francisco in the 1960s, collecting her data by observing and interviewing hippies in the area. See also Truzzi 1975, 906–911.

19. The taping for this *Young People's Concert* was on 18 December 1971. *The Planets* was performed on a regular subscription concert of the Philharmonic on 24 November 1971 (email message to the author from Richard Wandel, Associate Archivist Emeritus of the New York Philharmonic Archives, 21 July 2008; Shanet 1975 stops at the end of the 1970–1971 season).

20. Several articles that examine the "powerful, ongoing role that Boston's Jewish immigrant community" had in shaping Bernstein's identity and character are found in the *Journal of the Society for American Music* 3, no. 1 (2009). See also Gottlieb 2010, 1–15 and Pearlmutter 1985.

21. The "Summer of Love" and the Monterey Rock Festival in June 1967 established this link. Fischer, 2006, 307–312. Fischer includes a copious, current bibliography of sources on the 1960s classified by issues.

22. Tom Buckley wrote about "restless youngsters" coming to New York in his article, "Little Girl's Search Led to Death: . . . Lure of Hippie Life Proved Too Much for 13-Year-Old," *New York Times*, 12 August 1968.

23. Bernstein's lifelong asthma is woven through H. Burton 1994. This makes it even more surprising that he was so addicted to cigarettes.

24. A brief history of the social aspects of smoking is found in Tollison 1986, 167–188.

25. Only 23 percent of the population smoked by 2000.

26. Cheryl Krasnick Warsh, "Smoke and Mirrors: Gender Representation in North American Tobacco and Alcohol Advertisements before 1950," *Histoire sociale/Social History* 31 (1998), 220, quoted in Holt 2006, 233.

27. By the end of the 1960s, Jamie and Alexander must have had a good relationship with their father since they accompanied him on a five-week goodwill tour of Western Europe in 1968 (H. Burton 1994, 376).

28. Bernstein mentions reading the *New York Times* to Jonathan Cott (2013, 67).

29. Stanley F. Yolles explained various drugs and their deleterious effects to parents in "Before *Your* Kid Tries Drugs: Why Do Drug-Taking Kids Want to Ward Off Reality," saying that young people were more likely to respond to knowledge than threats (*New York Times*, 17 November 1968).

30. Two articles on drugs are in the April 1970 issue of *Psychology Today*.

31. The message in this program is so subtle that it was lost on James H. North (2006, 432). North watched the twenty-five *Young People's Concerts* on DVD. Of this program, he says, "Having once told us that music doesn't mean anything but music [in "What Does Music Mean?" (18 January 1958)], Bernstein now talks of nothing but the drama [in *Symphonie fantastique*]." It seems likely that his desire to warn against hallucinogenics caused the change of focus. Nonetheless, while Bernstein allowed the drama to organize the "talk" on the program, he did not neglect the music taking time to relate musical ideas to dramatic ideas. He used this technique when explaining the story of *Petrouchka* in "Happy Birthday, Igor Stravinsky" (26 March 1962), Ottorino Respighi's *The Pines of Rome* in "The Anatomy of a Symphony Orchestra" (24 May 1970), Franz Liszt's *Faust Symphony* in "Liszt and the Devil" (13 February 1972), and in "Holst: *The Planets*" (26 March 1972). Of these four, only the Stravinsky program was available on DVD when North published his book, so he probably did not see the other three programs.

32. The hippie credo is described by Charles Reich in the national bestseller *The Greening of America* (1970, 308).

33. The note in question is written as a C# in the exposition, but as a D-flat in the recapitulation.

34. For more information on *West Side Story*, see Simeone 2009 and Wells 2011. For more information on *Mass*, see André 1979; J. A. Bernstein 2001; Cottle 1978; De Sesa 1985.

35. See Allen Kozinn, "Bernstein and Thomas Head New Pacific Music Festival," *New York Times*, 19 January 1990.

CHAPTER 7

1. Theodor W. Adorno discusses the "opposing extremes" of music as represented by Stravinsky and Schoenberg in his 1949 book *Philosophy of Music* (3–4). It is safe to assume that a seeker of knowledge like Bernstein would have been aware of Adorno's thoughts.

2. Morgan (1998) and Simms (1999) offer valuable introductions and selected writings regarding twentieth-century music.

3. Critic Alex Ross offers a comprehensive survey of musical politics in the twentieth century, covering reactionary and avant-garde composers, styles, critiques, and polemical writings (2007). For more on this, see chapter 3. Emily Abrams Ansari offers excellent overviews of music during the Cold War and of the participation of American classical composers in federally funded activities during the Cold War (Emily Abrams Ansari, "Cold War, the," *Grove Music Online*, *Oxford Music Online*, Oxford University Press, accessed 8 January 2014, http://www.oxfordmusiconline.com/subscriber/article/grove/music/A2228066; 2010). See Watkins (1988) and Watkins (1994) for surveys of twentieth-century music. Grant (1998) discusses contemporaneous critics.

4. For entertainingly dreadful reviews of such concert standards as Beethoven's Fifth and Ninth Symphonies, see Slonimsky (1953) 2000.

5. Kopp 2006. The conflict between the existing European style and developing American style is presented in Oja 2000, 177–200, 231–236.

6. "Nicolas Nabukov," University of Texas at Austin, Harry Ransom Center, accessed 8 May 2014, http://norman.hrc.utexas.edu/fasearch/findingAid.cfm?eadid=00097.

7. *La Revue musicale* 212 (April 1952), 119: "*affirmon, à notre tour, que tout musician qui n'a pas ressenti—nous ne dison pas compris, man bien ressenti—la nécessité du langage de décaphonique est INUTILE.*" From the issue devoted to Masterpieces of the XXth Century.

8. Babbitt's original title for the article was "The Composer as Specialist." The title was changed by his editor, much to Babbitt's displeasure (Simms 1999, 153).

9. I would like to thank Mark Eden Horowitz for showing me Adams's letter with Bernstein's response before Simeone's book was published. Simeone 2013, 477.

10. The italics are in the original.

11. An incomplete list of his writings on these subjects includes: an *Omnibus* script titled "Introduction to Modern Music" for broadcast on 13 January 1957 (Bernstein [1959] 2004, 192–235); a script for a 13 May 1961 "Young People's Concert" for performance in Toronto titled "Modern Music from All Over" that was not broadcast; his talks during the 1964 Philharmonic festival of avant-garde music (Bernstein 2000, CD 9); two articles written after his 1964–1965 sabbatical "What I Thought . . . ," and ". . . and What I Did" (Bernstein 1982, 230–238); the introduction and "An Informal Lecture: Something to Say . . ." in *The Infinite Variety of Music* (Bernstein 1966, 9–13, 265–286); and his 1973 Norton Lectures (Bernstein 1976), in particular, lectures five and six (263–324, 325–425). He also is quoted in the September 1965 "Entrances and Exits" (a monthly column in the New York Philharmonic program) about his survey of the twentieth-century symphony for the 1965–1966 Philharmonic season (Ardoin 1965, 12, 30, 37). My thanks to Richard Wandel, Associate Archivist emeritus of the New York Philharmonic Archives, for placing the article in the context of Philharmonic programs in an email to the author (1 September 2010).

12. Bernstein brought the chimes that preceded concerts and summoned the audience back to their seats after intermission up-to-date by using tone rows rather than the Big Ben motif. Gottlieb was in charge of selecting fifteen rows and creating the recording on celesta that broadcast through the halls intermittently from 1965 through 2009. With Bernstein's approval, Gottlieb selected rows by the Second Viennese School, Stravinsky ("its polar opposite"), and Bernstein (Gottlieb 2010, 144–145).

13. Avant-garde composers John Cage and Iannis Xenakis, reactionary Randall Thompson, and jazz-influenced French composer Milhaud all wrote expressing their gratitude for Bernstein presenting their works (Simeone 2013, 452–453, 458, 498, 413).

14. The Philharmonic commissioned a total of twenty-six works by twenty-five composers during Bernstein's tenure as music director. Most of them were performed during either the 1967–1968 season to celebrate the Philharmonic's 125th season (eleven works) or the 1962–1963 season when Philharmonic Hall at Lincoln Center opened (seven works). Many composers were primarily reactionary but experimented with the avant-garde (serialism, and so forth). Fourteen were American and twenty

were primarily reactionaries. The composers so honored are listed here with their nationality and musical bent (despite the risk of attaching simplistic labels): Gunther Schuller (American reactionary, jazz-influenced), Copland (American reactionary, jazz-influenced), William Schuman (American reactionary, jazz/pop influenced), Darius Milhaud (French reactionary, jazz-influenced), Samuel Barber (American reactionary), Francis Poulenc (French reactionary), Paul Hindemith (German reactionary, moved to United States in 1940), Hans Werner Henze (German reactionary), Alberto Ginastera (Argentine nationalistic reactionary), Carlos Chavez (Mexican nationalistic reactionary), Alan Hovhaness (American reactionary), Tōru Takemitsu (Japanese reactionary), Roberto Gerhard (Spanish, avant-garde), Nicolas Nabokov (American of Russian origin, reactionary), Rodion Shchedrin (Soviet reactionary), Richard Rodney Bennett (English, avant-garde), Roy Harris (American reactionary), Howard Hanson (American reactionary), Walter Piston (American reactionary), Virgil Thomson (American reactionary), Roger Sessions (American, avant-garde), William Schuman (American reactionary), Luciano Berio (Italian, avant-garde), William Walton (American, reactionary), Milton Babbitt (American, avant-garde). See "Works Commissioned by or Written for the New York Philharmonic (Including the New York Symphony Society)," accessed 2 June 2014, http://archives.nyphil.org/Commissions.pdf.

15. For more on the survey, see H. Burton 1994, 350. See also the New York Philharmonic release "Leonard Bernstein and New York Philharmonic Announce Program Plans for Next Two Seasons," NYpa, 019-03-01.

16. Burton briefly discusses both the minimalist survey and the avant-garde survey (1994, 314, 342). See also Harold C. Schonberg, "Music: Avant-Garde at the Philharmonic: Bernstein Conducts 14 Minutes of the New," *New York Times*, 3 January 1964. Four concerts in January 1964 comprised the avant-garde survey. The section of the concerts with modernist works bore the titles "New Orchestral Sounds" (featuring works by Zenakis and Ligeti), "The Jazz Trend" (Copland and Larry Austin), without title (Stefan Wolpe), and "The Electronic Influence" (Edgard Varese). My thanks to Richard Wandel for sending me copies of the Philharmonic programs for this series. Bernstein 2000, CD 9 offers the avant-garde works in the series along with Bernstein's opening remarks.

17. Schuller also spends two paragraphs pointing out why Bernstein should have included Webern in this program (Simeone 2013, 357). Perhaps coincidentally Webern appeared in the first *Young People's Concert* a year later (341).

18. Of the three early masters of serial composition (Schoenberg, Webern, and Berg), Berg often intentionally created rows with tonal implications.

19. *This I Believe* was a five-minute radio program that ran from 1951 through 1955 on the CBS Radio Network created and financed by Ward Wheelock and hosted by acclaimed journalist Edward R. Murrow. The series included credos by Bernstein and other luminaries, such as Eleanor Roosevelt, as well as cabdrivers, teachers, and secretaries. The program was so popular that the essays were released in a book that was a Top-10 bestseller for three years, and Columbia Records released a best-selling two-record set. "This I Believe" became an international phenomenon, translated into six languages and broadcast daily on the Voice of America during the

Cold War (Gediman 2006, 266). The series was revived by NPR from 2005–2009 and is now subsumed into other public radio shows. "About This I Believe," accessed 8 May 2014, http://thisibelieve.org/about/.

20. See also Cott 2013, 77.

21. "The Legacy of Leonard Bernstein," *The Independent: Classical Wednesday,* 16 September 2009, accessed 8 May 2014, http://www.independent.co.uk/.

22. For more on this script, see chapter 2.

23. "Dear Dr. Bernstein . . . : A look at Leonard Bernstein's 'Young People's Concerts' mail," cover story in *Senior Scholastic* [magazine], 2 December 1964, 39. pa, 019-04-01.

24. This quote comes from a talk Bernstein gave at Thursday evening preview concert of Nielsen's *Masquerade* Overture (5 April 1962).

25. Bernstein makes some comment on modernism in programs no. 1: 40–41 revised; no. 10: many; no. 13: many; no. 17: 6, 16–17, 20–21; no. 18: 5, 6, 7, 17–18; no. 21: 4, 27; no. 25: 13; no. 26: many; no. 27: 3; no. 29: many; no. 32: many; no. 33: 34; no. 38: many; no. 42: 15; no. 43: 9; no. 45: many; no. 50: 6, 8, 10, 15–21; no. 52: 9–10; no. 53: 25.

26. A cursory glance of the repertory of and performances by the Philharmonic during Bernstein's tenure shows that he programmed very few pieces in the avant-garde idiom, usually two or three out of well over one hundred works per season, for example: Sessions, Concerto for Violin and Orchestra, 19, 20, 21 February 1959 (Shanet 1975, 622); Varese, *Arcana,* 27, 28, 29, 30 November 1958 (622); Webern, *Passacaglia for Orchestra, Opus 1,* 21, 22, 23, 24 January 1960 (630); Foss, *Phorion,* 27, 28, 29 April, 1 May 1967 (691); Varese *Intégrales,* 6, 7, 8, 10 October 1966 (693); Xenakis, *Eonta,* 27, 28 February, 1, 3 March 1969 (712). See also Adams 2008, 197–203. One practical reason is that such innovative works require a great deal of rehearsal time.

27. See also program no. 13 (5–6) and no. 25 (13).

28. Before Bernstein had studied theory formally, he sensed the function of chords. His first student, Sid Ramin, remembers him talking about pre-finishing chords, finishing chords, governing chords, and so forth (Simeone 2013, 556).

29. Bernstein does not take the opportunity to mention such techniques when he performs Richard Strauss's *Don Quixote* in either "What Does Music Mean?" (18 January 1958) or "Fantastic Variations (*Don Quixote*)" (25 December 1968). Perhaps he felt that was a less important feature of this work, so he focused on other aspects due to the limited air time.

30. For "crazy modern music," see program no. 1 (40–41 revised, regarding Webern); "spooky effect," no. 10 (25, regarding the Theramin); "indigestion" and "nightmare," both in no. 29 (12, 14, regarding Charles Ives's *The Fourth of July*).

31. A few of the sources on Copland include: Crist and Shirley eds. 2006; Oja and Tick eds. 2005; Crist 2005; Copland and Perlis 1984; Copland and Perlis 1999; and their correspondence, some of which is in Simeone 2013.

32. About the Philharmonic performances of Foss's works and Foss as soloist, see New York Philharmonic Performance History Search, accessed 8 May 2014, http://history.nyphil.org/nypwcpub/dbweb.asp?ac=a1.

CHAPTER 8

1. The New York Philharmonic began life as the Philharmonic Society of New York, founded in 1842. It merged with New York's National Symphony Orchestra (no connection to the ensemble based in Washington, D.C.) in 1921, with the City Symphony in 1923, and with the Symphony Society of New York in 1928. While the official name of the orchestra since the last merger is the Philharmonic-Symphony Society of New York, Inc., it is commonly referred to as the New York Philharmonic. New York Philharmonic "infoplease," accessed 10 March 2014, http://www.infoplease.com/encyclopedia/entertainment/new-york-philharmonic.html. See also Shanet 1975, 79–86, 234–257.

2. Shanet 1975, 102. Shanet offers many examples of the Philharmonic's support of American music throughout its history. The mission was revisited later in the plan developed by the Philharmonic's Board of Directors prior to the opening of the 1922–23 season, with the goal of drawing in and retaining a wider audience for the orchestra. Chairman Clarence Mackay described what he called the "Greater Americanization of the Philharmonic," which was intended to "offer definite encouragement to the native American composer of orchestral music" by giving the "widest possible hearing" of those American works they deemed "merit presentation" (235).

3. Shanet 1975 lists the opportunities the orchestra missed to encourage home-grown composers on pp. 110, 116, 117, 194, 272–273, and 275–256.

4. Shanet also documents the increase of American personnel in the orchestra during this time. By 1969, 83 of the 103 musicians (78 percent) were born in America (347–348).

5. Shanet 1975, 347. During Bernstein's tenure, the largely European repertory chosen by some guest conductors kept the number of American works down. Under Bernstein the Philharmonic compared favorably to other American orchestras in its support of American composers. According to Kate Hevner Mueller, "Boston has been the most consistently generous orchestra to the Americans, keeping well above average through all decades [1900–1970] and all conductors" (1973, xlix). The New York Philharmonic (like the orchestras in Indianapolis and Utah) played more American music toward the end of the period in the study under consideration as new conductors sought to promote native composers. In other words, the Philharmonic under Bernstein was among the leading orchestras when it came to performing American compositions (1).

6. Memo from Leonard Bernstein, recipient unspecified, "Programs—General Plan/Season 1958–1959," 4 February 1958, NYpa, Minutes of Policy Committee, 8 January 1957 through 2 May 1962. Dimitri Mitropoulos was the Philharmonic's director before Bernstein, from 1949 to 1958.

7. The document suggests "such composers as Charles Ives, Edward MacDowell, etc." Bernstein also indicates that Columbia Records is "very much interested in the idea" and that they will cooperate in coordinating recording sessions with the orchestra's plans. He is already synergizing the concert and recording repertory in his first season with the Philharmonic.

8. Two *Omnibus* programs, "The World of Jazz" (16 October 1955) and "The American Musical Comedy" (7 October 1956) (Bernstein 1959, 106–131, 164–191); "Dvořák: Symphony No. 9 in E minor, Opus 95 'From the New World'" (Bernstein 1966, 149–169). This is a transcript of his remarks before a performance given on 9 January 1956; *Lincoln Presents* program, "Jazz in Serious Music" (25 January 1959) (Bernstein 1966, 49–64); and *The Unanswered Question: Six Talks at Harvard* (Bernstein 1976). For more on *The Unanswered Question: Six Talks at Harvard*, known as the Norton Lectures, see chapter 4.

9. For more on Bernstein's use of the word "Negro," see chapter 6.

10. Bernstein gave an example of the blues scale: C, D, E-flat/E, F, G-flat/G, A, B-flat/B, C (Bernstein 1982, 52).

11. As a young student with limited experience of American music, Bernstein's idea of showcasing Copland was a superb choice. Kate Havner Mueller shows that in the time block from 1900 through 1970, Copland tied with Gershwin as the American symphonic composer most frequently performed by American orchestras (Mueller 1973, lvii). Ives came in third.

12. As evidence, Block points out that Copland had arranged a performance of seven Ives songs in 1932 and published an article about Ives's *114 Songs* in *Modern Music* two years later, all before Bernstein began his thesis (Block 1982, 58–59). In 1938, Bernstein wrote to Copland asking for advice in selecting composers for his thesis who would validate his ideas about American music and requesting help in finding their scores, mentioning Ives as a possibility (Simeone 2013, 24).

13. See note 8.

14. For more on jazz as cultural diplomacy during the Cold War, see Von Eschen 2006 and Davenport 2009. For more on the committee's actions and members, see chapter 7.

15. The Harvard thesis is sixty-three single-spaced pages as typeset and published in Bernstein, *Findings*. His *Young People's Concerts* script is thirty-one pages, typed, double-spaced using only about half the page (the left half of the page is left blank for notes), and devotes an entire page to only the title of longer works. If this script were single spaced, full page, it would cover only seven pages.

16. There are 117 boxes of fan mail spanning 1938 to 1990, so I read only fan mail from selected years (1958, 1964, and 1967). Nonetheless, this is a logical assumption since Bernstein's *Young People's Concerts* fan mail offers either a general compliment or a response to a specific program.

17. The maestro briefly alludes to or expounds on American music in fifteen programs. Extended discussions appear in programs: no's. 2, 11, 13, 17, 23, 27, 29, 38, and 50. Brief mentions appear in: no. 6: 4, 5; no. 10: 30; no. 15: 4, 8, 9, 20–21; no. 24: 9, 10; no. 39: 5; and no. 45: 15.

18. Jazz appears in eighteen programs. At length discussions appear in programs no's. 2, 5, 13, and 27. Brief mentions appear in no. 3: 9; no. 4: 12; no. 10: 24; no. 15: 9; no. 16: 14; no. 17: 5–6; no. 21: 4; no. 23: 18; no. 24: 9–10; no. 29: 6; no. 35: 15; no. 36: 37; no. 42: 20, 21; no. 50: 9.

19. Ten programs mention both American music and jazz: no's. 2, 10, 13, 15, 17, 23, 24, 27, 29, and 50.

20. George W. Chadwick, Henry F. Gilbert, Roy Harris, Edward MacDowell, Roger Sessions, and Virgil Thomson appear only in "What Is American Music?" while Schuman and Randall Thompson appear in that program and one other ("What Is Orchestration?" 8 March 1958 and "A Tribute to Teachers," 29 November 1963, respectively).

21. See chapter 7.

22. Thirteen composers are represented in those seventeen programs. See chapter 2. The three programs devoted to Copland are: "*The Second Hurricane* by Copland" (24 April 1960), "Aaron Copland Birthday Party," and "A Copland Celebration."

23. For a list of the programs that featured Copland's compositions (with specific works), see either appendix F or G.

24. Mozart received eighteen performances in fourteen programs (four were young performers programs), but none were devoted to this beloved Viennese composer alone. The timings are given in bold; **NT** indicates no time was given. The information comes from box/folder 990/3. Serenade no. 10 for Thirteen Instruments, K. 361/370a (program no.3: **0:50**); no. 4: Symphony no. 41 in C, K. 551, "Jupiter" (no. 4: **6:30**; no. 28, I, **8:00**; no. 40, III: **3:35**); no. 5: Concerto no. 21 in C, K. 467 (I, **0:25**; II **1:30**), *The Marriage of Figaro*, K. 492 (Overture, no. 5: **3:50**; no. 19: **4:15**; no. 43: **3:55**, orchestral examples: **0:20**); *Musical Joke*, K. 522 (no. 6: **0:30**); Sinfonia Concertante (no. 7: **6:20**); Symphony no. 39 in E-flat, K. 543 (III, no. 15: **3:45**); Symphony no. 35 in D, "Haffner," K. 385 (no. 21: **0:07**), Symphony no. 40 in g, K. 550 (I, no. 21: **5:50**); Piano Concerto in A, K. 488 (no. 22: **10:05, 6:03, 7:45**); no. 28: Sonata in C (no. 28: **2:30**); Piano Concerto no. 20 in d, K. 466 (no. 30: **14:00**); *The Magic Flute*, K. 620 (no. 37: "In diesen heil'gen Hallen:" **4:00**); Contradanse no. 41, K. 605, no.3 (no. 40: **2:25**). Beethoven received eighteen performances (many less than thirty seconds) in fifteen programs: Sonata no. 21 in C major, "Waldstein", opus 53 (no. 1: **0:10**); Symphony no. 6 in F, op. 68 (I, no. 1: **2:40**); Symphony no. 3 in E-flat, "Eroica," op. 55 ("horn call," no. 2: **0:10**; fourth mvt. theme, no. 4: **1:00**; no. 41: **0:20**); String Quartet in C, op. 131 (no. 3: **0:25**); Symphony no. 5 in c, op. 67 (opening theme, no. 4: **0:15**; no. 5: **NT**; no. 16: **NT**; no. 21: **0:20**; I, no. 41: (**6:20**); III, no. 33: **0:03**; IV, no. 36: **1:00**); Egmont Overture, op. 84 (no. 5: **8:00**); Leonore Overture no. 3, op. 72 (no. 12: **12:54**; no. 41: **13:10**); Symphony no. 7 in A, op. 92 (no. 21: **0:10**; no. 33: **0:10**; no. 40: **4:30**); no. 34: Symphony no. 9 in d (IV excerpt, no. 34: **0:30**; no. 43: **0:10**); Piano Concerto no. 4 in G, op. 58 (II, III, no. 41: **15:05**). Two programs featured solely Beethoven's works (see above for timings): no. 41: "Forever Beethoven!" Symphony no. 5, Symphony no. 3, Piano Concerto no. 4, Leonore Overture no. 3; and no. 49: "*Fidelio*: A Celebration of Life," excerpts from the opera *Fidelio* (**0:30, 10:52, 5:37, 5:55, 4:46**).

25. *An American in Paris* and *Rhapsody in Blue* are performed on "What Is American Music?"; *An American in Paris* again in three programs: no's. 6, 17, and 33; and an excerpt from *Porgy and Bess* in no. 39.

26. Two programs have excerpts from Ives's compositions: "Folk Music in the Concert Hall": finale of Symphony no. 2; "Charles Ives: American Pioneer": *The Gong on the Hook and Ladder, or Firemen's Parade on Main Street*, "Washington's Birthday" from *Holiday Symphony*, *The Circus Band*, "Lincoln, the Great Commoner," and *The Unanswered Question*.

27. For more on the importance and definition of fun to Bernstein, see chapter 3.

28. Bernstein's encomium to Copland as seen in "Aaron Copland Birthday Party" is discussed in connection with modernism in chapter 7.

29. Jazz is discussed in chapter 3, avant-garde modernism in chapter 7, and troubles under the Red Scare in chapter 5. For more on Copland's role as an advocate for American music, see Kopp 2006.

30. Copland conducted his Symphony no. 3 in "What Is American Music?" and his *El Salón México* in "Aaron Copland Birthday Party," and he performed as soloist in his *Concerto for Piano and Orchestra* in "Jazz in the Concert Hall." See appendix G.

31. *Parkersburg News*, November 1944, as quoted in H. Burton 1994, 134.

32. Babbitt is not included here because the excerpt from his Composition for 12 Instruments performed on "Farewell to Nationalism" was very short. Bernstein did not showcase this composer.

33. See chapter 7.

EPILOGUE

1. Humphrey Burton mentions one occasion when Bernstein obliquely speaks against the Vietnam War in "*Fidelio*: A Celebration of Life" (29 March 1970) in *Leonard Bernstein* (H. Burton 1994, 388).

2. African Americans rioted in Memphis, Tennessee, on 27 July 1967. A June 11 radio broadcast from Cairo of "Voice of the Arabs" reported to Egyptians that the United States was "the hostile force behind Israel . . . the enemy of all peoples, the killer of life, the shedder of blood that is preventing you from liquidating Israel." The Soviet Union played to Arab sentiment by verbally attacking the United States and severing relations with Israel. Macrohistory and World Timeline, accessed 11 April 2014, http://www.fsmitha.com/time/1967.htm.

3. It would be interesting to know if Shostakovich benefited, financially or otherwise, from performances, broadcasts, and LP sales of his works.

4. A study of the correlation between Bernstein's television performances and comments and the sales of LPs of these composers would give valuable information on the influence of the programs in this regard.

5. Kramer lists sixteen characteristics found in postmodern classical music (16–17). It: 1) is neither a continuation nor repudiation of modernism, but is both an extension and a break from it; 2) is somehow ironic; 3) does not honor boundaries between the past and the present; 4) breaks down barriers between highbrow and lowbrow styles; 5) does not value structural unity; 6) deems that populist and elitist values are not mutually exclusive; 7) employs more than one method of structuring form (for example, the entire work will not be entirely tonal or serial); 8) considers music not divorced from but relevant to cultural, political, and social contexts; 9) references or quotes the music from many cultures and traditions; 10) believes technology is integral to both the essence and production of music; 11) "embraces contradictions"; 12) "distrusts binary oppositions"; 13) incorporates discontinuities and fragmentations;

14) "encompasses pluralism and eclecticism"; 15) "presents multiple meanings and multiple temporalities"; 16) places the meaning and even structure of a work in the listener more than in the composer, performer, or score.

6. Martin Steinberg, "Young People's Concerts Return to TV," *prelude, fugue & riffs* (Spring/Summer, 2002), 1–2.

7. *BBC Music Magazine* 16, no. 3 (November 2007). Inside are articles on Bernstein by Humphrey Burton (Bernstein's biographer), Sedgwick Clark (editor of *Musical America*), and Edward Seckerson (writer and broadcaster). Some of Bernstein's influence is evidenced by the fact that, of these three, only Burton knew Bernstein personally.

8. "This Month's Contributors," *BBC Music Magazine* 16, no. 3 (November 2007): 3.

9. Ibid.

10. See "Q&A" on Marin Alsop's home page, accessed 7 June 2014, http://www.marinalsop.com/about/marin-qa/.

11. This initiative is so successful that it won the Atlanta Symphony Orchestra a $1 million three-year grant from the Andrew W. Mellon Foundation. "Atlanta School of Composers" at http://www.atlantasymphony.org/about/atlantaschoolcomposers.aspx (accessed 6 June 2014). Barbara Jepson, "New Music with a Tonal Twist," *Wall Street Journal*, 1 June 2010. Jepson observes that "tonal music still elicits disdain from diehard modernists. Mr. Spano chalks it up to elitism—'If people like it, it can't be that good.'"

12. Baltimore Symphony Orchestra, accessed 7 June 2014, http://www.kdschmid.de/orchestradetail/items/baltimore-symphony-orchestra.html.

13. "Baltimore Symphony Orchestra, Musicians," accessed 7 June 2014, https://www.bsomusic.org/musicians/musician/marin-alsop.aspx.

APPENDIX A

1. The lecture and program on development in German music were filmed for American television and are described in Jonathan Rosenberg, "An Idealist Abroad," in Bernstein and Haws 2009, 131–132.

APPENDIX C

1. The information regarding video technology comes from Richard Wandel, Associate Archivist at the New York Philharmonic (pers. comm.). A CBS-generated list of all the programs in the series accompanied a letter from John Walker to Harry Kraut, Amberson Productions, n.d., (box/folder 924/02); according to CBS, "Overtures and Preludes" (8 January 1961) was the first program in black and white on two-inch videotape.

2. This is the program title as it appears on the final script. Gottlieb gives the title as "Happy Birthday Igor Stravinsky" (1998, 72).

3. Display Ad 50, *New York Times*, 24 May 1968.

4. The final page of the version of the last four scripts housed at the Library of Congress lists the double sponsorship.

APPENDIX E

1. Cambridge University Press, Historical Statistics of the United States, accessed 19 April 2014, http://hsus.cambridge.org.

2. "Television History—The First 75 Years," accessed 25 July 2014, http://www.tvhistory.tv/Annual_TV_Households_50-78.JPG.

Bibliography

ARCHIVES

Leonard Bernstein Collection, Library of Congress, Washington, DC.
Leonard Bernstein Office, New York, NY.
New York Philharmonic Archives, New York, NY.

BOOKS, ARTICLES,
DISSERTATIONS, THESES, AND VIDEOS

Adams, John. 2009. *Hallelujah Junction: Composing an American Life.* New York: Farrer, Straus, and Giroux.
———. "An American Voice." 2008. In *Leonard Bernstein, American Original,* Bernstein and Haws, 193–205. New York: HarperCollins for Philharmonic-Symphony Society of New York.
Adorno, Theodor W. (1949) 1973. *Philosophy of Modern Music.* Translated by Anne G. Mitchell and Wesley V. Blomster. New York: Seabury.
———. (1951) 2005. *Minima Moralia: Reflections on a Damaged Life.* Translated by E. F. N. Jephcott. New York: Verso.
Ames, Evelyn. 1970. *A Wind from the West: Bernstein and the New York Philharmonic Abroad.* Boston: Houghton Mifflin.
André, Don A. 1979. "Leonard Bernstein's *Mass* as Social and Political Commentary on the Sixties." DMA diss., University of Washington.
Ansari, Emily Theodosia Abrams. 2010. "'Masters of the President's Music': *Cold War* Composers and the United States Government." PhD diss., Harvard University.
———. 2011. "Aaron Copland and the Politics of Cultural Diplomacy." *Journal of the Society for American Music* 5(3): 335–364.

———. 2012. "Leonard Bernstein and the New York Philharmonic in Moscow: Educational Television, Diplomacy, and the Politics of Tonal Music." Annual meeting of the American Musicological Society, New Orleans, LA.

———. 2012. "Shaping the Policies of Cold War Musical Diplomacy: An Epistemic Community of American Composers." *The Journal of the Society for Historians of American Foreign Relations.* 36(1): 41–52.

Ardoin, John. 1965. "Entrances and Exits," *Philharmonic Hall Program,* (September): 12, 30, 37. Box/folder 110/03.

Babbitt, Milton. 1958. "Who Cares If You Listen?" *High Fidelity,* vii.2: 38–40, in *Composers on Modern Musical Culture: An Anthology of Readings on Twentieth-Century Music,* ed. Bryan R. Simms, 152–159. New York: Schirmer, 1999.

Barnouw, Erik. 1970. *The Image Empire (From 1953),* Vol. 3 of *A History of Broadcasting in the United States.* New York: Oxford University Press.

———. 1978. *The Sponsor: Notes on a Modern Potentate.* New York: Oxford University Press.

———. 1990. *Tube of Plenty: The Evolution of American Television.* Rev. ed. New York: Oxford University Press.

Bernstein, Burton. (1982) 2000. *Family Matters: Sam, Jennie, and the Kids.* Lincoln, NE: iUniverse.com.

Bernstein, Burton, and Barbara B. Haws. 2008. *Leonard Bernstein, American Original: How a Modern Renaissance Man Transformed Music and the World during His New York Philharmonic Years, 1943–1976.* New York: HarperCollins for Philharmonic-Symphony Society of New York.

Bernstein, Jeffrey Alexander. 2001. "The Expressive Use of Musical Style and the Composer's Voice in Leonard Bernstein's Mass." PhD diss., University of California, Los Angeles.

Bernstein, Leonard. (1959) 2004. *The Joy of Music.* New York: Simon and Schuster. (Repr., Pompton Plains, NJ: Amadeus).

———. (1962) 2005. *Leonard Bernstein's Young People's Concerts.* Edited by Jack Gottlieb. Rev. ed. Pompton Plains, NJ: Amadeus.

———. 1966. *The Infinite Variety of Music.* New York: Simon and Schuster.

———. 1976. *The Unanswered Question: Six Talks at Harvard.* Cambridge, MA: Harvard University Press.

———. 1982. *Findings.* New York: Simon and Schuster.

———. 2000. *Bernstein LIVE.* New York: The Philharmonic-Society of New York Special Editions, NYP 2003 (10 compact discs).

———. 2004. Roger Englander, Charles Dubin, New York Philharmonic, and Kultur Video. *Leonard Bernstein's Young People's Concerts with the New York Philharmonic.* West Long Branch, NJ: Kultur Video.

———. 2013. Roger Englander, Charles Dubin, New York Philharmonic, and Kultur Video. *Leonard Bernstein's Young People's Concerts with the New York Philharmonic, volume 2.* West Long Branch, NJ: Kultur International Films.

Block, Geoffrey. 2008. "Bernstein's Senior Thesis at Harvard: The Roots of a Lifelong Search to Discover an American Identity." *College Music Symposium* 48: 52–68.

Boddy, William. 1993. *Fifties Television: The Industry and its Critics.* Urbana: University of Illinois Press.

Boulez, Pierre. 1952. "Schoenberg Is Dead." In *Composers on Modern Musical Culture,* ed. Bryan R. Simms, 145–151. New York: Schirmer, 1999.

Bourdieu, Pierre. 1984. *Distinction: A Social Critique of the Judgement of Taste.* Translated by Richard Nice. Cambridge: Harvard University Press.

Bower, Robert T. 1985. *The Changing Television Audience in America.* New York: Columbia University Press.

Britten, Benjamin. 1964. "On Winning the First Aspen Award." In Simms, 175–181. 1999.

Brodie, Janet Farrell, and Marc Redfield, eds. 2002. *High Anxieties: Cultural Studies in Addiction.* Berkeley: University of California Press.

Brooks, John. 1983. "Highbrow, Lowbrows, Middlebrow, Now." *American Heritage* 34:4 (June, July), http://www.americanheritage.com/content/highbrow-lowbrows-middlebrow-now.

Brown, Malcolm Hamrick, ed. 2004. *The Shostakovich Casebook.* Bloomington: Indiana University Press.

Bryant, J. Alison. 2007. *The Children's Television Community.* Mahwah, NJ: Lawrence Erlbaum.

Burton, Humphrey. 1994. *Leonard Bernstein.* New York: Doubleday.

———. 2007. "Bernstein: The Communicator." *BBC Music Magazine* 16:3 (November): 29–30.

Burton, William Westbrook, ed. 1995. *Conversations about Bernstein.* New York: Oxford University Press.

Carpenter, Charles A. 1999. *Dramatists and the Bomb.* Westport, CT: Greenwood.

Cavan, Sherri. 1972. *Hippies of the Haight.* St. Louis, MI: New Critics Press.

Chapin, Schuyler. 1991. "Leonard Bernstein—The Television Journey." *Television Quarterly* xxv(2): 13–19.

———. 1992. *Leonard Bernstein: Notes from a Friend.* New York: Walker.

Clark, Robert S. 1985. "Congruent Odysseys," *Leonard Bernstein: The Television Work,* 17–25. New York: Museum of Broadcasting.

Clark, Sedgewick. 2007. "Bernstein: The Conductor," *BBC Music Magazine,* 16:3 (November): 26–27.

Collier-Thomas, Bettye, and V. P. Franklin. 2000. *My Soul Is a Witness: A Chronology of the Civil Rights Era 1954–1965.* New York: Henry Holt.

Comstock, George, et al. 1978. *Television and Human Behavior.* New York: Columbia University Press.

Comstock, George, and Erica Scharrer. 1999. *Television: What's On, Who's Watching, and What It Means.* New York: Academic Press.

Copland, Aaron. 1927. "Jazz Structure and Influence." *Modern Music* 4:2 (January-February), 9–14.

Copland, Aaron, and Vivian Perlis. 1984. *Copland, 1900 through 1942.* New York: St. Martin's Griffin.

———. 1999. *Copland: Since 1943.* New York: St. Martin's Griffin.

Cott, Jonathan. 2013. *Dinner with Lenny: The Last Long Interview with Leonard Bernstein.* New York: Oxford University Press.

Cottle, William A., Sr. 1978. "Social Commentary in Vocal Music in the Twentieth Century as Evidenced by Leonard Bernstein's *Mass.*" DA diss., University of Northern Colorado.

Crist, Elizabeth Bergman. 2005. *Music for the Common Man: Aaron Copland during the Depression and War.* New York: Oxford University Press.

———. 2006. "Mutual Responses in the Midst of an Era: Aaron Copland's *The Tender Land* and Leonard Bernstein's *Candide.*" *The Journal of Musicology* 23:4 (Fall): 485–527.

———. 2007. "The Best of All Possible Worlds: The Eldorado Episode in Leonard Bernstein's *Candide.*" *Cambridge Opera Journal* 19:3 (November): 223–248.

Crist, Elizabeth Bergman, and Wayne Shirley, eds. 2006. *The Selected Correspondence of Aaron Copland.* New Haven: Yale University Press.

Cullen, Jim. 2002. *The Art of Democracy: A Concise History of Popular Culture in the United States.* New York: Monthly Review.

Davenport, Lisa E. 2009. *Jazz Diplomacy: Promoting America in the Cold War Era.* Jackson: University Press of Mississippi.

DeLapp, Jennifer. 1997. "Copland in the Fifties: Music and Ideology in the McCarthy Era." PhD diss., University of Michigan.

De Sesa, Gary. 1985. "A Comparison between a Descriptive Analysis of Leonard Bernstein's Mass and the Musical Implications of the Critical Evaluations Thereof." PhD diss., New York University.

Dizard, Wilson P. 2004. *Inventing Public Diplomacy: The Story of the U.S. Information Agency.* Boulder CO: Lynne Rienner Publishers.

Englander, Roger. 1985. "No Balloons or Tap Dancers: A Look at the Young People's Concerts." *Leonard Bernstein: The Television Work*, 29–36. New York: Museum of Broadcasting.

———. 1993. "Behind the Scenes: The Young People's Concerts in the Making." *prelude, fugue & riffs* (Fall): 1, 5.

Farber, David, and Beth Bailey, et al. 2001. *The Columbia Guide to America in the 1960s.* New York: Columbia University Press.

Finkler, Elizabeth. 1993. "Cutlets and Addbergers." *prelude, fugue & riffs* (Fall): 4.

Fischer, Klaus P. 2006. *America in White, Black, and Gray: The Stormy 1960s.* New York: Continuum.

Friedan, Betty Friedan. 1963. *The Feminine Mystique.* New York: W. W. Norton.

Gans, Herbert J. 1974. *Popular Culture and High Culture: An Analysis and Evaluation of Taste.* New York: Basic.

Garofalo, Reebee. 2002. *Rockin' Out: Popular Music in the USA.* Upper Saddle River, NJ: Prentice-Hall.

Gediman, Dan. 2006. "The History of This I Believe: The Power of an Idea" in *This I Believe: The Personal Philosophies of Remarkable Men and Women*, eds. Jay Allison and Dan Gediman, 260–271. New York: Holt.

Gelleny, Sharon. 1991. "Leonard Bernstein's Young People's Concerts: A Critical Overview." M.A. thesis, McMaster University.

———. 1999. "Leonard Bernstein on Television: Bridging the Gap between Classical Music and Popular Culture." *Journal of Popular Music Studies* 11–12, no. 1 (March): 48–67.

Gentry, Philip. 2011. "Leonard Bernstein's The Age of Anxiety: A Great American Symphony during McCarthyism." *American Music* 29 no. 3 (Fall): 308–331.

Gottlieb, Jack. 1988. *Leonard Bernstein: A Complete Catalog of his Works Celebrating his 70th Birthday.* New York: Jalni.

———. 1998. *Leonard Bernstein, August 25, 1918–October 14, 1990, a Complete Catalogue of His Works Celebrating His 80th Birthday Year: 1998–1999. Volume I: Life, Musical Compositions & Writings.* New York: Leonard Bernstein Center.

———. 2004. *Funny, It Doesn't Sound Jewish: How Yiddish Songs and Synagogue Melodies Influenced Tin Pan Alley, Broadway, and Hollywood.* Albany, NY: State University of New York.

———. (1962) 2005. Introduction to *Leonard Bernstein's Young People's Concerts.* Rev. and expanded ed. Milwaukee, WI: Amadeus.

———. 2010. *Working with Bernstein: A Memoir.* Milwaukee, WI: Amadeus.

Grad, Karene Esther. 2006. "When High Culture Became Popular Culture: Classical Music in Postwar America, 1945–1965." PhD diss., Yale University.

Grant, Mark N. 1998. *Maestros of the Pen: A History of Classical Music Criticism in America.* Boston: Northeastern University Press.

Gray, Francine du Plessix. 1970. *Divine Disobedience: Profiles in Catholic Radicalism.* New York: Knopf.

Greenberg, Clement. 1939. "Avant-Garde and Kitsch." *Partisan Review* 6(5): 34–49. http://www.sharecom.ca/greenberg/kitsch.html, accessed 14 June 2014.

Gruen, John. 1968. *The Private World of Leonard Bernstein.* New York: Viking.

Gunter, Brian, and Adrian Furnham. 1998. *Children as Consumers: A Psychological Analysis of the Young People's Market.* New York: Routledge.

Hall, Stuart, and Paddy Whannel. 1964. *The Popular Arts.* Boston: Beacon.

Halle, David. 2007. "Highbrow/Lowbrow." In *Blackwell Encyclopedia of Sociology*, edited by George Ritzer. Malden, MA: Blackwell Publishing. Accessed 6 August 2013. http://www.sociologyencyclopedia.com.

Helgert, Lars Erik. 2008. "Jazz Elements in Selected Concert Works of Leonard Bernstein: Sources, Reception, and Analysis." PhD diss., Catholic University of America.

Hellman, Lillian. 1976. *Scoundrel Time.* Boston: Little, Brown.

Henderson, Amy. 1988. *On the Air: Pioneers of American Broadcasting.* Washington, DC: Smithsonian Institution Press.

Henze, Hans Werner. 1982. *Music and Politics: Collected Writings, 1953–1981*, trans. Peter Labanyi. Ithaca, NY: Cornell University Press.

Hill, Thomas H. 1970. "Ernest Schelling (1876–1939): His Life and Contributions to Music Education through Educational Concerts." PhD diss., Catholic University of America.

Hindemith, Paul. 1945. *The Craft of Musical Composition.* New York: Associated Music Publishers.

Ho, Allan B., and Dmitry Feofanov, eds. 1998. *Shostakovich Reconsidered.* London: Toccata.

Holt, Mack P. 2006. *Alcohol: A Social and Cultural History.* New York: Berg.

Horowitz, Joseph. 1987. *Understanding Toscanini: How He Became a Culture-God and Helped Create a New Audience for Old Music.* New York: Alfred A. Knopf.

———. 1993. "Professor Lenny." *The New York Review,* 40:11 (10 June): 39–44.

———. 2007. *Classical Music in America: A History.* 2nd ed. New York: W. W. Norton.

Hubbs, Nadine. 2004. *The Queer Composition of America's Sound: Gay Modernists, American Music, and National Identity.* Berkeley: University of California Press.

Jackendoff, Ray. 1974. "Leonard Bernstein's Harvard Lectures." *High Fidelity/Musical America,* 24 (April): 8–10.

———. 1977. "Bernstein: The Unanswered Question." *Journal of the Linguistic Society of America* 53(4): 883–894.

———. 1990. *Semantics and Cognition.* Cambridge, MA: MIT Press.

Johnson, Victoria E. 2008. *Heartland TV: Prime Time Television and the Struggle for U.S. Identity.* New York: New York University Press.

Kammen, Michael. 1999. *American Culture, American Tastes: Social Change and the 20th Century.* New York: Alfred A. Knopf.

Kapur, Tribhuwan. 1981. *Hippies: A Study of Their Drug Habits and Sexual Customs.* New Delhi, India: Vikas.

Kopp, Christina Lee. 2006. "'A School of New Men': Composing an American Identity in the Early Twentieth Century." PhD diss., Boston University.

Kramer, Jonathan D. 2002. "The Nature and Origins of Musical Postmodernism." In *Postmodern Music: Postmodern Thought,* edited by Judy Lochhead and Joseph Auner, 13–26. NY: Routledge.

Laird, Paul R. 2002. *Leonard Bernstein: A Guide to Research.* New York: Routledge.

Leibowitz, René. 1949. *Schoenberg and His School: The Contemporary Stage of the Language of Music,* trans. Dika Newlin. New York: Philosophical Library.

Levine, Lawrence W. 1988. *Highbrow/Lowbrow: The Emergence of Cultural Hierarchy in America.* Cambridge, MA: Harvard University Press.

Levine, Michael L. 1996. *African Americans and Civil Rights: From 1619 to the Present.* Phoenix, AZ: Oryx.

Libbey, Theodore. 1995. *The National Symphony Orchestra.* Washington, DC: The NSO Book Project.

Locke, Ralph P., and Cyrilla Barr, eds. 1997. *Cultivating Music in America: Women Patrons and Activists since 1860.* Berkeley: University of California Press.

Lopes, Paul. 2002. *The Rise of a Jazz Art World.* New York: Cambridge University Press.

Lowenthal, Abraham F., ed. 1991. *Exporting Democracy: The United States and Latin America.* Baltimore: Johns Hopkins University Press.

Lynes, Russell. 1949. "Highbrow, Lowbrow, Middlebrow: Which Are You?" *Harper's Magazine* 198:1185 (February): 19–28.

———. 1949. "Highbrow, Lowbrow, Middlebrow." *Life* (11 April): 99–101.

———. 1967. "After Hours: Highbrow, Lowbrow, Middlebrow Reconsidered." *Harper's Magazine* 235:1407 (August): 16–20.

Lytle, Mark Hamilton. 2006. *America's Uncivil Wars: The Sixties Era from Elvis to the Fall of Richard Nixon.* New York: Oxford University Press.

Macdonald, Dwight. 1960. "Masscult and Midcult: I." *Partisan Review* 27:2 (Spring): 203–233.

———. 1960. "Masscult and Midcult: II." *Partisan Review* 27:4 (Fall): 589–631.

MacInnis, John Christian. 2009. "Leonard Bernstein's and Roger Englander's Educational Mission: Music Appreciation and the 1961–1962 Season of Young People's Concerts." MM thesis, Florida State University.

Maltese, Anthony Michael. 1967. "A Descriptive Study of Children's Programming on Major American Television Networks from 1950 through 1964." PhD diss., Ohio University.

Melcher, Rita Mary. 1968. "Leonard Bernstein: His Impact on the Field of Music Education." MA thesis, Catholic University of America.

Minow, Newton N. 1964. *Equal Time: The Private Broadcaster and The Public Interest*, ed. Lawrence Laurent. New York: Antheneum.

Moore, James Walter. 1984. "A Study of Tonality in Selected Works by Leonard Bernstein." PhD diss., Florida State University.

Morgan, Robert P., ed. 1998. *Strunk's Source Readings in Music History: The Twentieth Century*. Vol. 7. New York: W. W. Norton.

Moseley, Carlos. 1993. "The Fabled Music Lessons That Captured Them All." *prelude, fugue & riffs* (Fall): 8.

Mueller, Kate Hevner. 1973. *Twenty-Seven Major American Symphony Orchestras: A History and Analysis of Their Repertoires Seasons 1842–43 through 1969–70*. Bloomington, IN: Indiana University Studies.

Museum of Broadcasting. 1985. *Leonard Bernstein: The Television Work, September 27–November 14, 1985*. Exhibition catalogue. New York: Museum of Broadcasting.

Nielsen Television Index Reports. 1958–1978. Northbrook, IL: A. C. Nielsen Company.

North, James H. 2006. *New York Philharmonic: The Authorized Recordings, 1917–2005: A Discography*. Lanham, MD: Scarecrow.

O'Brien, Orin. 2000. "His Love of Music Overcame Every Other Aspect of His Personality." Liner notes to *Leonard Bernstein LIVE*. The Philharmonic-Society of New York Special Editions, NYP 2003 (10 compact discs).

Oja, Carol J. 2000. *Making Music Modern: New York in the 1920s*. New York: Oxford University Press.

Oja, Carol J., and Judith Tick, eds. 2005. *Aaron Copland and His World*. Princeton, NJ: Princeton University Press.

O'Neil, Thomas. 1993. *The Grammys: The Ultimate, Unofficial Guide to Music's Highest Honor*. New York: Berkley Publishing Group.

Page, Christopher Jarrett. 2000. "Leonard Bernstein and the Resurrection of Gustav Mahler." PhD diss., University of California, Los Angeles.

Pearlmutter, Alan J. 1985. "Leonard Bernstein's Dybbuk: An Analysis Including Historical, Religious, and Literary Perspectives of Hasidic Life and Lore." DMA diss., Peabody Institute, Johns Hopkins University.

Peyser, Joan. 1998. *Bernstein: A Biography*. Rev. New York: Billboard.

Pollack, Howard. 1999. *Aaron Copland: The Life and Work of an Uncommon Man*. New York: Henry Holt.

Presnell, Don, and Marty McGee. 1998. *A Critical History of Television's "The Twilight Zone," 1959–1964.* Jefferson, NC: McFarland.

Red Channels: The Report of Communist Influence in Radio and Television. 1950. New York: American Business Consultants.

Rees, James Lester. 1966. "Leonard Bernstein's Informative Speaking in the 1965–66 Young People's Concerts." MA thesis, Syracuse University.

Reich, Charles. 1970. *The Greening of America: How the Youth Revolution Is Trying to Make America Livable.* New York: Random House.

Rodgers, Mary. 1993. "Such a Good Time." *prelude, fugue & riffs* (Fall): 4.

Rose, Brian G. 1986. *Television and the Performing Arts: A Handbook and Reference Guide to American Cultural Programming.* Westport, CT: Greenwood.

———. 1992. *Televising the Performing Arts: Interviews with Merrill Brockway, Kirk Browning, and Roger Englander.* Westport, CT: Greenwood.

Rosenberg, Jonathan. 2008. "An Idealist Abroad," in Burton and Haws, 117–133.

Ross, Alex. 2007. *The Rest Is Noise: Listening to the Twentieth Century.* New York: Farrar, Straus, and Giroux.

Rozen, Brian David. 1997. "The Contributions of Leonard Bernstein to Music Education: An Analysis of His 53 *Young People's Concerts.*" PhD diss., University of Rochester, Eastman School of Music.

Rubin, Joan Shelley. 1992. *The Making of Middle-Brow Culture.* Chapel Hill: University of North Carolina Press.

Sachar, Howard M. 1992. *A History of Jews in America.* New York: Alfred A. Knopf.

Samuel, Lawrence R. 2001. *Brought to You by: Postwar Television Advertising and the American Dream.* Austin: University of Texas Press.

Sanjek, Russell. "The War on Rock," 1972. *Downbeat Music '72 Yearbook.* Chicago: Maher.

Sargeant, Winthrop. 1949. "In Defense of the Highbrow," *Life* (11 April): 102.

Saunders, Frances Stonor. 1999. *The Cultural Cold War: The CIA and the World of Arts and Letters.* New York: The New Press.

Schaffler, Robert. 1929. *Beethoven, the Man Who Freed Music.* Garden City, NY: Doubleday.

Schiff, David. 1998. *The Music of Elliott Carter,* 2nd ed. Ithaca, NY: Cornell University Press.

Schonberg, Harold C. 1981. *Facing the Music.* New York: Summit.

Schrecker, Ellen. 1998. *Many Are the Crimes: McCarthyism in America.* Boston: Little, Brown.

Seckerson, Edward. 2007. "Bernstein: The Composer," *BBC Music Magazine,* 16:3 (November): 24–25.

Secrest, Meryle. 1994. *Leonard Bernstein: A Life.* New York: Knopf.

Seldes, Barry. 2009. *Leonard Bernstein: The Political Life of an American Musician.* Berkeley: University of California Press.

Shanet, Howard. 1975. *Philharmonic: A History of New York's Orchestra.* Garden City, NY: Doubleday.

Sherman, Robert. 2010. *Leonard Bernstein at Work: His Final Years, 1984–1990.* Milwaukee, WI: Amadeus.

Shultz, Gladys Denny. 1962. *Jenny Lind: The Swedish Nightingale*. Philadelphia: J.B. Lippincott.

Simeone, Nigel. 2009. *Leonard Bernstein: West Side Story*. Burlington, VT: Ashgate.

———. ed. 2013. *The Leonard Bernstein Letters*. New Haven, CT: Yale University Press.

Simms, Bryan R., ed. 1999. *Composers on Modern Musical Culture: An Anthology of Readings on Twentieth-Century Music*. New York: Schirmer.

Slonimsky, Nicolas. (1953) 2000. *Lexicon of Musical Invective: Critical Assaults on Composers since Beethoven's Time*. New York: Norton.

———. 1994. 5th ed. *Music since 1900*. New York: Schirmer.

Stravinsky, Igor. 1982–1985. *Stravinsky: Selected Correspondence*. Vol. 2, ed. Robert Craft. New York: Knopf.

Television Network Program Procurement: Report of the Committee on Interstate and Foreign Commerce, House of Representatives, 88th Congress, 1st Session. 1963a. Washington, DC: GPO.

Television Network Program Procurement: Report Pursuant to Section 136 of the Legislative Reorganization Act of 1946, Public Law 601, 79th Congress, and House Resolution 17, 8th Congress. 1963b.

Thomas, Michael Tilson. (1962) 2005. Introduction to new edition, *Leonard Bernstein's Young People's Concerts*. Rev. ed. Milwaukee, WI: Amadeus.

Thomas, Naomi. 2004. "Bernstein's *Unanswered Question*: A Journey from Linguistic Deep Structure to the Metaphysics of Music." MA thesis, Florida Atlantic University.

Thomson, Charles A., and Walter H. C. Laves. 1963. *Cultural Relations and U.S. Foreign Policy*. Bloomington: Indiana University Press.

Thomson, Virgil. 1962. *The State of Music*, 2nd ed., revised. New York: Vintage.

Titus, Q. Constadina, and Jerry L. Simlich. 1990. "From 'Atomic Bomb Baby' to 'Nuclear Funeral': Atomic Music Comes of Age, 1945–1990." *Popular Music and Society* 14:4 (Winter): 11–37.

Tollison, Robert D., ed. 1986. *Smoking and Society*. Lexington, MA: Lexington Books.

Tomkins, Calvin. 1968. *The Bride and the Bachelors: Five Masters of the Avant Garde*. New York: Viking.

Tracey, Sarah W., and Caroline Jean Acker, eds. 2004. *Altering American Consciousness: The History of Alcohol and Drug Use in the United States, 1800–2000*. Boston: University of Massachusetts Press.

Travis, Trysh. 2002. "Print and the Creation of Middlebrow Culture." In *Perspectives on American Book History: Artifacts and Commentary*, edited by Scott E. Caspar, Joanne D. Chaison, and Jeffrey D. Groves, 339–366. Boston: University of Massachusetts Press.

Truzzi, Marcello. 1975. "Astrology as Popular Culture." *Journal of Popular Culture* 8:4 (Spring): 906–910.

Turow, Joseph. 1981. *Entertainment, Education, and the Hard Sell: Three Decades of Network Children's Television*. New York: Praeger.

Von Eschen, Penny M. 2006. *Satchmo Blows Up the World: Jazz Ambassadors Play the Cold War*, Cambridge, MA: Harvard University Press.

Wald, Elijah. 2009. *How the Beatles Destroyed Rock 'n' Roll: An Alternative History of American Popular Music*. New York: Oxford University Press.

Ware, W. Porter, and Thaddeus C. Lockard Jr. 1980. *P.T. Barnum Presents Jenny Lind: The American Tour of the Swedish Nightingale*. Baton Rouge: Louisiana State University Press.

Watkins, Glenn. 1988. *Soundings: Music in the Twentieth Century*. New York: Schirmer.

———. 1994. *Pyramids at the Louvre: Music, Culture, and Collage from Stravinsky to the Postmodernists*. Cambridge, MA: Belknap Press of Harvard University Press.

Wells, Elizabeth A. 2011. *West Side Story: Cultural Perspectives on an American Musical*. Lanham, MD: Scarecrow.

Wolfe, Charles K., and James E. Akenson. 2005. *Country Music Goes to War*. Lexington: University of Kentucky.

Wolfe, Tom. 1970. *Radical Chic & Mau-Mauing the Flak Catchers*. New York: Farrar, Straus, and Giroux.

Woolery, George W. 1985. *Children's Television: The First Thirty-Five Years, 1946–1981, Part II: Live, Film, and Tape Series*. Metuchen, NJ: Scarecrow.

Woolf, Virginia. 1942. *The Death of the Moth and Other Essays*. New York: Hartcourt, Brace.

Young, Edgar B. 1980. *Lincoln Center: The Building of an Institution*. New York: New York University Press.

Zicree, Marc Scott. 1989. *The Twilight Zone Companion*. 2nd ed. New York: Bantam.

SELECT WEBSITES

Leonard Bernstein Collection, Library of Congress: http://memory.loc.gov/ammem/collections/bernstein/.

New York Philharmonic Digital Archives: http://archives.nyphil.org/.

New York Times: www.nytimes.com.

Official Leonard Bernstein website: leonardbernstein.com.

Index

The following abbreviations are used in this index: LB for Leonard Bernstein, NYP for the New York Philharmonic, and YPCs for Leonard Bernstein's *Young People's Concerts*.

Americans with Disabilities Act, 121
"Anatomy of a Symphony Orchestra,"
    18, 31, 157, *188, 201, 203, 211,*
    242–43n52, 259n31; on Vietnam,
    110, *122,* 190. *See also* orchestration
"appreciation racket." *See* Thomson,
    Virgil
art, abstract, 148
art music. *See* classical music
the Association, 47, 64, 137, 151
astrology, xxvii, 113, 123, 124–26, 194,
    202
astronomy, 125, 247n39
asymmetrical meter, 145, 161
AT&T, 71, 84–85; YPCs episodes
    sponsored, *81, 209–10;* YPCs films,
    distributor of, 85, 239n12; YPCs,
    questionnaire to teachers about LB's
    YPCs, 17, 33, 85, 252n48; YPCs, as
    sponsor of, 17. *See also* sponsors
Atlanta School of Composers, 198
atomic bomb. *See* nuclear weapons
atonality, 99, 137–168, 178, 192, *223.*
    See also Copland, Aaron–composer;
    Foss, Lukas; Hindemith, Paul
audience: of the future, 139; gap
    between composer and, 151. *See also*
    avant garde; Bernstein, Leonard,
    author/composer; fan mail
Austin, Larry, 178, 186, *188, 223, 227,*
    261n16
avant garde, xxviii, 45, 137–168;
    audience issues, 139–143; LB
    acknowledges audiences right to hear,
    98,150; LB and Copland experiment
    with, 182; LB's definition of, 94,
    138, 178, 223; LB's reaction to, 137,
    192, 194; LB predicts future of avant
    garde, 197; LB's postulates reasons
    composers choose avant garde, 154,
    156–157; LB suggests young people
    understand better than older people,
    98,150, 159; composer reactions
    to, 144; composers thank LB for
    performing their works, 149; conflict

between avant-garde and reactionary
    modernism, 138–145; cosmopolitan
    rather than nationalistic, 178–79;
    as highbrow, *41;* Ives and the,
    179–82; NYP commissions to avant
    garde composers, 260–261n14;
    politicized, 141, 143–44, 145, 259n3;
    reactionaries distained, 141–42; in
    YPCs, 157–68, 192, *266. See also*
    Adorno, Theodore; The Avant
    Garde; atonality; audience; Berg,
    Alban; bitonality; Copland, Aaron,
    composer; extended techniques;
    Foss, Lukas; modernism; New York
    Philharmonic; Schoenberg, Arnold;
    serialism; Socialist Realism; Webern,
    Anton
The Avant Garde (NYP series), 138,
    149, 150, 158, 260n11; reviews of,
    148, 261n16

Babbitt, Milton, 142–43, 148, 179,
    226, 227, 260n8, 266n32; NYP
    commission, 260–61n14; Barber,
    Samuel, 144, 177; NYP commission,
    260–61n14
Bartók, Béla, *41,* 48, 144, *215, 223,*
    238n8
the Beatles (rock group), xvi, 47, 56,
    63–64, 65, 123, 194, 244n7, 248n57;
    Help! (movie, 1965) 55, 61; as
    inspiration for "What Is a Mode?" 18
Beethoven, Ludwig van, 138, 154,
    188, 242n40, 259n4; centennial,
    201; folk music in, 56; in Harvard
    Norton Lectures, 56; *Omnibus*
    program on, xxxi, 52, 53; in *Peanuts,*
    58, figures 35 and 36; YPCs, works
    in, 179, 265n24. *See also "Fidelio,*
    A Celebration of Life"; "Forever
    Beethoven!"
Bell System Associated Companies,
    10; *The Bell Telephone Hour,* 71;
    YPCs films, as distributor of, 33, 85,
    243n57, 252n48; YPCs, as sponsor

resignation, xxvii, 88; sabbatical, 147, 156, 167, 238n4, 260n11. *See also* "Leonard Bernstein and the New York Philharmonic in Moscow"; New York Philharmonic

Bernstein, Leonard, reviews, 147; *Age of Anxiety*, 24; of LB compositions incorporating popular styles, 174; LB response to bad, 241n36, 241n38; as composer, 24, 146; as conductor, 24; fans support after bad, 241n34; of Norton Lectures, 246n27; of his presentations/scripts, 149; of YPCs, 4–5, 24, 65

Bernstein, Leonard, television series: *Ford Presents*, xxxi; *Lincoln Presents*, xxxi, 89, 264n8. *See also* Norton Lectures; *Omnibus*

Bernstein, Nina (daughter), 124, 153; birth of, xxxiii, 246n33; role in LB legacy xxxiii; scripts written with Nina in mind, 57, 58. *See also* Blitzstein, Marc; JALNI Publications

Bernstein, Sam (father), xxix, xxx

Bernstein, Shirley Anne (sister), x; in *Carmen* parody xxx (figure 16); ideas for programs, 18

Billboard magazine, 125

"A Birthday Tribute to Shostakovich," 21, 100–01, 156, *188*, 193, *201*, *203*, *209*, 238n7, 252n48; achievements, 111, 122, 190; deletions from, 5; Iron Curtain, artist's life behind, 99; production crew meetings observed, xvii, 8–9, 235n19; program title, evolution of, 238n3; self-censorship in, 88; bitonality, 138, 161–162, *223*

Black Panthers, 115–16, 256n2

blacklist, 1, 86, 114. *See also* Bernstein, Leonard, challenges; Hollywood Blacklist

Blitzstein, Marc: as American composer, 170; on Cuban trip with LB, 103, 107, 255–56n25; as source for names of LB's children, 233n8

Bloch, Ernest, 17, 104; *Prayer*, 214; *Schelomo*, 95, 224. *See also* "The Road to Paris"

Block, Geoffrey, 171–74

boogie woogie, negative influence on LB's career, xxxii, 48

Boulez, Pierre, 141–42, 143, 147

Brahms, Johannes, 198, 242n40; audience joyously anticipated new work by, 56, 151; film biography of, 54; Symphony no. 4, *28*, 31, 160; upper-middlebrow, classified as, 41, 48, 51

Britten, Benjamin: in avant garde festival 141; modernism, approach to, 144; *Young Person's Guide to the Orchestra*, *213*, 224, 238n9

"brow" or taste cultures, xxvii, 35–65; cultural artifacts or activities classified, *40–41*, 246n30; definitions of, 36–38, 243n2, 244n4, 244n5, 244n6; factors that predict, 39–41; hierarchy changes, 38–39; highbrows seek to educate middlebrows and lowbrows, 70; television viewer, decline in brow level, 70–71; sources, 243n1, 244n4; syncopation, definition tailored to brow level, 54; YPCs, brow of audience, 49, 51. *See also* highbrow; lowbrow; middlebrow.

Buddhism: and John Cage, 141; and hippies, 123; Burton, Humphrey, xvii, xxi; on abstract art and LB, 148; audience rejects aleatoric music when LB absent, 149; on LB and cigarettes, 127, 258n23; on LB and critics, 240n30, 240n31; on LB's death, 128; on *Dybbuk*, 126; on Felicia as LB's stabilizer, 88, 195; on *Fidelio* as LB's reaction to Vietnam War, 109–10; on Foss, Lukas, 164-65; fun, on LB's definition of, 48–49; on Gruen's book on LB, 258; homosexual, on LB's "coming out" as, 195; Latin America, on LB's love

Chomsky, Noam, 50
Civil Rights Act (1964), 114
civil rights, African Americans,
114–116, 256n29, 266n2. *See also*
Bernstein, Leonard, activist; fan
mail; Negro; "The Negro in Music";
Serling Rod
classical music, xv, xxvi, xxvii, 18,
196, 244n9, 246n32, 247n44;
African Americans in, 115; LB
links lowbrow music with, 63,
193; composers withdrawing from
audience, xxv, 142–43; definition of,
xxiii; during the cultural explosion,
67; as fun, 58; as savior of society,
46; and State Department, 94; teens
and, 64, 194; new trends in, 198.
See also American classical music;
avant garde; Bernstein, Leonard, fun;
jazz; Toscanini, Arturo; "What Is
Classical Music?"
Coates, Helen, xix, xxx, 22, 94, 232n7,
235n19, 239n10, 239n12 (figure 3)
Cohn, Felicia Montealegre. *See*
Bernstein, Felicia (wife)
the Cold War, xxvii, 91–112, 139, 190,
201; arts as tool, 93; end of, 144; fall
of Berlin Wall, 134; music in cultural
arsenal of, 138, 139, 174, 254n12,
259n3, 261n19, 264n14; YPCs in
cultural arsenal, 76
Columbia Records, 30, 77
Comden, Betty, 48, 95
comics/cartoons: *Dick Tracy*, 58;
Disney, 57; *Heckle and Jeckle*, 249; as
influence, bad, 75; *Mutt and Jeff*, 57,
65; *Peanuts*, 58, figures 35 and 36;
Carl W. Stalling, 198; *Terry and the
Pirates*, 58; *Woody Woodpecker*, 249
commercials: LB listened to radio jingles
as child, xxix; multiple sponsors, 80;
Nielsens data used to sell commercials,
251n28; primetime TV commercials,
sales of, 79; woven into programs
in 1950s by single sponsor, 80; *YPC*

commercial breaks, scheduling of,
9–10; YPCs contract regarding
commercials, CBS restrictions on
83–84; YPCs, jingles mentioned in,
xxvii; YPCs, original TV commercials
unavailable, 84; YPCs, commercials
are sacrifice but give opportunity,
9–10. *See also* AT&T; Bell Telephone;
Eastman-Kodak; Kitchens of Sara
Lee; Shell Oil Corp; sponsors; *Young
People's Concerts*
commissions: influence on composer,
156. *See also* Taubman, Harold; New
York Philharmonic
communication. *See* unity, international
communism, 254n3; accessible music,
linked to, 94, 139, 141, 144–45;
and Masscult, 43; rock 'n' roll as
communist plot, 46. *See also* the
Cold War; Dubin, Charles S.; the
Red Scare; *Red Channels*; Socialist
Realism
Communist Party, 96, 97, 100, 101, 111
Como, Perry, *41*, 63
Coney Island, 58
Congress for Cultural Freedom, 141
Copland, Aaron, 28, 157, 162, 193,
262n31, 264n11, 266n29; American
music, definition of, 185; American
music, helping shape LB's concept
of, 171; avant garde, LB letter about,
166; blacklisting of, xxxii; figures
30, 32; and HUAC, 93, 254n3; Ives
and, 264n12; NYP commission,
260–61n14; as Norton Professor of
Poetry Chair at Harvard, 50; NYP
Russian tour, LB letter from, 96; in
Red Channels, 93; at Tanglewood,
108; YPCs devoted to Copland, list
of, 265n22; YPCs, performs on, 266;
YPCs without LB, ran, *230*; YPCs,
works in, 179, *187–88*. *See also*
"*The Second Hurricane* by Copland";
"Aaron Copland Birthday Party"; "A
Copland Celebration"

encores, *28*, 96, 234n12

Englander, Roger, xviii, 2, 235n19, 235n33, 253n55; as LB's friend, 6 (figure 17); memos to or from, 240n20, 243n53, 251n39; as producer/director, 1, 4, 17, 20, 23, 32, 92, 158, *205*, 231n1, 237n47, 239n14; on production crew, 6, 7, 9; role in inception of YPCs, 77; sponsor issues, 88

Entartete Kunst, 139

Entartete Musik, 139

extended techniques, 145, 161, 162, 165, 166

Falla, Manuel de, 104, 135, 161, 162, *224*

Fancy Free (LB; 1944), xxxii, 61, 93, 103, 145, 179, *224*, *227*

fan mail about YPCs: adults write more than children, 2; African Americans, from, 118; ages of viewers revealed by, 85; American music, praising LB's support of, 177–78; avant garde, dislike of, 154–155, 168; avant garde, like it after LB's explanations, 155, 182; LB read fan mail, xix, 194–95; cartoons, YPCs superior to, 74; CBS, praising network for YPCs, 5; complaints about TV's intrusion at concerts, 236–37n45; delivery, on LB's unaffected, 11; feminism, 120–21; figures 34 and 35; fun, viewers thank LB for showing classical music as, 58–59; inspiring program "Humor in Music," 18, 58; Ives, LB helped fans appreciate, 182; jazz, praise LB for support of, 5; "The Latin American Spirit," 108; LPs, fans bought, 30; numbers of viewers revealed by, 83; praise for YPCs, 5, 195; rock 'n' roll, dislike of, 46; rock 'n' roll, praise for LB's support of, 64; size of collection of LB's fan mail, xix, 122, 232n7, 264n16; from teachers, 5, 11, 58, 83, 118, 154, 195

"Fantastic Variations (*Don Quixote*)," 14, 22, 60, *188*, 189, *201*, *203*, *210*, *225*, 234n15, 251n37, 262n29. *See also* Strauss, Richard

"Farewell to Nationalism," 61, 155, 157, 158–159, 178, 179, 180, *188*, *200*, *203*, *208*, 266n32

Fascism. *See* Nazis

Fearing, Kenneth, 59

Federal Bureau of Investigation (FBI). *See* Bernstein, Leonard, Challenges, Hollywood Blacklist, *Red Channels*

feminism, xxvii, 113, 114, 119–121, 122, 190, 231n4

Fernández, Oscar Lorenzo, 105, 107, 108

"*Fidelio*, A Celebration of Life," 18, 55, 122, *188*, *201*, *203*, *211*, 236–237n45, 242n52, 265n24; Juilliard soloists used in *Fidelio*, controversy over, 239n19; Vietnam War, *Fidelio* as veiled comment on 109–110, 122, 190, *201*, 266n1. *See also* Beethoven, Ludwig van

films: Bergman, Ingmar, 45; big Hollywood musicals, 41; Charlie Chaplin's films, 41; *La dolce vita* (1960), 55, 246n30; *Don Quixote* (1965), 60; *Dr. Strangelove* (film; 1965), 102; *Duck and Cover* (civil defense film; 1951), 254n2; *Fantasia* (1940), 45, 60; *Fail-Safe* (1964), 102; *Forbidden Planet* (film 1956), 162; foreign, 41, 246n30; D. W. Griffiths's films, 41; Hollywood, 54–55; *Lilies of the Field* (1963), 115; *The Mouse That Roared*, 253–54n1; *The Music Man* (1957), 60; *Psycho* (1960), 162; *The Red Violin* (1998), 198

films mentioned in YPCs: *The Bridge over the River Kwai*, 55, 61; cowboy films, 74; list, 248n49; road pictures (Bing Cosby and Bob Hope "road" films; 1941–1962), 52–53, *200*;

bitonality in 161–62; nationalism in, 162; *Petrushka* in, 31, 259n31; Picasso in, 59. *See also* Stravinsky, Igor

Harrell, Lynn, 33, 120, *213*, 243n53 (figure 17)

Harris, Roy, 177; as American composer, 170, 177, 265n20; in LB's Harvard thesis, 173, 175, *176*; blacklisted, xxxii; NYP commission, 260–61n14; symphonies of, 148, 157, 185, *224*, *228*

Harvard University (Cambridge, MA), 42; LB as student at, 30, 47; Copland and LB at, 182; discovered Hindemith at, 26; discovered Ives at, 180; as highbrow, 64; "Leonard Bernstein: Boston to Broadway," xviii, 147, 152–53, 231n5, 241n38, 245n20; *Omnibus* about, 248. *See also* "Absorption of Race Elements into American Music"; Norton Lectures

Haydn, Franz Joseph, 17, 56, 95, *215*

Hellman, Lillian, 93, 254n4

Henze, Hans Werner, 141, 143; NYP commission, 260–61n14; highbrow, xvi, xxvii, 193, 194, *200*, 245n18; in LB's childhood, xxix; cultural artifacts, 246n30; education of the masses as goal of, 70, 245n19; market, 86; *Partisan Review* as highbrow periodical, 244n4; highbrow sport of sailing, LB enjoying (figure 18); State Department tours, highbrow music selected for, 144; television, early owners of, 70. *See also* "brow" or taste cultures; postmodernism

Hindemith, Paul, 144, 148, *216*, 240n29, 245n11; Adorno on, 140; NYP commission, 260–61n14; newspaper articles on Hindemith's death in LB's files, 240n27; YPCs, number of works in, 158, *224*. *See also* "The Genius of Paul Hindemith"

hippies, xxvii, 113, 122, 191, 258n18; and astrology 124–127, *202*; definition of, 123; and drugs, 127–131, *201*; and freedom, 131–133

Hiroshima, 102, 154

Hitler, Adolph, 68, 103, 132, 190; influence on the arts, 25, 139, 140

Hollywood, xxxii; films, 38, *41*, 44, 54, 55

Hollywood Blacklist, 92, 93

Holocaust, LB family members lost to, 26

"Holst: *The Planets*," 188, *202*, *203*, *211*, 242–43n52, 259n31; aleatoric music added to, 161; and astrology, 125–126, 194; war, LB's allusions to, 110, 122, 190; House Un-American Activities Committee (HUAC), 87, 92; artists testify before, 93. *See also* Dubin, Charles S.

Ian, Janis, 47, 118, 257n

impressionist art, 59

indeterminacy. *See* aleatoric music

India, 15, 123, 245n16

intellectual ghetto. *See* cultural ghetto

"Inside Pop—The Rock Revolution," 47, 118, 191–192, 245n17

Israel, 246n28, 266n2; performers from, 135, *213*, *214*

Ives, Charles, *41*, 96, 148, 175, 242n9; as an American composer, 179–182, *228*, 264n12; in LB's Harvard thesis, 151, 173, *176*; LB championed, 186, 192, 193; fan mail about, 155; fun as motivation, 180, 181; as highbrow, *41*; as modernist composer, 155, 158, 192, *225*, *226*, 262n30; popularity with U.S. orchestras, 198, 264n11; recordings, 263n7, 257n6; YPCs, works performed in, 265n26; *See also* Bernstein, Leonard, fun; "Charles Ives: American Pioneer"; Copland, Aaron, LB's mentor; "Farewell to Nationalism"; "Folk Music in the

Schuller, Gunther, 148, 150, 178, 186, 261n17; *Journey into Jazz*, 225, 228; NYP commission, 260–61n14. *See also* "Jazz in the Concert Hall"

Schumann, Robert, xvi, 29, 54

Schuman, William, 29, 144, 148, 157, 170, 175, 176, 177, 185, *225*, *228*, 265n20; NYP commission, 260–61n14; "*The Second Hurricane* by Copland," 20, 177, *187*, *199*, *203*, *206*, *224*, *227*, 265n22; Bernstein family adored it, 239n16; only opera on YPCs, 18

serialism: avant garde, within definition of, 138, 145, 192, *223*; Berg's rows with tonal implications, 261n18; LB's use of, 145; Foss and, 165; NYP commission, 260–61n14; old-fashioned by mid-1960s, 167; opposition to by composers, 143; postmodernism, as a part of, 266–67n5; total serialism, 140–41, 141–42; *See also* avant garde

Serling, Rod, 86–87, 253n52

Sessions, Roger, xxxii, 144, 148, 172, 173, *176*, *225*, *226*, *228*, 262n26, 265n20; NYP commission, 260–61n14

Shell Oil Company: YPCs, commercials on, 84, 86; YPCs sponsored, *81*, *206–208*. *See also* sponsors

Shostakovich, Dmitri, 91, 96, 98, 99, 140, 148, 195, 266n3; LB increased visibility of, 192; reactionary, criticized as, 142; YPCs, works in, *225*. *See also* "A Birthday Tribute to Shostakovich"; Cultural and Scientific Conference for World Peace

Sibelius, Jean, 65, 148, *225*. *See also* "A Tribute to Sibelius"

Simon and Garfunkel, 137, 151, 248n57

Sinatra, Frank, 46

Socialist Realism, 94, 99, 139, 141

Sondheim, Stephen, 18, 239n15

"The Sound of a Hall," 60, *200*, *203*, *207*

Soviet Union. *See* New York Philharmonic; Pasternak, Boris

Spiegel, Mildred, 255–56n25

sponsors, xxvii, 12, 15, 16, 30, 75, 124, 195; censorship, 86–88; children's programming, 72–75, 249n11; cosponsor, 80, 84, 85; early television and arts programming, 70–72; trends in sponsorship 72–73; YPCs, cosponsors, *210*, 239n12, 268n4; YPCs, censorship, 17, 97–99, 253n54; YPCs, sponsors, *81*, *205–211*; YPCs, pre-broadcast review by, 9, 14; YPCs, struggle to find sponsor, 3; YPCs, overview of sponsors and commercials, 80–86; YPCs, sponsorship representative of trends, 80, 89–90. *See also* advertising; AT&T; Bell Telephone; Eastman-Kodak; Kitchens of Sara Lee; Nielsen ratings; Shell Oil Corp

sports in YPCs: baseball, xi, 45, 58, 244n, 246n29 (figure 19); baseball analogy for tonality, 54; boxing, *40*, *41*, 54, 246n29; football, *40*, 43, 45, 47, 54, 58, 82, 120, 245n15, 246n29; foot racing, 246n29; golf, *41*, 54, 82; list of references, 246n29; pole vaulting, 246n29; sailing, *41*, 47 (figure 18); skiing, *41*, 47, 48, 54; swimming, 47, 58, 246n29; target practice, 246n29; wrestling, *40*, 45; YPCs, television scheduling lead-in for, 82

Stalin, Joseph, 139, 140

Stalling, Carl W., 198

Stockhausen, Karlheinz, 143, 150

Strauss, Johann, Jr., *28*, 60

Strauss, Richard, 14, 23, 158, 262n29; *Also Sprach Zarathustra*, 21–22, 61, 242–43n52. *See also* "Fantastic Variations (*Don Quixote*)"; "Thus Spake Richard Strauss"

About the Author

Alicia Kopfstein-Penk is an enthusiastic postmodernist who teaches at American University. As a performer, she has sung Bernstein at the Metropolitan Opera, Beatles with her guitar at supper clubs, Bach on classical guitar at the Kennedy Center, and jazz on ukulele at local venues. As a scholar, she has written articles for *Soundboard* magazine and podcasts for the Washington National Opera, as well as presented for the National Opera Association. Her interests range from Elizabethan lute music to ergonomics for musicians to the life and television work of Bernstein. Her research has won recognition from the American Musicological Society, the Cosmos Club Foundation, and other organizations. Her forthcoming book, *Making Music with Heart and Mind*, incorporates her innovative and successful approach to musicianship that links the intellectual with the emotional.